REAL ESTATE FINANCE

THIRD EDITION

RONALD W. MELICHER
Professor of Finance
University of Colorado

MAURICE A. UNGER
Professor Emeritus of Real Estate
University of Colorado

FX63CA
PUBLISHED BY
SOUTH-WESTERN PUBLISHING CO.
CINCINNATI   WEST CHICAGO, IL   CARROLLTON, TX   LIVERMORE, CA

PREFACE

THE PRACTICE OF real estate has undergone significant change in recent years. For example, the adjustable-rate mortgage now competes directly with the traditional fixed-rate, long-term mortgage. Government legislation has altered financial institution channels and sources for securing real estate funds. Investor acceptance of mortgage-backed securities has led to the development of a viable secondary mortgage market. Recent changes in tax laws relating to depreciation write-off periods and investment credits have altered real property financing and investment decisions. Without question, these and other developments have increased the uncertainty associated with the practice of real estate. However, these recent developments also provide greater opportunities for the successful real estate professional.

Organization and Changes

The Third Edition of *REAL ESTATE FINANCE* is designed to provide the student and real estate professional with a basic understanding of the instruments, procedures, methods, institutions, and markets involved in the financing of real estate. We have substantially reorganized the sequence in which major topics and chapter materials are presented. These changes were made to reflect recent developments in real estate finance and to improve the flow from topic to topic. This Third Edition contains six parts.

Part 1 focuses on a discussion of real estate instruments. We begin with the fundamentals and legal aspects of mortgages and deeds of trust. The third and final chapter in Part 1 discusses variations in mortgage financing available to lenders and borrowers.

In Part 2 we focus on real estate credit and mortgage markets. We begin with a discussion of factors that affect the supply of real estate funds and then discuss the characteristics and role of major real estate lenders. Mortgage banking's facilitating role and secondary mortgage market activities and procedures are then covered, followed by a discussion of government real estate assistance programs.

Part 3 discusses financing costs, investment returns, and risk. In the first of a two-chapter sequence, we cover interest rates and other loan factors. This is followed by coverage of investment returns and risk factors. Part 4 focuses on real estate financing methods. We begin with a discussion of seller financing methods and follow with chapters on the financing of real estate with junior liens and financing by means of long-term leases.

In Part 5 we shift our attention to the coverage of construction and permanent financing practices. Builder-developer financing fundamentals are considered first followed by a discussion of construction financing methods and procedures. The remaining two chapters in Part 5 cover tract and special purpose financing topics, and high ratio or leverage financing practices.

Part 6 focuses on real estate practices and settlement procedures. In the first of two chapters we discuss loan application, analysis, and closing topics. We conclude the book with a chapter covering mortgage default and foreclosure issues.

In addition to a major reorganization of chapter sequences, we have thoroughly updated chapter materials to reflect recent real estate financing developments. The chapter discussing variations in mortgage financing has been completely rewritten to reflect recent changes. Likewise, recent developments in secondary mortgage market activities have been incorporated in the Third Edition. The impact of recent banking legislation (i.e., the Depository Institutions Deregulation and Monetary Control Act of 1980 and the Garn-St. Germain Depository Institutions Act of 1982) on real estate lender characteristics and practices is covered. We also consider the implications of changes in tax laws (i.e., from the Economic Recovery Tax Act of 1981 to the Tax Reform Act of 1986) on real estate financing and investment decisions throughout the book.

Teaching and Learning Aids

The Third Edition of *REAL ESTATE FINANCE* incorporates a number of features designed to aid the teaching and learning process. At the beginning of each chapter, we provide several *learning objectives* that identify important topics covered in the chapter and which should be understood by the reader. At the end of each chapter, a list of *key terms* is presented. Each term is defined in the chapter and also is included in the *glossary* at the end of the book.

Most of the chapters contain *boxed items* which focus on current real estate finance developments, as well as tax implications relating to real estate financing and investment topics. End-of-chapter *questions and problems* can be used to aid class discussion and to test how well students understand the chapter materials.

An instructor's manual is available to teachers who adopt this book. General comments are provided concerning the purpose and organization of a real estate finance course. A test bank of true-false and multiple-choice questions also is provided for each chapter. In addition, the manual describes the use of the *Decision Assistant* software, a computerized toolkit designed to help students master specific *REAL ESTATE FINANCE* concepts.

Acknowledgments

We thank users of earlier editions of this book for their helpful suggestions, many of which have been incorporated in this Third Edition. We also wish to acknowledge the constructive comments provided by several reviewers of this book. Finally, we thank present and past colleagues at the University of Colorado for their useful suggestions.

Ronald W. Melicher

Maurice A. Unger

CONTENTS

PART 1

REAL
ESTATE
INSTRUMENTS

FUNDAMENTALS OF MORTGAGES AND DEEDS OF TRUST

LEARNING OBJECTIVES

After studying this chapter, you should be able to do the following:

Distinguish between the mortgage and the deed of trust.

Describe the three theories of real estate mortgages.

Explain the use of a promissory note in conjunction with mortgages.

Identify and describe each of the three basic types of mortgages.

Briefly describe the budget mortgage and the package mortgage.

Briefly describe open, blanket, and open-end mortgages.

Discuss and describe the home equity mortgage and the purchase money mortgage.

THE LOGICAL PROGRESSION in a real estate transaction consists of first a contract for the sale of real estate and then a deed conveying the title of the real property to a buyer. However, nearly every contract for the sale of real property calls for financing of the property, either by an institution, the seller, or some other third party. The property becomes the security for the loan and this is evidenced either by a mortgage or a deed of trust.

THE MORTGAGE AND DEED OF TRUST

What is a Real Estate Mortgage?

The use of the mortgage in the United States had its origin in early English Common Law. One of the forms of transfer of real property as security for a debt was called *mortuum vadium*. It was so called because under the ancient law the pledgee became entitled to the rents and profits from the land, hence the land was "dead" to the debtor. Another form of pledge was called *vivum vadium*, wherein the profits from the land were applied to the payment of the loan.

Out of these two forms of mortgage there gradually evolved the so-called "common-law mortgage," which, in the final analysis, was a transfer of the property subject to a condition—the condition being that upon the payment of the debt, by a certain time, the estate of the transferee would terminate.

In early law, the condition that the debt had to be paid by a certain time was strictly enforced. The result of this was that the debtor lost the property if the sum due was not paid by the stated time, even though a partial payment may have been made on the debt. To relieve this obvious hardship on the debtor, the courts, about the middle of the seventeenth century, gave the debtor the right to pay off the debt even after it became due. The debtor was given the right to redeem the property, and this right became known as the equity of redemption. This concept in turn worked a hardship on the creditor, who might never receive the money owed. This resulted in placing a time limit on the equity of redemption, by a decree of foreclosure issued by a court. By virtue of the decree of foreclosure, the right to redeem was cut off unless the debt was paid by the time named in the decree.

Nearly all modern real property transfers involve the use of the property itself as security for part of the payment of the purchase price. Often, too, real property is used as security for a debt when no transfer takes place. In all of these transactions where land is given as security for a debt, there are two instruments involved. Sometimes these instruments are, for brevity's sake, combined into one form, but essentially they remain two separate and distinct instruments. These instruments are the promissory note and the mortgage. The details of the mortgage will be discussed later, but for the moment let it suffice that a *mortgage* is the creation of an interest in property as security for the payment of a debt or the fulfillment of some obligation. The two parties to a mortgage are the *mortgagor* (borrower) and the *mortgagee* (lender).

What is a Real Estate Deed of Trust?

A *deed of trust* is a deed absolute to secure the payment of a debt. There are three parties to the deed of trust: the *trustor* (borrower), the *beneficiary* (lender), and the *trustee*. The loan is given to the trustor, who in turn transfers the trust deed to the trustee for the benefit of the beneficiary. In the event of default by the trustor, the trustee forecloses for the benefit of the beneficiary.

In most instances in financing real estate there are two instruments signed by the borrower: a note and a mortgage or deed of trust.[1] There are a number of states that use a deed of trust (or trust deed or trust indenture, as it is sometimes called) in the nature of a mortgage.[2] In many of these states the lender is given a choice of using either a mortgage or a deed of trust as the security for a real property loan.

In an ordinary mortgage transaction there are usually only two parties: the mortgagor and mortgagee. In the deed of trust, however, there are three parties to the transaction. The borrower executes the deed of trust, which conveys the property to a third person, known as the trustee, who receives from the conveyance sufficient title to carry out the trust. This trustee holds for the benefit of the owner of the note executed by the borrower at the time of the transaction. The note is the evidence of the debt. If the borrower defaults, the property is either transferred to the lender, after proper legal proceedings have been completed, or disposed of at a public sale at which the trustee transfers title to the purchaser.

Depending upon state law, the trustee is either a private trustee whose only qualification is the possession of contractual capacity, or the trustee is a public trustee. Generally speaking, the public trustee is either the county clerk or an individual appointed by the governor of the state. The public trustee in these states is bonded and handles all of the trust deeds recorded in the state.

Contractual Implications

The legal aspects of mortgages and deeds of trust will be discussed in some detail in Chapter 2. However, it is important to recognize at this time that both the mortgage and deed of trust are contracts. Therefore, the instrument creating the mortgage or deed of trust must embrace the "elements" of a contract, namely:

1. Competent parties
2. Offer and acceptance
3. Legality of object
4. Compliance with the Statute of Frauds (written and signed)

The forms for the mortgage and the deed of trust shown in Appendix A are the uniform Federal National Mortgage Association, Federal Home Loan Mortgage Corporation forms. Actually, these forms are "uniform" only inso-

---

[1]In Georgia neither a mortgage nor deed of trust is used. There, a security deed is used. Basically, the deed secures payment of a debt and grants power of attorney to sell the property upon default, and payment of the debt cancels the deed.

[2]Alabama, Alaska, California, Colorado, Delaware, District of Columbia, Illinois, Mississippi, Missouri, Nevada, New Mexico, Oregon, Tennessee, Texas, Utah, Virginia, Washington, and West Virginia. The Small Tract Financing Act (Sec. 52–401 et seq. Revised Code of Montana) provides for a deed of trust, but "only for parcels not exceeding three (3) acres." The 1957 Act of Idaho provides a deed of trust for 20 acres or less.

far as the first seventeen clauses are concerned. After clause seventeen, nonuniform covenants may be added, and these vary among the states.

Although many of the clauses in the standard residential mortgage are common to the mortgages and deeds of trust in commercial-type mortgages, e.g., apartment house projects, shopping centers, etc., it should be noted that the commercial-type mortgages are vastly more complex and, in most cases, much longer.

THE THREE THEORIES OF REAL ESTATE MORTGAGES

There are three theories of mortgages used in the United States. These theories are the title theory, the lien theory, and the intermediate theory.

The Title Theory

The basic concept of the *title theory*[3] is that upon making the mortgage, the mortgagor (borrower) passes title to the property, the subject of the mortgage, to the mortgagee (lender) subject to a condition subsequent. This condition subsequent is the payment of the debt. Upon fulfillment of the condition, title to the property divests (reverts) to the mortgagor.

For example, A (the mortgagor) mortgages real property to B (the mortgagee) in a title state. Under the terms of the instrument, title passes to B. However, the instrument will state that if A complies with the condition (makes payment), then the instrument will be void.

During the period of the mortgage, by virtue of a provision in the mortgage, A is generally entitled to remain in possession of the property even though title has passed to the mortgagee.

The Lien Theory

The majority of the states use the *lien theory* of mortgages.[4] Under this theory, title remains with the mortgagor, and the mortgage that is placed on the property is a charge on the title. The mortgage instrument says nothing about title, but states: "The mortgagor does hereby mortgage to. . . ." After the recording of the instrument, it becomes a lien on the property described in the mortgage.[5]

---

[3]The states using the title theory are: Alabama, Arkansas, Connecticut, Maine, Maryland, Massachusetts, New Hampshire, Pennsylvania, Rhode Island, Tennessee, Vermont, Virginia, West Virginia, and The District of Columbia.

[4]The states using the lien theory are: Alaska, Arizona, California, Colorado, Delaware, Florida, Georgia, Hawaii, Idaho, Indiana, Iowa, Kansas, Kentucky, Louisiana, Michigan, Minnesota, Missouri, Montana, Nebraska, Nevada, New Mexico, New York, North Dakota, Oklahoma, Oregon, South Carolina, South Dakota, Texas, Utah, Washington, Wisconsin, and Wyoming.

[5]Oddly enough, in some lien theory states, for example, Texas, the deed of trust states that the borrower transfers title to the trustee for the benefit of the lender. However, the Courts in all lien theory states have ruled that while it is *said* the trustee receives title, the trustee is not given the right of possession.

The rule regarding the priority of mortgages, whether in title or lien states, is substantially the same rule as that regarding the priority of deeds: the instrument recorded first, in the absence of fraud, is the operative one. For example, *A* mortgages real property to *B* on October 15 with the instrument bearing that date. On the following day *A* mortgages the same property to *C*. *C* records the mortgage before *B*. In the absence of fraud, *C* has a valid enforceable mortgage. To avoid such circumstances, mortgages should be recorded immediately.

The Intermediate Theory

The *intermediate theory* involves a combination of the title and lien theories.[6] When the mortgage is written, it is a lien. If the borrower defaults, title passes to the lender, who then proceeds to foreclose.

What Difference Do These Theories Make?

So long as neither party (particularly the mortgagor) has breached any of the covenants or promises in the mortgage, there is, for all practical purposes, no difference. However, in the event of a breach, the processes of foreclosure, acceleration, and the appointment of a receiver, as will be pointed out later, are quite different depending on the mortgage theory that is used in the particular state.

USE OF A PROMISSORY NOTE

A promissory note is employed as evidence of the debt, the real property being used as collateral security for the note. A *promissory note* is defined as a written promise by one person to pay money to another. Thus, the note must spell out the terms of payment, the rate of interest, prepayment clause, if any, and the amortization period. The note often is made in the form shown in Figure 1–1. This is a standard Federal National Mortgage Association/Federal Home Loan Mortgage Corporation uniform instrument. The reason behind this standardization is that FNMA and FHLMC are the largest purchasers of home mortgages in what is called the "secondary market." They have insisted that institutions selling mortgages and deeds of trust to them standardize both the notes and mortgages or deeds of trust.

The uniform note is exactly the same regardless of the state, except for part of one sentence. In states using the deed of trust it reads, "The indebtedness evidenced by this Note is secured by a Deed of Trust . . ." In states using the mortgage it reads, "The indebtedness evidenced by this Note is secured by a Mortgage . . ."

---

[6]The states using the intermediate theory are: Illinois, Mississippi, New Jersey, North Carolina, and Ohio.

NOTE

US $ .42,500.00...............

Denver,
.........................., Colorado
City
.........June 18,.........., 19.--.

FOR VALUE RECEIVED, the undersigned ("Borrower") promise(s) to pay MIDLAND FEDERAL SAVINGS AND LOAN ASSOCIATION, or order, the principal sum of Forty-Two Thousand Five Hundred----....Dollars, with interest on the unpaid principal balance from the date of this Note, until paid, at the rate of Thirteen (13)..... ....percent per annum. Principal and interest shall be payable at 1418 - 17th Street, Denver, Colorado ...., or such other place as the Note holder may designate, in consecutive monthly installments of . Eight Hundred Sixteen and 00/100 --------------. ....Dollars (US $816.00 ....), on the.....5th........... ....day of each month beginning....July 5,..............., 19.--.. Such monthly installments shall continue until the entire indebtedness evidenced by this Note is fully paid, except that any remaining indebtedness, if not sooner paid, shall be due and payable on...July 5, 20.--......................

If any monthly installment under this Note is not paid when due and remains unpaid after a date specified by a notice to Borrower, the entire principal amount outstanding and accrued interest thereon shall at once become due and payable at the option of the Note holder. The date specified shall not be less than thirty days from the date such notice is mailed. The Note holder may exercise this option to accelerate during any default by Borrower regardless of any prior forbearance. If suit is brought to collect this Note, the Note holder shall be entitled to collect all reasonable costs and expenses of suit, including, but not limited to, reasonable attorney's fees.

Borrower shall pay to the Note holder a late charge of five (5) percent of the principal and interest of any monthly installments not received by the Note holder within fifteen (15) days after the installment is due.

Borrower may prepay the principal amount outstanding in whole or in part. The Note holder may require that any partial prepayments (i) be made on the date monthly installments are due and (ii) be in the amount of that part of one or more monthly installments which would be applicable to principal. Any partial prepayment shall be applied against the principal amount outstanding and shall not postpone the due date of any subsequent monthly installments or change the amount of such installments, unless the Note holder shall otherwise agree in writing. If, within five years from the date of this Note, Borrower make(s) any prepayments in any twelve month period beginning with the date of this Note or anniversary dates thereof ("loan year") with money lent to Borrower by a lender other than the Note holder, Borrower shall pay the Note holder (a) during each of the first three loan years ......Four...............percent of the amount by which the sum of prepayments made in any such loan year exceeds twenty percent of the original principal amount of this Note and (b) during the fourth and fifth loan years ......Six.................percent of the amount by which the sum of prepayments made in any such loan year exceeds twenty percent of the original principal amount of this Note.

Presentment, notice of dishonor, and protest are hereby waived by all makers, sureties, guarantors and endorsers hereof. This Note shall be the joint and several obligation of all makers, sureties, guarantors and endorsers, and shall be binding upon them and their successors and assigns.

Any notice to Borrower provided for in this Note shall be given by mailing such notice by certified mail addressed to Borrower at the Property Address stated below, or to such other address as Borrower may designate by notice to the Note holder. Any notice to the Note holder shall be given by mailing such notice by certified mail, return receipt requested, to the Note holder at the address stated in the first paragraph of this Note, or at such other address as may have been designated by notice to Borrower.

The indebtedness evidenced by this Note is secured by a Deed of Trust, dated....June 18, 19.--......... ...., and reference is made to the Deed of Trust for rights as to acceleration of the indebtedness evidenced by this Note.

/s/ Marvin J. Miller
....

368 Stout Street
....

/s/ Cynthia Miller
....

Denver, Colorado
....
Property Address

....
(Execute Original Only)

COLORADO—1 to 4 Family—6/75—**FNMA/FHLMC UNIFORM INSTRUMENT**

M-501

FIGURE 1–1. Promissory Note

BASIC TYPES OF MORTGAGES

There are three basic types of mortgages: FHA, VA, and conventional, which are discussed in the following paragraphs.

The FHA-Insured Mortgage

The primary feature of the **FHA-insured mortgage** as far as the lender is concerned is that the loan is insured. A loss as a result of failure of the mortgagor to meet the payments will be covered by the Federal Housing Administration, which was instituted under the National Housing Act of 1934. It is now under the jurisdiction of the Department of Housing and Urban Development. This insurance feature enables lending institutions to lend a higher percentage of the appraised value than they would under ordinary circumstances.

FHA-insured loans are limited to the extent that FHA standards for the property and the borrower are met. In early 1988, the maximum loan limit on an FHA-insured single-family home loan was $90,000 (this limit has been increased periodically). Interest rates on FHA mortgage loans are set by the Secretary of Housing and Urban Development, with frequent changes being common in recent years.

A maximum *loan-to-value ratio,* which is the percentage of loan permitted on the appraised value of the property, is also established for FHA-insured loans. The formula for loan-to-value ratios permitted FHA-insured mortgage lenders is:

97 percent on the first $25,000 and
95 percent on the value in excess of $25,000

For example, if the appraised value of a single-family home is $75,000, the maximum loan permitted would be:

$$.97 \times \$25,000 = \$24,250$$
$$.95 \times \$50,000 = \underline{\ \ 47,500}$$
$$\text{Maximum} \quad \$71,750$$

Maximum loan limits on FHA-insured loans actually differ by type of property. In addition to the $90,000 limit on single-family homes, the following limits also were in effect as of 1988:

Duplex $101,300
Triplex.   122,650
Fourplex   142,650
Condominium.   90,000

The VA-Guaranteed Mortgage

The **VA-guaranteed mortgage,** or the so-called GI mortgage, is a part of the Servicemen's Readjustment Act of 1944 (as amended). The crux of the law pertaining to real property is that the Veterans Administration will guarantee a

VA AND FHA HOME MORTGAGE LOAN ACTIVITY

Although the dollar amount of home mortgage loans made annually is dominated by conventional mortgage loans, VA-guaranteed and FHA-insured mortgage loans continue to play important roles in financing homes. Following are data for mortgage loans made, expressed in millions of dollars, as reported in the U.S. League of Savings Institutions' annual *Sourcebook*.

YEAR	VA-GUARANTEED HOME MORTGAGES	FHA-INSURED HOME MORTGAGES
1960	$ 1,985	$ 4,601
1965	2,652	7,465
1970	3,440	8,114
1975	8,884	6,165
1980	14,500	16,458
1981	7,903	10,279
1982	5,428	8,087
1983	17,966	26,572
1984	12,728	14,525
1985	13,046	23,964
1986	24,720	—

Notice that while the amount of VA and FHA loans made fluctuates widely from year to year, there has been a general upward trend since the 1960s. Also note that FHA-insured annual home loan activity almost always exceeds the amount of VA-guaranteed loans.

The volatility of the dollar amount of VA and FHA loans made during the 1980s reflects, in part, the wide swings in interest rates and economic activities. Record high interest rates during the first part of the 1980s, along with two economic downturns, caused activity in VA and FHA home loans in 1982 to drop below 50 percent of the 1980 level. This was followed by a threefold increase in home loan activity amounts in 1983 over the 1982 level for both VA and FHA loans.

certain percentage of a mortgage loan to a veteran up to a maximum amount to qualified lenders who lend money on homes purchased by veterans. The amount of the maximum guarantee, the rate of interest, and the length of the loan can be changed by an act of Congress. They have varied in the past and will probably be changed again.

The mortgage is said to be guaranteed because the Veterans Administration will guarantee the lending institution, in case of default, a certain amount (currently 60 percent of the loan or $66,000, whichever is the lesser).

In some areas, under changes in the law made by Congress, the Veterans Administration has loaned money directly to veterans. For example, from time to time sums of money have been allotted to various counties to be loaned to veterans within that county who have been unable to obtain a VA loan from a bank or other lending institution. In these cases, the veteran obtains a letter from each of two lending institutions, which indicates that they will not lend money to the veteran. After having done this, the veteran makes direct application to the Veterans Administration.

There are five groups of veterans entitled to mortgage loan benefits under the GI Bill:

1. Members of the armed forces during World War II (September 10, 1940–July 25, 1947) for 90 days or longer or those discharged or released from active duty due to a service-incurred disability.
2. Members of the armed forces during the Korean conflict (June 27, 1950–January 31, 1955) serving anywhere in the world for 90 days or longer or those discharged or released from active duty due to a service-connected disability.
3. "Cold War" veterans who, as members of the armed services, served 180 days or more in active duty since January, 1955.
4. Unremarried widows of veterans who died from a service-incurred disability, are missing in action, or were captured or detained by a foreign government or power while performing in the line of duty. The veteran spouse must have been missing in action for 90 days or more before eligibility commences.
5. American citizens who during World War II served as members of the armed forces of a government *allied* with the United States and who meet other requirements of the law, including residency in the United States at the time benefits are sought.

The Conventional Mortgage

The term *conventional mortgage* as it is presently used refers to a mortgage that is neither FHA-insured nor VA-guaranteed. In general it can be said that the down payment on the conventional mortgage is higher than either the FHA or VA mortgages. However, since 1972 home buyers have been able to borrow from savings and loan associations up to 95 percent of the value of the home, provided the loan is guaranteed or insured by a mortgage insurance company which is determined to be "a qualified private insurer" by the Federal Home Loan Mortgage Corporation.

The standards for underwriting the privately insured conventional mortgages are established by insurance companies themselves. One of the leading insurance companies, Mortgage Guarantee Insurance Corporation, called "MGIC," suggests the following guidelines for underwriting the insurance:

1. Total monthly house payments must not exceed 25 percent of the borrower's gross monthly income.
2. Total monthly house payments plus total monthly installment obligations (on loans of ten months or more) may not exceed 33 percent of gross monthly income. Other factors such as the borrower's net worth, age, and number of dependents are also considered.
3. The borrower's payment attitude must be assured by the possession

of a good credit rating.
4. The borrower must present evidence of job stability or income stability.

On applying for an "insured" conventional loan, the prospective borrower must pay an application fee. Furthermore, the borrower, if the insurance is approved, must pay the insurance premiums. Because the companies are in the private sector, their premiums vary. To begin with, the entire amount of the loan is not insured, only the top end is. This varies from 20 to 25 percent. For example, assume a loan-to-value ratio of 95 percent for a home valued at $200,000. The down payment is $10,000 ($200,000 $\times$ .05). Assume the insurance covers the top 25 percent of the loan. Then the coverage comes to 25 percent of the 95 percent loan: in this case, 25 percent of $190,000, or $47,500. Put another way, the amount "at risk" for the lender is $142,500. On a $200,000 home, this is a substantial cushion in the event of default by the borrower.

Generally premiums amount to 1 percent of the loan for the first year and $1/4$ of 1 percent of the loan balance in each succeeding year. Another plan might be $1/2$ of 1 percent of the loan balance for three years and $1/4$ of 1 percent of the loan balance thereafter. Again it depends on the company.

OTHER MORTGAGE TYPES OR VARIATIONS

In addition to the basic FHA, VA, and conventional mortgages, several other mortgage types, or variations, are frequently used. The more important variations are briefly described here, some of which receive greater attention in later chapters.

The Budget Mortgage

The *budget mortgage* is a further development of the self-amortizing mortgage. The self-amortizing mortgage provides for monthly payments of part interest and part principal to enable the mortgagor to build equity in the property from the beginning of the mortgage. In addition, the budget mortgage includes in the monthly payments one twelfth of the year's taxes, a proportionate amount of the yearly fire insurance premiums, and any other charges which might, if left unpaid, constitute a basis for the foreclosure of the mortgage. Generally, when the mortgagor enters into a budget mortgage, six months of taxes are paid in advance at the title closing in order to provide the lender with a revolving fund. Any surplus in the fund is returnable to the mortgagor when the final payment has been made on the mortgage.

The Package Mortgage

The *package mortgage* is a mortgage that goes a step further than the budget mortgage. Usually, it incorporates all the features of the budget mortgage plus payments for certain mechanical equipment put in the home, e.g., a washer and dryer. In this manner all charges are met in one payment.

The Open Mortgage

The term *open mortgage* refers to a mortgage that has reached the due date but has not yet been paid. The mortgagee in these cases can demand payment at any time, but if security is good and the mortgagee is receiving a fair return on the investment, the mortgagee may be content to allow the mortgagor to continue paying interest and leave the mortgage "open."

It should be remembered that there is a statute of limitations on mortgages in most states. Thus, if there is no payment of interest or principal for six years, the mortgagor has a defense in the event of a foreclosure action by the mortgagee.

The Blanket Mortgage

A *blanket mortgage* is briefly defined as a mortgage that covers more than one parcel of real property. It is a type of instrument that is often used by builders to cover construction loans.

The *partial release clause* is generally used in conjunction with the blanket mortgage. It is a clause that is inserted in a mortgage stating that upon partial payment on the mortgage, the mortgagee will issue a partial satisfaction piece that releases a particular parcel or lot from the terms of the mortgage. It would be worded substantially as follows:

> The mortgagee agrees to release any lot from the lien of this mortgage upon payment to the mortgagee by the mortgagor or mortgagor's assigns of the sum of $500 per lot upon the lands so released.

The Open-End Mortgage

The *open-end mortgage* is a mortgage in which the borrower is given a limit on the amount which may be borrowed. For example, the loan may be authorized up to $40,000, and the borrower may initially borrow only $30,000; but at a later date the loan may be increased to the maximum authorized, in this case $40,000, without changing the terms of the original agreement.

The Home-Equity Mortgage

The *home-equity mortgage* is a variation of the open-end mortgage. The home-equity mortgage amounts to a revolving line of credit based on the equity in a home. For example, a homeowner may be eligible for a $20,000 credit line; i.e., the owner can borrow up to $20,000. While the ordinary open-end mortgage adds the amount of the loan to your first mortgage and is repayable at a fixed rate, the home equity mortgage is a "second" mortgage at

RECENT DEVELOPMENTS IN HOME-EQUITY LOANS

Home-equity borrowing turned into the "hot" consumer product of the mid-1980s. Lenders, by offering relatively low rates, discovered previously untapped lending opportunities. Borrowers flocked to home-equity loans, sometimes called HELS, because rates were much lower and the terms much longer relative to those on other consumer loans.

In addition to banks and thrifts, home-equity loans are made by brokers, such as the Loan Depot Corporation in Boston. These brokers offer speed and convenience and charge about $1/2$ of 1 percent more than do banks. These loans are then resold to major investors such as Travelers Insurance and Ford Motor Credit companies.

A *Business-Week*-Harris poll conducted in early 1987 indicated that 13 percent of over 800 home or condominium owners surveyed indicated that they had, or were seriously considering taking out, a home-equity loan. When asked "Why did you? (or Would you?) take out an HEL, 24 percent indicated to pay off other debt and 19 percent to pay for home improvements.

Also of interest was the belief by survey respondents that home-equity loans carried only a moderate risk (65 percent), versus high risk (15 percent), or hardly any risk (20 percent). Furthermore, 63 percent of the respondents felt the growth of home-equity loans would do more good than harm for the economy. For further discussion of HELs, see: "The Home Equity Gold Rush," *Business Week* (February 9, 1987): 64-70.

a variable rate. After the enactment of the Tax Reform Act of 1986, financial institutions vigorously solicited home equity loans and they now hold nearly $200 billion of such loans.

The reason for the appeal of home-equity loans is that the Act provides for mortgage interest on a principal residence to be fully deductible up to the amount of the home's cost plus the cost of any improvements. This means, for example, if the fair market value of the home, including improvements, is $100,000 and there is a $60,000 existing mortgage, the owner's equity is $40,000. If the original mortgage is increased in the amount of $40,000 through a second mortgage, the interest on the entire $100,000 can be deducted. Interest on consumer loans is not deductible; hence, the financial institutions say: "Go buy a car, charge it to your home equity loan, and deduct the interest." So far it has worked well for the institutions. However, the dangers of borrowing money through home equity mortgages are very clear:

1. Home-equity loans are variable-rate mortgages. If rates go up, the borrower pays more.
2. Lending institutions frequently offer very low "teaser rates." These loan rates typically are rock-bottom charges which, in some cases, are raised within a few months.
3. Very few home equity loans have "caps" and thus there usually are no maximum interest rate limits on these variable-rate mortgages.
4. Upfront fees are generally high.

5. If the economy declines, a borrower may be unable to make the additional payments on the home-equity mortgage and as a consequence may lose his or her home.
6. If, as the 1986 Tax Act promises, tax rates drop significantly, the need for tax deductions will be less.

The Purchase Money Mortgage

The *purchase money mortgage* is a mortgage given as part of the consideration for the sale of real property. In practice, the seller agrees to finance part of the selling price by "taking back" a mortgage as part of the purchase price. The purchase money mortgage is discussed in further detail in Chapter 10.

KEY TERMS

beneficiary	mortgagor
blanket mortgage	open mortgage
budget mortgage	open-end mortgage
conventional mortgage	package mortgage
deed of trust	partial release clause
FHA-insured mortgage	promissory note
home-equity mortgage	purchase money mortgage
intermediate theory	title theory
lien theory	trustee
mortgage	trustor
mortgagee	VA-guaranteed mortgage

QUESTIONS FOR REVIEW

1. Briefly explain the evolution of the concept of a mortgage.
2. Explain the major or principal differences between a mortgage and a deed of trust.
3. Describe each of the following three theories relating to real estate mortgages: (a) title theory, (b) lien theory, and (c) intermediate theory.
4. What are the elements of a mortgage or deed of trust contract?
5. How is a promissory note used with a mortgage or deed of trust?
6. Explain the principal differences among an FHA-insured mortgage, a VA-guaranteed mortgage, and a conventional mortgage.
7. Briefly define the budget mortgage and the package mortgage.
8. Differentiate between: (a) an open mortgage, and (b) an open-end mortgage.
9. Briefly define a *blanket mortgage* and the *purchase money mortgage.*
10. Describe the home equity mortgage and briefly explain why the use of these mortgages has shown rapid growth.

PROBLEMS

1. Mr. and Mrs. Morris want to obtain an FHA-insured mortgage on a $75,000 home they are interested in purchasing. Based on the current formula for loan-to-value ratios, what is the maximum loan they could receive? To what extent is this affected by the current maximum limit established for FHA loans? What would be the Morris' minimum required down payment?

2. The Veterans Administration guarantees VA mortgages in case of default. On an outstanding VA loan of $45,000, what would be the extent of the guarantee? What would be the amount of guarantee on a $60,000 VA loan?

3. Insured conventional loans do not involve full coverage of the entire amount of the loan. What amount does the lender have at risk if: (a) the loan-to-value ratio is 90 percent; (b) the home is appraised at $70,000; and (c) insurance is on the top 20 percent of the loan.

4. Dr. Jill Walker is considering the purchase of a $130,000 single-family home. Based on the 1988 loan limits, how much of a down payment would be necessary if she borrowed the maximum amount allowed on an FHA-insured loan. Also determine the maximum loan amounts which would be available on FHA-insured loans on single-family homes with appraised values of: (a) $100,000, and (b) $90,000. If each of these homes could be purchased at its appraised value, what would be the size of the required down payment?

5. Joji Akita is considering purchasing a duplex with an appraised value of $120,000, a triplex with an appraised value of $130,000, or a fourplex with a $175,000 appraised value. He expects to be able to borrow the maximum amount allowed on an FHA-insured loan on each type of property. Furthermore, he wants to minimize his down payment. Which type of property should he purchase and what will be his required down payment?

2

LEGAL ASPECTS OF MORTGAGES AND DEEDS OF TRUST

LEARNING OBJECTIVES

After studying this chapter, you should be able to do the following:

Describe how real property can be taken over "subject to" an existing mortgage.

Describe how an existing mortgage can be "assumed."

Define and discuss the use of the due-on-sale or nonassumption clause.

Describe how and when a wraparound mortgage is used.

Identify and briefly discuss the six general clauses typically found in a mortgage.

Identify and briefly discuss the most common special clauses typically inserted in the mortgage form.

Explain how a mortgage is acknowledged.

Explain the terms "satisfaction of mortgage" and "assignment of mortgage."

A COMPLETE DISCUSSION of the legal aspects of mortgages and deeds of trust would fill several volumes. Consequently, the discussion here is limited to some of the more common aspects.[1]

TRANSFERS INVOLVING EXISTING MORTGAGES

Where permitted, a person may purchase a piece of real property and "take over" the mortgage. The buyer either takes the property "subject to" or "assumes" the mortgage. The distinction between these two terms is subtle, but important to understand.

Subject To

When a parcel of property is purchased *subject to* a mortgage, there is inserted in the *deed* this statement:

> This deed is made subject to the following: a certain first mortgage in the amount of $10,000, and interest to date, made by Isabel Soto to Arturo Diaz on January 2, 1985, recorded January 3, 1985, in the office of the Clerk of the County of _____, State of _____, in Liber 2159 of Mortgages at page 5.

This statement means that the purchaser recognizes the *existence* of a mortgage on the property. For example, the buyer moves into a house and makes the payments that are due on the property mortgage. At this point things run smoothly; however, what happens if the buyer fails to meet the payments? The seller, who had the mortgage placed on the property originally, signed a note along with the original mortgage. When payments are not met, the mortgagee will commence foreclosure proceedings. The property will be sold and the buyer will be ousted. Suppose, however, that there is a deficiency of $1,000 due the mortgagee after the foreclosure sale has been completed. The question now is: Who is liable for the deficiency—seller, the mortgagor, or buyer, who took the property "subject to" the mortgage? The buyer promised nothing by taking the property "subject to" the mortgage. In effect, the buyer merely recognized the existence of the mortgage. The seller, however, promised to pay the mortgagee by signing the note. Therefore, the mortgagee will have recourse to the seller for the $1,000 deficiency.

When the seller sells the property "subject to" a mortgage, the seller may be liable for any deficiency. On the other hand, when the purchaser buys "subject to" the mortgage, the buyer is not liable for any deficiency; and the most that the buyer can lose in the event of foreclosure is any equity that has built up in the property.

Assuming the Existing Mortgage

Assumption of a mortgage is a contractual arrangement whereby a purchaser of property takes over or assumes the obligations of an existing mortgage. For

---

[1]The standard residential mortgage and the standard deed of trust are found in Appendix A.

example, *A* has an existing mortgage of $25,000. The sales price is $35,000. *A* agrees to sell to *B,* who gives *A* $10,000 in cash and agrees to assume *A*'s $25,000 mortgage.

The initial agreement whereby *B* agrees to assume the mortgage will appear in the Contract for Sale of Real Property. The second place where it appears is in the deed from *A* to *B* written substantially as follows:

> The conveyance hereunder is subject to a certain mortgage executed by *A* as mortgagor to Personal Savings and Loan Association as mortgagee, which mortgage is dated April 2, 19_____ and was recorded April 3, 19_____ in the office of the Clerk of the County of _____ in liber 1348 of mortgages page 87 on which mortgage there is now due $25,000 with interest thereon at the rate of $7^{3/4}$ percent per annum and that the grantor hereby assumes and covenants to pay such mortgage debt and interest as part of the consideration of this conveyance.

Assumption Statement. In the case above, *A* has informed *B* that the amount to be assumed is $25,000. The question is, how does *B* know it amounts to $25,000 and not, say, $30,000? The person who knows is the lender: in this case, the Personal Savings and Loan Association. If a real estate broker is handling the transaction, one of three things will be requested from the lender, depending on the state. In some cases the Mortgagor's Information Letter will be requested. Essentially, this is a letter from the lender stating the amount due on the loan as of the date of closing. In some states the lender will sign and deliver a Mortgagee's Certificate of Reduction similar to the one shown in Figure 2–1.

In most states the broker or seller will request what is termed either an "assumption statement" or a "statement for assumption of loan." An example of the statement for assumption of loan is shown in Figure 2–2.

Loan Assumption and Transfer Fees. As explained previously, the Contract for the Sale of Real Property will call for *B* to assume *A*'s mortgage. The contract will also contain a statement regarding loan assumption or, as they are sometimes called, transfer fees. Typically, the buyer pays the fee, although sometimes it is paid by the seller. The contract will state: "The purchaser agrees to pay the assumption fee," or there may be a limitation in the contract, namely, "the purchaser agrees to pay the assumption fee up to $100, the balance being paid by the seller."

What then is the *assumption fee*? It is a fee charged by the lending institution, as they put it, to "change their records and otherwise process the records for the new debtor." Although the suggested amount for both FHA and VA is under $100, some institutions charge an assumption fee as a percentage of the sale price.

Tax Stamps. Whether property is sold by having the buyer assume the mortgage or with new financing, tax stamps are affixed to the deed. The underly-

MORTGAGEE'S CERTIFICATE OF REDUCTION

THE UNDERSIGNED, the owner   and holder   of the following mortgage   and of the bond ~~- -or note~~ secured thereby:

Mortgage dated the   14th   **day of**   August   , 19-- , made
by   William D. Link

in the principal sum of $68,000.00   and recorded in (Liber) (Record ~~Liber~~) ~~(Reel)~~
       672   ~~of section~~   of Mortgages, page 14   , in the office of the   Clerk   of the
County of Westchester, State of New York,

covering premises situate

(here follows a complete legal description of the property)

in consideration of the sum of one dollar, the receipt of which is hereby acknowledged, **DO HEREBY CERTIFY,** that there is now owing and unpaid upon said ~~bond - - -or note~~   and mortgage
                         the principal sum of Fifty-Four Thousand and 00/100
($54,000.00)--- Dollars,
with interest thereon at the rate of   Seven (7)   per centum per annum from the 9th
day of   July   , 19-- ; and that said mortgage   is
       now a lien   on the premises covered thereby only to the extent of the said last mentioned principal
sum and interest.

DATED, the   7th   **day of**   August   19-- .

IN PRESENCE OF:

/s/ Jacquelyn P. Skahill

/s/ Judith J. DeFore

(Acknowledgment)

Standard Form of New York Board of Title Underwriters

FIGURE 2–1. Mortgagee's Certificate of Reduction

ing purpose of this is to give both the assessors and appraisers an idea of the value of the property. The rates are nominal. The methods of computing the tax vary from state to state. In some states it is based on the purchase price. In others, it is based on so many cents per thousand dollars of taxable consideration, which is the sales price minus existing loans and encumbrances.

Release from Liability. When a VA loan is assumed, the veteran seller can be released from liability on the note. For example, assume the veteran's home is sold and the mortgage to be assumed is $32,000. Under the normal assumption, the seller is still liable on the note. However, when the seller has a VA-guaranteed loan, a release from the liability ($32,000 in this case) can be obtained from the lender.

E<small>AST</small> L<small>AKE</small> S<small>AVINGS</small>

STATEMENT FOR ASSUMPTION OF LOAN

(Figures effective through...)

To: RE: .... Loan ....
                                                .... Rate ....

The following amounts must be paid before the assumption can be completed:

.... $...........................
....
Due Tax Reserve ....
Due Insurance Reserve...   ....
       TOTAL AMOUNT THAT MUST BE PAID BEFORE LOAN CAN BE ASSUMED .... $_____

Balances:

....
....

           Principal Balance................................ $...........................
                Tax Reserve .... $ ....
                Insurance Reserve......... ....
                Total Reserves................................ $...........................

The monthly payment is:
                Principal and Interest................ $ ....
                Payment to Tax Reserve ....
                Payment to Insurance Reserve.......... ....
                Total Monthly Payment.......... $ _____

       Payments are due the 1st of each month and become delinquent after the 10th. Following the assumption of
       this loan, the next monthly payment will be due..

       According to our records, taxes for the year.............. were paid in the amount of $...........................

Insurance Information: (1)   (2)

	(1)		(2)	
Company	....		....	
Agent	....		....	
Amount	....	Dwg.	....	Dwg.
	....	HHG	....	HHG
Structure	....		....	
Type	....		....	
Term	....		....	
Expires	....		....	
Premium	....		....	
	....		....	

TO ASSIST US IN CHANGING OUR RECORDS, WILL YOU PLEASE COMPLETE THE FOLLOWING:

   1. *Have present owners and purchasers sign enclosed assumption form.*
   2. *Have present owners and their insurance agent execute enclosed insurance assignments.*
   3. *Send us the above forms together with your check for any amounts due.*
   4. *Record the Warranty Deed without delay. If there is an abstract, it should be certified and returned to us
      promptly.*

                                   CUSTOMER SERVICE DEPARTMENT

Date:...   By ....

FIGURE 2–2.   Statement for Assumption of Loan

The Due-on-Sale or Nonassumption Clause

The *due-on-sale clause,* also called a **nonassumption clause,** often has been inserted by lenders in conventional mortgages and deeds of trust since the early seventies. In brief, the clause states that the mortgagor cannot have a buyer assume the mortgage without the consent of the lender. The reasoning behind this is quite simple from the viewpoint of institutional lenders, particularly savings and loan associations. For example, suppose a mortgage carries an interest rate of 9³/₄ percent. If the market rate drops to 9 percent, permission for the assumption will be readily given if a buyer is foolish enough not to refinance. However, if the rate rises to, say, 14 percent for conventional mortgages, the institution will refuse permission for the assumption unless the buyer agrees to pay the new rate. It should be noted that the due-on-sale clause is prohibited in FHA and VA mortgages as well as in most variable-rate mortgages.

By early October, 1982, some twenty states, either by statute or court ruling, held that due-on-sale or nonassumption clauses were unenforceable. However, on October 15, the Garn-St. Germain Depository Institutions Act of 1982 was signed into law and called for the due-on-sale clause to be enforced, notwithstanding any state constitutional or judicial provisions. Furthermore, the law applies not only to loans made by financial institutions, but to "all" real estate loans, including purchase money mortgage financing provided by private lenders.

The Garn-St. Germain Act did permit several exclusions or exceptions to the enforcement of the due-on-sale clause. These exceptions involve:

(a) transfers to a relative resulting from the death of a borrower,
(b) transfers resulting from divorce or a separation agreement,
(c) transfers to a spouse or child not affecting possession of the property transferred, and
(d) other transfers pursuant to regulations of the Federal Home Loan Bank Board.

The Act also provided that in those states where the due-on-sale clause had been invalidated prior to October 15, 1982, mortgages that had been assumed were exempt, except for those loans "originated" by savings and loan associations.

The Wraparound Mortgage

Strictly speaking, the **wraparound mortgage** is not a mortgage *per se* but is a covenant or promise written as a mortgage. Its roots lie both as a device to "get around" usury laws and as a "sweetener" or "kicker" to entice a seller to sell and finance the property.

A mortgage greater than the "lawful contract rate" has generally been considered usurious. Historically, to circumvent this, the wraparound was used by a seller. For example, suppose a seller has an assumable mortgage of $50,000 with a 9 percent mortgage and that any rate over 11 percent is considered usurious. The seller is willing to finance $25,000; thus, the total to be financed is $75,000. The entire amount is wrapped at 11 percent. As a result, the seller has an effective yield of more than 11 percent because 11 percent is being earned on the $25,000 and an additional 2 percent is being earned on the $50,000 mortgage which is being assumed.[2]

As a sweetener, the wraparound was often used to persuade a seller to sell to a person with a relatively *small* down payment when the institutional lenders would refuse to lend on that basis. The argument to the seller was that if the seller personally financed the property, a higher rate of interest would be received.

In either of the above cases, the wraparound mortgage was junior to the first mortgage. In states using the deed of trust, the wraparound is called an "all inclusive deed of trust."

In recent years the wraparound mortgage has become a device to circumvent the due-on-sale or nonassumption clause, which was inserted in mortgages by lenders to render the mortgages *nonassumable*. The thinking behind this was that the lenders would not discover the existence of the wrap. Various devices have been used in an attempt to hide the sale from lenders. For example, the new buyer makes a payment to an escrow agent who, in turn, splits the payment between the seller and the lending institution.

Another method commonly used takes this form: Tom Jones is selling the property to, say, Frank Smith, with a wraparound. A deed is made by Tom Jones to Tom Jones Properties. Frank Smith, the buyer, then files a Certificate of Doing Business under the name and style of Tom Jones Properties. Smith then makes payments to an escrow agent who again splits the monies between the lender (first mortgagee) and Tom Jones (the seller). If the buyer, Smith, later decides to sell the property, he simply signs a deed, say to Harry Wilson, as grantor doing business under the name and style of Tom Jones Properties.

In any case, if the lending institution discovers this subterfuge, the transaction can be foreclosed upon under the terms of the due-on-sale clause.

SOME MORTGAGE CLAUSES AND THEIR MEANINGS

In general most of the statutory forms of the mortgage require: (1) a date, (2) the names of the parties, (3) the amount of the debt, and (4) a statement that the "mortgagor hereby mortgages to the mortgagee" certain described property.

General Clauses

Following the description of the property, the statutory form of mortgage

---

[2]In some states the wraparound has been ruled usurious because it is argued that the seller has derived interest plus the exaction of a collateral advantage from the borrower (the buyer) and hence usury. Commercial Credit Plan v Chandler, 218 S.W.2d, 1009 (1951).

contains this statement.

And the mortgagor covenants with the mortgagee as follows:

Here follow the general clauses or covenants found in the statutory mortgages in most states. They will vary slightly among the states, but in general they are as described below.

Covenant to Pay Indebtedness. The *covenant to pay indebtedness* states "that the mortgagor will pay the indebtedness as hereinbefore provided." This is self-explanatory.

Covenant of Insurance. The *covenant of insurance* is a promise that the premises shall be covered by fire insurance in a stated amount for the benefit of the mortgagee and that the mortgagor will assign and deliver the policies to the mortgagee. Depending upon the location of the property, a statement should be added to the mortgage in regard to an extended coverage endorsement. The reason for this is that the standard fire policy specifically exempts damage from wind and rain. In hurricane or frequent storm areas, this means that the mortgagee has insufficient protection with the fire policy alone because of the possibility that damage might be done by wind and rain.

Generally speaking, the mortgagee doesn't have to pay any insurance money it receives to "fix up" the premises, although in most cases of residential property, it in reality does.

In the case of a commercial-type loan, the mortgagor should attempt to rewrite the clause so that in the event of destruction or partial destruction of the premises the mortgagor can elect to use the proceeds to restore the premises or to pay off the mortgage.

Covenant Against Removal. The *covenant against removal* is often included in the statutory form of mortgage and states that the mortgagor will not remove or demolish any building without the consent of the mortgagee. This clause is necessary because the amount generally loaned is based on an appraisal that includes both land and buildings. One case involving this clause arose when a mortgage was given on a farm. The mortgagor, anticipating a possible default and having heard that real property consisted of land and things that were attached to the land, built all of the outbuildings on skids. The mortgagor did default on the mortgage, and then hauled the buildings on the skids off the land. The court held that despite the fact that the buildings were not physically attached to the land, they were still under the terms of the mortgage. Thus, the mortgagee was entitled to the foreclosure on those buildings.

Covenant to Pay Taxes. The *covenant to pay taxes* is a promise by the mortgagor that the taxes and assessments that might be levied against the property will be paid. Together with this covenant there is generally an acceleration clause stating that if the taxes or assessments are not paid after a certain time has elapsed, the mortgagee has the option to declare the entire amount of principal and interest due. This clause, in effect, gives the mortgagee the right to foreclose after a stated period in the event that the taxes or assessments are not paid.

One reason for inserting this clause is that if the mortgagor fails to pay real property taxes, the mortgagee would be forced to pay them. This amount, in turn, would be added to the loan and might raise the amount of the loan above the legal maximum loan-to-sale ratio.

Acceleration Clause. The mortgage form contains an *acceleration clause.* This clause specifies that, if the mortgagor fails to keep the covenants or if the title is defective, then the entire debt will become due and collectible at the option of the mortgagee.

In mortgages or deeds of trust containing the nonassumption or due-on-sale clause, the acceleration clause also states in effect that if the borrower sells the property without the consent of the lender, then the balance shall be due and payable.

In some states the acceleration right of the lender has been changed either by statute or court decisions. Here the mortgagor can "cure." This means that prior to the actual foreclosure sale the mortgagor can reinstate the mortgage by paying delinquent principal, interest, costs, expenses, late charges, and attorneys' fees.[3]

Warrant of Title. Most statutory forms of mortgage contain a *warrant of title clause.* It states simply that the mortgagor warrants title to the premises. It means in effect that the mortgagor guarantees the title to the property. This will be discussed in detail later in this chapter.

These six clauses are in general use in nearly every type of simple mortgage in all of the states.

Special Clauses

In addition to the general clauses, there are many other clauses that can be and are inserted into the mortgage form to cover special situations. The most common ones are discussed in the following paragraphs.

Covenant to Pay Attorneys' Fees. In states where a *covenant to pay attorneys' fees* is required, the mortgagor promises to pay reasonable attorneys' fees together with costs and disbursements if the mortgagee finds it necessary to foreclose. Some states do not require a covenant to pay attorneys' fees inasmuch as the mortgagee may demand reasonable fees in the event of foreclosure without the statement being included in the instrument.

---

[3]Cal. Civ. Code Ann. Sec. 2924e [West 1974, Colo.Rev. Stat. Sec. 38–39–118(i)(a) 1978 Supp., Ill. Rev. Stat. Ch. 95 Sec. 57(1976), Penn. Stat. Ann. Titl. 41 Sec. 404 (Purden 1974)].

RECENT FORECLOSURE RATES AND DEVELOPMENTS

Failure to comply with the covenant to pay indebtedness, in conjunction with the acceleration clause, often results in foreclosure. Data reported in the U.S. League of Savings Institutions annual *Sourcebook* indicate the following recent foreclosure rates:

YEAR	FORECLOSURE RATE
1980	.38%
1981	.44
1982	.67
1983	.67
1984	.73
1985	.81
1986	.98

Notice that mortgage foreclosures by all lenders as a percentage of all mortgage loans has increased dramatically from less than .4 percent in 1980 to nearly 1 percent in 1986. Furthermore, the 1986 rate is nearly double the highest foreclosure rates reached during the 1960s and 1970s.

A major contributor to the increased foreclosure rate has been costly housing market collapses. Housing prices have plummeted by more than one-half in certain areas of the country. As a result, voluntary "walk away" foreclosures have been taking place in increasing numbers. Home abandonments often look attractive when mortgage payments are much larger than what a similar home in the same area can be rented for after a housing market collapse. For further discussion of these developments, see: Steve Frazier, "Housing-Market Bust in Houston," *Wall Street Journal* (February 5, 1987): 1, 20.

Receiver Clause. The *receiver clause* states that in any action to foreclose a mortgage the holder of the mortgage shall be entitled to the appointment of a receiver. The receiver is one who will collect any rents and profits from the property and maintain the property. This clause is intended to protect the mortgagee during the interval between the commencement of the foreclosure action and the final order of the court. If the receiver, after having satisfied the mortgagee's claim, has a net balance, the mortgagor is credited with that balance.

This clause is especially important when the sale concerns a parcel of real property on which there is a business. For example, suppose *A* sells *B* real property on which there is a shoe store. *B* is really purchasing three things: the land and building, the stock in the store, and the goodwill of the store, this often being regarded by business people as having the greatest value. The goodwill is referred to by business as "the key." Suppose that *A* is going to finance the purchase in part by becoming the mortgagee for part of the purchase price. Commonly it is said that *A* "takes back" the mortgage. When a person "takes back" a mortgage as part of the purchase price, that person is said to have a purchase money mortgage, which will be discussed in detail later.

Assume that *B* defaults on the payments. *A* has security for the value of the land in the land itself and has probably been paid for the stock, but what about the goodwill or "key"? This may have given the sale its greatest value. Between the time of default and the time of termination of foreclosure action, *B* might operate the business in such a way as to destroy the value of the goodwill.

With a receiver clause in the mortgage, *A* can readily have a receiver appointed who will run the business in a satisfactory manner and thus preserve the value of the goodwill.

The appointment of a receiver may be easy or difficult, depending on whether the state is a title-theory state or a lien-theory state.

In title-theory states, many of the court decisions point to the fact that the mortgagee has title. Consequently the courts say that the lender must, therefore, bring an action of ejectment. *Ejectment* means a turning out of possession. This proceeding is very time-consuming.

In most lien-theory states, the appointment of a receiver can be made with little or no difficulty. However, in some lien-theory states, the mortgagee must show waste is threatened before being entitled to a receiver. *Waste* is defined as an abuse or destructive use of property by one in possession.

Estoppel Clause. The *estoppel clause* states that upon the request of the mortgagee (lender), the mortgagor (borrower) will furnish a written statement "duly acknowledged of the amount due on this mortgage and whether any offsets or defenses exist against the mortgage debt." In some states this is known as a Certificate of No Defense.

Although it might appear strange for the mortgagee to make a request of the mortgagor of how much the mortgagor owes on the mortgage, the inclusion of this is extremely important in the event the mortgagee desires to sell the mortgage. If the mortgagee decides to sell the mortgage in order to raise capital for a further investment, when the mortgagee approaches a third party to sell the mortgage, the third party will want to know the present value of the mortgage. The third party can demand to see the mortgage, but this will not disclose the present value because part of the face value may have been paid. If the mortgage contains an estoppel clause, the mortgagee can demand an estoppel certificate from the mortgagor indicating the present value of the mortgage. In addition, the mortgagor will certify that there are no defenses up to date in the event of a foreclosure action. After having certified that there are no defenses to a foreclosure, the mortgagor cannot later assert in court that a defense existed as of that time. Technically, the mortgagor is said to be "estopped."

In construction financing, as will be detailed in Chapter 14, there are two loans: the construction loan (interim financing) and the permanent loan (permanent financing). Consequently, before making the permanent loan, the permanent lender will require that an estoppel certificate be signed by the borrower under the construction loan.

Good Repair Clause. The *good repair clause* states that if the mortgagor does not keep the premises in "reasonably good repair" or if the owner fails to comply with the requirements of any governmental department within three months, then the mortgagee may foreclose. The test of what is in "reasonably good repair" is that the mortgagee is entitled to foreclose if the security is being impaired.

The inclusion of this clause came about as a result of the condemning of buildings by municipalities as being unfit for human habitation. For example, *A* is the mortgagee on an apartment building and *B* the owner and mortgagor. *B* has tenants in the building and allows the building to deteriorate to such a state of disrepair that the municipality feels it necessary to take action. *B* abandons the building, leaving *A* with a worthless building, in the sense of being untenantable. With a "good repair" clause inserted in the action, *A* could foreclose on the mortgage prior to the time that the municipality takes action and thus protect the security for the debt.

Sale in One Parcel Clause. The *sale in one parcel clause* is generally written as follows: "that in case of a sale, said premises, or as much thereof as may be affected by this mortgage, may be sold in one parcel." This clause is applicable when more than one lot is covered by the terms of the mortgage. In the event of a foreclosure, the mortgagee must offer the lots for sale one at a time until the amount due under the mortgage is paid. If the mortgagor has sold any of the lots "subject to the mortgage," the mortgagee must sell those lots in inverse order of their sale. In short, those lots still owned by the mortgagor must be sold and then those that the mortgagor has already sold, but in inverse order of their sale, last ones first. After they are sold, if this does not bring in enough money, the mortgagor may sell them in bulk. The sale of the individual lots is tentative until it is ascertained that they have brought sufficient funds to cover the debt.

Owner Rent Clause. The *owner rent clause* creates a landlord-tenant relationship between the mortgagee and the mortgagor in the event of a foreclosure. By means of this clause the owner agrees to pay a reasonable rent for the premises during the time of possession of the building after the commencement of the foreclosure action. In some states, even if a receiver under the terms of the mortgage has been appointed, the receiver cannot collect any money except that due on property contracts that the owner had. The owner rent clause enables the receiver to collect rent from the owner of the property.

Prepayment Clause. A *prepayment clause* inserted in a mortgage generally states that the mortgagor may pay the entire amount or a stated amount prior to the due date of the mortgage. In the absence of such language in a mortgage, the lender does not have to permit the borrower to make such payment(s).

In the home loan, the prepayment clause usually contains a prepayment penalty. It may take the form of payment of additional interest, e.g., two months' interest. Or the penalty may take the form of a "scale down," e.g., $3,000 penalty if paid the first year, $2,000 if paid the second year, and so forth.

On May 1, 1972, the FHA suspended loan prepayment penalties. The regulation suspended prepayment penalties to borrowers who paid off their loans before the first ten years of the amortization period had passed. The effect of this regulation was to make the FHA loans more competitive with the VA loans under which no prepayment charges were imposed.

It should be noted that, in the event of condemnation or fire where the proceeds go to pay off the mortgage, there are no prepayment penalties.[4]

ACKNOWLEDGMENT AND RECORDING

Both the mortgage and deed of trust must be acknowledged. The county clerk,[5] recorder, or some other designated person is required to record and index certain instruments as provided by the statute. The county clerk is not required, however, to record these instruments until they have been properly acknowledged. An **acknowledgment** is a formal declaration made before some public officer, usually a notary public, by a person who has signed a deed, mortgage, or other instrument stating that the instrument is that person's act and deed. The instrument to be recorded is usually signed in the presence of a notary or other public officer with the acknowledgment attached substantially in the following form:

State of _____, County of _____ ss.:

On this _____ day of _____ 19_____ before me came _____, known to me to be the said person(s), described in and who executed the foregoing instrument, and duly acknowledged to me that (he, she, they) executed the same as (his, her, their) free act and deed.

_____, Notary Public
(Seal)

The Satisfaction of Mortgage

The **satisfaction of mortgage** or what in some states is called the "release of mortgage," is a receipt signed by the mortgagee stating that the amount due under the mortgage has been paid and may be discharged of record (see Figure 2–3 for an example). This means that upon recording, the county clerk will

---

[4]The IRS regards prepayment penalties as interest which are therefore deductible.
[5]In Connecticut instruments are recorded in the office of the town clerk.

SATISFACTION OF REAL ESTATE MORTGAGE
(INDIVIDUAL)

Know all Men by these Presents:

That Gardner Jones, residing at 23 Elm Street, City of Pullman, County of Whitman, State of Washington,

do es *hereby certif* y *that a certain real estate mortgage bearing date* June 18, 19____, *in volume* 142 *page* 18 *of mortgage records of* Whitman *County, State of Washington made and executed by* Mawa Keyes and John Keyes

as Mortgagor to Gardner Jones

as Mortgagee has been fully paid, and is hereby satisfied, released and discharged, and the real estate covered thereby is hereby released from the lien thereof.

IN WITNESS WHEREOF I *ha* ve *hereunto set* my *hand and seal said* 18th *day of* December *, 19___.*

/s/ Gardner Jones

STATE OF WASHINGTON

} ss.   (INDIVIDUAL ACKNOWLEDGMENT)

County of Whitman

I, Jane Ott , Notary Public in and for the State of Washington, do hereby certify that on this 18th day of December , 19____, personally appeared before me Gardner Jones to me known to be the individual described in and who executed the within instrument and acknowledged that be signed and sealed the same as his free and voluntary act and deed for the uses and purposes herein mentioned.

GIVEN UNDER MY HAND AND OFFICIAL SEAL this 18th day of December , 19___.

/s/ Jane Ott

Notary Public in and for the State of Washington, residing at Pullman in said County.

FIGURE 2–3. Satisfaction of Mortgage

stamp the photostat or typewritten copy of the mortgage as being paid. This instrument is acknowledged and recorded. The effect upon recording is to clear the record of the mortgage.

Many states have statutes imposing criminal penalties upon mortgagees who refuse to deliver the satisfaction when the debt has been paid.

Too much emphasis cannot be placed upon the desirability of immediately recording the satisfaction piece. Without the satisfaction being placed on record, the opportunity presents itself for a fraudulent assignment of the mortgage because a prospective assignee upon examining the record will be led to believe that the mortgage has not been paid and satisfied. Further difficulties are apt to arise if the mortgagor, after having paid a mortgage, fails to record the satisfaction, then attempts to sell the property or to obtain a new mortgage. The record will show the mortgage as not having been paid. In addition, failure to record a satisfaction piece may cause difficulties in the case of death of the mortgagor.

In order to avoid this and to prevent fraudulent assignments, some states require that the mortgage be delivered to the county clerk together with the satisfaction piece in order for the mortgage to be properly discharged of record. The clerk will then efface the original mortgage, which tends to prevent fraudulent negotiation of mortgages which have been paid. To efface the mortgage, the clerk stamps in the margin of a copy of the mortgage filed in the office either "discharged" or "satisfied" and gives also the book and page number where a copy of the satisfaction piece is kept.

Some states, notably New York, prohibit more than one mortgage from being discharged by a single satisfaction piece. If there are two mortgages, there must be two satisfaction pieces. In New York, if the mortgage has been assigned, the assignment must be stated in the satisfaction together with the date of each assignment in the chain of title of the persons signing the instrument. The interest assigned and the book and page where each assignment is recorded must be stated. In the event that the mortgage has not been assigned, the satisfaction piece must state it. Furthermore, if the mortgage is held by a fiduciary, including an executor or administrator, the certificate must recite the name of the court and venue of the proceedings.

Assignment of Mortgage

The *assignment of mortgage* or deed of trust is an instrument used by a mortgagee to transfer interest in a mortgage to a third party. The mortgagee, who is the maker of the assignment, is called the assignor. The person to whom the assignment is made is called the assignee. The instrument names the parties and the consideration and states that the assignor "hereby assigns unto the assignee" interest in the mortgage being transferred. The mortgage is identified by giving, among other things, the book and the page number in which the mortgage is recorded in the county clerk's office. In some states the assignment makes provision for the description of the property assigned, which should be verified against the premises described in the recorded mortgage. Some assignments may contain a covenant by the assignor to the effect that there are no defenses to the mortgage in case it becomes necessary to foreclose, and the assignor verifies the amount due on the mortgage at the time of the assignment (see Figure 2–4).

The signature of the assignor is acknowledged and the assignment is sent to the office of the county clerk, in the county in which the property is located, to be recorded. The assignment is given a book number and a page number, is entered in the book, and a photostatic copy is made. At the same time the county clerk will make a notation on the margin of the photostat of the assigned mortgage indicating the book and page where the assignment has been entered. This enables anyone later searching the records to have notice of the assignment.

A prospective purchaser of a mortgage should have the records searched to determine whether or not a mortgage has been satisfied, has been previously assigned, or whether there are any actions pending on the property described in the mortgage being considered.

ASSIGNMENT OF MORTGAGE WITH COVENANT

KNOW THAT Pauline Rich, residing at 220 Tulip Lane, Borough of Brooklyn, County of Kings, State of New York,

, assignor,

in consideration of Eighty Thousand and 00/100   ($80,000.00)

dollars,

paid by Richard W. Tracy, residing at 2200 Ocean Avenue, Sayville, County of Suffolk, State of New York,

, assignee,

hereby assigns unto the assignee,

Mortgage dated the   8th   day of   June   , 19-- made by Ronald W. Stanton

to Pauline Rich

in the principal sum of $ 80,000.00   and recorded on the 19th   day of June   19-- ,
in ~~(Liber)~~ ~~(Record Liber)~~ (Reel) 1492   of Section 8   of Mortgages, page   , in the office
of the   Clerk   of the County of Suffolk   covering premises

(here follows complete legal description of the property)

TOGETHER with the bond ~~or note or obligation~~ described in said mortgage , and the moneys due and to grow due thereon with the interest,

TO HAVE AND TO HOLD the same unto the assignee and to the successors, legal representatives and assigns of the assignee forever.

AND the assignor covenants that there is now owing upon said mortgage   , without offset or defense of any kind, the principal sum of Eighty Thousand and 00/100 ($80,000.00)

dollars,

with interest thereon at 13-3/4   per centum per annum from the
3rd   day of   March   , nineteen hundred — —

The word "assignor" or "assignee" shall be construed as if it read "assignors" or "assignees" whenever the sense of this instrument so requires.

IN WITNESS WHEREOF, the assignor has duly executed this assignment the 4th   day of January   , 19--.

In presence of:
/s/ Rosemary Roe   /s/ Pauline Rich

(Acknowledgment)
Standard Form of New York Board of Title Underwriters

FIGURE 2–4. Assignment of Mortgage with Covenant

Action on Payment of the Indebtedness Under a Deed of Trust

Depending on the laws of a particular state, either one of two things happens upon the payment of the indebtedness under the terms of the trust deed. In one case an instrument called a reconveyance is used to release the security (the land and improvements) from the trust. There are two types of reconveyance. One is a full reconveyance which is made by the trustee and evidences satisfaction in full and release of the security. Secondly, there is a partial reconveyance which is made by the trustee and evidences satisfaction in part and the release of a portion of the security.[6] Both full and partial reconveyances must describe the deed of trust accurately and in detail, and a partial reconveyance must contain the legal description of the security being released.

The other way the deed of trust is handled upon payment of the indebtedness is as follows: The beneficiary under the trust deed signs an instrument known as a Request for Release of Deed of Trust. This is then presented either to the private, or in most cases, to the public, trustee together with the canceled note and the deed of trust. The trustee then signs a Release of Deed of Trust. As in the case of the mortgage, this release may be complete or partial. The Release of Deed of Trust is then recorded in the office of the county clerk or recorder of the county in which the property is located.

KEY TERMS

acceleration clause	good repair clause
acknowledgment	nonassumption clause
assignment of mortgage	owner rent clause
assumption (of a mortgage)	prepayment clause
covenant against removal	receiver clause
covenant of insurance	sale in one parcel clause
covenant to pay attorneys' fees	satisfaction of mortgage
covenant to pay indebtedness	subject to (a mortgage)
covenant to pay taxes	warrant of title clause
due-on-sale clause	wraparound mortgage
estoppel clause	

QUESTIONS FOR REVIEW

1. What is meant when real property is purchased "subject to" a mortgage?
2. What is meant by "assuming" a mortgage?

---

[6]Some states use a "marginal release," Tennessee and Maryland, for example. A marginal entry is made on the record in the office where the mortgage is recorded, or a release of mortgage is written on the original and then filed in the office where the mortgage is recorded. Cf. Md. Code, Art. 21, Secs. 38–44.

3. Describe the use of the due-on-sale or nonassumption clause.
4. What is included in the lender's assumption statement? Why is it necessary?
5. Describe the meaning and use of the wraparound mortgage.
6. A number of general clauses or covenants are usually found in statutory mortgages. Briefly explain each of the following general clauses: (a) covenant of insurance, (b) covenant to pay taxes, and (c) acceleration clause. Describe some additional general clauses.
7. A number of special clauses may be inserted into the mortgage form. Briefly describe each of the following clauses designed to cover special situations: (a) receiver clause, (b) estoppel clause, (c) good repair clause, and (d) prepayment clause. What are some additional special clauses?
8. Explain what is meant by "acknowledgment and recording" of mortgages and deeds of trust.
9. What does "assignment" of a mortgage or deed of trust mean?
10. Explain what happens upon the payment of the indebtedness under the terms of a deed of trust.

PROBLEMS

1. Mae White agrees to purchase a parcel of property for $40,000 and "take over" the existing $20,000 mortgage. If she fails to make the required payments, and a foreclosure sale takes place at $13,000, what would be the implications?
2. Assume that you are the mortgagee on a piece of property valued at $100,000. The mortgagor purchased the property from you at $90,000 and added portable buildings worth $10,000. You agreed to a mortgage of $80,000 to be paid over 20 years at a 10 percent interest rate. After making only a couple of payments, the mortgagor has missed the most recent payment date.
   a. What will happen if the mortgage contains only the general clauses found in nearly every type of simple mortgage?
   b. What kind of special mortgage clauses might be important to this problem? Describe briefly.
3. Identify recent articles and data relating to home mortgage foreclosures and developments. Compare your findings with the foreclosure rate data and discussion presented in the chapter.

3

VARIATIONS IN MORTGAGE FINANCING

LEARNING OBJECTIVES

After studying this chapter, you should be able to do the following:

Explain how the "quick-pay" and "growing-equity" mortgages relate to the traditional long-term fixed-rate mortgage.

Define and explain what is meant by an adjustable-rate mortgage.

Briefly describe buy-down mortgages and shared-equity financing.

Describe interest-only loans and indicate what is meant by a "moveable" mortgage.

Identify and describe both the graduated-payment mortgage and the shared-appreciation mortgage.

Define and explain the renegotiable-rate mortgage and the price-level-adjustment mortgage.

Identify and describe three types of less-than-full amortization mortgages.

Briefly describe zero-interest loans and replacement loans.

IN THE EARLY eighties, as the result of rapidly rising interest rates, double-digit inflation, and a downswing in the economy, many forms of alternative mortgage financing were developed to protect lenders and to enable more home buyers to qualify for loans.

In the latter part of the eighties, inflation and high interest rates had subsided and there was a return to more normal types of mortgage financing. Some of the "alternatives" used in the early eighties are still being used, while others might be said to be "waiting in the wings." It might be argued that more of the alternative types of mortgage instruments and financing may return if conditions warrant.

For the above reasons, the discussion here will be divided into two parts: (1) common types of mortgage financing, and (2) alternative (or uncommon) types of mortgage financing.

COMMON TYPES OF MORTGAGE FINANCING

The Fixed-Rate Mortgage (FRM)

This type of mortgage has been in existence since the Great Depression of the thirties. Early in its history it was a 20-year fixed-rate mortgage. Today the term is commonly for 30 years. This simply means that both the interest rate and the term are fixed for 30 years. For example, on a 30-year fixed-rate mortgage of $60,000 at 10 percent, the monthly payments would be $526.50. It should be noted that generally monthly payments of insurance and taxes are added to that.

As frequently happens in similar situations, variations of this mortgage have sprung up—with different names. One is the so-called "quick-pay" mortgage. This is simply a 15-year fixed-rate mortgage. Both the down payment and the monthly payments are higher than in the 30-year fixed-rate mortgage. For example, using the normal standard of the Federal National Mortgage Association and the Federal Home Loan Mortgage Corporation for secondary market purchases of mortgages—monthly principal and interest payments should not exceed 28 percent of the home buyer's gross monthly income—it takes a monthly income of $3,000 to qualify for a 30-year $9^{1}/_{2}$ percent $100,000 mortgage, but for a similar 15-year mortgage, a monthly income of $3,729 is required. The big advantages of the quick-pay mortgages are (1) interest payments over the life of the loan are reduced, and (2) equity in the home increases at a faster rate.

A second variation of the fixed-rate mortgage is the "biweekly" mortgage. This is sometimes called the "yuppie mortgage" because of its appeal to young, upwardly mobile professionals who are interested in the fast buildup of equity in their homes in order that they might sell them and move to a better home sooner. Instead of one monthly payment being made monthly, half the normal payment is collected every other week. This results in the equivalent of one extra month's payment being made each year. In addition, there is a steady reduction of principal every 14 days instead of every 30 or 31 days. Thus at $9^{1}/_{4}$ percent interest, a biweekly $100,000 loan pays off in a little over 21 years instead of 30 years, saving $63,819 in interest. On a 20-year fixed mortgage, the saving is $127,637.

Many of the mortgage companies who have developed these loans sell them to Goldman, Sachs & Co., who package them into blocks and sell them to institutional investors as mortgage-backed securities.

The "growing-equity mortgage" is a variation of the quick-pay mortgage. A *Growing-Equity Mortgage* (GEM) is also sometimes referred to as an "equity buildup," "early ownership," "accelerated equity," or "rapid pay-off" loan. In the GEM, the mortgage loan is based on a 25-year schedule. In short, the monthly payments are initially set *as if* the loan is to be paid off in equal monthly payments over 25 years. The interest rate is fixed—it does not move up and down with changes in an index as does the adjustable rate mortgage. However, the monthly payments are increased by 4 percent on March 1 of every year. These 4 percent payment increases constitute payments on *principal,* not interest. As a result of the payments on principal, the scheduled maturity is reduced to 15 years or less. Therefore, the homeowner will have the home paid for in 15 years. Furthermore, the total interest paid by the homeowner will amount to approximately 50 percent less than on the equivalent 25-year, fixed-rate level-payment loan.

The lenders are thrift institutions, mortgage bankers, and commercial banks. The major advantage to them of the GEM loan is liquidity. There are weekly auctions conducted by the Federal Home Loan Mortgage Corporation (FHLMC), and as originators of the GEM loans, these institutions sell their GEM loans and in turn receive GEM participation certificates issued by the FHLMC (or Freddie Mac as it has been dubbed). The *Participation Certificate* is an undivided interest in specified GEM loans underwritten and purchased by the Federal Home Loan Mortgage Corporation. Freddie Mac guarantees interest on the unpaid balance of the loan and the collection on principal. In essence, the Participation Certificate is backed by a pool of GEM loans.

Simultaneously as the lending institution commits to *exchange* its GEM loans for a Participation Certificate, a commitment is made to sell the GEM Participation Certificate to either Merrill Lynch or Salomon Brothers, who, in turn, sells the GEM PC to an institutional investor.

The GEM loan may have up to a 95 percent loan-to-value ratio. The *loan-to-value ratio* is the maximum mortgage loan allowable as a percentage of the property's purchase price. All loans exceeding an 80 percent loan-to-value ratio must have mortgage insurance for the principal amount exceeding 75 percent. For example, if there is a 95 percent loan-to-value ratio and the loan is for $100,000, the homeowner puts down $5,000 and the mortgage insurance is on the next $20,000 of the loan.

The Adjustable-Rate Mortgage (ARM)

What was originally termed a "variable-rate mortgage" is now called an "adjustable-rate mortgage." The rates of an *adjustable-rate mortgage* are pegged to an index, and in March of 1981 the Federal Home Loan Bank Board, under its Adjustable Mortgage Loan Rules, removed all restrictions on rates and payment increases for federal savings and loan associations. This means that the loans can be set up so that adjustments are made as frequently as monthly and at an indexed rate. Some are adjusted every ninety days, some semiannually, and some annually.

Depending on the particular ARM, changes in rates may be reflected in changes of monthly payments by the borrower or monthly payments may be kept constant. When the monthly payments remain constant, both increases and decreases are reflected in the length of the term of the loan or in the amount of the principal balance.

Figure 3–1 shows a standard Federal Home Loan Mortgage Corporation Adjustable Rate Note used in conjunction with the ARM. In paragraph 4(B), Setting the New Interest Rate, it states in effect that the change in the interest rate is to be the change between the Base Index figure and the Current Index figure.

Typically the Base Index figure is the initial interest rate—say, 13 percent. If the index is, for example, FHLBB's "National Average for All Types of Lenders," and it rises by one percentage point, then the new rate becomes 14 percent.

In reality, the Base Index figure can be any figure, say 8 percent, with an initial interest rate of 13 percent. If the index rises 1 percent, the change between the Current Index figure and the Base Index figure is still 1 percent, resulting in a new rate of 14 percent.

For example, assume at the time of the loan the T-Bill rate is 8.75 percent and that this is the index. Suppose that initially the rate on the mortgage is 13.5 percent. If the T-Bill rate rises to 10 percent, or a 1.25 percentage point rise, then the interest rate on the mortgage goes up to 14.75 percent.

A variation of the standard ARM is the *convertible adjustable-rate mortgage.* It gets its name because the buyer is given the option of converting an ARM to a fixed-rate mortgage. Recently the popularity of these mortgages has increased, since the Federal National Mortgage Association (or Fannie Mae as it has been dubbed), the largest investor in home mortgages, changed the circumstances under which it would buy convertible loans. It now permits the buyer to convert from an ARM to a 30-year fixed-rate mortgage from the 13th to the 60th month of the loan. Although Fannie Mae had previously purchased such mortgages, borrowers could convert only during the third, fourth, or fifth anniversaries of the loan. ARMs afford several advantages to the borrowers:

1. Generally it is easier for a borrower to qualify for an ARM than for a fixed-rate mortgage, and initial rates of interest are typically lower for an ARM than for a fixed-rate mortgage.
2. If rates drop, the borrower may refinance the loan, but the costs generally are much higher than the cost the borrower must pay in

ADJUSTABLE RATE NOTE

**NOTICE TO BORROWER: THIS NOTE CONTAINS A PROVISION ALLOW-
ING FOR CHANGES IN THE INTEREST RATE. INCREASES IN THE
INTEREST RATE WILL RESULT IN HIGHER PAYMENTS. DECREASES
IN THE INTEREST RATE WILL RESULT IN LOWER PAYMENTS.**

. . . . ,19. . . . .,. . . . .
                                                                          City   *State*

. . . .:. . . . .
Property Address   *City*   *State*   *Zip Code*

1. BORROWER'S PROMISE TO PAY
In return for a loan that I have received, I promise to pay U.S. $. . . . . (this amount will be
called "principal"), plus interest, to the order of the Lender. The Lender is . . . .
. . . .

I understand that the Lender may transfer this Note. The Lender or anyone who takes this Note by transfer and
who is entitled to receive payments under this Note will be called the "Note Holder".

2. INTEREST
Interest will be charged on that part of outstanding principal which has not been paid. Interest will be charged
beginning on the date I receive principal and continuing until the full amount of principal I receive has been paid.

Beginning on the date of this Note, I will pay interest at a yearly rate of . . . .% (the "Initial Interest Rate"). The interest rate that I will pay will change in accordance with Section 4 of this Note until my loan is paid.
Interest rate changes may occur on the . . . . . day of the month beginning on . . . . ,
19. . . . . and on that day of the month every . . . . months thereafter. Each date on which the rate
of interest may change will be called a "Change Date".

3. PAYMENTS
(A) Time and Place of Payments
I will pay principal and interest by making payments every month. I will make my monthly payments on the
. . . . . day of each month beginning on . . . . ,19. . . . . . I will make these payments
until I have paid all of the principal and interest and any other charges, described below, that I may owe under this
Note. I will pay all sums that I owe under this Note no later than . . . ., ...
(the "final payment date").

I will make my monthly payments at . . . .
. . . . .or at a different place if required by the Note Holder.

(B) Borrower's Payments Before They Are Due
I have the right to make payments of principal at any time before they are due. A payment of principal only is
known as a "prepayment". When I make a prepayment, I will tell the Note Holder in writing that I am doing so. I may
make a full prepayment or a partial prepayment without paying any penalty. The Note Holder will use all of my
prepayments to reduce the amount of principal that I owe under this Note. If I make a partial prepayment, there will be
no delays in the due dates of my monthly payments unless the Note Holder agrees in writing to those delays. My partial
prepayment will reduce the amount of my monthly payments after the first Change Date following my partial prepayment. However, any reduction due to my partial prepayment may be offset by an interest rate increase.

(C) Amount of Monthly Payments
My initial monthly payments will be in the amount of U.S. $. . . . . If the interest rate
that I pay changes, the amount of my monthly payments will change. Increases in the interest rate will result in higher
payments (unless my prepayments since the last Change Date offset the increases in my monthly payments). Decreases
in the interest rate will result in lower payments. The amount of my monthly payments will always be sufficient to repay
my loan in full in substantially equal payments by the final payment date. In setting the monthly payment amount on
each Change Date, the Note Holder will assume that the Note interest rate will not change again prior to the final payment date.

COLORADO—ADJUSTABLE RATE LOAN NOTE—6/81—FHLMC UNIFORM INSTRUMENT

EL 263 (7 30-81)

FIGURE 3–1. Adjustable Rate Note

4. INTEREST RATE CHANGES

   (A) The Index

      Any changes in the interest rate will be based on changes in an interest rate index which will be called the "Index". The Index is the: [*Check one box to indicate Index.*]

      (1) □* "Contract Interest Rate, Purchase of Previously Occupied Homes, National Average for all Major Types of Lenders" published by the Federal Home Loan Bank Board.

      (2) □* . . . .
. . . .

      If the Index ceases to be made available by the publisher, or by any successor to the publisher, the Note Holder will set the Note interest rate by using a comparable index.

   (B) Setting the New Interest Rate

      To set the new interest rate, the Note Holder will determine the change between the Base Index figure and the Current Index figure. The Base Index figure is . . . . The Current Index figure is the most recent Index figure available . . . . days prior to each Change Date. If the amount of the change is less than one-eighth of one percentage point, the change will be rounded to zero. If the amount of the change is one-eighth of one percentage point or more, the Note Holder will round the amount of the change to the nearest one-eighth of one percentage point.

      If the Current Index figure is larger than the Base Index figure, the Note Holder will add the rounded amount of the change to the Initial Interest Rate. If the Current Index figure is smaller than the Base Index figure, the Note Holder will subtract the rounded amount of the change from the Initial Interest Rate. The result of this addition or subtraction will be the preliminary rate. If there is no change between the Base Index figure and the Current Index figure after rounding, the Initial Interest Rate will be the preliminary rate.

      [*Check one box to indicate whether there is any maximum limit on interest rate changes; if no box is checked, there will be no maximum limit on changes.*]

      (1) □ If this box is checked, there will be no maximum limit on changes in the interest rate up or down. The preliminary rate will be the new interest rate.

      (2) □ If this box is checked, the interest rate will not be changed by more than . . . . percentage points on any Change Date. The Note Holder will adjust the preliminary rate so that the change in the interest rate will not be more than that limit. The new interest rate will equal the figure that results from this adjustment of the preliminary rate.

   (C) Effective Date of Changes

      Each new interest rate will become effective on the next Change Date. If my monthly payment changes as a result of a change in the interest rate, my monthly payment will change as of the first monthly payment date after the Change Date.

   (D) Notice to Borrower

      The Note Holder will mail me a notice by first class mail at least thirty and no more than forty-five days before each Change Date if the interest rate is to change. The notice will advise me of:

      (i)   the new interest rate on my loan;

      (ii)   the amount of my new monthly payment; and

      (iii) any additional matters which the Note Holder is required to disclose.

5. BORROWER'S FAILURE TO PAY AS REQUIRED

   (A) Late Charge for Overdue Payments

      If the Note Holder has not received the full amount of any of my monthly payments by the end of . . . . calendar days after the date it is due, I will pay a late charge to the Note Holder. The amount of the charge will be . . . .% of my overdue payment of principal and interest. I will pay this late charge only once on any late payment.

   (B) Notice from Note Holder

      If I do not pay the full amount of each monthly payment on time, the Note Holder may send me a written notice telling me that if I do not pay the overdue amount by a certain date I will be in default. That date must be at least 30 days after the date on which the notice is mailed to me.

   (C) Default

      If I do not pay the overdue amount by the date stated in the notice described in (B) above, I will be in default. If I am in default, the Note Holder may require me to pay immediately the full amount of principal which has not been paid and all the interest that I owe on that amount.

      Even if, at a time when I am in default, the Note Holder does not require me to pay immediately in full as described above, the Note Holder will still have the right to do so if I am in default at a later time.

   (D) Payment of Note Holder's Costs and Expenses

      If the Note Holder has required me to pay immediately in full as described above, the Note Holder will have the right to be paid back by me for all its reasonable costs and expenses to the extent not prohibited by applicable law. Those expenses may include, for example, reasonable attorneys' fees.

6. WAIVERS

      Anyone who signs this Note to transfer it to someone else (known as an "endorser") waives certain rights. Those rights are (A) the right to require the Note Holder to demand payment of amounts due (known as "presentment") and (B) the right to require the Note Holder to give notice that amounts due have not been paid (known as "notice of dishonor").

FIGURE 3–1. Adjustable Rate Note (continued)

7. GIVING OF NOTICES

Except for the notice provided in Section 4(D), any notice that must be given to me under this Note will be given by mailing it by certified mail. All notices will be addressed to me at the Property Address above. Notices will be mailed to me at a different address if I give the Note Holder a notice of my different address.

Any notice that must be given to the Note Holder under this Note will be given by mailing it by certified mail to the Note Holder at the address stated in Section 3(A) above. Notices will be mailed to the Note Holder at a different address if I am given a notice of that different address.

8. RESPONSIBILITY OF PERSONS UNDER THIS NOTE

If more than one person signs this Note, each of us is fully and personally obligated to pay the full amount owed and to keep all of the promises made in this Note. Any guarantor, surety, or endorser of this Note is also obligated to do these things. The Note Holder may enforce its rights under this Note against each of us individually or against all of us together. This means that any one of us may be required to pay all of the amounts owed under this Note.

Any person who takes over my rights or obligations under this Note will have all of my rights and must keep all of my promises made in this Note. Any person who takes over the rights or obligations of a guarantor, surety, or endorser of this Note is also obligated to keep all of the promises made in this Note.

9. LOAN CHARGES

It could be that this loan is subject to a law which sets maximum loan charges and that law is interpreted so that the interest or other loan charges collected or to be collected in connection with this loan would exceed permitted limits. If this is the case, then: (A) any such loan charge shall be reduced by the amount necessary to reduce the charge to the permitted limit; and (B) any sums already collected from me which exceeded permitted limits will be refunded to me. The Note Holder may choose to make this refund by reducing the principal I owe under this Note or by making a direct payment to me. If a refund reduces principal, the reduction will be treated as a partial prepayment.

10. THIS NOTE SECURED BY A DEED OF TRUST

In addition to the protections given to the Note Holder under this Note, a Deed of Trust, dated . . . . , 19 . . . . . protects the Note Holder from possible losses which might result if I do not keep the promises which I make in this Note. That Deed of Trust describes how and under what conditions I may be required to make immediate payment in full of all amounts that I owe under this Note. One of those conditions relates to any transfer of the property covered by the Deed of Trust. In that regard, the Deed of Trust provides in paragraph 17:

17. Transfer of the Property; Assumption. If all or any part of the Property or an interest therein is sold or transferred by Borrower without Lender's prior written consent, excluding (a) the creation of a lien or encumbrance subordinate to this Deed of Trust, (b) the creation of a purchase money security interest for household appliances, (c) a transfer by devise, descent or by operation of law upon the death of a joint tenant or (d) the grant of any leasehold interest of three years or less not containing an option to purchase, Lender may, at Lender's option, declare all the sums secured by this Deed of Trust to be immediately due and payable. Lender shall have waived such option to accelerate if, prior to the sale or transfer, Lender and the person to whom the Property is to be sold or transferred reach agreement in writing that the credit of such person is satisfactory to Lender and that the interest payable on the sums secured by this Deed of Trust shall be at such rate as Lender shall request. If Lender has waived the option to accelerate provided in this paragraph 17, and if Borrower's successor in interest has executed a written assumption agreement accepted in writing by Lender, Lender shall release Borrower from all obligations under this Deed of Trust and the Note.

If Lender exercises such option to accelerate, Lender shall mail Borrower notice of acceleration in accordance with paragraph 14 hereof. Such notice shall provide a period of not less than 30 days from the date the notice is mailed within which Borrower may pay the sums declared due. If Borrower fails to pay such sums prior to the expiration of such period, Lender may, without further notice or demand on Borrower, invoke any remedies permitted by paragraph 18 hereof.

An Adjustable Rate Loan Rider supplements the Deed of Trust and provides:

If there is a transfer of the Property subject to paragraph 17 of the Security Instrument, Lender may require (1) an increase in the current Note interest rate, or (2) an increase in (or removal of) the limit on the amount of any one interest rate change (if there is a limit), or (3) a change in the Base Index figure, or all of these, as a condition of Lender's waiving the option to accelerate provided in paragraph 17.

. . . .(Seal)
Borrower

. . . .(Seal)
Borrower

. . . .(Seal)
Borrower
(Sign Original Only)

* *If more than one box is checked or if no box is checked, and Lender and Borrower do not otherwise agree in writing, the first Index named will apply.*

FIGURE 3–1.   Adjustable Rate Note (concluded)

order to exercise the conversion privilege.
3. Many individuals find themselves psychologically unable to handle an ARM in the sense that they worry about a rapid increase in interest rates. The convertible ARM gives these persons an "out" and thus more peace of mind.

The Buy-Down Mortgage (BDM)

The *buy-down mortgage* is really not a mortgage but a financing device. The purpose of the buy-down mortgage is to reduce the monthly payments to home buyers. It involves the use of a front-end payment to set up an annuity-type fund to reduce the initial monthly payments of a borrower.

There are two basic types of buy-downs:

1. Fixed Buy-Down. For example, a buyer needs a $50,000 mortgage, and the interest rate is, say, $15^1/2$ percent for a 30-year loan. Without a buy-down, monthly principal and interest payments are $652.26. Let's assume that this payment is too large for the buyer to qualify for the loan. What can be done?

One possibility might be for the seller (generally a builder) to agree to pay perhaps a 2 percentage point buy-down for three years. The 2 percent is subtracted from the $15^1/2$ percent to equal monthly payments at $13^1/2$ percent on the loan, or $572.71. Thus the monthly payments to the borrower become $79.55 ($652.26 – $572.71) less than before the buy-down and might allow the buyer to qualify for the loan. The total cost to the seller in this case would be $2,863.80 ($79.55 × 36 months).

When an FHA-insured mortgage is to be used under FHA Title 245, the normal maximum FHA loan amount will prevail. This program is limited to owner-occupied single-family homes or approved condominiums. The term of the loan is always 30 years. Co-mortgagors are allowed under this program. The buyer will be qualified on the basis of whether he or she meets FHA financial standards at the time the loan is applied for.

2. Graduated Buy-Down. In this case, the $15^1/2$ percent loan is reduced to $12^1/2$ percent in the first year, resulting in payments of $533.63 per month. During the second year, the buyer would make monthly payments based on a $13^1/2$ percent loan rate. The rate for the third year would be $14^1/2$ percent. Beginning in the fourth year and thereafter the buyer would pay $652.26 per month. The cost of the buy-down to the seller would be the difference between $652.26 and the monthly payments made by the buyer during the first three years of the loan. Because a person is qualified on the basis of size of payments during the first year, the buyer could qualify more easily under a graduated buy-down plan.

The cost of the buy-down is placed in escrow at the closing and contributes to the monthly payments on a schedule agreed upon by the participants. The buy-down can be made by anyone—the seller, the buyer, or a third

RECENT MORTGAGE FINANCING DEVELOPMENTS

Mortgage interest rates dropped during 1986 and early 1987. As fixed-rate mortgages (FRMs) became more affordable, the share of conventional loans closed held by adjustable-rate mortgages (ARMs) declined. Even so, ARMs continued to account for between one-fourth and one-third of new conventional loans. As interest rates rose during the latter part of 1987, the ARMs' share of total conventional loans closed increased to about the 50-percent level.

Adjustable-rate mortgages also have become more standardized. Increased secondary market activity has contributed to this greater standardization by requiring tighter underwriting standards for ARMs. The Treasury-indexed ARM has annual adjustments and contains periodic and lifetime caps, while the monthly adjustable ARM is tied to the 11th Federal Home Loan Bank District Cost-of-Funds index. Both of these ARMs are widely available to borrowers.

Also of note is the recent revival of convertible adjustable-rate mortgages which were initially introduced during the high-interest-rate early 1980s. Borrowers like them because it now is relatively easy, quick, and cheap to convert the convertible ARM to a FRM. Convertible ARMs also are attractive to lenders because the loans are kept outstanding and servicing fees are maintained. Furthermore, convertible ARMs cost less to process than do mortgage loan refinancings.

For further discussion of these developments, see: *Freddie Mac Reports,* "ARMs Poised for Big Gains" (August 1987) and "Convertibles Cruise to New Popularity" (November 1987).

party (e.g., the buyer's parents).

Sometimes, if the institution intends to keep the loan, the buy-down may be for as long as five years. At the end of that time period, a balloon payment may be agreed upon, giving the buyer an option to refinance at the then current market rate.

Shared-Equity Financing

As defined by the IRS, *shared-equity financing* is an agreement under which two or more persons acquire qualified ownership interests in a dwelling unit as a principal residence, and occupant-owners are required to pay rent to the nonoccupant co-owners.

According to the IRS, "qualified ownership interest" is an undivided interest for more than 50 years in the entire dwelling unit and the land.[1] For all practical purposes, this means a fee simple interest rather than anything that could be construed as a lease.

The transaction works like this:

There is a seller of a home, a buyer of a home, and an investor. In

---

[1]Internal Revenue Code, Section 280A(d)(3)(D).

most cases, the seller is the investor. For example, assume the home is valued at $80,000 with 20 percent down. The seller or some other investor puts up 75 percent of the down payment, or $12,000 ($16,000 down × .75), the buyer $4,000, leaving a balance of $64,000. Assume that the loan is at 14 percent for 25 years. This would make the monthly payments $770.41.

The buyer and the investor receive a deed as tenants in common. The agreement calls for the buyer to pay all operating expenses, plus 50 percent of the mortgage payments, real property taxes, and interest. In addition, the buyer agrees to pay the co-owner rent. Out of the rent, the co-owner pays 50 percent of the mortgage payments, real property taxes, and interest on the mortgage. A split in any profits from a sale are agreed upon.

Fifty percent of the $770.41 is $385.20. Assume the buyer agrees to pay rent of $300 to the investor; then the buyer's total out-of-pocket payments would be $685.20, with the owner-investor picking up the balance.

In addition to holding a 50 percent share in the property, the owner-investor can deduct real property taxes, interest, and depreciation from income taxes. Prior to mid-1982, this could not be done because depreciation could not be deducted when a home was used by an owner for "personal" purposes. Personal purposes, as defined by the IRS, referred to a dwelling used by the taxpayer or any other person who had an interest in such unit.[2] However, in mid-1982, an amendment was passed that approves of the depreciation by an owner-investor provided:

1. The rental charged is fair;
2. The owner-occupant uses the premises as his/her personal residence; and
3. The rental is made pursuant to a shared-equity financing agreement.[3]

Interest-Only Loans (IOL)

Interest-only loans, as their name implies, require the payment of interest *only* over a number of years and are generally set up in one of two ways. The first scenario is essentially as follows: *A* sells *B* a home for $75,000, with interest *only* to be paid at 13 percent for five years; at the end of five years, the principal is to be paid. The note that is signed is said to be a "balloon" note because the loan is not amortized but is due in a lump sum.

In the early eighties millions of dollars were lost by buyers who had signed balloon notes. Because interest rates had risen and the real estate market had flattened as a result, buyers were not able to refinance the loans nor sell the property.

However, in 1987 Fannie Mae announced that it would buy balloon notes, and the result was a rapid rise in the use of these financing instruments. Because of their high risk, lenders and Fannie Mae both require a

---

[2]Internal Revenue Code, Section 280A(d)(2)(A).
[3]Internal Revenue Code, Section 280(d)(3)(B)(ii) and Internal Revenue Code, Section 280A(d)(3).

down payment of at least 20 percent, and in many cases as much as 25 percent. Interest rates are generally lower for these loans than the 30-year fixed-rate loans because the term is generally only seven or ten years. Since down payments are relatively high and statistics suggest that the "average" American moves every six years, Fannie Mae does not regard this type of balloon note as a problem.

Another method for handling this type of loan is a variation of the "balloon" mortgage. It requires the borrower to pay interest *only* for five years, and then payments are increased to include *principal and interest* so that the mortgage is fully amortized over the remaining term of the mortgage.

The Moveable Mortgage

The *moveable mortgage* is a commercial type of mortgage recently coming into use which permits borrowers to transfer the balance of their income property loan to another property without paying "points." *Points* are an extra charge by the lender for having obtained the money, and one point is equal to one percent. If the loan is increased, points are paid only on the incremental amount. For example, an investor buys a property for $1.1 million, renovates it, and then sells it for a profit within two years. A loan was received for $700,000 with 1.5 points, or $10,500. Buyer then purchases a second property with a loan of $800,000, the old loan of $700,000 is moved to the new property, and the borrower instead of having to obtain a new loan for $800,000 and pay 1.5 points, merely has to pay points on the incremental $100,000, or an additional $1,500. If the dollar amount remains flat, meaning that the loan remains the same, there are no points.

Generally the moveability of the loan is limited to one move a year and as yet there is no limitation on how many times this sort of rollover may be made by an investor. These loans are payable at the rate of a 30-year amortization with maturities between 10 and 15 years. The rates are adjustable and are generally pegged to $2^{1}/_{2}$ to $2^{3}/_{4}$ percentage points above a picked Federal Reserve District Cost of Funds.

ALTERNATIVE TYPES OF MORTGAGE FINANCING

The Graduated-Payment Mortgage (GPM)

In the *graduated-payment mortgage,* payments are stepped up at an agreed future date. For example, a loan may be offered to a home purchaser at 14 percent interest on $50,000 for 30 years. The monthly payment of principal and interest on this loan amounts to $592.44. If the lender's loan policy is on a 1:4 ratio basis, meaning that the loan payments cannot be greater than 25 percent of the person's income, then, to qualify, the potential borrower must earn $2,369.76 ($592.44 ÷ .25) per month. If this criterion is not met, the borrower fails to obtain the loan. The GPM, in contrast, permits lower payments of principal and interest during, for example, the first five years of the loan; then payments are increased. Interest which has not been paid during the first five years is added to the balance due on the loan.

The *Graduated-Payment Adjustable Mortgage* (GPAM) is similar to the GPM except that at the time of the step-up in the payments on the loan, the borrower has to pay the prevailing rate of interest at that time. It should be noted that on both the GPM and the GPAM there can be more than one step-up in the payment period. For example, it could be arranged that payments increase every five years until the loan has been repaid.

The Shared-Appreciation Mortgage (SAM)

Under the *shared-appreciation mortgage,* a lender shares in any appreciation over and above the original purchase price of the property. The maximum period for SAMs cannot exceed 10 years, but the time period can be less if the property is sold sooner. If the property does not sell in 10 years, the lender can have the home appraised and the borrower must pay the lender a lump sum equal to the lender's proportion of the appreciation. For example, assume a home is bought now for $100,000 and the agreement calls for equal sharing of appreciation. In 10 years the fair market value as determined by an appraisal is $200,000. The lender can demand $50,000 of the $100,000 appreciation. If the homeowner lacks the $50,000 lump sum due, the lender must refinance the loan, including the amount of the appreciation, at the then-prevailing rate of interest.

The SAM raises a number of problems, both to the consumer and to the lender.

Consumers face the following possible problems:

1. Refinancing might cause the homeowner's monthly payments to rise to a level that the homeowner cannot afford, with foreclosure as a result.
2. The homeowner might lose the hedge against inflation.
3. Upon the sale of the home, under current law, there is a possibility that the seller might have to pay a capital gains tax on the appreciation even though part of the profit goes to the lender.

Lenders, too, might have problems:

1. There is no way lenders can accurately forecast future income or losses on outstanding loans.
2. Current antidiscrimination laws can force the making of SAMs in depressed or market value-declining areas.

The *Equity-Participation Mortgage* (EPM) is slightly different from the SAM. In the SAM, the lender's share is in the appreciation only. In the EPM, the lender shares in the appreciation *plus* any down payments and other increases in the homeowner's equity.

Mortgages with Special Features

The Renegotiable-Rate Mortgage (RRM). The *renegotiable-rate mortgage* is set up for a long term, generally for 30 years. This means that the monthly payments are relatively low. The interest rate is adjusted periodically: at perhaps three-, four-, or five-year intervals. The rate is determined by a national mortgage index published by the Federal Home Loan Bank Board. The maximum upward change for the life of the loan is 5 percent, and there is a maximum change upward of $1^1/2$ percent per year. The upward changes are at the option of the lender, however, and reductions in rates are mandatory.

The Price-Level-Adjustment Mortgage (PLAM). In the *price-level-adjustment mortgage,* two rates of interest are used with the net result being that the loan principal becomes variable rather than the interest rate. The borrower pays the "real" or "true" rate of interest. This rate is determined by subtracting the rate of inflation, at the time of the loan, from the mortgage rate of interest at the time of the loan. For example, if the mortgage rate is 16 percent and the rate of inflation is 10 percent, then the "true" rate is 6 percent.

Six percent becomes the rate paid by the borrower and the monthly payments are at this rate. At the end of the first year and subsequent years, the balance owed the lender is adjusted by the rate of inflation. The effect of this is to give the lender purchasing power equal to that realized from the original loan principal. For example, if the rate of inflation is 10 percent and the balance is $100,000, the new balance due the lender becomes $110,000. At this point, the monthly payment of the borrower is adjusted upward to reflect this balance, still at 6 percent interest, for the second year, and so on.

The danger in this to the borrower is an implied assumption that the income of the borrower will rise at the rate of inflation and consequently the borrower will be able to pay the increased monthly payments. Very often, this is not the case. To avoid this burden on the borrower, some institutions are willing to permit the increase in the loan to become a balloon payment on the sale of the house.

Less-Than-Full Amortization Mortgages

These are simply loans in which (a) payments never fully amortize the loan, or (b) the buyer never takes title to the land, as in the case of a lease.

The Reverse-Annuity Mortgage (RAM). Although the *reverse-annuity mortgage* was authorized by statute in Connecticut in the late seventies, it wasn't until July, 1981, that federal savings and loan associations were given the authority to become involved with this type of mortgage. The purpose of the mortgage is to supplement the monthly income of retirees. The mortgage is handled in one of two ways:

1. A lender purchases an annuity for the borrower based on the value of

the property. A mortgage is then placed against the property. The mortgage is paid out of the estate of the retired person.

2. Rather than the lender purchasing an annuity for the borrower, the lender pays the borrower a fixed monthly payment, again to be paid out of the estate of the borrower.

In some cases the annuity is a lifetime annuity, and in other cases the pay-out period to the retiree is for 10 years. In the latter situation, the homeowner is protected because there is a guarantee of either a rollover of the RAM or outright financing.

It should be added that the July, 1981, authorization given to savings and loan associations to make RAMs also gave them authority to make RAMs with adjustable rates.

The Residential Ground Lease. The *residential ground lease,* which has been used in Maryland and Hawaii for many years, is increasing in popularity. It is used to enable more persons to qualify for loans and to reduce down payments. For example, assume a property worth $100,000 with an 80 percent loan-to-value ratio: the down payment would be $20,000 and the property could be sold only to those persons qualifying for an $80,000 loan. If the land were valued at $20,000 and leased, the down payment would be $16,000 ($80,000 × .20) and the purchaser could qualify for a $64,000 ($80,000 – $16,000) loan rather than for an $80,000 loan.

In these cases, the buyer is given an option to purchase the land; however, the leases call for an annual percentage increase in the purchase price. For example, the buyer can buy during the first year at $20,000, but in the second year it will cost the buyer an additional 5 percent, or whatever rate is negotiated, the third year another 5 percent, and so on.

In most cases the ground rent is at a flat rent for 15 years, but after that it escalates. The reason for the flat rental is that the Federal Home Loan Bank Board requires a flat rental for 15 years in order to make the mortgage eligible for sale in the secondary market.

Because lenders will demand a first lien, they will require that the seller's fee interest in the land be subordinated.

The Graduated-Payment Ground Lease. The *graduated-payment ground lease* is a variation of the straight residential ground lease and is used by some builders. For example, a home including the land is priced at $130,000 and the fee may be purchased at this price. If the buyer wants to lease the land, let's assume the price of the home becomes $100,000 and the land is valued at $30,000. The term of the lease is 99 years; the rent for the first year is 2 percent (or $600). The rent increases 2 percent per year until it reaches 10 percent in Year 5. It remains at that level for the rest of the term. However, the rent paid by the home owner is figured on the assumption that the value of the land is increasing at the rate of, say, 5 percent per year. For example, the first year's rent on the $30,000 lot is $600 ($30,000 × .02); in the second year the assumed value of the lot is $31,500 and the rent is $1,260 ($31,500 × .04); and so forth. The lessee is given an option to buy the land at any time at the appreciated value.

Unusual Financing Arrangements

There are a number of unusual types of financing used either by individuals or financial institutions in various parts of the country. These methods may become more commonplace in the future.

Zero-Interest-Rate Loans. In parts of the Midwest, some builders are making *zero-interest-rate loans.* In most of these instances, home purchasers must have a down payment of a third of the purchase price. The balance is financed by a five-year zero-rate mortgage payable in 60 equal monthly payments. For example, for a $90,000 home there is a down payment of $30,000 with the $60,000 balance being paid off in 60 monthly payments of $1,000 each.

One of the problems facing purchasers in this kind of arrangement is that in some cases the purchase price of the home is raised to cover the loss of interest. For example, in at least one case, the conventional mortgage contract price is quoted at $58,000; with a zero-interest loan, however, the contract price is quoted at $71,000—an increase of $13,000—and the down payment is $23,666 compared with a down payment of $5,800 when conventionally financed. For all practical purposes, the $13,000 increase in price can be considered interest paid in advance out of the increase in down payment and the increase in the purchase price.

Replacement Loans. *Replacement loans* are loans made by individual financial institutions at below-market rates. The institution simply announces that it will make loans at below market rates to home purchasers who buy homes on which that institution has an existing loan. For example, A owns a home on which a particular institution has an old existing loan of, say, 8 percent. If B wants that home, the institution offers, say, 12.5 percent, even though the market rate may be 14 percent. In this way, the institution is able to get the old 8 percent mortgage off its books. Of course, this makes the older home both easier to sell and easier to buy.

However, the loan made by the institution has an adjustable rate, adjustable every six months. Generally, the loan agreement calls for monthly payments to remain the same for five years with necessary raises in monthly payments every five years thereafter. The net effect of this is if rates are raised during any five-year period with monthly payments remaining the same, less is paid on principal and more is paid in interest.

KEY TERMS

adjustable-rate mortgage
buy-down mortgage
convertible adjustable-rate
    mortgage
equity-participation mortgage
graduated-payment adjustable
    mortgage
graduated-payment mortgage
growing-equity mortgage
interest-only loans

moveable mortgage
price-level-adjustment mortgage
replacement loans
renegotiable-rate mortgage
residential ground lease
reverse-annuity mortgage
shared-appreciation mortgage
shared-equity financing
zero-interest-rate loans

QUESTIONS FOR REVIEW

1. What does the term "quick-pay" mortgage mean? Also describe the grow-ing equity mortgage.
2. Identify and briefly describe what is meant by an "adjustable-rate mort-gage." Also describe a convertible ARM.
3. What is a *buy-down mortgage*?
4. Describe what is meant by "shared-equity financing."
5. What are *interest-only loans*?
6. Briefly describe the: (a) graduated-payment mortgage, and (b) shared-appreciation mortgage.
7. What is meant by the: (a) renegotiable-rate mortgage, and (b) price-level-adjustment mortgage?
8. There are several types of less-than-full amortization mortgages. Identify and provide a brief explanation of each type.
9. Two unusual types of real estate financing include (a) zero interest rate loans, and (b) replacement loans. Give a brief explanation of each.

PROBLEMS

1. The First Savings and Loan Association makes fixed-rate, long-term first mortgage home loans. In order to qualify for a mortgage loan, your maxi-mum monthly loan payments cannot exceed 30 percent of your monthly income. A $60,000, 11 percent, 30-year mortgage loan will require pay-ments of $571.40 per month.
   a. What would be the necessary amount of monthly income for you to qualify for the loan?
   b. If your salary is currently $1,800 per month and is expected to increase at six percent per year, how long would it take before you could qualify for the mortgage loan?

2. The Wolfstats are trying to qualify for a mortgage loan on a new $100,000 home. They have a $20,000 down payment and the remaining $80,000 balance can be financed with a 12 percent, 30-year mortgage loan requiring monthly principal and interest payments of $822.90. Monthly mortgage payments would be only $702.07 on a comparable mortgage carrying a 10 percent interest rate. The lender requires that income be four times the annual principal and interest payments to qualify for a loan.
   a. What annual income would the Wolfstats need to qualify for the $80,000 12 percent loan?
   b. If the builder of the new home agrees to a 2 percent fixed buy-down for two years, what annual income would the Wolfstats need in order to qualify for the loan? What would be the builder's monthly and total costs associated with the buy-down?
3. Assume that the Rusher-Lindsey family wants to buy a home for a price of $110,000. However, since they have only a $20,000 down payment, they are unable to qualify for a conventional fixed-rate long-term mortgage loan. Instead they are considering some possible equity-sharing alternatives. One option is a 50 percent shared-appreciation mortgage with a local real estate lender. A second option would be for the present owner-seller to put up an additional down payment of $20,000 in return for a 50 percent shared equity so that the Rusher-Lindseys could qualify for a $70,000, 11 percent, 25-year conventional mortgage requiring monthly payments of $686.10.
   a. Under a shared appreciation mortgage, show how equity sharing would be handled if the home were sold for $150,000 at the end of five years. What would have happened if the lender's interest had been only 30 percent?
   b. Under the shared-equity option with the present owner-seller, describe what would happen if the home were sold for $160,000 at the end of six years.

PART 2

REAL ESTATE CREDIT AND MORTGAGE MARKETS

4

FACTORS AFFECTING
THE SUPPLY OF
REAL ESTATE FUNDS

LEARNING OBJECTIVES

After studying this chapter, you should be able to do the following:

Describe what is meant by financial intermediation and identify the financial institutions that are involved.

Briefly identify the major instruments used to raise funds in the credit markets and describe the role of mortgage funds.

Briefly describe what has happened to interest rate levels and changes during the 1980s.

Identify and describe the major U.S. economic goals.

Describe and discuss the general controls used by the Federal Reserve System to conduct its monetary policy.

Identify selective credit and other controls that are or have been available for use by the Federal Reserve System.

Briefly describe what is meant by fiscal policy and debt management by the U.S. Treasury.

Briefly discuss and trace major developments relating to the economy since the 1960s, with particular emphasis on the 1980s.

GROWTH THROUGH CAPITAL formation is a basic economic objective. Capital is formed by adding to the existing stock of homes, equipment, roads, etc. Of course, funds (savings) must be made available in order to carry out these investments.

In this chapter, we first examine where investment funds come from and how they are used. Then, we turn our attention to the cost of funds as reflected in interest rate levels. This is followed by a discussion of U.S. economic goals and the impact of the Federal Reserve and fiscal policy on the availability of funds. The final section traces developments in the economy during recent decades.

SOURCES AND USES OF FUNDS

The basic source of funds supplied to the credit markets comes from *savings* which represent the accumulation of cash and other financial assets such as savings accounts, insurance policies, and pension plan reserves. Savings are provided primarily by individuals, and to a lesser extent by businesses who "save" when current incomes exceed tax payments plus other current expenditures. Governments also can save when their revenues exceed expenditures.

The supply of funds available for investment is affected by both the level and rate of savings. The level of personal income, and thus potential personal savings, in any given year is affected by existing economic conditions. After paying taxes and making other necessary payments, individuals must decide what to do with the remaining disposable personal income. Since disposable personal income can be spent or saved, the *personal savings rate* is measured as personal savings divided by disposable personal income. In recent years, individuals in the U.S. have been saving only about 5 to 6 percent of their disposable personal incomes, which is much lower relative to the savings rates in Japan and in the industrialized countries of Western Europe.

The savings of individuals may be directly invested in corporate bonds and stocks or even real estate mortgages. However, it is more typical for investors to invest indirectly in corporate securities and mortgages by placing their savings first in financial institutions and intermediaries. Financial institutions are important to many savers because they can offer liquidity, safety of principal, and often are willing to accept savings in small amounts.

The process of accumulating savings in financial institutions and then lending or investing (supplying) funds is called *intermediation.* Financial institutions through the intermediation process bring together or "match" savings (sources of funds) and investments (uses of funds). Intermediation traditionally has been important in directing accumulated savings into real estate mortgages because direct investment was generally inconsistent with individual saver objectives.

When individuals choose to withdraw savings and/or not accumulate new savings in institutions, the opposite of intermediation, or *disintermediation,* occurs. This bypassing of financial institutions generally developed in

PERSONAL SAVINGS RATES IN THE U.S.

The savings of individuals are crucial to the formation of new capital such as homes and equipment. Individuals choose between current spending (consuming) or saving their disposable personal incomes.

Since the savings of individuals represents the most important source of funds in the U.S., it is important to develop some understanding of savings rate levels and trends. Following are U.S. personal savings as a percent of disposable income for selected years as reported in the U.S. League of Savings Institutions' annual *Sourcebook*.

U.S. PERSONAL
SAVINGS RATES

1960	5.8%
1965	7.0
1970	8.1
1975	9.2
1980	7.1
1985	5.1

It can be seen that the personal savings rate increased from about 6 percent in 1960 to 9 percent by 1975 before falling to the 5 percent level by 1985. These relatively wide swings in savings rates, associated (at least in part) with the many changes in tax laws during the last three decades, contribute to the volatility of economic activity in general and the construction of homes and commercial property in particular.

U.S. income tax laws since the great depression of the 1930s have generally been designed to encourage spending (to stimulate economic activity) rather than saving by heavily taxing savings. Lower personal income tax rates in the mid-1960s and in the 1970s may have contributed to the rise in the personal savings rate. However, the savings rate fell during the 1980s again even though income tax rates were lowered even further in 1981. Whether the 1986 tax law changes (lower tax rates but less favorable deductions) will lead to an increase in the savings rate remains to be seen.

the past when other high quality investments such as short-term U.S. Treasury securities provided proportionately higher yields or returns. Savings accounts and certificates then were bypassed for direct investments in these securities. In the past, disintermediation severely affected mortgage investment funds because savings diverted from financial institutions traditionally have not gone into mortgages. Recent legislation which has removed ceilings on the rates that financial institutions can pay to savers should reduce the degree of disintermediation that is likely to occur in the future.

Sources of Funds Supplied to the Credit Markets

Table 4–1 indicates the sources of funds supplied to credit markets in recent years. Total funds supplied (excluding corporate equities) increased from

TABLE 4–1   Sources of Funds to Credit Markets in the United States (In Billions of Dollars)

	1984	1985	1986
Total Funds Supplied to Domestic Nonfinancial Sectors	753.9	854.8	833.4
Private Financial Intermediation			
Commercial banking	168.9	186.3	194.7
Savings institutions	150.2	83.0	105.8
Insurance and pension funds	121.8	156.0	175.9
Other finance intermediaries	118.9	154.2	249.6
Total Funds Advanced by Private Financial Institutions	559.8	579.5	726.1
Financial Intermediation Funds/Total Funds Supplied	74.3	67.8	87.1

Note: Corporate equities were not included above.

Source: *Federal Reserve Bulletin* (December 1987): A43.

about $754 billion in 1984 to $833 billion in 1986. The importance of private financial intermediation is shown by the fact that 87 percent of the 1986 total funds were supplied through intermediation. This was substantially higher than the 74 percent rate in 1984 and the nearly 68 percent rate for 1985. Funds supplied through commercial banking, insurance and pension funds, and other finance intermediaries increased in each of the three years. However, funds supplied through savings institutions to the credit markets declined sharply in 1985 (compared with 1984) and exhibited only a slight recovery in 1986. These figures undoubtedly reflect the problems faced by savings institutions during the past couple of years.

Funds Raised in the Credit Markets

Table 4–2 shows how funds were raised in the credit markets over the 1984 through 1986 period. Borrowing by households represented the most important borrowing sector in each of the three years and accounted for about 34 percent of the total in 1986. Borrowing by the U.S. government ranks second in importance and in 1986 accounted for about 26 percent of the total borrowings.

Corporate borrowing ranks third in importance and accounts for about 23 percent of the total. Borrowings by state and local governments peaked in 1985. Also note the continued negative net borrowing by the farm sector which reflects the farming difficulties during the 1980s.

Table 4–2 also indicates borrowing activity by type of instrument. Mortgage borrowing amounted to $298 billion in 1986 which accounted for about 36 percent of total borrowings. U.S. government securities rank second in importance and accounted for about $214 billion in funds raised during 1986, or 26 percent of total borrowings. Corporate bonds were in third place in borrowing importance in 1986 surpassing the role of state and local governments in the raising of funds in the credit markets. Corporations also raise

TABLE 4–2 Funds Raised in the Credit Markets (In Billions of Dollars)

	1984	1985	1986
Total Net Borrowing By Domestic Nonfinancial Sectors	753.9	854.8	833.4
BY BORROWING SECTOR			
U.S. government	198.8	223.6	214.3
State and local governments	27.4	91.8	46.4
Households	234.6	293.4	279.9
Farm	-.1	-13.9	-15.1
Nonfarm noncorporate	97.1	93.1	115.9
Corporate	196.0	166.7	192.0
Total	753.9	854.8	833.4
BY INSTRUMENT			
U.S. government securities	198.8	223.6	214.3
Tax-exempt obligations	50.4	136.4	35.4
Corporate bonds	46.1	73.8	121.7
Mortgages	217.1	237.7	298.0
Consumer debt	90.4	94.6	65.8
Bank loans	67.1	38.6	66.5
Other debt	84.0	50.1	31.7
Total	753.9	854.8	833.4
Note: External corporate equity funds not included above.			
Total Net New Share Issues	-36.4	19.9	91.6

Source: *Federal Reserve Bulletin* (December 1987): A42.

funds by issuing shares of stock and they raised nearly $92 billion this way in 1986.

Now let's examine more closely mortgage funds raised in recent years by type of mortgage. Table 4–3 shows that home mortgages constitute the primary type of mortgage funds raised in recent years and represented nearly two thirds of total mortgage funds raised in 1986. Mortgages on commercial property rank second in importance and are followed by multifamily residential mortgages. Farm mortgage funds have actually contracted during recent years.

Holders of Mortgage Debt

The major suppliers of mortgage funds are financial institutions, which as we previously noted receive their funds through the intermediation process. Table 4–3 indicates that nearly 59 percent of total mortgage debt was held by financial institutions in 1986. While this declined from about 63 percent in 1984, the importance of financial institutions cannot be overlooked. Savings institutions (savings and loan associations and mutual savings banks) held about 30 percent of the total mortgage debt outstanding in 1986. This was a drop from the 35 percent level in 1984 and reflects the operating difficulties faced by savings institutions in recent years. Commercial banks rank second with

TABLE 4–3 Mortgage Funds Raised and Mortgage Debt Outstanding (In Billions of Dollars)

	1984	1985	1986
ANNUAL FUNDS RAISED			
Home mortgages	129.7	151.9	199.4
Multifamily residential	25.1	29.2	33.0
Commercial	63.2	62.5	73.9
Farm	-.9	-6.0	-8.3
Total Mortgages	217.1	237.7	298.0
MORTGAGE DEBT OUTSTANDING			
1- to 4-family	1,318.5	1,467.4	1,666.4
Multifamily	185.6	214.1	246.9
Commercial	419.4	482.0	555.8
Farm	111.7	105.7	96.8
All Holders	2,035.2	2,269.2	2,565.9
PERCENT OF TOTAL MORTGAGE DEBT HELD BY TYPE OF HOLDER			
Commercial banks	18.7	18.9	19.6
Savings institutions	34.9	33.6	30.3
Life insurance companies	7.7	7.5	7.5
Finance companies	1.2	1.4	1.3
Total Financial Institutions	62.5	61.4	58.7
Federal and related agencies	7.8	7.4	7.9
Mortgage pools or trusts	16.3	18.3	20.7
Individuals and others	13.4	12.9	12.7
All Holders	100.0	100.0	100.0

Source: *Federal Reserve Bulletin* (December 1987): A39 and A42.

nearly 20 percent of the total. Life insurance companies hold about 8 percent of total mortgage debt outstanding compared with only about 1 percent for finance companies.

According to the data in Table 4–3, mortgage pools or trusts have been increasing in importance and in 1986 accounted for about 21 percent of total mortgage debt holdings. Mortgages in the pools are insured or guaranteed by agencies such as the Federal Home Loan Mortgage Corporation (FHLMC), the Government National Mortgage Association (GNMA), the Federal National Mortgage Association (FNMA), and the Farmers Home Administration (FmHA).

Nearly 13 percent of total holdings are held by individuals and others (i.e., real estate investment trusts, mortgage companies, noninsured pension funds, credit unions, and state and local retirement funds). Finally, federal and related agencies (i.e., the FHLMC, GNMA, FNMA, FmHA, FHA, VA, and the Federal Land Banks) account for about 8 percent of the mortgage debt that is outstanding. Government assistance programs have been developed to aid in both the primary and secondary real estate markets. We will examine the role of government assistance programs as they aid the primary and secondary markets in Chapter 6.

INTEREST RATE LEVELS AND CHANGES

Interest rates reflect the basic price or cost of funds in the marketplace and are determined by the demand for and the supply of funds. The demand for real estate and other funds is directly affected by prevailing economic conditions and the level of interest rates. When the economy is growing and interest rates are relatively low, more attractive investment opportunities are identified and the demand for borrowed funds increases. The opposite occurs when economic activity is declining and interest rates are high.

In addition to the level of savings, the supply of funds available for investment is dependent upon the size of the money supply. Monetary policy actions by the Federal Reserve System affect the availability of credit and the money supply itself. A reduction in the supply of money relative to the demand for funds will cause interest rates to rise, and vice versa.

Government fiscal policies relating to the balance between tax receipts and expenditures directly affect economic activity. A resulting change in the demand for funds could also alter interest rate levels. Debt financing procedures employed by the U.S. Treasury also impact on interest rate levels because government demand for funds must compete against the demand for funds by the private sector.

Figure 4–1 shows the developments in long-term interest rates during recent years. Interest rates have fallen from their record high levels of the early 1980s. As we will see later in the chapter, this decline in interest rates has been accompanied by relatively low inflation rates and somewhat slow real growth in economic activity.

Long-term interest rates at any point in time reflect a risk-free component as depicted by the rate on long-term treasury securities (interest rates on state and local bonds are lower only because they are exempt from federal income taxes). A major factor influencing the rate on long-term treasury securities is the then-prevailing attitude of investors concerning expectations about long-run inflation rates.

In addition to the risk-free component, investors expect a risk premium or added compensation for investing in riskier securities such as corporate AAA (highest quality) bonds. The size of the risk premium at any time will reflect investor attitudes concerning the outlook for economic activity. An increase in the risk premium occurs when investors are pessimistic, and vice versa.

Notice that the FHA mortgage rates also declined sharply after reaching levels above 17 percent in early 1982. FHA rates bottomed slightly below the 9 percent level in early 1987 before increasing to about the 11 percent level by the end of 1987. As mortgage rates declined from their early 1982 levels, real estate construction (both residential and commercial) increased rapidly as we moved into the mid-1980s. However, tax legislation in 1986 and the upward movement in interest rates during 1987 has since slowed new real estate investments.

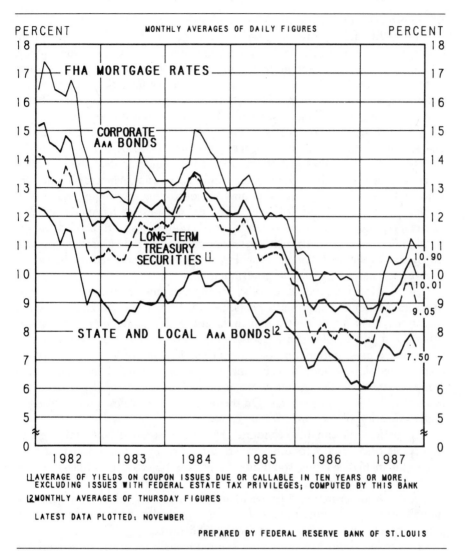

PERCENT   MONTHLY AVERAGES OF DAILY FIGURES   PERCENT

LLAVERAGE OF YIELDS ON COUPON ISSUES DUE OR CALLABLE IN TEN YEARS OR MORE,
EXCLUDING ISSUES WITH FEDERAL ESTATE TAX PRIVILEGES; COMPUTED BY THIS BANK

L2MONTHLY AVERAGES OF THURSDAY FIGURES

LATEST DATA PLOTTED: NOVEMBER

PREPARED BY FEDERAL RESERVE BANK OF ST.LOUIS

FIGURE 4–1. Long-Term Interest Rates

ECONOMIC GOALS OR OBJECTIVES

An effective financial system begins with a medium for exchanging goods and services. We often refer to this medium of exchange as *money*. Money also serves as a standard of value by providing a convenient method for comparing prices or values. Money is important to the savings-investment process since it, or money substitutes such as savings accounts and government and corporate securities, permits the storing of value. Additionally, since debts are generally expressed in terms of money, money is used as the basis for handling future promises to pay (i.e., it is a standard of deferred payment).

In addition to a medium of exchange, an effective financial system needs a monetary system for creating, controlling, and transferring money. The system also must contain institutions and facilities for channeling savings into investment. Finally, because of the long-term characteristics of many investments, an effective financial system must have markets designed to facilitate the buying and selling of securities and other claims to wealth.

The U.S. economy is based on the existence of an effective financial system. Rather than allowing economic activity to be decided solely by chance or the "free" market, efforts are made to guide or steer the economy. This done primarily through monetary and fiscal policy. *Monetary policy* involves efforts to "manage" the economy by controlling the supply and cost of money and the availability of credit. The Federal Reserve System establishes monetary policy. Efforts to "manage" the economy also are carried out by *fiscal policy* through government spending, taxation of individuals and institutions, and public debt management. Fiscal policy is established by the executive and legislative branches of government.

Monetary and fiscal policy attempts to guide the economy in terms of several economic objectives or goals. Some of the objectives can be traced to the Employment Act of 1946 and include sustainable economic growth, stable prices, and full employment. *Economic growth* is frequently measured in terms of the gross national product or the total output of goods and services over a stated time period. Real sustainable economic growth is associated with rising standards of living, and is important because too rapid growth often leads to inflation and recessions. On the other hand, too slow growth leads to underutilization of economic resources.

Real sustainable economic growth is associated with stable prices or a stable price level. Economic growth due to rising prices or inflation does not result in higher living standards. Thus, the objective of *stable prices* is consistent with the maintaining of purchasing power.

Another major objective focuses on achieving full employment. Although difficult to define, *full employment* is generally reached when a 3 to 5 percent unemployment rate exists for the labor force.

We would like to achieve simultaneously the goals of sustainable economic growth, full employment, and stable prices. Recent history indicates, however, the difficulties associated with trying to achieve these multiple objectives through monetary and fiscal policy actions. Economic growth has not been sustained. This is reflected in the business cycles characteristic of the U.S. economy in recent years. Purchasing power of the dollar has declined as reflected in rising prices in the form of inflation, while at the same time unemployment rates have fluctuated between 5 and 10 percent in recent years. Thus, while it may be possible to "manage" the economy to achieve all three objectives at the same time, it is apparent that the task is not an easy one.

A fourth objective of monetary and fiscal policy is concerned with achieving a *long-run balance in international payments*. Inflows and outflows of funds occur because of foreign trade, investments and loans, foreign aid, and military expenditures. International bankruptcy is possible unless a long-run balance of payments is achieved. Monetary policy attempts to balance this objective in conjunction with the objectives of economic growth, stable prices, and full employment.

THE FEDERAL RESERVE SYSTEM

The Federal Reserve System was established with the passage of the Federal Reserve Act in 1913. Twelve Federal Reserve districts, each with individual regional problems, were established. A Federal Reserve Bank was formed in each district through the purchase of stock by commercial banks operating within each district. These subscribing banks are known as "member banks" and technically "own" the Federal Reserve Banks. In actual practice, the Federal Reserve System is the central bank in the United States and monetary policy decisions are made and carried out by the Board of Governors of the Federal Reserve System. Monetary policy is implemented, or carried out, through the use of both general and selective controls.

General Monetary Controls

General monetary controls are used by the Federal Reserve to regulate and control the level and changes in the supply of money and the availability of credit. The regulation of the money supply in conjunction with the demand for money by governments, businesses, and individuals leads to an indirect regulation of interest rates. Regulation of money supply and credit impacts initially on short-term interest rates. The impact of general controls is slower in terms of long-term interest rates.

Reserve Requirements. The Federal Reserve System's most powerful general control has been the ability to establish reserve requirements against member bank deposits. The commercial banking system in the United States is referred to as a *fractional reserve system* because banks are not permitted to lend 100 percent of their deposits. Congress traditionally established a range for reserve requirements on demand deposits or checking accounts and a range for time deposits or savings accounts. The Board of Governors has the authority to specify and change the legal reserve requirements within the established range.

Changes in reserve requirements impact member banks in two basic ways. First, when reserve requirements against existing deposits are changed, excess reserves are created or destroyed. Assuming that member banks are holding the correct amount of required reserves, an increase in required reserves (say from 10 percent to 20 percent) leads to a contraction in bank credit and generally a reduction in the money supply. A reduction in reserve requirements generally results in an expansion in bank credit and money supply. Second, under a fractional reserve system the amount of deposits that can be supported by a given volume of reserves is affected by reserve requirement changes. The commercial banking system has the capability of expanding and contracting deposit credit. For example, given a 20 percent reserve requirement, $10,000 of new reserves injected into the banking system could expand and thus support $50,000 in new deposits. A lowering of the reserve requirement to 10 percent in the above example would allow the expansion and support of $100,000 in new deposits. Thus, the potential change in deposits is calculated as the dollar amount of initial excess reserves divided by the reserve requirement percentage stated in decimal form, e.g., $10,000/.10 = $100,000.

In March 1980, the Depository Institutions Deregulation and Monetary Control Act of 1980 (DIDMCA) became law. It has been described as the most significant banking legislation since passage of the Federal Reserve Act. Title I of the DIDMCA is referred to as the Monetary Control Act of 1980 and provided for the implementation of universal reserve requirements on all depository institutions. This legislation broadened the ability of the Board of Governors of the Federal Reserve System to manage and control the availability of credit and the nation's money supply.

Reserve requirements for existing member banks were phased in over a three- to four-year period, while reserve requirements for nonmember depository institutions were phased in evenly until they became comparable with member bank requirements. Reserves have to be maintained against transaction accounts (demand and share draft deposits, negotiable order of withdrawal deposits, and deposits subject to telephone or automatic transfer) at commercial banks, mutual savings banks, savings and loan associations, and credit unions. Initial reserve requirements called for the holding of 3 percent of transaction account deposits up through $25 million (with this upper limit subject to change annually) and 12 percent of reserve amounts in excess of $25 million. In addition, initial reserves of 3 percent were set on nonpersonal time deposits (including savings deposits) held by depository institutions. Nonpersonal time deposits generally reflect the situation where the depositor is not a natural person, although the category also includes some transferable time deposits held by natural persons.

A number of different definitions of money supply or money stock exist. In the narrowest traditional sense (prior to passage of the DIDMCA), money supply was defined as demand deposits in commercial banks plus currency (including coins) held by the public. Today broader-based definitions are used. For example, the M1 definition includes currency and commercial bank demand deposits held by the nonbank public (excluding deposits held by foreign banks and official institutions), plus other checkable deposits of all depository institutions, plus travelers' checks. The "other checkable deposits" category includes negotiable order of withdrawal (NOW) and automatic transfer service (ATS) accounts at commercial banks and thrift institutions, demand deposits at mutual savings banks, and credit union share draft (CUSD) accounts. A somewhat broader definition of the money supply, M2, includes, in addition to the M1 components, savings and small time deposits at all depository institutions, commercial bank overnight repurchase agreements, overnight Eurodollars, and money market mutual fund shares. *M3* is a third measure of the money supply that adds to the *M2* definition: large-denomination time deposits at all depository institutions, term repurchase agreements at commercial banks and savings and loans, and institution-only money market mutual funds. The Federal Reserve System is concerned with growth rates in all three of these measures of money supply and their impact on the availability of credit in the U.S. economy.

The Discount Rate. The Federal Reserve System also provides a source for loans to member banks and other depository institutions.[1] The interest rate charged by Federal Reserve Banks can be altered and thus constitutes a second general tool, or control, for administering credit policy. Member banks traditionally could borrow against either their own notes generally secured by government obligations or by rediscounting notes and other debt instruments contained in their own portfolios. Thus, the *discount rate* represents the cost of borrowing from the Fed.

In some instances member banks have borrowed from Federal Reserve Banks to meet reserve requirements rather than borrowing from other commercial banks or by selling short-term securities from their portfolios. Reserves that qualify to meet legal reserve requirements include vault cash and deposits held in their district Federal Reserve Bank. When the discount rate is increased, banks may be more inclined to meet reserve requirements by borrowing short-term funds known as *federal funds* from other commercial banks with excess reserves. This could result in higher federal funds interest rates. On the other hand, member banks also might sell some of their short-term government securities in order to meet reserve requirements. This greater supply would tend to lower short-term government security prices and thus raise their interest rates.

Changes in the discount rate also convey psychological implications. It is thought by many that discount rate changes are used by the Federal Reserve System to signal the intended direction of future credit policy.

Open-Market Operations. The Federal Reserve System's most important general credit tool is its open-market operations. Through the Open Market Committee, policy is established in terms of the Federal Reserve's buying and selling of government securities. In essence, the Federal Reserve System possesses a massive portfolio of U.S. government securities to which securities may be added or from which securities may be sold. By selling securities in the open market, the Federal Reserve system moves to constrain credit expansion and money supply growth. When the purchasers pay for the securities with checks drawn on their demand deposits at member banks, the member bank reserves are reduced. Credit expansion capabilities are thus constrained.

---

[1]Prior to the passage of the Monetary Control Act of the DIDMCA in 1980, only member banks could borrow from the Fed. This law extended borrowing privileges at the discount window to nonmember commercial banks, savings and loan associations, mutual savings banks, and credit unions that maintain reserves with the Fed.

If a large amount of government securities are sold, member bank reserves may fall below the legal reserve requirements. This could cause a contraction in bank credit and a reduction in money supply. Just as the commercial banking system can create a multiple credit expansion given an increase in new reserves, a reduction in reserves below the required level can cause a multiple impact in terms of credit contraction and reduction in the money supply. In addition, the selling of government securities by the Federal Reserve increases the supply, which causes prices to fall and interest rates to rise. Open-market operations are concerned primarily with the buying and selling of short-term government securities. The buying of securities by the Federal Reserve generally leads to credit expansion.

Moral Suasion. Moral suasion is considered by some to be an additional tool of monetary policy. It is sometimes referred to as "jawbone" policy in that Federal Reserve statements and comments are used to let commercial banks know how they are supposed to behave in light of Federal Reserve objectives.

Selective Credit Controls

In some instances it is desirable to regulate particular uses of money or credit. The Federal Reserve accomplishes this through the use of selective credit controls. *Selective credit controls* are designed to operate directly on the availability of credit in contrast with the general monetary controls, which operate on commercial bank reserves. In the past the Federal Reserve has possessed the power to regulate consumer credit, real estate credit, and stock and bond market credit. At present, the Federal Reserve regulates only securities market credit by setting margin requirements. This power was established under the Securities Exchange Act of 1934.

    Margin requirements represent the minimum down payment that is required to purchase securities. Margin purchases are permitted primarily on stocks and bonds listed on national exchanges. *Regulation T* is the most common example of margin requirements in that it is designed to regulate broker-dealer loans to customers. Loans against securities by commercial banks and other lenders also are regulated. Margin requirements are used to stimulate or constrain investor interest and speculation. During recessions and periods of depressed stock prices, margin requirements are lowered—often to levels of down payments in the 50–60 percent range. These requirements are often raised during periods of excessive security speculation.

    From time to time Congress has provided the Federal Reserve with other selective credit controls. For example, in 1941 the Federal Reserve established specific "curbs" on the use of credit to finance the purchase of automobiles and other consumer durable goods. The objective was to avoid excessive upward pressure on prices because of the prevailing situation of increased purchasing power and consumer durable goods shortages.

    The passage of the Production Act of 1950 permitted regulation of real estate financing. *Regulation X* was established and administered by the

Federal Reserve System. The principal amount of real estate loans was regulated on the basis of maximum loan amounts and repayment time periods. Minimum periodic payments also were set. Restrictions on consumer durable goods and real estate credit were removed in 1952. However, the Board of Governors currently has the authority to regulate disclosure of credit terms under the Truth in Lending Act of 1968.

Other Controls

Before passage of the DIDMCA of 1980, the Federal Reserve System had the authority to set interest rate ceilings on member bank time and savings deposits. These rates were established under *Regulation Q*. Interest rate ceilings were set after consultation with the Federal Deposit Insurance Corporation and the Federal Home Loan Bank Board. Interest rate ceilings for nonmember, insured banks were regulated by the Federal Deposit Insurance Corporation while the Federal Home Loan Bank Board regulated dividend rates on member and other savings and loan associations.

Regulation Q offered the Federal Reserve System an additional form of control for influencing economic activity. However, in practice the setting of interest rate ceilings seemed to have contributed to the magnitude of the swings between periods of intermediation and disintermediation. When Regulation Q rates were higher than interest rates on competing investments (government and corporate securities), intermediation or the accumulation of savings in financial institutions took place. In contrast, the availability of funds was constrained due to disintermediation as investors chose to bypass financial institutions and invest directly when competitive investments offered yields higher than those set by Regulation Q on time and savings deposits.

Title II of the Depository Institutions Deregulation and Monetary Control Act is referred to as the Depository Institutions Deregulation Act of 1980 and provided for the phaseout of limitations on maximum interest and dividend rates that can be paid by depository institutions. To insure an orderly phaseout, a Depository Institutions Deregulation Committee was established consisting of the Secretary of the U.S. Treasury, the Chairman of the Board of Governors of the Federal Reserve System, the Chairman of the Federal Home Loan Bank Board, the Chairman of the Board of Directors of the Federal Deposit Insurance Corporation, and the Chairman of the National Credit Union Administration Board. In addition to these voting members, the Comptroller of the Currency was a nonvoting member. The Deregulation Committee increased existing interest and dividend rate ceilings to market rate levels, after which the Committee ceased to exist.

FISCAL POLICY

Fiscal policy is concerned with government spending and how that spending is financed. Federal government expenditures are so large that they dwarf other U.S. institution and government expenditures. Federal government taxation provides the basis for meeting these expenditures. The combination of expenditures and tax receipts produces the federal budget. When expenditures exceed receipts, we have a *deficit budget.* Tax receipts larger than expenditures result in a *surplus budget.* Deficit budgets act as a stimulus to the economy while surplus budgets tend to constrain the economy.

A deficit budget results in a national debt that must be financed by the United States Treasury by issuing and selling government securities. Deficit budgets have had a cumulative effect in recent years with the result being a substantial increase in the amount of outstanding federal debt.

Debt Management

Debt management involves the financing of outstanding federal debt and new debt arising from deficit budgets. The method of financing deficits influences the impact of deficits on the economy. The U.S. Treasury can finance deficits in three basic ways. Government securities can be sold to: (1) the nonbank public, (2) commercial banks, and (3) Federal Reserve Banks. When individuals, businesses, and nonbank financial institutions purchase government securities from the Treasury, bank reserves are not affected but there might be added upward pressure on interest rates. This is because the Treasury must compete against the private sector for the available supply of funds. If the Treasury sells government securities directly to commercial banks, bank reserves decrease and thus the ability of banks to expand credit is constrained. This is a form of competition between the public and private sectors of the economy in terms of bank reserves. Of course, if the Treasury spends some of its acquired funds, bank reserves will be restored.

The least initial impact of debt management on interest rates occurs when the Treasury sells government securities directly to Federal Reserve Banks. The Treasury thus is not in direct competition with the private sector for available funds or bank reserves. In fact, bank reserves are actually increased when the Treasury deposits the funds from the sale of the government securities in commercial banks. This allows for possible further bank credit expansion.

U.S. Government Obligations

The federal government issues both marketable securities and nonmarketable obligations. *Nonmarketable* issues can be redeemed only by turning them in to the Treasury, and are primarily in the form of savings bonds. Series EE bonds (sold at a discount) and Series HH bonds (paying a specified interest rate) are available for sale to the public. A more important role in the financing of the national debt is played by *marketable securities* which may bought and sold through financial institutions and intermediaries. A secondary market exists for marketable government securities. In addition to marketable and nonmarketable issues, some obligations are designed for specific ownership by government agencies.

Marketable securities are distinguished primarily on the basis of their maturity periods at time of issuance. *Treasury bills* are short-term securities with maturities ranging from 91 days up to one year. In contrast with other marketable government issues, Treasury bills are sold at a discount and mature at par. *Treasury notes* have maturities greater than one year but with a maximum of seven years. *Treasury bonds* generally have maturities in excess of five years and may exceed 20 years. Both Treasury notes and bonds are issued at specified interest rates.

Commercial banks are the largest holders of Treasury bills. These government issues provide both liquidity and safety of principal. Businesses and individuals seeking liquidity and safety also are investors in Treasury bills. Savings and time deposits are in direct competition with Treasury bills for the savings dollar. Treasury notes also are largely held by commercial banks. However, Treasury notes also compete against financial institutions for the savings of individuals and others. Life insurance companies and pension funds are heavy investors in Treasury bonds.

The ability of commercial banks, savings and loan associations, and mutual savings banks in performing the intermediation function of channeling savings into real estate mortgages is dependent on being able to compete effectively for the savings dollar. Since liquidity and safety of principal also are provided by Treasury bills and notes, time and savings accounts must be able to compete on a yield or return basis in order to avoid problems of disintermediation.

THE ECONOMIC ENVIRONMENT

Ideally, monetary and fiscal policy should be combined so as to achieve the economic objectives of real sustainable economic growth, stable prices, and full employment. Emphasis on achieving these goals should be conducted in light of also maintaining a long-run balance in international payments. In actual practice, however, results pertaining to the simultaneous achievement of these goals have been less than desirable. In many instances, rather than working together, monetary and fiscal policy seem to have been in conflict with one another. Insight into monetary and fiscal policy activities can be better understood in terms of trends and changes in the economic goals.

Monetary and Fiscal Policy in the 1960s

The United States was in a mild recession during the last half of 1960. Thus, in early 1961 the private sector was characterized by excess capacity, and unemployment approached the 7 percent level. Prices were reasonably stable as measured by low levels of inflation. At the same time, there was increased concern over our continued deficits in international payments and the meeting of these deficits with gold and dollar payments. Thus, beginning with the Kennedy Administration, a concerted effort was made to seek real sustainable economic growth, full employment, and a sustainable balance in international payments while maintaining reasonable price stability.

In order to achieve these objectives, the Federal Reserve undertook an expansionary monetary policy that lasted until mid-1965. Growth in the money supply and availability of bank credit relative to demand helped to hold interest rates down. At the same time, fiscal policy also was directed at stimulating the economy. For example, attempts were made to stimulate investment expenditures in the private sector in 1962 by enacting an investment tax credit (designed to reduce tax liabilities when making capital expenditures) and by liberalizing depreciation guidelines (permitting the use of accelerated depreciation methods and shorter depreciation lives). In addition, the Revenue Act of 1964 provided for the reduction in personal and corporate income taxes. Real GNP growth, declining unemployment rates, and relatively stable prices prevailed during this period.

However, inflationary pressures became pronounced beginning in mid-1965. Along with expansionary monetary policy and stimulative fiscal policy came rapid escalation of the Vietnam War. Increased military expenditures led to even larger deficit budgets. The private sector began operating at very high capacity levels, demand for funds rose, and labor shortages developed. This, in turn, led to price increases. Monetary policy became restrictive during the first half of 1966. Slowing of money supply growth along with continued demand for money pressures led to a "credit crunch" and rapidly rising interest rates. There was little restraint on the part of fiscal policy during this period.

The economy was on the verge of a recession at the beginning of 1967 and the Federal Reserve subsequently moved to rapid expansion of the money supply during 1967 and 1968. This, coupled with continued stimulative fiscal policy, resulted in even higher inflation rates.

In 1969 the Federal Reserve moved to a monetary policy of restraint. This, along with a small surplus budget for fiscal 1969, contributed to the mild recession of 1969–70. Interest rates peaked at high levels during 1969 and disintermediation became a major problem. However, strong inflationary pressures persisted and prices continued to rise during the recession.

Developments During the 1970s

The recession which began in the third quarter of 1969 continued through most of 1970. Economic recovery developed in 1971 and 1972 but was associated with rapidly increasing prices. To combat this inflation, wage and price controls were instituted in 1971. After experimentation with a voluntary wage and price control program at the beginning of 1973, a price freeze was imposed in mid-1973. The Arab oil embargo began in late 1973 and contributed further to the upward pressures on prices.

Economic activity slowed in 1973 before turning down sharply in 1974 and bottoming out in the first quarter of 1975. This downturn was followed by subsequent economic growth that continued through the remainder of the 1970s.

A downturn in economic growth is associated with rising unemployment rates. The 1974–75 recession led to a sharp increase in unemployment rates from about 5 percent at the beginning of 1974 to 9 percent during the first half of 1975. The unemployment rate fell gradually throughout the remainder of the 1970s but never reached as low as the rate that existed at the beginning of 1974. Full employment was not achieved when viewed in terms of historical norms.

To summarize, the decade of the 1970s was characterized by two periods of economic downturn, substantial price inflation, and high levels of unemployment. In addition, the U.S. continued to operate with deficits in its international payments.

While monetary and fiscal policy had difficulty in achieving the economic objectives, it is important to have an understanding of the efforts that were made. The Federal Reserve entered into a period of monetary expansion beginning in 1970 and continuing until mid-1973. Money supply growth was constrained sharply during 1974 and this contributed to the 1974–75 recession. During the last few years of the 1970s the money supply was allowed to grow at rates that were in excess of 7 percent annually.

At the beginning of the 1970s fiscal policy attempted a new approach to management of the economy with particular emphasis on controlling inflation. A price freeze was ordered in mid-1971 and was followed by institution of wage and price controls as was previously indicated. By early 1974 remaining mandatory and voluntary controls were removed. High inflation rates remained and the conclusion was that wage and price controls were a failure.

Fiscal policy through the enactment of the Tax Reduction Act of 1975 then moved to stimulate the economy by cutting both corporate and individual income taxes and by increasing the investment tax credit. Additional tax legislation was passed in 1976 and 1977, with these actions being followed by the Revenue Act of 1978, which further reduced corporate income tax rates, liberalized investment tax credits, and reduced individual capital gains tax rates. These various tax cuts, along with government expenditures, led to large deficit budgets throughout the latter part of the 1970s.

The Decade of the 1980s

The same elusive economic goals set out at the beginning of the 1970s remained unachieved as the U.S. moved into the 1980s. Figure 4–2 depicts economic output in terms of Gross National Product shown in 1982 dollars and in current dollars. Use of 1982 dollars provides an estimate of "real" growth in GNP and business cycle changes. A brief but deep economic downturn occurred in early 1980 followed by a slight recovery and then a second downturn beginning during the third quarter of 1981 and continuing through the fourth quarter of 1982. Economic activity then grew rapidly at a 7 percent real rate between the fourth quarter of 1982 and the second quarter of 1984. Since then, the economy has continued to grow but only at a moderate rate of

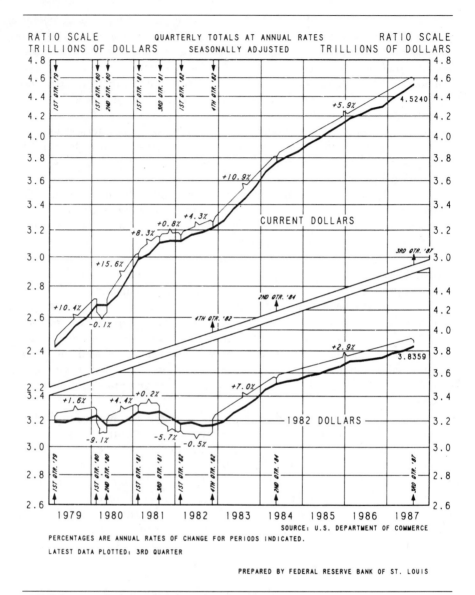

FIGURE 4–2. Gross National Product

about 3 percent.

The difference between the real growth in GNP stated in 1982 dollars and the GNP growth in current dollars indicates inflation in the economy. Notice in Figure 4–2 that the GNP growth rate in 1982 dollars between the second quarter of 1980 and the first quarter of 1981 was 4.4 percent compared with a growth rate for GNP in current dollars of 15.6 percent over the same time period. The difference between these two figures is explained by the double-digit inflation which prevailed during the early 1980s. Since the end of 1982, the inflation rate has slowed dramatically. For example, the constant dollar (1982) GNP growth rate from mid-1982 through the third quarter of 1987 was 2.9 percent. This compares with a current dollar GNP growth rate of 5.9 percent over the same period and reflects the fact that inflation has averaged only about 3 percent in recent years.

Rising unemployment rates typically coincide with downturns in economic activity and the early 1980s were no exception. Figure 4–3 shows that the unemployment rate during 1979 was about 6 percent before rising close to 8 percent during mid-1980, reflecting the sharp economic downturn which occurred during the second quarter of 1980. Then, after a slight improvement, the unemployment rate rose sharply as the economy started to decline again during the latter part of 1981. The unemployment rate finally peaked in late 1982 at close to 11 percent as a trough in economic activity was occurring. Since the end of 1982, the unemployment rate first dropped sharply as the economy recovered sharply in 1983 and early 1984. Since then, the moderate real growth in economic activity has been associated with gradual

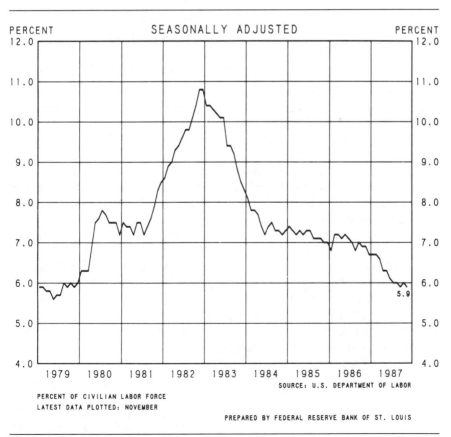

FIGURE 4–3. Unemployment Rate

improvement in the unemployment rate until the 6 percent level was reached during the latter part of 1987.

In an effort to stimulate economic activity, the Economic Recovery Tax Act of 1981 was passed. Both individual and corporate tax rates were cut and personal and real property depreciation guidelines were liberalized. As we noted above, economic activity rebounded sharply beginning in 1983. Housing and commercial property construction also rebounded sharply from their 1980–1982 depressed levels. In fact, concern about the possibility of real estate overexpansion surfaced during the mid-1980s. Then in 1986, the Tax Reform Act was passed. While individual and corporate tax rates were reduced further, some depreciation guidelines, particularly those for real property, were sharply curtailed. Because these Tax Acts of 1981 and 1986 have impacted heavily on real estate financing and investment decisions, they will be discussed in greater detail in Chapter 9.

KEY TERMS

disintermediation
fiscal policy
general monetary controls
intermediation

monetary policy
personal savings rate
savings
selective credit controls

QUESTIONS FOR REVIEW

1. What are *savings* and why are they important to the U.S. financial system?
2. Briefly describe the terms: (a) *intermediation* and (b) *disintermediation.*
3. A substantial portion of funds available for investment purposes are directed into mortgages annually. Who are the major suppliers of these mortgage funds?
4. Briefly describe what has happened to real estate mortgage rates and other long-term interest rates during the 1980s.
5. Briefly outline the general economic goals and objectives developed for the United States.
6. Identify and explain the Federal Reserve's general monetary controls. How do these differ from selective credit controls?
7. The commercial banking system is sometimes referred to as a fractional reserve system. Define and describe what this means.
8. There are a number of different definitions of money supply. Explain.
9. How do the federal budget and debt management combine to control or administer fiscal policy?
10. There are a number of U.S. government securities or obligations. First, explain the difference between marketable and nonmarketable issues. Second, list and describe the different types of marketable securities.

11. Briefly trace developments in the economy during recent years.

PROBLEMS

1. An understanding of the flow of funds into mortgages is important to the development of an overall recognition of the importance of real estate financing. Assume that you have been asked to describe the sources of funds supplied for mortgages. In your description indicate the relative importance of institutions and other suppliers of mortgage funds.
2. Assume that the Federal Reserve purchases $1,000,000 in U.S. government securities from a commercial bank. If the reserve requirement is 15 percent, what is the total amount of deposits that can be created in the commercial banking system?
3. The economic environment impacts heavily on real estate finance. Indicate and describe the degree of success in recent years (be as current as possible) in achieving the economic goals set for our country.
4. Obtain a current issue of the *Federal Reserve Bulletin*. For the most current year of information, answer the following:
   a. Determine the amount of the sources of funds supplied to the credit markets. Also indicate the relative importance of financial institutions in the financial intermediation process.
   b. Indicate the relative significance of funds raised in the credit markets by both borrowing sector and by instrument.
   c. Indicate the relative importance of financial institutions as holders of mortgage debt. Also identify the current roles of mortgage pools or trusts, as well as federal and related agencies, as holders of mortgage debt.

5

REAL ESTATE LENDERS

LEARNING OBJECTIVES

After studying this chapter, you should be able to do the following:

Discuss the impact of recent banking legislation on depository institutions that supply real estate funds.

Briefly describe major operating characteristics of savings and loan associations and indicate their significance as real estate lenders.

Briefly describe major operating characteristics of mutual savings banks and indicate their significance as real estate lenders.

Briefly describe major operating characteristics of commercial banks and indicate their significance as real estate lenders.

Briefly describe major operating characteristics of life insurance companies and indicate their significance as real estate lenders.

Identify and briefly describe some additional suppliers of real estate funds.

FINANCIAL INSTITUTIONS AND facilities have long played an essential role in the U.S. financial system by channeling savings into investments. Commercial banks date back to the 1700s, while mutual savings banks and savings and loan associations were first formed during the early 1800s. Credit unions began during the early 1900s. Each of these four types of depository institutions evolved and thrived because they focused on meeting different saver and borrower needs. However, there has been a growing movement to encourage greater competition among depository institutions.

Passage of the Depository Institutions Deregulation and Monetary Control Act of 1980 led to fewer differences among depository institutions and further has altered the roles of traditional suppliers of real estate funds. This Act and other recent banking legislation will be discussed in the first section of this chapter. Then, traditional real estate-related characteristics of the four types of depository institutions are discussed.

The remainder of the chapter will cover other traditional lenders or suppliers of real estate funds. Included are discussions of life insurance companies, pension funds, and real estate investment trusts.

RECENT BANKING LEGISLATION

The *banking system* today is comprised of the four basic depository institutions—commercial banks, savings and loan associations, mutual savings banks, and credit unions. Sometimes savings and loan associations and mutual savings banks are grouped together and are referred to as just "savings institutions." Additionally, savings and loans, mutual savings banks, and credit unions are often referred to as "thrift institutions." No matter what nomenclature we use, these four financial institutions comprise the banking system, and changes in banking laws affect them all.

The Depository Institutions Deregulation and Monetary Control Act of 1980

The Depository Institutions Deregulation and Monetary Control Act (DIDMCA) of 1980 has been heralded by some as the most significant banking legislation since the Federal Reserve Act was passed in 1913. Others choose to refer to the DIDMCA as the most significant banking and finance legislation since the 1930s when the Glass-Steagall Act of 1933 and other laws were passed as a result of the banking collapse of the early 1930s. The Glass-Steagall Act specifically provided that interest could not be paid on demand deposits and that the Federal Reserve could set interest rate ceilings on time and savings deposits that could be paid by commercial banks which were members of the Fed.

Review of the title of the DIDMCA suggests two distinct parts to the legislation. In the way of broad objectives, a portion of the Act was directed toward the improvement of monetary control procedures by the Federal Reserve. Rather than deregulation, this portion of the Act provided for added regulation, or, if you prefer, "reregulation." The second major area of objectives was directed at deregulation by allowing increased competition in the financial markets among depository institutions and by expanding the powers of thrift institutions.

Monetary Control Act of 1980. Title I of the DIDMCA is referred to as the *Monetary Control Act* of 1980. As its name implies, efforts were made to improve the Fed's ability to control the nation's money supply and to implement monetary policy. Provision was made for imposing universal reserve requirements on all depository institutions and equal reserve requirements are now in place.

The Federal Reserve Board also has the authority to impose a supplemental reserve requirement on depository institutions if deemed necessary for monetary control purposes. This supplemental reserve cannot exceed 4 percent of a depository institution's total transaction accounts.

The Monetary Control Act also provided for the Fed to charge for services it provides to depository institutions. Services covered in the Fed's fee schedule include check clearing and collection, wire transfers, securities safekeeping, and the providing of an automated clearinghouse. Possible new services such as the electronic transfer of funds also would be included in the fee structure. Also, access to the Fed's discount window has been extended to depository institutions with reserves at the Fed.

Depository Institutions Deregulation Act of 1980. Title II of the DIDMCA is referred to as the *Depository Institutions Deregulation Act* of 1980. Its purpose was to phase out and finally eliminate interest rate ceilings on interest and dividends that could be paid by depository institutions. This action effectively rescinded the Glass-Steagall Act provision allowing the Fed to set maximum rates that could be paid by member banks (as well as other legislation pertaining to nonmember banks and thrift institutions).

Recall in our discussion in the last chapter that the setting of maximum rates under Regulation Q often contributed to wide swings in savings flows in the forms of intermediation and disintermediation, depending on whether alternative investments carried higher or lower rates. It was anticipated that by allowing depository institution savers to earn market rates (after the phaseout) on their savings that savings flows would become more stable resulting in lesser swings between intermediation and disintermediation. It was further hoped that this legislation would encourage individuals to save, allow depository institutions to effectively compete for funds, and provide a stable source of funds for home mortgages and other real estate financing needs.

The law provided for the formation of a Depository Institutions Deregulation Committee to carry out an orderly phaseout of interest and dividend rate ceilings. All interest rate payment differentials between commercial banks and thrift institutions also were to be phased out. Voting members of the Depository Institutions Deregulation Committee came from the Federal Reserve Board (Chairman of the Board of Governors); the Federal Home Loan Bank Board (Chairman); the National Credit Union Administration Board (Chairman); the U.S. Treasury (Secretary); and the Federal Deposit Insurance Corporation (Chairman of the Board of Directors). The Committee ceased to exist once rate ceilings were eliminated.

Consumer Checking Account Equity Act of 1980. Title III of the DIDMCA is referred to as the Consumer Checking Account Equity Act of 1980. Insurance limits were raised from $40,000 to $100,000 on accounts held at federally insured commercial and mutual savings banks, credit unions, and savings and loan associations.

The ability of depository institutions to offer negotiable order of withdrawal (NOW) accounts was extended nationwide by Title III. Previously NOW accounts were authorized only in the New England states. Thus, while the Glass-Steagall Act's prohibition of the payment of interest on demand deposits was not eliminated, interest payments were permitted on NOW accounts, which represent accounts that are payable on demand and are close substitutes for checking accounts. NOW accounts may be held by individuals and nonprofit organizations.

Title III also provides for the continued use of automatic transfer services (ATS) by banks and thrift institutions, and share draft accounts by credit unions. Recall from the last chapter that share draft, ATS, and NOW accounts are all now included in the *M1* definition of the money supply.

Powers of Thrift Institutions. Title IV of the DIDMCA allowed new investment opportunities for federally chartered savings and loan associations by amending the Home-Owners' Loan Act of 1933. These associations were permitted to invest up to 20 percent of their assets in consumer loans, corporate debt securities, and commercial paper. There also was a limited opportunity to invest in shares of certain mutual funds or open-end investment companies that hold portfolios consistent with savings and loan association objectives. Title IV also permitted federal mutual savings banks to make commercial loans in amounts up to 5 percent of their assets and could even accept demand deposits from these commercial borrowers. These and other provisions allowed thrift institutions to become more like commercial banks if they so chose.

Federal savings and loan associations also received expanded authority concerning the making of real estate loans. Geographical and first mortgage (or first-lien) loan restrictions on residential real estate were removed. In addition, loan limits were raised to 90 percent of loan-to-value ratios (instead of a prior $75,000 limit). Added authority to make construction and real estate development loans was also provided by Title IV of the DIDMCA.

On the liability side of their balance sheets, savings and loan associations were permitted to issue mutual capital certificates which could be considered as part of their net worth. These capital certificates were subordinated to savings accounts, savings certificates, and other debt obligations.

Other Provisions. The DIDMCA contained a number of additional titles (nine in total). Those particularly relevant to real estate finance include Title V on state usury laws and Title VI, which is referred to as the Truth in Lending

Simplification and Reform Act. State usury laws pertaining to first mortgage residential real property and limiting the amount or rate of interest and finance charges, or discount points, were preempted by a federal usury override contained in Title V. Title VI made Truth in Lending disclosures more understandable to consumers and reduced some of the prior detailed reporting requirements.

The Garn-St. Germain Depository Institutions Act of 1982

Expected benefits from the DIDMCA were initially hindered by high interest rates in 1980 and 1981. Savings and loan associations were particularly hard hit as depositors shifted to negotiable order of withdrawal (NOW) accounts from lower-interest passbook savings accounts, causing the cost of funds to rise. Even so, rate ceilings on the NOW accounts kept the savings and loan associations at a disadvantage because money market mutual funds could offer an even higher interest rate. These developments, as well as other economic factors, led to passage of the Garn-St. Germain Depository Institutions Act of 1982.

The *Garn-St. Germain Act,* while containing many provisions, focused primarily on assisting the savings and loan industry (including mutual savings banks). All depositories were permitted to issue a new money market deposit account which did not have an interest rate ceiling. Furthermore, savings and loan associations were permitted to issue adjustable-rate mortgages, commercial loans, and nonresidential real estate loans.

SAVINGS AND LOAN ASSOCIATIONS

The origin of savings and loan associations can be traced back to 1831 when the first "building" association was formed. In some states, savings and loan associations continue to be referred to as "cooperative banks" or "homestead associations." Savings and loan associations traditionally have specialized in home financing and thus have sought to encourage home ownership. Association members were offered liquidity, safety of principal, and a return for saving in these thrift institutions. Funds "pooled" from a number of savers were lent to other members who needed financing for homes.

Structure and Operation

All of the early savings and loan associations were chartered by the states within which they operated. Beginning in 1933, however, the Home Owners' Loan Act provided for federal chartering of savings and loan associations. There are over 3,000 savings and loan associations in operation today. Approximately 45 percent are federally chartered associations. They control over 55 percent of all association assets, which were about $963 billion at the end of 1986.

Federally chartered associations were initially required to organize as depositor-owned or *mutual* associations. That is, they did not sell stock in the associations, and thus they did not have stockholders. However, in recent years a number of federally chartered mutual associations have been permitted to convert to *stock* associations in order to raise capital by selling stock to shareholders. State-chartered associations also may be mutual or stock associations since approximately one half of the states permit their chartered associations to issue shares of stock. About 70 percent of the savings and loan associations continue to operate as mutuals.

Mutual associations are further characterized by the fact that both savers and borrowers are members. Savings represent shares of ownership, and thus payments on savings are technically dividends rather than interest. However, with the passage of the Housing and Urban Development Act of 1968, federally chartered savings and loan associations were permitted to refer to savings accounts as deposits and be classified as deposit institutions. Some state-chartered mutual associations also were permitted similar classifications.

Regulation and Control

Prior to the Depression of the 1930s, savings and loan associations were loosely regulated. Only individual state regulations existed. In 1932 the Home Loan Bank Act was passed. The Act provided for the creation of the Federal Home Loan Bank System with organizational characteristics similar to those of the Federal Reserve System. The FHLB System consists of the Federal Home Loan Bank Board, 12 regional banks, and the financial institutions that are members of the system. All federal savings and loan associations must belong to the FHLB System.

State-chartered savings and loan associations, along with other qualified financial institutions involved in home mortgage loans, may become members of the system. Approximately 82 percent of state-chartered savings and loan associations belong and, together with the federally chartered members, control approximately 99 percent of the assets held by all savings and loan associations. However, aside from savings and loan association members, 594 mutual savings banks and five life insurance companies belong to the FHLB System.[1]

The Federal Home Loan Bank System, through its role as a central credit facility, assists member institutions by providing: (1) secondary liquidity to meet withdrawal demands; (2) funds to reduce seasonal differences between savings flows and mortgage loan demands; and (3) a mechanism for shifting funds between geographical areas where imbalances exist between savings supply and mortgage loan demand. The FHLB System has been particularly active in attempting to provide stability in residential financing during periods of disintermediation.

---

[1]Savings Institutions *Sourcebook* (Chicago: United States League of Savings Associations, 1987), 48 and 59.

The Federal Savings and Loan Insurance Corporation was created under the National Housing Act of 1934. Insurance is provided for savings accounts held at savings and loan associations. Currently, savings accounts are insured up to $100,000 each. All federal savings and loan associations must belong to the FSLIC and are subject to annual audits.

State-chartered savings and loan associations may apply for insurance under the FSLIC. While only 82 percent of the state-chartered associations are FSLIC-insured, 99 percent of all savings and loan association assets are FSLIC-insured.[2]

Importance of Savings Flows

Savings and loan associations are dependent upon the savings deposits of their shareholders as their principal source of funds. Table 5–1 shows that the dollar amount of savings has grown rapidly since the latter part of the 1970s. In 1966, with the passage of the Interest Rate Adjustment Act, the Federal Home Loan Bank Board was authorized to set maximum interest rates on savings and loan association passbook accounts and savings certificates. The FHLB Board also was permitted to authorize new forms of savings accounts and certificates under the Housing and Urban Development Act of 1968, for example, certificates of deposit.

The significance of savings flows is made clear by the fact that about 77 percent of total savings and loan association liabilities are in the form of savings balances. Mortgage lending and other investment decisions thus are heavily dependent on the level and changes in savings flows. Advances from the Federal Home Loan Bank System and the net worth of savings and loan associations provide only a partial cushion against the volatility of savings flows.

The passbook account historically represented the major type of savings instrument available at savings and loan associations. Today, more than two thirds of the savings held at these institutions is in the form of savings certificates and certificates of deposit. In mid-1978 a six-month money market certificate (MMC) was introduced requiring a minimum $10,000 deposit. These MMCs have a fixed interest rate over their maturity. However, rates are determined weekly and are based on the higher of the average yield on the most recent weekly auction of six-month Treasury bills or on the average of the four most recent auction rates. Their success is indicated by the fact that they accounted for about one third of the savings balances held at savings and loan associations during the early 1980s.

In 1980, 30-month savings certificates were introduced to help meet demand by small savers with savings investments of less than $10,000. Other actions include the creation of the one-year tax-exempt "All Savers" certificate by Congress in 1981 and the elimination of rate ceilings on longer-

---

[2]Savings Institutions *Sourcebook,* 48.

TABLE 5–1   Assets and Liabilities of Savings and Loan Associations (in Billions of Dollars)

	1977		1981		1986	
	Amount	Percent	Amount	Percent	Amount	Percent
ASSETS						
Mortgage loans	381.2	83.0	518.3	78.1	553.6	57.5
Cash and invest- ment securities	39.2	8.5	62.8	9.5	142.8	14.8
Real estate owned	1.9	.4	2.8	.4	20.9	2.2
FHLB stock	3.2	.7	5.3	.8	N.A.	—
Other assets	33.8	7.4	74.6	11.2	245.9	25.5
Total Assets	459.3	100.0	663.8	100.0	963.2	100.0
LIABILITIES AND NET WORTH						
Savings deposits	386.9	84.2	524.4	79.0	740.9	76.9
FHLB and other advances	27.8	6.1	89.1	13.4	158.8	16.5
Loans in process	9.9	2.2	6.3	1.0	N.A.	—
Other liabilities	9.5	2.0	15.6	2.3	20.6	2.1
Net worth	25.2	5.5	28.4	4.3	42.9	4.5
Total Liabilities and Net Worth	459.3	100.0	663.8	100.0	963.2	100.0

N.A. = Not available.

Source: Savings Institutions *Sourcebook,* 1987, 71.

term IRA and Keogh accounts. Also, as previously cited, NOW accounts were authorized on a nationwide basis. One result of this rapid change in account structures has been a rapid rise in the cost of funds to savings and loan associations.

Investment Policies

Savings and loan associations face a maturity problem in trying to match their savings accounts with their lending and investing policies. They borrow short-term and lend long-term. For example, savings account withdrawals usually are honored upon request even though technically associations have the right to require at least 30 days notice prior to withdrawal. Savings certificates have average maturities of only a few years.

On the other hand, mortgage loans of 25 to 30 years traditionally have been common. Thus, sources of funds often are relatively short-term and volatile, whereas the use of funds in the form of mortgage loans is long term. As a result, liquidity problems arise during periods of disintermediation.

Table 5–1 shows that mortgage loans now account for less than three fifths of the total assets of savings and loan associations in contrast with a much higher historical percentage.

About 80 percent of outstanding loans are of the 1- to 4-family

TERMS OF CONVENTIONAL MORTGAGES ON NEW HOMES

An indication of development and trends in conventional mortgages on new homes can be identified by examining recent mortgage terms or characteristics. The following data were gathered from selected issues of the *Federal Reserve Bulletin.*

CONVENTIONAL MORTGAGE TERMS	1984	1985	1986
Purchase Price ($ Thousands)	96.8	104.1	118.1
Amount of Loan ($ Thousands)	73.7	77.4	86.2
Loan/Price Ratio (Percent)	78.7	77.1	75.2
Maturity (Years)	27.8	26.9	26.6
Fees and Charges (% of Loan Amount)	2.64	2.53	2.48
Contract Rate (% Per Annum)	11.87	11.12	9.82

Notice the continued increase in both average purchase prices and average loan amounts in recent years. At the same time, loan to price ratios declined indicating that the increase in average purchase price was greater than the increase in average loan size. Average loan maturities also declined indicating a trend toward somewhat shorter maturities.

Contract interest rates on conventional mortgages on new homes declined sharply over the 1984 through 1986 period. A slight decline in fees and charges also occurred.

home type. The other mortgage loans are approximately equally distributed among multifamily and commercial and other mortgage loans. Approximately 9 out of 10 mortgage loans made by savings and loan associations are conventional loans.

In recent years savings and loan associations have been moving toward alternative mortgage instruments and away from the traditional long-term, fixed-rate mortgage loans. As we have previously indicated, these newer instruments include graduated-payment and adjustable-rate mortgages as well as a variety of other alternative financing methods.

Liquidity is of particular concern to savings and loan associations. In 1950 liquidity requirements were written into the Federal Home Loan Bank Act. The Federal Home Loan Bank Board also controls liquidity requirements in terms of liquidity ratios (savings deposits and short-term borrowings relative to liquid assets) and by specifying which assets qualify as liquid assets. The Board can vary the liquidity ratio between 4 percent and 10 percent. These relatively low liquidity ratios, along with the short-term liabilities versus long-term assets operating positions, indicate why savings and loan associations are heavily affected by changes in savings flows.

MUTUAL SAVINGS BANKS

Mutual savings banks, the oldest type of savings institution in the United

States, provide an important real estate credit source in the Northeast. The approximately 450 banks are concentrated in New York, New Jersey, and the New England states. Safety of principal is stressed in conjunction with the thrift savings of bank members. From the beginning, mutual savings banks stressed investment in real estate mortgages.

Structure and Operation

As their name implies, mutual savings banks were organized for the mutual benefit of depositors and are owned by their depositors. Depositors are entitled to all earnings after provisions are made to insure adequate reserves. All mutual savings banks are state-chartered and thus are regulated by their respective states. Mutual savings banks are managed by boards of trustees.

While mutual savings banks are primarily concentrated in the Middle Atlantic and New England states, they have had an important role in the national mortgage market since 1950. Mutual savings banks currently hold well over $100 billion in mortgages.

Regulation and Control

Mutual savings banks are regulated by the states within which they operate. Legal restrictions have generally prevented geographical extension of the industry. These restrictions are tempered, however, by the fact that laws in several major states permit mutual savings banks to acquire mortgages outside their state boundaries.

The deposits in mutual savings banks are insured largely by the Federal Deposit Insurance Corporation (although three banks have FSLIC insurance as do savings and loan associations). The remaining banks are insured by state funds such as the Mutual Savings Central Fund of Massachusetts.

Importance of Savings Flows

The primary source of funds for mutual savings banks is savings deposits. Table 5–2 shows that deposits account for about 81 percent of total liabilities. Thus, like savings and loan associations, mutual savings banks are affected tremendously by changes in savings flows as reflected in periods of intermediation and disintermediation.

Mutual savings banks have not relied very heavily on borrowings to meet liquidity needs. The credit facilities of the Federal Home Loan Bank System are, of course, available to member banks. Furthermore, the states of New York and Massachusetts provide state-based liquidity facilities for their mutual savings banks in an attempt to cushion the impact of changes in savings flows.

As is the case with savings and loan associations, significant changes have taken place in mutual savings bank deposits in recent years. The six-month money market certificates contributed significantly to the shift in

TABLE 5–2   Assets and Liabilities of Mutual Savings Banks (in Billions of Dollars)

	1977		1981		1986	
	Amount	Percent	Amount	Percent	Amount	Percent
ASSETS						
Mortgage loans	88.2	59.9	100.0	56.9	118.3	49.9
Other loans	6.2	4.2	14.7	8.4	35.2	14.9
U.S. government, state and municipal securities	8.7	5.9	12.1	6.9	16.4	6.9
Corporate and other securities	37.9	25.7	37.8	21.5	46.3	19.6
Cash and other assets	6.3	4.3	11.1	6.3	20.7	8.7
Total Assets	147.3	100.0	175.7	100.0	236.9	100.0
LIABILITIES AND RESERVES						
Deposits	134.0	91.0	155.1	88.3	192.2	81.1
Other liabilities	3.3	2.2	10.6	6.0	26.6	11.2
General reserve accounts	10.0	6.8	10.0	5.7	18.1	7.7
Total Liabilities and Reserves	147.3	100.0	175.7	100.0	236.9	100.0

Source: *National Fact Book of Mutual Savings Banking* and *Federal Reserve Bulletin* (selected issues).

savings mix and at the beginning of the 1980s accounted for over one third of the total savings and time deposits.

Investment Policies

Mortgage loans continue to represent the major investment objective of mutual savings banks. According to Table 5–2 mortgage loans accounted for about 50 percent of the industry's assets in 1986. However, this represents a decline from the 1977 level. During the same period mutual savings banks have been increasing their investments in corporate bonds and mortgage-backed securities.

The dominant form of mortgage loan is in 1- to 4-family homes. In contrast with savings and loan associations, mutual savings banks have a relatively larger percentage of their mortgage loan portfolios invested in multifamily mortgages. Mutual savings banks have made much heavier commitments in their mortgage portfolios to FHA and VA mortgage loans than have savings and loan associations. But, conventional loans have been growing in importance in recent years.

Liquidity and safety of principal are major objectives of mutual savings banks. Legal restrictions require managements to follow conservative lending and investment policies. Regulations identify the types of qualified investments as well as the minimum levels of quality acceptable for such investments. Certain investments also are restricted in amount relative to total assets or deposits. Even so, mutual savings banks have suffered in recent years from liquidity problems associated with periodic deposit outflows. Mutual savings banks currently hold approximately 9 percent of their total assets in cash or in securities maturing within one year.

COMMERCIAL BANKS

Banking in the United States can be traced back to the colonial period. Considerable uncertainty and instability characterized banking, however, until the Federal Reserve Act of 1913 created a central banking system. Commercial banks have differed traditionally from thrift institutions in that they are permitted to provide "checking deposit" facilities.

As was noted earlier, commercial banks traditionally have been the second largest institutional supplier of mortgage credit. This is sometimes overlooked, though, because commercial banks are also substantially committed to numerous other types of loans.

Structure and Operation

All commercial banks are stock companies and are operated for the benefit of their stockholders. Commercial banks are either state chartered or federally chartered. Banks receiving federal charters are known as national banks and must become members of the Federal Reserve System. These banks receive their charters from, and are supervised by, the Comptroller of the Currency. State-chartered banks are under the supervision of state agencies. State banks also have the option of joining the Federal Reserve System.

There are over 14,000 commercial banks in the United States. While less than 6,000 banks are members of the Federal Reserve System, these banks control over three fourths of all commercial bank assets.

Regulation and Control

Member banks, all national banks, and state banks that have joined are under the regulation of the Federal Reserve System. Control is exercised over all bank reserves and the cost of borrowing from the Fed. The significance of Federal Reserve System activities was discussed in the last chapter.

Insurance for deposits held in commercial banks dates back to the Glass-Steagall Act of 1933. In 1935 a permanent deposit insurance plan established the Federal Deposit Insurance Corporation. Membership in the FDIC, with a current maximum insurance of $100,000 per account, is required of all national banks and state bank members of the Federal Reserve System. FDIC membership is also available to state banks that are not members of the Federal Reserve System. Approximately 98 percent of all commercial banks are insured by the FDIC.

Importance of Savings Flows

Commercial banks derive more than one half of their funds from time and savings deposits, according to Table 5–3. When combined with demand deposits, total deposits account for over 70 percent of total liabilities. This is roughly similar to the deposits to total liabilities ratios for savings and loan associations and mutual savings banks. The major difference, of course, is that demand or checking deposits are less stable than savings deposits. Thus, commercial banks must provide for greater liquidity cushions in the form of cash and short-term U.S. government securities. Liquidity problems associated with disintermediation affect commercial banks as well as thrift institutions.

Investment Policies

Investment by commercial banks in real estate loans accounted for about 18 percent of total assets in 1986 (see Table 5–3). This is due, in part, to a need to provide for some balance between short-term liabilities and longer-term asset maturities. Commercial banks, in contrast with savings and loan associations and mutual savings banks, have more varied loan and investment objectives. The importance of securities investments and other loans is shown in Table 5–3.

Even though real estate loans are a relatively small portion of total assets, the nearly $498 billion of outstanding mortgages ranks only behind the mortgage holdings of savings and loan associations. While mortgages on 1- to

TABLE 5–3 Assets and Liabilities of Commercial Banks (in Billions of Dollars)

	1977		1981		1986	
	Amount	Percent	Amount	Percent	Amount	Percent
ASSETS						
Cash and bank balances	16°.7	14.5	188.1	10.4	273.7	9.7
Securities investments	257.4	22.1	345.5	19.1	479.6	17.1
Real estate loans	177.2	15.2	286.8	15.9	497.5	17.7
Other loans	483.2	41.4	697.7	38.6	1,337.2	47.5
Other assets	79.6	6.8	288.7	16.0	224.8	8.0
Total Assets	1,166.1	100.0	1,806.8	100.0	2,812.8	100.0
LIABILITIES AND CAPITAL						
Demand deposits	383.0	32.8	377.7	20.9	691.1	24.6
Time and savings deposits	556.5	47.7	910.9	50.4	1,326.9	47.2
Other liabilities	146.6	12.6	386.7	21.4	614.2	21.8
Capital accounts	80.0	6.9	131.5	7.3	180.6	6.4
Total Liabilities and Capital	1,166.1	100.0	1,806.8	100.0	2,812.8	100.0

Source: *Federal Reserve Bulletin* (selected issues).

RECENT INTEREST RATES
ON NEW CONVENTIONAL MORTGAGES

Housing construction and sales activities are affected by the level of, and changes in, real estate mortgage interest rates. Annual yields on conventional mortgages are maintained by both the Federal Home Loan Bank Board (FHLBB) and the Department of Housing and Urban Development (HUD). Yields for both series are reported in the *Federal Reserve Bulletin* and were as follows for the 1980s:

YEAR	FHLBB SERIES	HUD SERIES
1980	12.65%	13.95%
1981	14.74	16.52
1982	15.12	15.79
1983	12.66	13.43
1984	12.37	13.80
1985	11.58	12.28
1986	10.25	10.07
1987 (Aug.)	9.38	10.37

Even when annual rates were reported, there were wide fluctuations during the first half of the 1980s. The FHLBB series was below 13 percent in 1980 before increasing and finally peaking above the 15 percent level in 1982. FHLBB rates then started a downward trend with a mid-1987 low of less than 10 percent. The FHLBB series reports effective interest rates on conventional loans that were closed.

The HUD series was even more volatile than the FHLBB series. Rates for 1980 were about 14 percent before increasing to about 16.5 percent in 1981. HUD series rates then fell to just above 10 percent by the end of 1986 and remained slightly above 10 percent as of mid-1987. The HUD series reports average rates on conventional first mortgage commitments.

4-family homes account for over one half of commercial bank mortgage portfolios, loans on commercial property are very important. Commercial banks also engage primarily in conventional mortgage loans.

LIFE INSURANCE COMPANIES

Life insurance companies are another major institutional supplier of funds to the primary mortgage market. At the same time it is important to recognize that life insurance companies were not organized primarily to finance mortgage needs. Thus, mortgage investments are in direct competition with other investment opportunities for the funds flowing into life insurance companies.

Savings flows that are important to thrift institutions and commercial banks are not of direct concern to life insurance companies. Rather than having to worry about periods of intermediation and disintermediation, the investment policies of life insurance companies are largely dependent upon the inflow of premiums paid by policyholders.

Structure and Operation

Life insurance companies may be organized as either mutual companies or as stock companies. Over 90 percent of the approximately 2,200 life insurance companies are stock companies owned by shareholders. However, mutual life insurance companies control over one half of the industry's total assets.

Regulation and Control

Life insurance companies are regulated by the states within which they are chartered and by states in which they do business. State regulations focus primarily on the investment policies of life insurance companies. Of interest is the fact that a number of states require life insurance companies, in order to conduct business in their states, to invest a certain percentage of assets or reserves within the state. Limitations and standards often are placed on real estate and mortgage loan investments.

Table 5–4 shows that the primary source of funds (liabilities) for life insurance companies is from policy reserves. These reserves comprise over 80 percent of the industry's total liabilities. State laws require life insurance companies to maintain their policy reserves at appropriate levels such that all policy obligations will be met as they come due. An actuarial basis calculation is used to determine the level of adequate policy reserves. Consideration is given to mortality experience, expected inflows of premium payments, and expected interest earnings rates. The surplus funds provide added reserves to meet unexpected contingencies such as an increase in policyholder death rates.

Investment Policies

Life insurance companies hold a variety of different types of assets. According to Table 5–4, the two dominant asset holdings are in the form of corporate bonds and mortgages. Mortgages account for over 20 percent of total assets. In addition, life insurance companies place approximately 3 to 4 percent of their assets in other forms of real estate investments.

Life insurance companies as a group represent the largest institutional holder of corporate bonds which are acquired largely in the form of direct or private placements based on direct negotiations with the issuers. Corporate stock investments by life insurance companies are regulated by strict state laws.

Since the beginning of the 1970s, life insurance companies have reduced the significance of 1- to 4-family home loans in terms of their mortgage portfolios. There also has been a recent drop-off in residential multifamily mortgage loans. Nonfarm, nonresidential mortgage loans have grown

TABLE 5-4   Assets and Liabilities of Life Insurance Companies (in Billions of Dollars)

	1977		1981		1985	
	Amount	Percent	Amount	Percent	Amount	Percent
ASSETS						
Government securities	23.6	6.7	39.5	7.5	124.6	15.0
Corporate bonds	137.9	39.2	193.8	36.8	296.8	36.0
Corporate stocks	33.8	9.6	47.7	9.1	77.5	9.4
Mortgages	96.8	27.5	137.7	26.2	171.8	20.8
Real estate owned	11.1	3.2	18.3	3.5	28.8	3.5
Other assets	48.5	13.8	88.8	16.9	126.4	15.3
Total Assets	351.7	100.0	525.8	100.0	825.9	100.0
LIABILITIES AND SURPLUS						
Policy reserves	281.0	79.9	428.0	81.4	665.3	80.6
Other obligations	47.1	13.4	60.4	11.5	103.9	12.6
Surplus funds	21.7	6.2	35.2	6.7	54.0	6.5
Capital (stock companies)	1.9	.5	2.2	.4	2.7	.3
Total Liabilities and Surplus	351.7	100.0	525.8	100.0	825.9	100.0

Note: Beginning in the mid-1980s balance sheet information is available only for odd-numbered years. Thus, data for 1986 were not available.

Source: *Life Insurance Fact Book,* 1986.

rapidly in the form of shopping centers, office buildings, and medical centers. To a lesser extent, growth has also occurred in the holdings of farm mortgages. Directly owned real estate largely reflects investments in residential and commercial properties, with about one fifth of the total represented by the firms' home and branch offices.

ADDITIONAL SOURCES OF MORTGAGE FUNDS

The primary mortgage market is dominated by savings and loan associations, mutual savings banks, commercial banks, and life insurance companies. Mortgage funds also are sometimes supplied to the primary mortgage market by mortgage companies, pension funds, credit unions, real estate investment trusts, and individuals. While their dollar amount of mortgage funds raised in recent years has been relatively small, they make a very important contribution to the primary mortgage market.

Mortgage Banking Companies

Mortgage banking companies, while not major suppliers of mortgage funds, perform a very necessary "merchandising" or facilitating function in financing real estate. They are private corporations that depend heavily on short-term bank borrowing in order to finance their merchandising function. Mortgage companies frequently originate or negotiate residential mortgages. But, rather than hold the mortgages, mortgage companies resell the mortgages to institutions. They often continue to service the mortgage loans for the institutional owners by collecting the interest and principal payments. Mortgage banking companies will be discussed in detail in Chapter 6.

Pension Funds

Private, noninsured pension funds have been small but positive suppliers of funds to the mortgage market. At the same time, state and local retirement funds have been even smaller suppliers of mortgage funds. In 1970 mortgage loans represented about 4 percent of the total assets of noninsured private pension plans. However, this ratio has declined while assets have grown to over $600 billion. Mortgages relative to total assets were at about the 12 percent level for state and local government retirement funds in 1970. Ratios, though, have been declining while assets now exceed $300 billion.[3]

The primary source of funds for noninsured or trusteed private pension funds is in the form of contributions from employers and employees. These funds are supplemented by investment income. State and local government retirement plans receive their sources of funds from government and employee contributions plus investment income. A significant portion of the liabilities of pension funds thus represent long-term commitments or obligations to employees. Consequently, pension plan investments also are predominantly long-term in nature. Noninsured private pension funds have a major portion of their assets committed to corporate common stocks and bonds. State and local government retirement funds also are heavily committed to investments in corporate common stocks and bonds.

Pension funds have been a major target for the federally underwritten mortgage passthrough securities. A special type of FHLMC passthrough security has been of interest to pension funds. This security is termed the "guaranteed mortgage certificate" with cash flow features similar to those for bonds instead of the more typical uneven cash flows associated with many mortgage pools.

Pension funds also have made direct real estate investments through the formation of "commingled funds" in recent years. A number of pension funds pool a portion of their capital for purposes of investing in real property and this sum becomes a commingled fund. Life insurance companies and commercial banks usually originate and administer these funds, with the pension funds being viewed as passive investors for tax purposes. Pension funds own shares in the commingled funds and income received from these investments is tax-exempt.

---

[3]Herbert E. Dougall and Jack E. Gaumnitz, *Capital Markets and Institutions,* 5th ed. (Englewood Cliffs, New Jersey: Prentice-Hall, Inc., 1986), 138 and 148.

Credit Unions

The first credit union was formed in 1909. Today, there are over 20,000 credit unions with approximately three fifths being federally chartered and the remainder state chartered. They represent a third type of thrift institution, along with savings and loan associations and mutual savings banks.

Credit unions are nonprofit financial cooperatives that are operated for the financial benefit of their members. Officers and directors are elected to their unpaid positions by each credit union's members and are responsible for setting policies.

In order to become a member of a credit union, an individual must meet the credit union's membership requirements. Nearly four fifths of credit unions in the U.S. are categorized as being occupationally related.

Credit unions have assets in excess of $150 billion with loans outstanding of more than $86 billion which are primarily consumer loans.[4] Thus, these thrift institutions have had little impact on real estate financing. The Federal Credit Union Act of 1934 and subsequent amendments, while not directly prohibiting real estate mortgage loans, created an effective barrier by imposing relatively short loan maturity limits. However, in 1977 legislation was passed that substantially revised the 1934 Act by allowing credit unions to engage in first mortgage residential real estate loans with maturities up to 30 years. Mobile home loans and real property loans for home improvement purposes could be made for as long as 15 years. Even so, recent data continue to show the emphasis by credit unions on making consumer loans.

Real Estate Investment Trusts

Some form of real estate investment trusts (referred to as REITs) can be traced back to the 19th century. In 1960 the Real Estate Investment Trust Act provided for separation of investment from management responsibilities and problems—much like the operation of mutual funds. Thus, small investors were provided with a means for participating in both large and diversified real estate investments. Real growth developed during the 1969–70 tight money period and REIT assets reached $21 billion by the end of 1974 before declining to a level of about $12 billion in the early 1980s. Liquidations and foreclosures have continued to plague the industry.

If REITs meet certain qualifications, they are exempt from corporate income taxes. One requirement is that they pay out at least 90 percent of their ordinary income to investors, with the remainder being taxed at the appropriate rate. Thus, retained earnings do not represent a major source of funds. The major source of funds for REITs has been in the form of term loans and lines of credit from commercial banks. Shareholders' equity, primarily in the form of new stock issues, has been the second largest source of funds. Commercial paper was also a significant source of funds during the

---

[4]*Federal Reserve Bulletin* (January 1988): A27.

early 1970s.[5]

REITs must derive annually at least 90 percent of their gross income from certain passive sources (such as real estate rentals or interest receipts) and at least 75 percent of the income must come from real estate sources. Also, the sale of real estate, if held for less than four years, plus short-term security profits cannot exceed 30 percent of annual gross income.

There are two basic types of real estate investment trusts. The 1960s saw a heavy emphasis on *equity trusts* whereby a proprietary interest was achieved through the purchase and operation of existing income-producing properties. More recently the emphasis has shifted to the *mortgage trust,* which, as its name implies, invests by purchasing mortgage obligations. Thus these trusts hold mortgage liens and become creditors rather than the holders of equity positions. Today, many hybrid combinations of the two types exist.

The assets of REITs are largely in the form of mortgage loans with property ownership usually representing less than 20 percent of assets. Construction loans are the largest type of mortgage loans made by real estate investment trusts. In the early 1970s over 40 percent of total assets were held in the form of first mortgage construction loans. This, coupled with the fact that over one half of REIT funds were derived from bank loan and commercial paper sources, resulted in the development of substantial REIT problems.[6]

REITs were substantial suppliers of mortgage funds during the 1971–73 period. However, beginning in 1974 the role of REITs in the primary mortgage market changed dramatically. Rising interest rates during 1973 and 1974 and the ensuing recession created havoc for the REIT industry. Not only were there substantial defaults by builders on loans, but REITs were further squeezed because they were forced to pay very high short-term interest rates on their borrowings while they were "locked-in" to rates previously committed to builders. REIT stock prices dropped dramatically, a number failed, and many of the surviving REITs are still trying to work out of their problems. The future role of REITs as suppliers of mortgage funds continues to depend on their ability to solve existing problems and to guard against the recurrence of similar problems.

Individuals

Individuals represent important sources of funds in both the primary and secondary mortgage markets. With the development of federally underwritten mortgage passthrough securities, it is now even easier for individuals to directly participate as suppliers of real estate funds. Indications are that this source of real estate funds will continue to expand in future years.

---

[5]*REIT Fact Book* (Washington, D.C.: National Association of Real Estate Investment Trusts), various editions.
[6]*REIT Fact Book.*

KEY TERMS

banking system
Depository Institutions
   Deregulation Act

Garn-St. Germain Act
Monetary Control Act

QUESTIONS FOR REVIEW

1. Provide a brief explanation of the major provisions of the Monetary Control Act of 1980.
2. Identify and briefly explain the purpose of the Depository Institutions Deregulation Act of 1980.
3. What are the major provisions of the Consumer Checking Account Equity Act of 1980?
4. Title IV of the Depository Institutions Deregulation and Monetary Control Act of 1980 alters the powers of thrift institutions. Explain.
5. Provide a brief description of the Garn-St. Germain Depository Institutions Act of 1982 in terms of how it impacted on savings and loan associations and other depositories.
6. Briefly describe and compare savings and loan associations with mutual savings banks in terms of: (a) structure and operation, (b) regulation and control, (c) significance of savings flows, and (d) investment policies.
7. Compare and contrast commercial banks with savings and loan associations and mutual savings banks on the basis of the four areas listed in question 6.
8. What is the role of life insurance companies as suppliers of mortgage and real estate investment funds?
9. In addition to the major depository institutions and life insurance companies, there are several other important suppliers of funds to the primary mortgage market. Briefly identify and describe these suppliers.

PROBLEMS

1. You are considering the purchase of commercial property that is appraised at $300,000 and are investigating the possibility of financing for the property. What type of institution is likely to be a potential financing source?
2. Assume that you are seeking FHA financing on a new home. Based on the fact that different institutions specialize in different types of loans, what type of institution would specialize in FHA financing?
3. Obtain current financial statement data for savings and loan associations, mutual savings banks, commercial banks, and life insurance companies. Examine their asset and liability structures to determine whether structural changes have occurred since the data presented in the chapter.

6

SECONDARY MORTGAGE MARKET ACTIVITIES AND PROCEDURES

LEARNING OBJECTIVES

After studying this chapter, you should be able to do the following:

Describe the three types of transactions or activities that take place in the mortgage market.

Define what is meant by a mortgage banker and briefly describe the role of mortgage banking in the financing of real property.

Describe and contrast developments in the secondary mortgage market during the 1950s and 1960s versus the 1930s and 1940s.

Briefly identify and discuss secondary mortgage market institutional developments during the 1970s and 1980s.

Define what is meant by mortgage-backed securities, describe the two basic types, and indicate the use of mortgage-backed securities in the secondary mortgage market.

Describe the basic role, structure, and organization of the Federal National Mortgage Association.

Discuss how the Federal National Mortgage Association has carried out its secondary mortgage market responsibilities in recent years.

A FINANCIAL SYSTEM, to be effective, must provide markets and procedures for handling and transferring claims to wealth. The *mortgage market,* broadly defined, involves three types of transactions or activities. As we have seen in the two previous chapters, the *primary mortgage market* involves the creation or origination of new mortgages. Savings are channeled into financial institutions which, in turn, perform the investment function by originating and holding mortgages. The holding of a mortgage represents one form of a claim to wealth.

In some instances, financial institutions and other financial intermediaries are involved in the process of origination of new mortgages but without the intention of holding mortgage claims to wealth. In essence, these originators act as middle persons or agents in distributing mortgages to other investors. This *facilitating function* represents the second major activity or transaction in the mortgage market. Mortgage banking firms perform this facilitating or intermediary function.

The third segment of the mortgage market involves the buying and selling of existing mortgage loans and mortgage-backed securities in the *secondary mortgage market.* Thus, the secondary mortgage market provides liquidity through improved marketability of mortgage claims to wealth. Mortgage bankers often sell their originated mortgages directly to institutions operating in the secondary mortgage market. And, just as stocks and bonds are traded in secondary markets, mortgage claims to wealth can be bought and sold in the secondary mortgage market.

NEED FOR A SECONDARY MORTGAGE MARKET

The origination of mortgages generally results in long-term claims to wealth. Since mortgage loans usually involve substantial dollar amounts, borrowers need long time periods over which to repay loan principal and interest obligations. Originators establish the terms of mortgage loans in the primary mortgage market. As we have previously seen, lender-originators such as commercial banks, mutual savings banks, and savings and loan associations often intend to hold the mortgage loans they originate until the loans mature. Returns on these claims to wealth are received in the form of interest payments. However, economic conditions influenced by monetary and fiscal policy actions has often resulted in periods of disintermediation for these financial institutions. Severe disintermediation can produce liquidity pressures or cash needs that may require the liquidation of some mortgage holdings.

From time to time other holders of mortgages such as pension funds, life insurance companies, and even individuals may find it necessary to meet liquidity needs. In other instances it might be desirable for institutions or individuals to sell some of their existing mortgage claims to wealth and purchase other mortgages or securities in order to meet their portfolio investment objectives. Thus, there is a need for a mechanism for facilitating the marketing of mortgage claims to wealth. In an effective financial system, markets need to be established to provide for the ready buying and selling of mortgages at reasonable prices and costs. Improved marketability of mortgage claims to wealth will result in greater liquidity for the holders of mortgages. Mortgage *marketability* thus relates to the time required to buy or sell mortgages as well as the cost involved in marketing secondary mortgage market transactions.

However, while the need for a well-functioning national secondary mortgage market is apparent, its early development was erratic. Lack of loan standardization practices and procedures undoubtedly contributed to the slow development of a national market. Historically, loan originators often employed different loan application standards and requirements across the United States. Compounding these differences has been the importance of geographical areas, within which the pledged properties are located, in traditionally assessing the quality of mortgage loans. Today, as further loan standardization practices and procedures continue to take place, the national secondary mortgage market is becoming quite efficient.

MORTGAGE BANKING'S FACILITATING ROLE

The facilitating function between the primary and secondary mortgage markets often is performed by mortgage banking firms. According to the 1946 Constitution of the Mortgage Bankers Association of America, a **mortgage banker** is: "Any person, firm, or corporation . . . engaged in the business of lending money on the security of improved real estate in the United States and who publicly offers such securities, or certificates, bonds, or debentures based thereon, for sale as a dealer therein, or who is an investor in real estate securities, or is the recognized agent of an insurance company or other direct purchaser of first mortgage real estate securities for investment only."

In actual practice, a distinction sometimes is made between mortgage brokers and mortgage bankers. A **mortgage broker** performs the loan origination function by bringing together lenders and borrowers in real estate loan transactions, which results in a mortgage placement fee for successful loan originations. Mortgage brokers specialize in commercial real estate properties and they seldom finance loans with their own capital. The role of a mortgage broker usually is terminated when the loan is placed. That is, mortgage brokers generally do not service loans after they have been delivered to the investor or lender.

Mortgage bankers also originate new real estate loans. They perform a significant role in residential real estate financings. While mortgage bankers sometimes finance or invest in the loans they originate, their more important role is as middle persons or agents in the distribution of mortgages to other investors. Mortgage bankers often perform a loan servicing function by collecting payments and inspecting real estate properties used as collateral for the loan they originated. Thus, mortgage bankers traditionally performed mortgage loan *origination, servicing,* and *placement* functions.

Mortgage Banker Operations

Traditional mortgage banking operations in an intermediary capacity can be illustrated with an example. Assume that a builder seeks the assistance of a mortgage banker in obtaining financing for a major real estate project. Two kinds of financing actually are needed: (1) a short-term construction or building loan, and (2) a long-term property mortgage loan. In practice, the two kinds of financing go hand-in-hand. A mortgage banker must be able to show that long-term mortgage funds can be obtained before short-term construction loans are acquired. The short-term building loan to cover construction activities is either supplied from the mortgage banker's own funds or is obtained through a short-term loan from a commercial bank. Security for the loan includes the underlying property plus the general credit of the builder and mortgage banker.

In order to obtain funds for a builder, the mortgage banker first secures the availability of long-term mortgage funds by obtaining an *advance* (or *forward*) *commitment* from the permanent investor, which often is an insurance company or mutual savings bank. The permanent investor makes or enters into a firm commitment to purchase mortgage loans which will be placed on the property. This is done in advance of construction. The mortgage banker agrees to deliver the mortgages at some future date on the homes that are to be constructed on the property by the builder.

A *take-out letter* represents the agreement for the advance commitment and covers the delivery date, amount of loans, and fees connected with the long-term mortgages. The take-out letter aids the mortgage banker in the attempt to obtain the necessary construction loan funds. However, in certain instances the mortgage banker is unable to obtain an immediate advance commitment. This frequently occurs during periods of high or rising interest rates and brings about the need for a *standby commitment.* In this situation, the commercial banker enters into a firm or standby commitment to purchase the mortgage if the mortgage banker cannot find a permanent investor by a specified date. The commercial banker pays a *forfeiture price* or discount price in the event that a permanent investor cannot be found during the stated time period.

Under certain conditions mortgage bankers find it desirable to "warehouse" mortgages. *Mortgage warehousing* is an interim loan made by a commercial bank designed to cover the time period between when the mortgage banker closes the mortgage loan and the mortgage is accepted by the permanent investor. The most prevalent type of warehousing occurs when a time lapse develops between the time the mortgage banker closes or originates the loan and the time the loan is, in turn, delivered to the permanent investor. During this interim period, the amount of the mortgage is lent by the commercial bank to the mortgage banker.

Recent Trends and Developments

Earlier in this century mortgage banking grew out of the need by life insurance companies and mutual savings banks located in the northeast to invest in out-of-state mortgages. The assets of these institutions expanded rapidly and their officers sought additional opportunities for investments offering relatively high but safe yields. Mortgage bankers provided necessary assistance in facilitating the making of these out-of-state loans.

Mortgage banking also grew because mortgage bankers performed a necessary role in the development of *mortgage loan participations.* Briefly, in situations when local financial institutions could not meet the total amount requested for a loan, mortgage bankers sought to arrange participation in the mortgage loan by additional lenders.

Mortgage bankers traditionally specialized in originating FHA-insured mortgage loans. Before the formation of the Federal Housing Administration (FHA) in 1934, the lack of standards for qualifying borrowers and collateral created substantial risks for investors lending funds on real estate mortgages. With the development of a standardized system for estimating property values and borrower credit capabilities, mortgage banking activity flourished. Emphasis on VA-guaranteed mortgage loans also developed rapidly after the passage by Congress of the Serviceman's Readjustment Act (commonly known as the GI Bill of Rights) in 1944. At the beginning of the 1970s FHA/VA loans comprised over 60 percent of the dollar amount of first mortgage loans closed by mortgage bankers. More recently, the figure has been in excess of 75 percent of the total amount of FHA/VA loans, making mortgage bankers the primary institutional originators of the federal loan programs.

Long-term mortgage loans closed during 1986 by mortgage bankers were in excess of $142 million and represented over one fifth of the total amount closed by savings and loan associations, commercial and mutual savings banks, life insurance companies, and mortgage bankers.[1] This compares with long-term mortgage loan closings by mortgage bankers of about $13 million in 1970 and $20 million in 1975.

Loans originated and often serviced by mortgage bankers were traditionally purchased by life insurance companies, depository institutions (savings and loan associations, commercial banks, and mutual savings banks) and federal credit agencies. Today, the primary placement of mortgage banker loan originations is through the Government National Mortgage Association's guaranteed mortgage pools. This development is consistent with the fact that the most rapid growth in mortgage passthrough securities has been in the form of GNMA guaranteed securities. The Federal National Mortgage Association represents the second major source or purchaser of federally underwritten mortgages originated by mortgage bankers. Life insurance companies represent the third most important purchaser of mortgage banker loan originations.

---

[1]"Mortgage Banking Activity," *Mortgage Banking* (December 1987): 101.

Mortgage bankers operate with very little of their own capital funds. Net worth of about 10 percent of total assets is not uncommon. Borrowed funds are primarily short-term and take the form of commercial paper (short-term unsecured promissory notes issued by the mortgage bankers) or lines of credit from commercial banks. Mortgage bankers are able to operate with small amounts of equity funds and short-term borrowed funds because their loan originations usually are made with existing purchase commitments and they hold relatively small amounts of mortgage loans in inventory over long time periods.

In addition to their important role as loan originators, mortgage bankers continue to service about three fourths of the long-term mortgage loans that they originate. Thus, mortgage bankers continue to perform a dominant, facilitating, or intermediary role in the overall mortgage market.

DEVELOPMENT OF THE SECONDARY MORTGAGE MARKET

Secondary securities markets are well developed for stocks and bonds. For example, organized stock exchanges such as the New York Stock Exchange date back to the last century. A secondary mortgage market lacks such a history. While undoubtedly some buying, selling, or exchanging of mortgages between financial institutions was carried out on a local level, little regional and virtually no national secondary mortgage activity occurred prior to the 1930s. Depository institutions such as commercial banks and savings and loan associations frequently faced problems of liquidity. These were compounded by the lack of marketability of mortgage loans.

Prior to the 1930s, only commercial banks that were members of the Federal Reserve System possessed a source that they could turn toward in order to temper liquidity pressures. As we saw in Chapter 4, member banks historically could borrow at the prevailing discount rate from Federal Reserve Banks. One way member banks did this was by rediscounting notes or other debt instruments contained in their own portfolios. This ability to borrow against certain outstanding loans helped temper the lack of an active secondary mortgage market.

Savings and loan associations were not as fortunate. Although Congressional hearings as early as 1919 considered the establishment of a central credit system for the purpose of aiding mortgage lending institutions, formal action was not taken until the financial crisis of the 1930s. As we saw in Chapter 5, savings and loan associations were "loosely" regulated until the passage of the Federal Home Loan Bank Act of 1932. One important purpose of the creation of the Federal Home Loan Bank System was to provide credit in the form of advances to member mortgage lending institutions. Member institutions are permitted to borrow against their savings balances. This has helped, at least since the 1930s, to temper liquidity pressures associated with the lack of marketability for mortgage loans.

However, the need for a well-developed national secondary mortgage market remains. The overall mortgage market continues to be highly volatile. Further improvement in the secondary mortgage market is expected to help reduce overall volatility. A number of legislative efforts have taken place to stimulate and encourage the continued development of an efficient secondary mortgage market. Major federal laws affecting the development of the secondary market are listed in Table 6–1 and provide the basis for further

TABLE 6–1. Major Federal Developments Affecting the Secondary Mortgage Market

Date	Federal Provisions and Developments
1934	NATIONAL HOUSING ACT Created the Federal Housing Administration. Also provided for the establishment of privately-owned mortgage institutions to operate a national secondary mortgage market.
1938	FEDERAL NATIONAL MORTGAGE ASSOCIATION (CREATION OF) The Reconstruction Finance Corporation provided capital for the establishment of the Federal National Mortgage Association which was to operate as a government-sponsored secondary mortgage market.
1950	FEDERAL NATIONAL MORTGAGE ASSOCIATION (TRANSFERENCE OF) Provision was made to move the FNMA from under the Reconstruction Finance Corporation to the Housing and Home Finance Agency which was created in 1942 to coordinate federal home financing activities.
1954	FEDERAL NATIONAL MORTGAGE ASSOCIATION CHARTER ACT The FNMA was rechartered as a federal agency with some corporate structural characteristics. It continued as an agency of the Housing and Home Finance Agency but was to become privately-owned.
1968	HOUSING AND URBAN DEVELOPMENT ACT The FNMA was reorganized as a separate, privately-owned corporation. At the same time, the Government National Mortgage Association was created as a wholly-owned government corporation under the direction of the Department of Housing and Urban Development.
1970	EMERGENCY HOME FINANCE ACT Created the Federal Home Loan Mortgage Corporation for purposes of providing a secondary mortgage market for savings and loan association members of the Federal Home Loan Bank System. Also permitted FNMA to purchase and sell conventional mortgages.
1978	FINANCIAL INSTITUTIONS REGULATORY AND INTEREST RATE CONTROL ACT Authorized the FHLMC to purchase packages of home improvement loans.
1980	HOUSING AND COMMUNITY DEVELOPMENT ACT Created a secondary market for FNMA mobile home loans and property improvement loans.
1984	SECONDARY MORTGAGE MARKET ENHANCEMENT ACT Secondary mortgage market issuers were exempted from state securities registration laws and the secondary mortgage market powers of FHLMC (Freddie Mac) and FNMA (Fannie Mae) were broadened.

discussion in this section. (Additional federal laws relating to real estate finance are listed in Appendix C.)

Federal Developments During the 1930s and 1940s

The Federal Housing Administration was established with the passage of the National Housing Act of 1934. The Act also provided for the establishment of privately-owned mortgage institutions to operate a national secondary mortgage market.

The Reconstruction Finance Corporation purchased some mortgages on urban commercial properties, while avoiding residential mortgages, during 1935. By 1938, it was apparent that a national secondary mortgage market was not developing. Consequently, legislation was enacted in 1938 which created the Federal National Mortgage Association (FNMA). The objective was to develop a government-sponsored secondary market for residential mortgages.

More specifically, the FNMA, which is commonly referred to as "Fannie Mae," was designed to provide a secondary market for Federal Housing Administration (FHA) insured mortgages. FHA-insured loans originated under the National Housing Act of 1934 when the Federal Housing Administration was created. It was anticipated that the development of FHA insurance of residential real estate loans would facilitate the establishment of a secondary market. However, a secondary market did not develop on a national level.

The Reconstruction Finance Corporation provided $10 million in capital to the FNMA when it was established in 1938. Additional funds could be raised by the FNMA by issuing its own notes when additional funds were needed. The FNMA had power to purchase FHA-insured mortgages from qualified sellers which, in turn, helped replenish available funds for making more FHA mortgage loans. In actual practice, however, the Federal National Mortgage Association purchased relatively few mortgages during most of the 1940s. It was 1948 before the FNMA's mortgage holdings began to increase substantially. This dramatic increase in holdings coincided with the broadening of the FNMA's operations in 1948 to allow purchase of Veterans Administration guaranteed loans.

Changes During the 1950s and 1960s

In 1950 the Federal National Mortgage Association was transferred from the jurisdiction of the Reconstruction Finance Corporation to the Housing and Home Finance Agency which was created in 1942 to coordinate federal home financing activities.

In 1954 FNMA was rechartered as a federal agency (it was previously a wholly-owned government corporation) under the Federal National Mortgage Association Charter Act. The FNMA continued as an agency of the Housing and Home Finance Agency but was to become privately-owned and have corporate structural characteristics. In other words, FNMA was to move from government ownership to private ownership. This was to be accomplished in the following fashion. First, preferred stock was to be issued to the U.S. Treasury so that the capital, surplus, and earnings of the old FNMA could be used for working capital.

Second, lenders doing business with FNMA were expected to become common stockholders of the secondary market facility. Lenders were required to invest 3 percent of the dollar amount of the loans they sold to FNMA in capital contributions that were then exchanged for common stock. This was changed to a stock purchase requirement of between 1 and 2 percent under the Housing Act of 1957. Further reductions in stock purchase requirements for sellers of mortgages to FNMA were made during the recessionary period of 1958.

The Charter Act of 1954 made three additional provisions relating to: (1) secondary market operations, (2) special assistance functions, and (3) management and liquidation functions. FNMA's secondary market operations were limited to FHA-insured (stemming from the 1938 National Housing Act) and VA-guaranteed (stemming from the 1944 Serviceman's Readjustment Act) mortgage loans. Under the 1954 Charter Act, insured or guaranteed loans could be purchased at par or discount prices depending upon prevailing economic and geographic conditions. The FNMA also was given discretion as to whether or not to accept submitted mortgages. That is, the FNMA could set its own mortgage acceptability standards. This flexibility permitted the FNMA to set profit objectives consistent with a movement toward private ownership.

The special assistance function provided the President with the power to authorize the FNMA to support special types of housing programs through advance commitments and purchases of mortgages. Special types of housing problems include urban renewal projects. FNMA assistance also has been used to stimulate the construction industry during recessionary periods. Another form of special assistance includes the purchase of mortgages on properties reconstructed after natural disasters.

The management and liquidation function provided in the 1954 Charter Act required that FNMA manage and liquidate its portfolio of mortgages acquired prior to November, 1954. Many of the mortgages owned by the FNMA prior to the 1954 Act did not meet new quality standards and were purchased during periods when the FNMA operated without profit objectives.

In 1965 FNMA became a subsidiary of the Department of Housing and Urban Development which replaced the Housing and Home Finance Agency. FNMA continued to operate in a quasi-public capacity, characterized by profit motives while maintaining U.S. Treasury support, until 1968.

Housing and Urban Development Act of 1968

The Federal National Mortgage Association was reorganized as a privately-owned corporation under the Housing and Urban Development Act of 1968. All stock owned by the U.S. Treasury was redeemed and replaced by the sale of common stock to the general public. The secondary mortgage operations remained with the new Fannie Mae. FNMA thus is a private corporation dealing in mortgage loan claims to wealth. The FNMA raises money by selling securities backed by its pool of mortgages. However, since this private corporation still has a public purpose, the U.S. Treasury still has the authority to purchase Fannie Mae obligations.

The special assistance and management and liquidation functions provided for under the 1954 Charter Act were reassigned to a new organization under the Housing and Urban Development Act of 1968. This new organization, the Government National Mortgage Association (GNMA), was created as a wholly-owned government corporation under the direction of the Department of Housing and Urban Development. As might be expected, it soon became known as "Ginnie Mae."

Fannie Mae and Ginnie Mae were designed to work together even though one is privately-owned and the other government-owned. FNMA raises funds to purchase mortgages by selling its common stock and by issuing mortgage-backed bonds and other debt instruments. Ginnie Mae, in turn, guarantees mortgage-backed bonds issued by FNMA. FNMA provides support for GNMA through its ability to purchase securities issued by GNMA.

Emergency Home Finance Act of 1970

FNMA's role in the secondary market was expanded with the passage of the Emergency Home Finance Act of 1970. After many years of exclusion, the FNMA was permitted to purchase conventional mortgages in addition to FHA-insured and VA-guaranteed mortgages. However, FNMA did not begin actual purchase of conventional mortgage loans until February, 1972. FNMA also was permitted to deal in mortgage loans issued to finance the construction and modernization of hospitals.

The Emergency Home Finance Act of 1970 also created the Federal Home Loan Mortgage Corporation (FHLMC) for purposes of providing a secondary mortgage market for savings and loan association members of the Federal Home Loan Bank System. The FHLMC, logically nicknamed "Freddie Mac," was permitted to purchase conventional, FHA-insured, and VA-guaranteed mortgages. Since savings and loan associations deal heavily in conventional mortgages, this is the area where the FHLMC was expected to be very active.

Recent Institutional Trends and Developments

Three major institutions or organizations have evolved as the secondary mortgage market developed over time. First was the evolution of FNMA which, since 1968, is a privately-owned but government-authorized corporation. In 1968, GNMA was created as a government-owned and government-operated secondary market institution. Then, in 1970, the FHLMC was formed as a secondary market subsidiary of the Federal Home Loan Bank. With FNMA operating by itself through most of the 1950s and 1960s, the secondary mortgage market was slow to develop.

Secondary mortgage operations changed with involvement by all three secondary market institutions during the 1970s and early 1980s. Development of the secondary market was supported by the Financial Institutions Regulatory and Interest Rate Control Act of 1978 which permitted the FHLMC to purchase home improvement loans. In 1980, a secondary market for FNMA mobile home loans and property improvement loans was created under the Housing and Community Development Act of 1980. Passage of the Secondary Mortgage Market Enhancement Act in 1984 exempted secondary mortgage market issuers from state securities registration laws and the secondary mortgage market powers of the FNMA and FHLMC were broadened.

DEVELOPMENT OF MORTGAGE-BACKED SECURITIES

The recent development and growth of the secondary mortgage market has been aided by both greater standardization of mortgage loans and the successful introduction of mortgage-backed securities. A *mortgage-backed security* is a security or investment instrument representing shares in an underlying pool of FHA, VA, or conventional mortgage loans. In essence, the security issued against the pool of mortgages is "collateralized" by the underlying mortgage loans which, in turn, are said to be "securitized."

For example, an originator such as a mortgage banker or a large holder of mortgage loans could "securitize" a pool of mortgages by first placing them with a bank or other authorized trustee. The pool of mortgage loans then becomes the backing or collateral for securities issued by the loan originator or holder and sold to investors. Monthly payments of interest and principal continue to be made by each mortgage loan borrower to the loan servicer which typically is the loan originator. These payments then are forwarded to the trustee who represents the interests of the security investors.

What makes this process work? First, there is a differential between the interest rate paid by the homeowner and the rate received by the security investor. For example, the homeowner, or mortgage loan borrower, might pay 10 percent on his or her mortgage while the security investor might receive, say, 9.25 percent. This differential allows the loan servicer, the trustee, and the issuer of the securities to be compensated for their efforts. Second, the security investors are willing to accept this lower rate of return because their interests can be easily traded and the underlying pool of mortgages often is guaranteed by the Government National Mortgage Association or is privately insured.

A *pass-through security* is a mortgage-backed security whereby the payments received by the trustee are passed through to the security holders in proportion to their ownership in the mortgage pool. Interest and principal payments typically are received monthly. However, in the event that some of the mortgage loan borrowers represented in the underlying pool of mortgages choose to prepay or refinance their loans, cash flow payments to the security holders will fluctuate instead of being stable over time.

The *Collateralized Mortgage Obligation* (CMO) represents another variation of the mortgage-backed security which was designed to offer cash flows to investors more like those received by holders of government and corporate bonds. An investor in a CMO owns one of several classes of "bonds" that are backed by a pool of mortgages, or even mortgage-backed securities. Interest is paid on all existing bonds, while principal repayments are made class by class.

Collateralized mortgage obligations were first issued by the Federal Home Loan Mortgage Corporation during the early 1980s. This was quickly followed by CMOs being issued by mortgage bankers and various real estate institutional lenders. Although CMOs, like pass-through securities, may be retired early due to mortgage borrower decisions to repay or to refinance, investors can at least decide beforehand whether they want to hold short-, intermediate-, or long-term mortgage-backed bonds.

For example, several classes (A, B, etc.) of bonds are designated in each CMO issue. Each class typically has a different maturity with the first class having the shortest maturity (e.g., two or three years), and so forth. Cash flows received by the CMO trustee, while still affected by mortgage borrower prepayments and refinancings, are used first to pay interest on the bonds and then to repay principal. The classes of bonds are retired in order of maturity beginning with the shortest maturity which typically is termed class A. In essence, after all current interest obligations are met, additional cash flows are used to pay off the principal on the class A bonds. All class A bonds must be retired before any principal repayments are made on class B bonds, and so forth.

The rapid growth of mortgage-backed securities will likely continue into the future because they offer liquidity and flexibility to the originators or holders of mortgage loans, as well as to investors. Mortgage originators or holders receive the proceeds from the sale of mortgage-backed securities and thus funds are freed up to enable the making or holding of new mortgage loans (or other investments). Investors like the diversification afforded by an interest in a pool of mortgages and can even choose different maturities by holding CMOs.

FEDERAL NATIONAL MORTGAGE ASSOCIATION

Our attention now turns to the operating characteristics of Fannie Mae. The operations of GNMA and the FHLMC will be examined in the next chapter, along with other government real estate finance programs and activities. However, we should not lose sight of the fact that many of the FNMA, GNMA, and FHLMC secondary mortgage market activities are interrelated.

The *Federal National Mortgage Association,* as we previously noted, was created as a government-owned organization in 1938. It became semiprivately owned in 1954 and completely privately owned in 1968. Its common stock is traded on the New York Stock Exchange.

Structure and Organization

FNMA still remains government-sponsored and is tied to the federal government in a number of ways. Fannie Mae is controlled by 18 directors. Thirteen members of the board are elected by FNMA's stockholders; and five members are appointed by the President. The Secretary of Housing and Urban Development also has regulatory authority over FNMA in a number of areas. For example, the Secretary can set FNMA size of debt and debt-to-capital ratio limits. FNMA also may be required to allocate a portion of its loan purchases for mortgages issued in conjunction with certain national housing programs.

FNMA's basic function is to provide a secondary market for residential mortgage claims to wealth by purchasing, servicing, and selling loans. FNMA is permitted to deal in conventional (since 1970), FHA-insured, and VA-guaranteed mortgage loans. FNMA traditionally has worked with mortgage bankers, although it may deal with virtually any organization in performing its secondary mortgage market functions.

As of year-end 1975, 93 percent of FNMA's total assets were in the form of FHA/VA mortgage loans or claims to wealth. By the mid-1980s, FHA/VA mortgages had declined in importance to about one half of total assets. Substantial growth occurred in the FNMA's holding of conventional mortgages, which increased from less than 10 percent of total assets to a level approaching one half of total assets.

The FNMA assets are financed almost exclusively with debt funds. Short-term debt is used to finance about 3 percent of the assets. Long-term debt provides nearly 95 percent of the financing requirements, as might be expected since FNMA's mortgage holdings tend to be largely long-term commitments. About 2 percent of the assets are financed with stockholder equity funds. FNMA raises new equity capital by (1) selling common stock to the public, and (2) having institutions selling mortgages to FNMA subscribe to common stock on the basis of the value of the mortgages sold. There currently are over 60 million shares outstanding.

It is apparent that FNMA depends heavily on its ability to sell debt obligations in order to purchase mortgages. Short-term debt often is in the form of discount notes (i.e., notes sold at a price below par value). Most financing comes from the issuing of debentures (secured by FNMA's general credit) and mortgage-backed bonds. Debentures convertible into common stock also are occasionally issued.

FNMA, rather than engaging in buying *and* selling secondary mortgage functions, has been operating more as a lender adding to its permanent loan portfolios. Table 6–2 shows that loan sales were engaged in during the early and mid-1970s and more recently during the mid-1980s.

TABLE 6–2. FNMA Activity (Millions of Dollars)

Year	Loan Purchases	Loan Sales	Total Portfolio (Year-end)	Mortgage-Backed Securities (Year-end)
1960	980	42	2,903	. . .
1965	757	46	2,520	. . .
1970	5,078	. . .	15,502	. . .
1971	3,574	336	17,791	. . .
1972	3,699	211	19,791	. . .
1973	6,127	71	24,175	. . .
1974	6,953	4	29,578	. . .
1975	4,263	2	31,824	. . .
1976	3,606	86	32,904	. . .
1977	4,780	67	34,370	. . .
1978	12,303	5	43,311	. . .
1979	10,812	. . .	51,091	. . .
1980	8,099	. . .	57,327	. . .
1981	6,112	2	61,412	717
1982	15,116	2	71,814	14,450
1983	17,554	3,528	78,256	25,121
1984	16,721	978	87,940	36,215
1985	21,510	1,301	98,282	54,987
1986	30,826	N.A.	97,895	97,174

N.A. = not available.
Note: Data adjusted to exclude functions transferred to GNMA in 1968.

Source: Savings Institutions *Sourcebook,* 1987, 66.

However, from an overall viewpoint, the FNMA has been an active purchaser of loans (particularly conventional loans) in recent years in an effort to support thrift institutions by providing mortgage liquidity through secondary market activities.

Previous Auction Market Operations

Prior to 1968 FNMA's procedure for carrying out its secondary market activities was based on setting in advance prices it would pay for the purchase of qualified mortgages. However, this was not felt to be a particularly efficient method for conducting a secondary mortgage market. Thus, in 1968 a *Free Market System Auction* was established.

The auction system operated as follows. FNMA announced, usually biweekly, the amount of funds it was willing to spend to purchase residential mortgages. Potential mortgage sellers could make either a competitive offering or a noncompetitive offering. In a *competitive offering,* the prospective seller specified the yield to be paid to FNMA. Then, after examining all competitive bids or offerings, FNMA decided which bids to accept by working downward from the highest bid or offering.

Noncompetitive offerings or bids did not specify a yield. Rather, yields or noncompetitive bids were established as the weighted average yield calculated for the competitive bids accepted by FNMA.

Both types of bids or offerings were made by phone. FNMA announced an offering date with a notice. Four-month, 9-month, and 12-month forward commitments were set for purchasing mortgages. Bids or offers were received on the offering date. The next day FNMA announced the offers which were accepted, the range of yields on offers accepted, and the weighted average yield for the accepted offers. Separate FNMA auctions were held for FHA/VA mortgages and conventional mortgages. FNMA could limit the maximum amount a mortgage bidder could sell in a given auction.

FNMA notified successful bidders in writing the amount of acceptable mortgages that would be purchased. Successful bidders were required to purchase a specified amount of FNMA common stock when the bid was accepted and again when the mortgages were delivered to FNMA. FNMA entered into agreements to hold committed funds for the specified time period for a commitment fee of 2 percent of the commitment amount. A two-basis-point fee also was charged for processing each competitive bid that was received. Successful bidders could elect to sell their mortgages to FNMA during the commitment period. As an alternative, the mortgages could have been sold to someone else or kept, with the commitment fee being FNMA's compensation for standing by.

Sellers of home mortgages were permitted to continue to service mortgages sold to FNMA. A minimum $3/8$ percent fee was traditionally paid by FNMA to have this loan-servicing function performed by mortgage sellers.

FNMA suspended its secondary market auction system involving forward mortgage purchase commitments at the end of February, 1983. Instead, a fixed price purchase program was instituted that required mandatory one-month or two-month delivery of accepted mortgages.

Recent FNMA Secondary Market Actions

In 1981, Fannie Mae entered into its first commitment in a *participation program* with lenders whereby the lenders kept a "stake," or position, in mortgage loans sold to FNMA. Required paperwork was diminished substantially compared to requirements for whole or complete loan sales. FNMA commitments continue to expand in importance today.

A master participation agreement is first executed between FNMA and the lender, such as a savings and loan association. Then, a pool of loans (either FHA/VA or conventional fixed-rate mortgages) is assembled by the lender. A participation interest in the pool that is to be sold to FNMA is set by the lender, which may range from 50 percent to 95 percent of the total. Mortgages in the pool must conform to FNMA loan limits and down-payment requirements set on whole loan FNMA purchases. Fannie Mae required yields on participations are available daily, and participation sale commitments can be made with a phone call to an FNMA regional office. There is no maximum on the amount of each participation sale, but a $250,000 minimum is required.

In 1981 FNMA also announced a program involving the sale of *conventional mortgage-backed securities* designed to appeal to pension funds and other investors interested in the conventional mortgage market. The program was patterned after the successful GNMA pass-through securities backed by pools of FHA/VA mortgages and guaranteed by GNMA. The FNMA-issued securities are guaranteed by the FNMA as to full and timely payment of both principal and interest. Securities certificates are issued in minimum amounts of $25,000 and represent fractional interests in pools of conventional home mortgages.

A conventional mortgage pool of $1 million or more can be put together by one lender with an FNMA security being issued against this specific pool. In such a pool, the mortgages are on properties in a particular geographical area and may appeal to certain investors such as pension funds. As an alternative, individual loan pool packages of $1 million or more each can be grouped together to back a "jumbo" security. Investors in the jumbo security would have the security backed by a geographically diversified portfolio of mortgages. A service fee is charged by Fannie Mae for issuing securities backed by each mortgage pool package, and FNMA will charge a monthly fee to cover the guarantee provision.

By 1982 the FNMA also began buying participations in pools of *second mortgages* originated by lenders. This program has been extended to the purchase of whole second mortgage loans originated by mortgage companies and others.

Fannie Mae will purchase fully amortizing (monthly payments will be sufficient to retire the principal balance at maturity) second mortgages, as well as balloon (a portion of principal will remain at maturity) second mortgages. To qualify for FNMA purchase, the combined amount of the first and second mortgages cannot exceed 80 percent of an owner-occupied home's value (70 percent if the home is owned for investment purposes).

In 1982 the FNMA also entered into its first *swap* or *exchange* of mortgage-backed securities for variable-rate home loans held by a savings and loan association. Previous swaps involved fixed-rate mortgages. Such swaps offer lenders greater liquidity because the mortgage-backed securities can be borrowed against or can be sold more easily than can a number of individual mortgages.

During the early 1980s Fannie Mae also began what has turned out to be a very successful program of purchasing adjustable-rate mortgages (ARMs). Since then, the types of standards for buying mortgage loans have become increasingly more flexible. For example, in 1987 Fannie Mae agreed to buy convertible adjustable-rate mortgages which allow borrowers to convert from an ARM to a 30-year fixed-rate mortgage after the first year. The FNMA also instituted a program to buy 10-year and 20-year mortgages, an action which was designed to increase the availability of such loans. In early 1988, Fannie Mae also initiated a plan to purchase biweekly mortgages.

In 1987 the FNMA also was granted clearance to issue a new type of mortgage-backed security called a "Remic" which stands for Real Estate Mortgage Investment Conduit. Remics are tax-advantaged securities, created under the Tax Reform Act of 1986, that offer investors greater flexibility and thus are expected to provide an additional source for raising mortgage funds.

KEY TERMS

advance commitment

Collateralized Mortgage Obligation

facilitating function

Federal National Mortgage
     Association

mortgage-backed security

mortgage banker

mortgage broker

mortgage loan participations

mortgage market

mortgage warehousing

pass-through security

primary mortgage market

secondary mortgage market

standby commitment

take-out letter

QUESTIONS FOR REVIEW

1. Explain what is meant by the statement that "the overall mortgage market involves three types of transactions or activities."
2. Why is there a need for a secondary mortgage market?
3. Mortgage banking operations often involve a number of activities. Explain what is meant by: (1) an advance or forward commitment, (b) a take-out letter, (c) a standby commitment, and (d) mortgage warehousing.
4. A number of major federal government developments and actions have affected the secondary mortgage market. Indicate and briefly describe these major laws and actions.
5. What do the nicknames Fannie Mae, Ginnie Mae, and Freddie Mac stand for? What are their relationships with the secondary mortgage market?
6. The Federal National Mortgage Association was initially created in 1938. How does its structure and organization differ today from when it was created?
7. Explain how FNMA's auction market system operated, before it was suspended, in terms of the secondary mortgage market.
8. Identify and provide a brief explanation of recent FNMA secondary market activities and developments.

PROBLEMS

1. Mortgage banking plays an important role in the overall mortgage market. Obtain current information on mortgage loans originated and closed by mortgage bankers. Compare and contrast your findings with the information provided in the chapter.
2. New developments in the secondary mortgage market have been occurring quite frequently in recent years. Attempt to identify important new developments in general, and in particular as they relate to the FNMA.

7

GOVERNMENT REAL ESTATE ASSISTANCE PROGRAMS

LEARNING OBJECTIVES

After studying this chapter, you should be able to do the following:

Describe the structure and organization of the Federal Home Loan Mortgage Corporation.

Discuss some of the recent secondary mortgage market actions taken by the Federal Home Loan Mortgage Corporation.

Describe the structure and organization of the Government National Mortgage Association.

Discuss the Government National Mortgage Association's mortgage-backed security program and other recent developments relating to the secondary mortgage market.

Identify what is meant by the Farm Credit System and describe how the System is organized.

Describe the role of the Farmers Home Administration in terms of making home ownership and other real property loans.

Describe the role of the Department of Housing and Urban Development as it relates to the financing of real property.

Briefly discuss the activities of state real estate assistance agencies in conjunction with the housing and mortgage markets.

 T HE FEDERAL GOVERNMENT impacts on real estate finance in a number of different ways. We saw in Chapter 4 that monetary and fiscal policy affect the availability and cost of funds for financing real estate projects. This included the activities of the U.S. Treasury and the Federal Reserve System. Regulation and control by the Federal Reserve, the Federal Home Loan Bank Board, and state regulatory bodies of institutions supplying real estate funds represents an additional form of government involvement.

The government also has made substantial contributions by providing insurance of thrift institution deposits and through insuring mortgage loans. Deposit insurance is provided by the Federal Deposit Insurance Corporation and the Federal Savings and Loan Insurance Corporation. And, as we saw earlier, Federal Housing Administration insurance and Veterans' Administration guarantees have been important to the development of real estate financing.

Other government activities will be explored in this chapter, namely, the secondary mortgage market roles of GNMA and the FHLMC. Attention then will shift to the government's role in farm loans and public housing.

FEDERAL HOME LOAN MORTGAGE CORPORATION

The passage of the Emergency Home Finance Act of 1970 resulted in the creation of the *Federal Home Loan Mortgage Corporation.* FHLMC is a federally chartered, nonprofit institution operating in the secondary mortgage market under the control of the Federal Home Loan Bank System.

Structure and Organization

The FHLMC was initially funded in 1970 through a stock subscription of $100 million purchased by the 12 regional Federal Home Loan Banks. The Federal Home Loan Bank Board directs the mortgage activities of the FHLMC.

Because of the seriousness of the 1969–1970 recessionary period, high interest rates and "tight money" led to substantial amounts of disintermediation. Savings and loan associations were hit particularly hard. As a result, the FHLMC's primary objective as a secondary mortgage market institution was to assist savings and loan associations (and to a lesser extent other lending institutions) in acquiring funds for making additional mortgage loans. This was to be accomplished by having the FHLMC purchase mortgage claims to wealth already owned by the lending institutions. Like FNMA, the FHLMC is permitted to deal in conventional, FHA-insured, and VA-guaranteed loans.

Over 90 percent of the FHLMC's total assets are in mortgage loans. The FHLMC is heavily committed to "participation in" or "wholly owned" conventional mortgages. These assets, as was the case with FNMA, are financed almost totally with debt. This is accomplished by issuing bonds or through advances or borrowings from the Federal Home Loan Banks. Capital accounts for less than 3 percent of funds available to meet financing needs. The FHLMC also actively sells mortgages from its portfolio (in contrast with the FNMA emphasis on purchases) as is shown in Table 7–1. The FHLMC loan portfolio has grown gradually in size with a substantial switch from FHA/VA mortgage holdings to conventional mortgage holdings since the mid-1970s. While the FHLMC's total mortgage loan portfolio now exceeds $12 billion, this pales in comparison with the FNMA's total mortgage loan portfolio of $98 billion.

Operations

The FHLMC originally was designed to do for conventional mortgages what FNMA was doing in the secondary market for FHA and VA mortgages. However, Freddie Mac purchased a larger volume of FHA/VA mortgages during its early operating years. This policy was attributed to the fact that greater loan standardization existed for FHA and VA mortgages. It was 1973 before FHLMC began purchasing greater dollar amounts of conventional loans relative to FHA/VA loans. The FHLMC has been actively involved in developing standardized procedures and documents for making conventional loans. These efforts by FHLMC are consistent with the objective of assisting savings and loan associations which deal largely in origination of conventional mortgages.

Members of the Federal Home Loan Bank System are eligible to sell mortgages to the FHLMC. In addition to savings and loan associations and mutual savings banks, it is possible for commercial banks, credit unions, and other nonmembers to receive FHLMC approval as eligible sellers. Mortgage bankers, or mortgage companies, have also been accepted as eligible nonmembers since 1979. Funds generated by selling mortgage loans to FHLMC are to be used by the seller to make additional mortgage loans. The seller/servicer is responsible for servicing mortgages sold in part or in whole to the FHLMC with the FHLMC traditionally paying a minimum $3/8$ percent servicing fee. The FHLMC also charges nonmember sellers an added fee of .5 percent of the purchases.

Mortgages can be sold to the FHLMC through its *immediate delivery* purchase program or its less used *forward commitment* purchase program. The immediate delivery program is somewhat a misnomer, since sellers have up to 60 days to make delivery. The FHLMC requires delivery of the loans committed for. Failure to deliver may result in the seller being banned from further sales to the FHLMC for two years.

An example of an FHLMC immediate delivery purchase contract form is shown in Figure 7–1. The FHLMC used an auction system that was similar to the FNMA one during the 1977–1983 period (prior to mid-1977 the yields were administratively set) where lenders submitted competitive bids or offers. After ranking and analyzing the competitive offers, the FHLMC determined a minimum acceptable net yield which was published in *The Wall Street Journal*. Competitive offers could range from a minimum of $100,000

FHLMC Form 1

△ TheMortgage Corporation

Federal Home Loan Mortgage Corporation

IMMEDIATE PURCHASE CONTRACT
CONVENTIONAL HOME MORTGAGES

Sale: The Federal Home Loan Mortgage Corporation ("The Mortgage Corporation" or "FHLMC") hereby accepts the offer of the Seller named below to sell to FHLMC, Conventional Home Mortgages or undivided interests in Conventional Home Mortgages, in total principal amount to be purchased by FHLMC as stated herein, on the terms stated below, and in accordance with the Purchase Documents as defined in the Sellers' Guide Conventional Mortgages as in effect on the date of Seller's offer, all of which are fully incorporated herein by reference.

Servicing: The Seller named below hereby agrees to service all mortgages sold hereunder, in accordance with the Purchase Documents as in effect on the date of Seller's offer, all of which are fully incorporated herein by reference.

Offer Accepted by The Mortgage Corporation	Contract Commitment Amount (FHLMC's Interest): $...
Date of Seller's Offer:	Net Yield to FHLMC .... percent
Date of Acceptance:	**Federal Home Loan Mortgage Corporation**
Purchase Contract No.:	By .... (Seal) VICE PRESIDENT
Required Delivery Date:	.... (Seal) ASSISTANT SECRETARY

Nonmember fee, if applicable, will be deducted from amount due Seller on Funding Date. If you have any questions, please call applicable FHLMC Regional Office.

Receipt of Contract Hereby Acknowledged by Seller:

Seller's FHLMC Seller/ Servicer No.:	Date of Acknowledgement .... 19.........
	By ....(Seal) AUTHORIZED REPRESENTATIVE
	.... (TYPE NAME AND TITLE)
	This contract is signed pursuant to a telephone offer.

FHLMC—1   8/78

FIGURE 7–1.   Example of a FHLMC Mortgage Purchase Contract

to a maximum of $5 million. A weighted average of competitive bids was used to set the net yield on noncompetitive offers. Today, the FHLMC decides on a daily basis whether to accept bids from prospective sellers.

The immediate delivery purchase program for conventional mortgages may involve whole loan purchases or participation purchases. Whole loan purchases include eligible single-family and multifamily residential mortgages. Participation purchases may be in the form of a Class A offering (whereby the FHLMC will buy a 50 to 85 percent interest in qualifying multifamily mortgages) or a Class B offering (whereby a 50 to 95 percent interest is purchased in 1- to 4-family home mortgages). There is also an immediate delivery purchase program for FHA/VA mortgages.

An example of a FHLMC forward commitment purchase contract form is shown in Figure 7–2. Forward commitments are made for six-month and eight-month periods involving conventional home mortgages. Delivery of the mortgages is at the option of the seller, as is the case with FNMA forward commitments. There is a nonrefundable commitment fee of .75 percent on six-month forward commitments and a 1.0 percent fee of the contract amount on eight-month forward commitments. However, the use of forward commitments declined with the elimination of the auction system in 1983.

Freddie Mac attempts to finance its secondary mortgage market activities in a number of ways. As we have seen, the FHLMC is active in selling mortgages from its mortgage portfolio and seems to follow a policy of selling existing mortgages to finance new purchases. Freddie Mac also depends heavily on borrowing from the Federal Home Loan Banks and generating debt funds by issuing mortgage-backed securities guaranteed by GNMA.

Three mortgage securities also were developed by the FHLMC to help meet its secondary market needs. The *Mortgage Participation Certificate* (PC) gives an ownership interest in a pool of mortgages. Monthly interest and principal payments are passed through to the security holder (investor) and the payments are guaranteed by the FHLMC. PCs have frequently been sold to thrift institutions. The second Freddie Mac designed mortgage certificate is referred to as the *Guaranteed Mortgage Certificate* (GMC) and is "bond-like" in that it provides for semiannual payment of interest from the underlying mortgage loans. Mortgage principal payments are passed through annually to investors. Sales of GMCs have been directed toward pension funds and other nontraditional mortgage investors. Freddie Mac also raises funds by issuing Collateralized Mortgage Obligations (CMOs). The importance of participation certificates is shown in Table 7–1 on page 118.

Recent FHLMC Secondary Market Actions

The FHLMC has been instrumental in the development of the Automated Mortgage Market Information Network (AMMINET). This nonprofit corporation provides a centralized secondary mortgage market for its subscribers in the form of a national electronic communications network over which specific mortgage buy and sell offers can be listed. Transactions then can be consummated by phone.

In mid-1982, Freddie Mac joined with Merrill Lynch and Salomon Brothers to offer a $500 million mortgage plan involving fast paydown loans

Execute in Duplicate and Submit Either Copy to Applicable FHLMC Regional Office

FHLMC Form 459

The Mortgage Corporation
Federal Home Loan Mortgage Corporation

FORWARD COMMITMENT PURCHASE CONTRACT
CONVENTIONAL HOME MORTGAGES

Sale: The Federal Home Loan Mortgage Corporation ("The Mortgage Corporation" or "FHLMC") hereby accepts the offer of the Seller named below to sell to FHLMC, Conventional Home Mortgages and/or undivided interest in Conventional Home Mortgages, in total principal amount to be purchased by FHLMC as stated herein. on the terms stated below, in accordance with the Purchase Documents as defined in the Sellers' Guide Conventional Mortgages as in effect on the date of Seller's offer, all of which are fully incorporated herein by reference.

Servicing: The Seller named below hereby agrees to service all mortgages sold hereunder, in accordance with the Purchase Documents as in effect on the date of Seller's offer, all of which are fully incorporated herein by reference.

Offer Accepted by
The Mortgage Corporation

Contract Commitment Amount
(FHLMC's Interest): $..

Date of Seller's Offer: ....

Net Yield to FHLMC .... percent

Date of Acceptance: ....

Nonrefundable Commitment Fee: $..........................
(The Commitment Fee must be submitted with an
executed copy of this Purchase Contract)

Purchase Contract No.: ....

Contract Expiration Date: ....

Federal Home Loan Mortgage Corporation

Delivery Option must be exercised
not later than: ....

By .... (Seal)
                        VICE PRESIDENT

.... (Seal)
                        ASSISTANT SECRETARY

Nonmember fee, if applicable, will be deducted from amount due Seller on Funding Date.
If you have any questions, please call applicable FHLMC Regional Office.

Receipt of Contract Hereby Acknowledged by Seller:

Seller's FHLMC Seller/
Servicer No.: ....

Date of
Acknowledgement .... 19.........

By ....(Seal)
                AUTHORIZED REPRESENTATIVE

....
                (TYPE NAME AND TITLE)

This contract is signed pursuant
to a telephone offer.

FHLMC—459 8/78

FIGURE 7–2.   Example of a FHLMC Forward Commitment Purchase Contract

in an effort to support the home mortgage market. The mortgage loans were referred to as *growing-equity mortgages* (GEMs) because they provided for accelerated principal repayments. For example, instead of a traditional 25-year, fixed-rate mortgage requiring monthly payments for 25 years, the GEM

TABLE 7–1.   Federal Home Loan Mortgage Corporation Activity (Millions of Dollars)

Year	Mortgage Transactions		Loan Portfolio (Year-end)			Participation Certificates (Year-end)
	Purchases	Sales	Total	FHA-VA	Conventional	
1970	325	. . .	325	325	. . .	. . .
1971	778	113	968	821	147	64
1972	1,297	407	1,788	1,502	286	444
1973	1,334	409	2,604	1,800	804	791
1974	2,190	53	4,586	1,961	2,625	780
1975	1,713	1,521	4,987	1,881	3,106	1,143
1976	1,127	1,797	4,269	1,675	2,594	1,900
1977	4,160	4,647	3,267	1,450	1,817	5,408
1978	6,526	6,426	3,091	1,299	1,792	10,152
1979	5,621	4,544	4,052	1,159	2,893	12,922
1980	3,723	2,526	5,056	1,090	3,966	14,785
1981	3,744	3,532	5,237	1,047	4,190	17,925
1982	23,671	24,170	4,733	1,009	3,724	41,182
1983	22,952	19,638	7,633	942	6,691	56,412
1984	21,885	18,417	10,399	881	9,518	70,920
1985	44,012	38,658	14,022	825	13,197	100,507
1986	103,474	98,302	12,159	N.A.	N.A.	N.A.

N.A. = not available.

Source: Savings Institutions *Sourcebook,* 1987, 64.

mortgage could be repaid in less than 15 years and the total interest paid would be about one half of the amount paid under the traditional mortgage loan. Groups of growing equity mortgage loans were packaged for sale as Freddie Mac *GEM Participation Certificates* (PCs). Prospective purchasers of these FHLMC-guaranteed PCs were pension funds and other institutional investors.

Freddie Mac, like Fannie Mae, began a successful program of purchasing adjustable-rate mortgages (ARMs) during the early 1980s. By the beginning of 1988, Freddie Mac also began buying convertible ARMs from mortgage lenders. The convertible loans can be exchanged for participation certificates or they can be sold to Freddie Mac through a cash-purchase program.

At the end of 1987, the FHLMC also began issuing securities backed by a new type of fixed-rate mortgage called a ROL or "reduction-option loan." ROLs are conventional fixed-rate, 30-year mortgages that allow borrowers to take advantage of any fall in interest rates between the first and fifth years of the mortgage.

GOVERNMENT NATIONAL MORTGAGE ASSOCIATION

The *Government National Mortgage Association* was created as a result of the passage of the Housing and Urban Development Act in 1968. GNMA is a wholly-owned government corporation and operates under the direction of the Department of Housing and Urban Development.

Structure and Organization

GNMA, with its establishment in 1968, inherited certain responsibilities that were previously under the domain of the old FNMA (that is, prior to the time FNMA became completely privately owned in 1968). Ginnie Mae was given responsibility for managing remaining FNMA mortgages that had been acquired prior to November, 1954. These mortgages were to be liquidated under the "management and liquidation function" responsibilities. Table 7–2 shows that after dropping to $80 million in 1984, this category of FNMA mortgage loans increased substantially in 1985 and 1986.

The second responsibility is known as the "special assistance function." GNMA has been involved in assisting the financing of urban renewal and experimental housing projects by providing low-income families with below-market loan rates. It also assists in tempering the impact of changes in interest rates on existing mortgage values. Table 7–2 shows that GNMA added over $3 billion in mortgages under its special assistance programs during 1974 and 1975. This increase was largely associated with the passage of the Emergency Home Purchase Act of 1974, which permitted GNMA to purchase home mortgages (including conventional ones) at below-market interest rates.

TABLE 7–2. GNMA Loan Portfolio, by Function (Millions of Dollars)

Year-end	Special Assistance	Management and Liquidation	Total Portfolio
1965	1,340	953	2,293
1970	3,401	1,821	5,222
1971	3,648	1,673	5,321
1972	3,824	1,287	5,111
1973	3,576	469	4,045
1974	4,440	409	4,849
1975	6,884	358	7,242
1976	4,102	305	4,407
1977	2,989	260	3,249
1978	2,521	220	2,741
1979	2,404	199	2,603
1980	2,806	162	2,968
1981	3,698	141	3,839
1982	3,977	125	4,102
1983	3,374	91	3,465
1984	3,060	80	3,140
1985	. . .	1,634	1,634
1986	. . .	884	884

Source: Savings Institutions *Sourcebook*, 1987, 66.

However, since then the GNMA has focused less on its special assistance function and more, as we will shortly see, on its third area of responsibility—the mortgage-backed security program. Notice that the special assistance loan portfolio was eliminated by the end of 1984 because Congress stopped funding the program.

GNMA and FNMA Tandem Programs

One part of the special assistance function has previously involved FNMA's role in reducing the impact of interest rate risk on mortgage lenders. Interest rate risk occurs because interest rates fluctuate over time. Since traditional mortgages carry fixed coupon or specified interest rates, mortgage values must change to reflect yields comparable to then prevailing market interest rates. In essence, there is an inverse relationship between interest rate changes and mortgage prices or values. For example, a 10 percent $80,000 mortgage will fall in value (i.e., be discounted) if mortgage rates rise to 12 percent. The size of discount will be sufficient to make the 10 percent mortgage provide a 12 percent yield.

Rising market interest rates cause existing mortgages to sell at discounts. GNMA absorbs some of this discount under its *Tandem Programs,* so named because Fannie Mae and Ginnie Mae work jointly on mortgage loan purchases. These programs are particularly valuable during periods of high interest rates when existing mortgages sell at deep discounts. First, a commitment to purchase a mortgage at a specified price is made by GNMA to the potential mortgage seller. Then, after GNMA acquires the mortgage, it is sold to FNMA at the existing or prevailing market value. Discounts between the price paid to the mortgage seller and the price received from FNMA are absorbed by GNMA. In the way of an illustration, assume that Ginnie Mae agrees or commits to pay a seller $1 million for a mortgage on a housing project. In the meantime, after the purchase commitment has been made, interest rates rise and the mortgage drops in value to, say, $950,000. The mortgage then is sold to FNMA for $950,000 and GNMA absorbs the $50,000 difference or discount.

In the case of high-risk mortgages such as those originated under Section 236, GNMA and FNMA share in any mortgage value discounts that may develop. By working together, GNMA has more funds available for financing special assistance projects.

A variation of the tandem program was developed in 1974 for handling conventional mortgages. Both FNMA and FHLMC can participate. A commitment is made, as an agent for Ginnie Mae, to buy from a private lender conventional mortgages that carry below-market interest rates. The commitment is made only if the lender agrees to pass the below-market rate on to the borrower. The resulting discounted mortgages are delivered to FNMA or FHLMC after the loans are closed. The discount is absorbed by GNMA. For example, assume that the going interest rate is 12 percent on conventional mortgage loans. A mortgage with a $1 million par value would immediately sell at a discount, say $950,000, if the mortgage were issued with a 10 percent below-market interest rate. FNMA or FHLMC would pay the $950,000 upon delivery of the mortgage and GNMA would pay the discount differential of $50,000 to the lender originating the mortgage loan.

However in recent years GNMA has made little use of the tandem program, choosing instead to focus on guaranteeing mortgage-backed security issues.

Mortgage-Backed Security Program

GNMA also issues guarantees of FHA, VA, and Farmers Home Administration mortgages. Its so-called *mortgage-backed security program,* supported by the credit and borrowing power of the U.S. government, guarantees timely payment of interest and principal to the mortgage holders. A sample of the GNMA guaranteed mortgage-backed certificate is shown in Figure 7–3.

The GNMA guarantee permits mortgage originators and dealers to pledge a pool of their existing mortgage loans as collateral underlying a securities issue. Repayment of the mortgages in the pool provides funds to pay off the securities issue. Securities pools are used in lieu of direct sale of the underlying mortgages. In order to pool mortgages together, certain homogeneous requirements must be met in terms of types of properties, interest rates, and maturities. For example, single-family mortgages cannot be packaged with multifamily mortgages. Also, acceptable mortgages cannot be over one year old at the time GNMA enters into its commitment.

An eligible GNMA mortgage-backed security issuer must be an FHA-approved mortgagee, be an acceptable GNMA seller-servicer, and have a minimum net worth. Mortgage bankers or mortgage companies are typical issuers of GNMA-backed securities because, as we have seen, they originate most FHA/VA mortgage loans. The lender or mortgagee must pay a $500 application fee when seeking a GNMA commitment to guarantee its mortgage pool worth at least $1 million. If GNMA agrees to guarantee the mortgage pool, the lender-issuer must continue to service the mortgages for a fee of 44 basis points and pass through monthly principal and interest payments to the certificate holders (FNMA uses a central paying agent for its conventional mortgage-backed securities). GNMA receives six basis points as its guarantee fee, resulting in combined fees of 50 basis points or .5 percent.

There are two basic types of mortgaged-backed securities. The *bond-type security* is long-term, pays interest semiannually, and provides for payments of principal at specified redemption dates. The *pass-through security* provides for monthly interest and principal payments on the underlying mortgages. Table 7–3 shows the importance of GNMA's mortgage-backed security program in recent years. The bond-type security, not sold since 1971, can be issued only by the federal secondary mortgage market institutions. Pass-through securities are much more prevalent. However, it also is important to recognize that the GNMA is selective in that many more applications are

FIGURE 7–3. GNMA Guaranteed Mortgage-Backed Certificate

ASSIGNMENT

I AM THE OWNER, OR THE DULY AUTHORIZED REPRESENTATIVE OF THE OWNER, OF THE WITHIN MORTGAGE BACKED CERTIFICATE AND FOR VALUE RECEIVED HEREBY ASSIGN THE SAME TO

_____

(ASSIGNEE)

AND AUTHORIZE THE TRANSFER THEREOF ON THE BOOKS OF THE ISSUER.

_____

(SIGNATURE OF ASSIGNOR)

PERSONALLY APPEARED BEFORE ME THE ABOVE NAMED PERSON, WHOSE IDENTITY IS WELL KNOWN OR PROVED TO ME, AND SIGNED THE ABOVE ASSIGNMENT, ACKNOWLEDGING IT TO BE HIS FREE ACT AND DEED. WITNESS MY HAND, OFFICIAL DESIGNATION, AND SEAL.

_____   _____

(SIGNATURE OF WITNESSING OFFICER)   (OFFICIAL DESIGNATION)

SEAL   DATED AT_____   _____, 19____.

ASSIGNMENT

I AM THE OWNER, OR THE DULY AUTHORIZED REPRESENTATIVE OF THE OWNER, OF THE WITHIN MORTGAGE BACKED CERTIFICATE AND FOR VALUE RECEIVED HEREBY ASSIGN THE SAME TO

_____

(ASSIGNEE)

AND AUTHORIZE THE TRANSFER THEREOF ON THE BOOKS OF THE ISSUER.

_____

(SIGNATURE OF ASSIGNOR)

PERSONALLY APPEARED BEFORE ME THE ABOVE NAMED PERSON, WHOSE IDENTITY IS WELL KNOWN OR PROVED TO ME, AND SIGNED THE ABOVE ASSIGNMENT, ACKNOWLEDGING IT TO BE HIS FREE ACT AND DEED. WITNESS MY HAND, OFFICIAL DESIGNATION, AND SEAL.

_____   _____

(SIGNATURE OF WITNESSING OFFICER)   (OFFICIAL DESIGNATION)

SEAL   DATED AT_____   _____, 19____.

SPECIMEN

INSTRUCTIONS

TO ASSIGN THIS MORTGAGE BACKED CERTIFICATE, THE OWNER, OR HIS DULY AUTHORIZED REPRESENTATIVE, SHALL APPEAR BEFORE AN OFFICER AUTHORIZED TO WITNESS ASSIGNMENTS, ESTABLISH HIS IDENTITY TO THE SATISFACTION OF SUCH OFFICER, AND IN HIS PRESENCE EXECUTE THE ASSIGNMENT, USING ONE OF THE ABOVE FORMS. THE WITNESSING OFFICER MUST THEN AFFIX HIS SIGNATURE, OFFICIAL DESIGNATION, AND SEAL, IF ANY, AND ADD THE PLACE AND DATE OF EXECUTION. OFFICERS AUTHORIZED TO WITNESS ASSIGNMENTS INCLUDE EXECUTIVE OFFICERS OF BANKS AND TRUST COMPANIES IN-CORPORATED IN THE UNITED STATES OR ITS ORGANIZED TERRITORIES, AND THEIR BRANCHES, DOMESTIC AND FOREIGN. IF ADDITIONAL ASSIGNMENTS ARE REQUIRED, A FORM SIMILAR TO THE ABOVE MAY BE WRITTEN OR TYPED HEREON. FULL INFORMATION REGARDING ASSIGNMENTS MAY BE OBTAINED FROM GOVERNMENT NATIONAL MORTGAGE ASSOCIATION.

--- **IMPORTANT** ---

THE PRESENT PRINCIPAL BALANCE OF THIS MORTGAGE BACKED CERTIFICATE IS NOT NECES-SARILY THE ORIGINAL PRINCIPAL AMOUNT SHOWN ON ITS FACE. THE PRESENT PRINCIPAL BALANCE OF THE CERTIFICATE MAY BE ASCERTAINED FROM THE ISSUER NAMED THEREON OR A DEALER IN SUCH SECURITIES.

FIGURE 7–3. GNMA Guaranteed Mortgage-Backed Certificate (concluded)

TABLE 7–3.   GNMA Mortgage-Backed Security Program (Millions of Dollars)

| Year | Pass-Through Securities | | Bonds Sold |
	Applications	Issues	
1970	1,126	452	1,315
1971	4,374	2,702	300
1972	3,854	2,662	. . .
1973	5,529	3,249	. . .
1974	6,203	4,784	. . .
1975	10,449	7,366	. . .
1976	25,394	13,765	. . .
1977	31,076	16,230	. . .
1978	35,014	15,359	. . .
1979	53,820	24,592	. . .
1980	58,701	20,648	. . .
1981	36,915	14,253	. . .
1982	38,865	16,012	. . .
1983	70,280	50,496	. . .
1984	36,101	27,857	. . .
1985	64,360	45,868	. . .
1986	152,911	98,169	. . .

Source: Savings Institutions *Sourcebook,* 1987, 66.

received than are guaranteed.

The most successful Ginnie Mae pass-through security is referred to as the single-family *fully modified pass-through.* Monthly fixed payments of principal and interest are paid to certificate holders whether or not the payments have been collected from the mortgagors. Foreclosure proceeds and prepayments also are passed on to the certificate holders when received. If the issuer fails to meet the payment obligations, GNMA takes over the mortgage pool and makes the payments. Pension funds, bank trusts, and even individuals are active purchasers of these GNMA-guaranteed securities, which are offered in a minimum denomination of $25,000.

Two other single-family pass-through securities have been inactive in recent years. These are the *straight pass-through,* which provided for the monthly payment of interest and principal to certificate holders *only when and if collected* from the mortgagors, and the *partially modified pass-through,* which provided for a set monthly interest payment (not principal) whether or not collected.

Ginnie Mae also guarantees other types of mortgage-backed securities including project loans for nursing homes, hospitals, and multifamily buildings. Packages or pools of mobile home mortgage loans that are FHA-insured or VA-guaranteed have also been accepted and guaranteed by GNMA for purposes of issuing mortgage-backed securities.

A futures market in GNMA pass-through securities was initiated in October, 1975, with trading taking place on the Chicago Board of Trade Exchange.

RECENT INTEREST RATES IN THE SECONDARY MORTGAGE MARKETS

Yields in the secondary mortgage markets were quite volatile during the first half of the 1980s. Indications of mortgage rates in the secondary markets are compiled by the Department of Housing and Urban Development (HUD) on FHA mortgages and in terms of Government National Mortgage Association (GNMA) securities. The following data were gathered from selected issues of the *Federal Reserve Bulletin*.

YEAR	FHA MORTGAGES	GNMA SECURITIES
1980	13.44%	12.55%
1981	16.31	15.29
1982	15.31	14.68
1983	13.11	12.25
1984	13.81	13.13
1985	12.24	11.61
1986	9.91	9.30
1987 (Aug.)	10.55	9.77

The HUD series indicates average gross yields on 30-year FHA-insured first mortgages available for immediate delivery in the private secondary mortgage market. Rates peaked at above the 15 percent level in 1982 before declining to below 10 percent in 1986.

The rates on GNMA securities reflect average net yields to investors on GNMA guaranteed, mortgage-backed, fully modified pass-through securities. Rates are based on the assumption of prepayment in 12 years on pools of 30-year FHA/VA mortgages. The yields on GNMA securities peaked in 1982 at above the 15 percent rate before declining sharply to single digit levels during 1986.

FARM CREDIT SYSTEM

The passage of the Federal Farm Loan Act of 1916 led to the establishment of the cooperative *Farm Credit System*. Rural homeowners, farmers, ranchers, and owners of businesses with farm-related activities have always required unique real estate financing arrangements because of crop uncertainties associated with climate conditions and supply and demand factors. The cooperative Farm Credit System was designed to assist in meeting these unique financing requirements.

The Farm Credit System is comprised of 12 autonomous Farm Credit Districts. Each district supplies one member to the Federal Farm Credit Board with a thirteenth member being appointed by the Secretary of Agriculture. The Board, in turn, appoints an administrative head of its supervisory agency located in Washington, D.C., and referred to as the Farm Credit Administration. The Farm Credit System is known as a cooperative system since it is owned by the farmers, ranchers, and business cooperatives that have business transactions with it.

Federal Land Banks and Associations

Twelve Federal Land Banks, one in each of the Farm Credit Districts, were established in 1917. Congress sought to provide low-cost, long-term mortgage loans tailored to meet the needs of rural homeowners, farmers, ranchers, and certain farm-related businesses. In addition to rural home mortgage loans, mortgage loans are available for agricultural land and farms, farm machinery and equipment, livestock, and so forth.

Federal Land Bank loans are issued on the average for 20 years and generally provide for regular repayment of principal and interest. In certain instances the loans may be specially tailored because of unique problems. Many of the loans are written with *variable interest rate* provisions. That is, loan interest rates can be adjusted to reflect the then prevailing mortgage market interest rates.

The Federal Land Banks are owned by over 500 Federal Land Bank Associations operating within the 12 districts. The Federal Land Banks depend heavily on debt capital to finance the mortgage loans they make. Capital stock held by the Associations account for about 6 percent of the total capital structure of the Federal Land Banks. Federal Land Banks meet most of their loan demands by issuing Consolidated Federal Land Bank Bonds (secured by all 12 Banks) and discount notes for purchase by the general public. In addition, Farm Credit Investment Bonds are sold to Bank borrowers. Associations are owned, in turn, by their borrower-members.

In order to borrow funds from a Federal Land Bank, one must be a member of a Federal Land Bank Association in that district. The procedure for obtaining a mortgage loan is as follows. First, the member must submit a loan application to the Association for approval. An approved loan, if endorsed by the district bank, becomes guaranteed by the Association. Each borrower must purchase stock from the Association equal to 5 percent of the loan. This provides some protection for the Association in the event there is a default on the loan. The District Bank also is protected in the event of a default because it holds reserves of the Association's stock amounting to 5 percent of the Association's approved loans. Federal Land Bank and Association loans currently exceed $50 billion.

Other Farm Credit System Organizations

The Agricultural Credit Act of 1923 established 12 Federal Intermediate Credit Banks with one being located in each of the Farm Credit Districts. Since the Federal Land Banks were designed to provide long-term farm-related mortgage funds, a need for short-term and intermediate-term funds remained. The Federal Intermediate Credit Banks were designed to provide these shorter-term funds needed to finance agricultural-related production and distribution efforts.

The organizational structure of the Federal Intermediate Credit Banks is similar to that for Federal Land Banks. Capital stock issued by the Credit Banks is owned by more than 400 Production Credit Associations. Borrower-members, in turn, own the Associations. The organization of local cooperative Production Credit Associations by farmers and ranchers was authorized with the passage of the Farm Credit Act of 1933. Production Credit Associations make loans to farmer and rancher members to finance their operations. These loans may be for as long as seven years and are generally secured by collateral in the form of equipment, crops, and livestock. Borrowers become members of the Credit Association since they must purchase stock in the Association equal to 5 percent of the amount of their loans.

Production Credit Associations finance most of their loans through equity capital generated from the purchase of stock by members and through the accumulation of savings over time. On the other hand, Federal Intermediate Credit Banks rely heavily on debt funds to finance their lending operations. Bonds and notes are sold to the general public as well as to members of the Production Credit Associations. The Federal Intermediate Credit Banks possess certain secondary market characteristics since they often provide funds to financial institutions by purchasing their farm-related loans on a discount basis. Production Credit Association loans currently exceed $22 billion.

The Farm Credit System also is aided by 13 Banks for Cooperatives. Each Farm Credit District has one of these "banks" designed to make seasonal and short-term loans to eligible cooperatives. The 13th bank is located in Denver, Colorado, and operates as a central bank for cooperatives and sometimes participates when large loans are requested. Assistance is made available to a variety of farm-related business cooperatives.

FARMERS HOME ADMINISTRATION LOANS

The *Farmers Home Administration* is a rural credit agency of the U.S. Department of Agriculture that was established in 1946. The extent of the lending activities of the FmHA is greater than its name implies. In addition to farm ownership loans available to qualified persons who receive a substantial share of their income from farming, other loans are available.

Home Ownership Loans

The FmHA provides loans for homes in rural areas. By definition, *rural areas* include open country and places with populations of 10,000 or less that are rural in character and not closely associated with urban areas. Loans may also be in towns with populations between 10,000 and 20,000 that are outside standard metropolitan statistical areas *if* the Secretary of Agriculture and the Secretary of Housing and Urban Development find there is a serious lack of mortgage credit.

While applications from eligible veterans are given preference, both veterans and nonveterans must be able to meet the same basic requirements. The home ownership loans are designed for low- and moderate-income families who:

1. Are unable to obtain a loan from commercial lenders on terms and conditions they can reasonably be expected to meet.
2. Have sufficient income to make house payments, insurance premiums, taxes, maintenance, and other debts and necessary living expenses. Persons with inadequate repayment ability may obtain co-signers.
3. Possess the character, ability, and experience to meet loan obligations.
4. Are without decent, safe, and sanitary housing.

FmHA Loan Terms

FmHA loans may be made for up to 100 percent of the FmHA appraised value of the site and the new home if construction-site inspections were made by FmHA, VA, or HUD. Homes over one year old are also eligible for 100 percent loans. The maximum repayment period for both new and older homes is 33 years.

Although the payment period can be made for 33 years, the FmHA mortgage (or deed of trust) provides for borrower refinancing. When the financial position of the family is such that the loan can be refinanced through a commercial lender, the loan contract provides that this shall be done.

FmHA Rural Rental Housing

Loans are obtainable from the FmHA to construct rural rental housing. This housing is limited to persons with low or moderate incomes and for persons 62 or older. In addition to actual construction costs, funds can be used to:

1. Buy and improve the land on which the buildings are to be constructed.
2. Provide streets and water and waste disposal.
3. Supply appropriate recreation and service facilities.
4. Install laundry facilities and equipment.
5. Landscape the property.

The maximum repayment period for the rental housing program is 50 years. However, when the financial position of the borrower reaches the point where the loan can be repaid or refinanced through a commercial lender, the borrower must do so.

The borrower may be either a nonprofit organization or an organization for profit. In both cases, the maximum loan is $750,000 per project. More than one project may be built if the need for housing is clearly shown. All applicants are required to provide initial operating capital equal to at least 2 percent of the cost of the project.

Loans to nonprofit organizations can be up to 100 percent of the appraisal value or the development costs, whichever is less. All other applicants are limited to not more than 95 percent of appraised value or development cost, whichever is less.

Construction or interim financing must be obtained through local lenders when available. When such funds are unavailable, the FmHA will provide interim financing.

Rural Housing Repair Loans

If an applicant is located in a rural area, the FmHA will make loans for repairs provided the applicant:

1. Has an urgent need for repairs.
2. Has sufficient money—including welfare payments—to repay the loan.
3. Has so little income that the applicant is unable to qualify for an FmHA loan to build or buy a new home.

HOUSING AND URBAN DEVELOPMENT (HUD)

As we saw in the last chapter, the Federal Housing Administration was created under the National Housing Act of 1934. In 1947 the FHA was moved under the Housing and Home Finance Agency. The Department of *Housing and Urban Development* (HUD) was created in 1965 to extend the programs and activities of the Housing and Home Finance Agency. At the same time, the FHA was made part of HUD.

HUD's Role in Housing and Mortgage Markets

Prior to the late 1960s, federal agency involvement in the housing and mortgage markets was of two basic types. One area involved the insuring of mortgage loans by the Federal Housing Administration along with the Veterans Administration's loan guaranteeing efforts. The second area focused on public housing programs. For example, the Housing Acts of 1954 and 1961 provided aid and assistance for urban renewal efforts.

The passage of the Housing and Urban Development Act of 1968 increased federal involvement in the housing and mortgage financing markets. First, as we saw in the last chapter, the Act of 1968 authorized the creation of the Government National Mortgage Association and placed GNMA under the direction of HUD. Thus, the Department of Housing and Urban Development now has administrative responsibilities over both the FHA and GNMA.

Second, the 1968 Act created two new subsidy programs designed to assist qualified families in rental housing and home ownership efforts. Section 235 was designed so that the government would pay a portion of the monthly interest on a home buyer's mortgage. Under Section 236, the government would pay a rent subsidy to the owner of an apartment. The intention is to keep monthly rental payments down to low levels. These subsidy programs were designed, of course, to assist low- and moderate-income families in obtaining adequate housing.

A substantial number of units were started under the interest subsidy program (Section 235) and the rent subsidy program (Section 236) during 1970, 1971, and 1972. However, in 1972 a number of program abuses were identified. Included were questionable construction activities and the falsifying of credit reports. These and other subsidy programs were suspended in January, 1973. Management was improved and certain program modifications were instituted before the programs were reinstated in 1975.

A new low-income housing subsidy program was provided in the Housing and Community Development Act of 1974 which amended Section 8 of the 1937 Housing Act. This new Section 8 program was intended to replace the Section 236 rent subsidy program. Assistance payments contracts are made on behalf of eligible low- or moderate-income families that live in qualifying housing. Owners, whether they be private or public housing agencies, can enter into assistance payments contracts with HUD before they construct new or substantially rehabilitate existing rental housing units. A maximum monthly rent is established based on comparable rents on other rental units in the area. The amount of Section 8 assistance, then, is determined as the difference between the maximum rent and the HUD-determined required rental contribution (based on a percentage of family income) to be paid by the occupant family.

Other HUD Activities

Besides the interest and rental subsidy programs cited above, the Department of Housing and Urban Development is involved in a number of other urban renewal, rehabilitation, and public housing projects and programs. For example, HUD provides funds for slum clearance and neighborhood renewal efforts. In addition, loans and grants are made available to owners and tenants interested in rehabilitating their properties located in urban areas.

Public housing programs prior to the mid-1960s often focused on the construction of new public housing units and projects. But beginning in 1965 HUD was authorized to provide financial assistance to local housing authorities to aid them in developing *turnkey* programs. In essence, the turnkey program is designed to make use of private industry efforts in the planning, construction financing, and construction phases of public housing project developments. One form of the turnkey program involves the acquisition of new, privately built housing or existing housing. The local housing authority also usually assumes operating responsibility for the turnkey project established for the benefit of low-income tenants.

Passage of the Demonstration Cities and Metropolitan Development Act of 1966 established the "demonstration cities" or "model cities" program. Under this program, loans and grants are made available for prototype projects to be planned and developed in certain cities. An example might be the renovation and redevelopment of a blighted downtown area by employing unique construction and mass transportation systems.

In 1968, the New Communities Act authorized HUD to support the development of new preplanned communities. Such communities are to reflect balanced housing, industrial, commercial, and recreational facilities.

Governmental support of community development projects changed markedly with the passage of the Housing and Community Development Act of 1974. Instead of having to conform to then existing federal programs, communities were allowed to develop their own plans to remove blighted real property or to prevent the development of slums. States, cities, and other local governmental units are eligible to make application to HUD for community development block grants and for HUD's guarantee of associated loans.

STATE REAL ESTATE ASSISTANCE AGENCIES

State governments have become increasingly involved in the housing and mortgage markets in recent years. State housing agencies had been formed in most states. These agencies attempt to improve the quality of housing and can assist local communities in attracting business and industry. A number of states provide their own real estate mortgage insurance programs to assist in special community real estate projects. Other state agencies assist in the development of industrial parks so that communities can attract new industry.

State housing finance agencies have attempted to provide mortgage funds at below-market interest rates in many states in an effort to help potential home buyers. This financing assistance, when not federally restricted, has been provided largely through the issuance of tax-exempt, single-family mortgage revenue bonds.

KEY TERMS

Farm Credit System
Farmers Home Administration
Federal Home Loan Mortgage
    Corporation
Guaranteed Mortgage Certificate

Government National Mortgage
    Association
Housing and Urban Development
    (Department of)
Mortgage Participation Certificate

QUESTIONS FOR REVIEW

1. Indicate a number of different ways in which the federal government impacts on real estate finance.

2. Describe briefly how the Federal Home Loan Mortgage Corporation was created and how it operates as a secondary mortgage market institution.
3. Identify the three mortgage securities developed by the FHLMC and describe some of the FHLMC's more recent secondary mortgage market activities.
4. The Government National Mortgage Association was created in 1968 and was given certain responsibilities that had been under the domain of the old FNMA in the past. What are these responsibilities? Give some indication as to how they have been carried out.
5. Explain what is meant by: (a) GNMA and FNMA Tandem Programs, and (b) GNMA's mortgage-backed securities program.
6. What is the purpose of the Farm Credit System? Within the System, what are the roles of Federal Land Banks and Associations? What other types of organizations are important to the effectiveness of the Farm Credit System?
7. Describe the role of the Farmers Home Administration as a provider of home loans.
8. Briefly describe the role of the Department of Housing and Urban Development in the housing and mortgage markets. What are some other activities undertaken by HUD?
9. What is a state real estate assistance agency?

PROBLEMS

1. Obtain recent FHLMC activity information relating to trends in mortgage transactions, loan portfolio size, and the importance of raising funds through participation certificates. Discuss your findings.
2. Major changes are continually taking place in the secondary mortgage market. Identify important new developments as they relate to the FHLMC.
3. Obtain recent information on the further development of the GNMA mortgage-backed security program. Discuss the program's significance in the development of the secondary mortgage market.

PART 3

FINANCING COSTS, INVESTMENT RETURNS, AND RISK

CHAPTER 8
Interest Rates and Other Loan Factors

CHAPTER 9
Investment Returns and Price-Risk Hedging

8

INTEREST RATES AND OTHER LOAN FACTORS

LEARNING OBJECTIVES

After studying this chapter, you should be able to do the following:

Explain what is meant by compound interest.

Describe the process of compounding more frequently than annually.

Differentiate between present value and future value.

Define the terms annuity, annuity due, and regular annuity.

Discuss and describe how constant-payment mortgage loans can be fully amortized.

Describe loan amortization characteristics for variable-rate and graduated-payment mortgage loans.

THE FINANCING OF real estate investments usually involves a period of years. This makes it necessary to consider and understand the concept of compound interest or the "math of finance." Some people are inclined to simply avoid considering compound interest because of an unfounded belief that the subject is very difficult and complex. This is simply not the case. Furthermore, erroneous decisions may be made if there is a failure to consider the *time value of money* which involves both the "cost" of money and "when" money flows in, or is paid out. Thus, interest rate levels and the timing of cash flows are important in making sound real estate financing and investment decisions.

FUTURE VALUE AND COMPOUND INTEREST

Future value is the worth at a specific point in the future of an amount received or paid today. Through the process of compounding, a current investment will "grow" or increase in value over time. This process utilizes the basic concept of **compound interest** whereby interest is earned on the original principal and on accrued interest (i.e., interest on interest).

Annual Compounding

Let's assume that you deposit $1,000 in a savings and loan association. You can earn 6 percent interest on your savings each year. At the end of 1 year your savings or investment will be worth $1,060. This is because you receive your original principal (P_0), or beginning amount, of $1,000 plus an *interest* (i) return of 6 percent of the principal or $60. This also may be expressed as $P_0(1 + i)$, which gives the compound or future value at the end of one year (P_1). In this example, $1,000(1.06) = $1,060. Thus, a $1,000 savings growing at 6 percent per year has a future value of $1,060 one year from now.

But what if you decide to leave your savings in the savings and loan association for two years before withdrawing the initial principal and accumulated interest? What is the future value of your investment? This involves *compounding* since you will earn "interest on interest" as well as interest on principal. Assuming annual compounding, this can be expressed as $P_2 = P_0(1 + i)(1 + i)$ or $P_0(1 + i)^2$. In our example, $P_2 = $1,000(1.06)(1.06) or $1,060(1.06). Thus, the future worth two years from now of $1,000 growing at 6 percent per year is $1,123.60 (or rounded to $1,124).

The compound interest concept can be stated in general terms as:

$$P_n = P_0(1 + i)^n$$

where

P_n = future value at the end of n years
P_0 = principal or initial amount at year 0
i = annual interest rate
n = number of years

To illustrate the usefulness of this formula, let us now assume that you will not withdraw your savings until the end of five years. This means that your earning of "interest on interest" will be even more beneficial. We can show this as follows:

$$P_5 = $1,000(1.06)^5$$
$$P_5 = $1,000(1.338)$$
$$P_5 = $1,338$$

The interest on principal, plus the interest on interest, is all captured in the $(1 + i)^n$ portion of the formula, which is referred to as the *future value interest factor* (FVIF) for a specified interest rate and time period.

While financial calculators make it easy to calculate specific interest factors, standardized tables are also available and widely used in practice. A partial "future value of $1" table is illustrated as Table 8–1.[1] A more comprehensive table is presented in Appendix B. As can be seen, FVIF factors are given for various interest rates and time periods in years. For example, the interest factor for one year at 6 percent is 1.060. Future value is determined by multiplying the interest factor by the principal or beginning amount. The interest factor for a two-year period at 6 percent is 1.124. An initial savings of $1,000 would "grow" to $1,124 in two years, i.e., $1,000(1.124) = $1,124. In other words, the 1.124 interest factor is the same as (1.06)(1.06) or $(1.06)^2$. Likewise, the FVIF for five years at 6 percent is 1.338 which corresponds to our previous calculation.

The significance of compounding at different interest rates is also illustrated in Table 8–1. For example, at a 6 percent interest rate with annual compounding, your initial $1,000 savings would grow to $1,791 ($1,000 × 1.791) at the end of 10 years. An alternative investment at 10 percent would be worth $2,594 at the end of 10 years. And, at a 16 percent rate of return per year for 10 years, your initial $1,000 would be worth $4,411.

More Frequent Compounding

Today many savings accounts and other investments provide for compounding of your money more than once a year. In order to handle such problems we must modify the previously stated compound interest formula that was given for annual compounding situations. Recall that $P_n = P_0(1 + i)^n$. We first de-

TABLE 8–1. Future Value of $1

Year	6%	7%	8%	9%	10%	12%	14%	16%
1	1.060	1.070	1.080	1.090	1.100	1.120	1.140	1.160
2	1.124	1.145	1.166	1.188	1.210	1.254	1.300	1.346
3	1.191	1.225	1.260	1.295	1.331	1.405	1.482	1.561
4	1.262	1.311	1.360	1.412	1.464	1.574	1.689	1.811
5	1.338	1.403	1.469	1.539	1.611	1.762	1.925	2.100
6	1.419	1.501	1.587	1.677	1.772	1.974	2.195	2.436
7	1.504	1.606	1.714	1.828	1.949	2.211	2.502	2.826
8	1.594	1.718	1.851	1.993	2.144	2.476	2.853	3.278
9	1.689	1.838	1.999	2.172	2.358	2.773	3.252	3.803
10	1.791	1.967	2.159	2.367	2.594	3.106	3.707	4.411

[1]These tables contain interest factors in three decimal places so as not to detract from our emphasis on illustration and application. This degree of accuracy is adequate for analyzing many problems. Tables also are available to six decimal places for greater accuracy when needed in specific real estate problems, as we will discuss later.

termine the number of times or intervals that compounding will take place *within one year.* We then divide the interest rate *i* by the number of intra-year compounding intervals which we will call *m.* Next we multiply the number of years *n* by *m* to reflect the *total number* of time periods involved in the specified problem. This revised formula can be expressed as:

$$P_n = P_0(1 + i/m)^{n \times m}$$

Let us now return to the $1,000 savings account example with a 6 percent stated annual yield and a two-year investment period. Assume that another savings and loan association also provides a 6 percent annual interest rate or yield but offers to compound your money *quarterly* or four times a year. Should this make any difference to you? Recall that annual compounding at 6 percent would amount to $1,124 at the end of two years. With quarterly compounding you would have:

$$P_n = \$1,000(1 + .06/4)^{2 \times 4}$$
$$P_n = \$1,000(1.015)^8$$
$$P_n = \$1,000(1.126)$$
$$P_n = \$1,126$$

While the added $2 might not be enough to cause you to switch your savings account, it does serve to illustrate the power of compounding more frequently than once a year. At some point, such as monthly or daily compounding, you might be enticed to switch your account because of an added savings differential. For example, the value at the end of two years given *monthly compounding* would be:

$$P_n = \$1,000(1 + .06/12)^{2 \times 12}$$
$$P_n = \$1,000(1.005)^{24}$$
$$P_n = \$1,000(1.127)$$
$$P_n = \$1,127$$

It also should be apparent that lengthening the total investment period from two years to, say, five years would make the more frequent compounding alternative even more preferable.

Lending institutions often distinguish between the annual yield when compounding annually and the *equivalent annual yield* when compounding occurs more than once a year. Recall that $1,000 invested at 6 percent with annual compounding would be worth $1,060 at the end of one year. The $60 interest amount divided by the initial $1,000 gives an annual yield of 6 percent. With quarterly compounding, the value at the end of one year would be: $1,000(1.015)^4 = $1,000(1.0614) = $1,061.40. This would produce an equivalent annual yield of 6.14 percent ($61.40/$1,000). Thus quarterly compounding would raise the effective annual return by .14 percentage points when the annual rate is 6 percent. To summarize, the effective or equivalent annual yield will always increase as we increase the frequency of the intra-year compounding interval. Furthermore, the effective annual yield calculated for the first year as we did above will be the same in every year for multiyear investments.

As is evident from the above, the reason behind compounding is that you begin to earn interest on your interest sooner. With annual compounding, interest is not credited until the end of the year; therefore, you don't earn interest on the interest earned during the year until the following year.

PRESENT VALUE OR WORTH

Most real estate and other finance problems involve making decisions now during the current or present time period. At the same time it is still necessary to forecast and estimate future values. However, since decisions are made in the present time period, future values are "brought back" or *discounted* so as to represent their present worth or value. In essence, **present value** is just the *opposite* of compound interest or future value. It is the worth today of an amount to be received (or paid) in the future.

Annual Discounting

Assume that you need $1,060 at the end of one year from now. If you can earn 6 percent interest (compounded annually) on your investment, how much would you have to invest now? Certainly, the required investment would be less than $1,060. In order to answer this question, we need to "bring back" or *discount* the future value to the present time period. It may be recalled that in compounding, the initial principal or current amount is multiplied by the sum of one plus the interest rate to arrive at next year's future value. In a similar fashion, the present value can be found by dividing the future value by the sum of one plus the interest rate. Present value in our example is determined as: $1,060/1.06 = $1,000.

Now, what is the present worth of $1,124 to be received in two years if the interest or discount rate is 6 percent? Since this is the reverse of compounding, we divide $1,124 by (1.06)(1.06) or 1.124. Thus, the present worth is $1,000. In other words, one would be indifferent between receiving $1,000 now or $1,124 two years from now if one's objective was to invest at a 6 percent interest rate.

In order to further aid our understanding of the process of discounting, we can rewrite the compound interest formula involving annual compounding, $P_n = P_0(1 + i)^n$, as:

$$P_0 = P_n/(1 + i)^n$$

This means that the present value (P_0) of the investment is equal to the future value (P_n) divided by the interest factor for a specific interest rate i and time period n. Using the above data at 6 percent for two years we have:

$$P_0 = \$1,124/(1.06)^2$$
$$P_0 = \$1,124/1.124$$
$$P_0 = \$1,000$$

The opposite process of discounting versus compounding also can be illustrated as follows:

Future Value   *Present Value*

Year 0▼ $1,000(1.000) = $1,000 ┌▶$1,124/1.124 = $1,000
Year 1 ├
Year 2 └▶$1,000(1.124) = $1,124▲ $1,124/1.000 = $1,124

In the future value example we start with $1,000 and earn 6 percent a year for two years. In the present value example we will receive $1,124 at the end of two years from now. However, since we are giving up the opportunity of earning 6 percent interest on our money, the present worth or value to us is only $1,000. That is, we are indifferent between having $1,000 today or $1,124 two years from now, assuming of course that we don't have any immediate spending plans for the money.

Most people prefer to multiply directly when working with present value concepts rather than dividing by future value interest factors. This is easily accomplished by rewriting the present value formula as follows:

$$P_0 = P_n/(1 + i)^n = P_n \left[\frac{1}{(1 + i)^n} \right]$$

For our two-year example we would have:

$$P_0 = \$1,124 \left[\frac{1}{(1.06)^2} \right]$$

$$P_0 = \$1,124 \left[\frac{1}{1.124} \right]$$

$$P_0 = \$1,124(.890)$$
$$P_0 = \$1,000$$

The $1/(1 + i)^n$ part of the formula is referred to as the *present value interest factor* (PVIF) and is the inverse of the $(1 + i)^n$ FVIF used for compound interest.

While financial calculators make it easy to calculate specific present value interest factors, standardized tables are also available and widely used in practice. A partial "present value of $1" table is illustrated as Table 8–2 and a more comprehensive table is presented in Appendix B. As can be seen, the PVIF value for a 6 percent discount rate and a two-year time period is .890, which is the same as we calculated above.

The significance of having to wait a long time to receive a payment can be very *costly* if you are giving up the opportunity of earning a high interest rate or receiving a high rate of return. For example, let's assume that we are willing to pay you $1,000 at the end of 10 years from now for work you are completing today. What is this offer worth to you? At a 6 percent discount rate with annual discounting, the present value of such an offer

TABLE 8–2.   Present Value of $1

Year	6%	7%	8%	9%	10%	12%	14%	16%
1	.943	.935	.926	.917	.909	.893	.877	.862
2	.890	.873	.857	.842	.826	.797	.769	.743
3	.840	.816	.794	.772	.751	.712	.675	.641
4	.792	.763	.735	.708	.683	.636	.592	.552
5	.747	.713	.681	.650	.621	.567	.519	.476
6	.705	.666	.630	.596	.564	.507	.456	.410
7	.665	.623	.583	.547	.513	.452	.400	.354
8	.627	.582	.540	.502	.467	.404	.351	.305
9	.592	.544	.500	.460	.424	.361	.308	.263
10	.558	.508	.463	.422	.386	.322	.270	.227

would be $558 ($1,000 × .558). However, if you could earn 10 percent per year if you had the money now, the present value would be only $386. Notice that the present value would be only $227 at a 16 percent discount rate.

Now that we have an understanding of fundamental present value concepts, assume that you have an opportunity to invest in raw land which could be resold for $1,927 per acre at the end of five years. During the period no cash will flow in or out. How much would you be willing to pay per acre? The answer, of course, depends on the discount rate. Let's assume that because of the availability of other investment opportunities you require a rate of return of 14 percent. Using the PVIF of .519 from Table 8–2 for five years at 14 percent allows us to make the following calculation:

$$P_0 = \$1,927(.519)$$
$$P_0 = \$1,000$$

This indicates that you should be willing to pay up to $1,000 per acre now. A lower purchase price, of course, would provide you with an even higher rate of return.

More Frequent Discounting

Discounting, like compounding, often involves the use of several time intervals within one year and thus requires an adjustment to reflect intra-year discounting. This is particularly true for real estate mortgage loans where payments or receipts typically take place on a monthly basis. Although we will not discuss the characteristics of mortgage loans until later, it is important that we give some consideration to the process of intra-year discounting at this time. This requires a modification of the basic present value formula used for annual discounting assumptions.

We first determine the number of times or intervals that discounting will take place *within one year* and we will denote this as m. We then divide the interest or discount rate i by m and also multiply the number of years n by m. The modified present value formula then becomes:

$$P_0 = p_n \left[\frac{1}{(1 + i/m)^{n \times m}} \right]$$

The present value of receiving $1,126 two years from now given a 6 percent discount rate and *quarterly* discounting would be:

$$P_0 = \$1,126 \left[\frac{1}{(1 + .06/4)^{2 \times 4}} \right]$$

$$P_0 = \$1,126 \left[\frac{1}{(1.015)^8} \right]$$

$$P_0 = \$1,126(.888)$$
$$P_0 = \$1,000$$

Notice that like annual compounding and discounting, intra-year compounding and discounting are also the opposite or inverse of each other.

ANNUITY CONCEPTS AND VALUES

Many real estate financing decisions and investment problems involve the periodic inflow or outflow of a constant dollar amount of cash. The term *annuity* is used to describe a series of payments or receipts of a fixed amount that will continue over several time periods. Time value of money concepts also apply to annuities.

Future Value of an Annuity

Instead of investing $1,000 now and determining its future value at the end of, say, three years, let's plan to invest $1,000 at the *beginning* of each year for three years. What would be the future value of our investment at the end of three years if we could earn 6 percent interest compounded annually? We can answer this question by returning to Table 8–1 and multiplying $1,000 by each of the FVIF values at the 6 percent rate for the three-year period as follows:

$$
\begin{aligned}
\text{Future Value} &= \$1,000(1.191) + \$1,000(1.124) + \\
&\quad \$1,000(1.060) \\
&= \$1,191 + \$1,124 + \$1,060 \\
&= \$3,375
\end{aligned}
$$

Alternatively, we could have added the three FVIF values and multiplied the sum (3.375) by the $1,000 annuity cash flow to arrive at the future value of $3,375. When the cash flow occurs at the beginning of each period, we refer to this as an *annuity due.* Notice that the first $1,000 investment earns interest compounded annually for three years, the second $1,000 earns interest for two years, and the final $1,000 earns interest for one year.

Cash flow payments or receipts also may occur at the end of each time period. We refer to such an annuity as a **regular** (or ordinary) **annuity.** Let's designate the future value or compound sum of such an annuity as S_n where n is the number of time periods involved. For the same three-year problem as above, except that $1,000 is invested at the *end of each year,* we could calculate the future value as:

$$S_3 = \$1,000(1.124) + \$1,000(1.060) + \$1,000(1.000)$$
$$S_3 = \$1,000(3.184)$$
$$S_3 = \$3,184$$

Notice that since the cash flows are at the end of the period, the first $1,000 earns interest for only two years, the second $1,000 earns interest for one year, and the last $1,000 earns no interest.

We also can state the regular annuity concept in general terms as:

$$S_n = PP(1 + i)^{n-1} + PP(1 + i)^{n-2} + \ldots + PP$$
$$S_n = PP(\text{FVIFA}, i\%, n \text{ yrs.})$$

where S_n is the future value of the regular annuity, PP is the periodic payment or investment, and FVIFA is the future value interest factor for an annuity at i percent for n years.

As is the case with future value interest factors involving a single cash payment or investment, standardized tables containing FVIFA values are available for regular annuities. A "future value of $1 ordinary annuity" table is presented in Appendix B, Table 3, for various interest rates and time periods assuming annual compounding. Notice that the FVIFA at 6 percent for three years is 3.184, the same as we computed above.

When compounding occurs more frequently than once a year, we would need to adjust the FVIFA value as we did the FVIF value involving a single payment in our earlier intra-year compounding illustrations. This is easily accomplished with the aid of a financial calculator and the FVIFA equation in Appendix B. Tables also are available for real estate problems utilizing monthly compounding.[2]

Determining Periodic Payments

In addition to determining future values of annuities, we can use the future value annuity equation to find the periodic payment that would be needed to accumulate a future dollar amount of, say, $50,000 at the end of five years. Let's further assume that a payment is to be made at the end of each year beginning one year from now and that we can earn 12 percent interest per year. This type of problem is frequently referred to as a "sinking fund" prob-

---

[2]Monthly compound interest tables are provided in Paul Wendt and Alan R. Cerf, *Tables for Investment Analysis* (Berkeley, California: Institute for Business and Economic Research, University of California, 1979). Comprehensive tables also are provided in the *Thorndike Encyclopedia of Banking and Financial Tables* (Boston: Warren, Gorham, and Lamont, Inc., 1973).

lem in that we are making constant payments in order to retire a debt obligation (or we might want to make a specific size investment at some future point in time).

To work the problem at hand, we can express the future value annuity equation as follows:

$$PP(\text{FVIFA}, i\%, n \text{ yrs.}) = S_n$$
$$PP(\text{FVIFA}, 12\%, 5 \text{ yrs.}) = S_5$$
$$PP(6.353) = \$50,000$$
$$PP = \$50,000/6.353$$
$$PP = \$7,870.30$$

The FVIFA value can be determined from Table 8–1 by summing the FVIF values at a 12 percent rate for year four down through year one (1.574 + 1.405 + 1.254 + 1.120) plus a value of 1.000 (since the last payment will not earn any interest) for an FVIFA of 6.353. As an alternative, we could have taken the FVIFA directly from Table 3 in Appendix B at 12 percent for five years. We would need to pay $7,870.30 annually in order to accumulate $50,000 at the end of five years.

Rather than having to divide the future value amount by the appropriate FVIFA, some real estate financial tables provide a *sinking fund factor* so that one can multiply instead of divide. The sinking fund factor is determined by dividing 1 by the FVIFA. For the above problem we would have a sinking fund factor of .157406. Multiplying this factor by the $50,000 future value annuity gives $7,870.30 for the periodic payment.

Present Value of an Annuity

Assume that you have the opportunity of purchasing real estate property that will provide you with a $10,000 return at the end of each year for three years. If you require a 12 percent return on your investment, how much would you be willing to pay for the property? Let's begin by stating the present value annuity concept in general terms as:

$$A_n = PR\left[\frac{1}{(1 + i)^1}\right] + PR\left[\frac{1}{(1 + i)^2}\right] + \ldots + PR\left[\frac{1}{(1 + i)^n}\right]$$
$$A_n = PR(\text{PVIFA}, i\%, n \text{ yrs.})$$

where A_n is the present value of an annuity, PR is the periodic receipt, and PVIFA is the present value interest factor for an annuity at i percent for n years.

Now we can determine the answer to our question by returning to Table 8–2 and obtaining the PVIF values at 12 percent for years one, two, and three. These values, then, would be multiplied by $10,000 as follows:

$$A_3 = \$10,000(.893) + \$10,000(.797) + \$10,000(.712)$$
$$A_3 = \$10,000(2.402)$$
$$A_3 = \$24,020$$

Thus you should be willing to pay $24,020 for a $10,000 three-year annuity if you require a 12 percent rate of return. Of course, if the property could be purchased for less than $24,020, your rate of return would be even higher.

Standardized tables containing PVIFA values for various interest rates and time periods also are available and are useful in that they eliminate the need to add the individual PVIFs. A "present value of $1 annuity" table is presented in Appendix B, Table 4. Notice that the PVIFA at 12 percent for three years is 2.402, the same as we computed above.[3]

When discounting occurs more frequently than once a year, we would need to adjust the PVIFA value as we did the PVIF value involving a single receipt in our earlier intra-year discounting illustrations. This is easily accomplished with the aid of a financial calculator and the PVIFA equation in Appendix B. Real estate financial tables that are based on monthly discounting also are available and will be referred to later when we discuss mortgage loan amortizations.

Determining Periodic Receipts

The present value annuity equation also can be used to find the periodic receipt that would be needed to justify a purchase price of, say, $100,000, for a real estate investment providing constant annual cash flows for five years with no *reversion value* (resale value) at the end of the fifth year. Assume that a 16 percent rate of return is required on the investment. We can answer this question by expressing the present value annuity equation as follows:

$$PR(\text{PVIFA}, i\%, n \text{ yrs.}) = A_n$$
$$PR(\text{PVIFA}, 16\%, 5 \text{ yrs.}) = A_5$$
$$PR(3.274) = \$100,000$$
$$PR = \$100,000/3.274$$
$$PR = \$30,543.68$$

The PVIFA value can be determined from Table 8–2 by summing the PVIF values at a 16 percent rate for years one through five (.862 + .743 + .641 + .552 + .476) for a PVIFA of 3.274. As an alternative, we could have taken the PVIFA directly from Table 4 in Appendix B at 16 percent for five years. We would need to receive $30,543.68 annually in order to justify paying $100,000 for the real estate investment.

MORTGAGE LOAN AMORTIZATION

During the past several decades, borrowers and lenders typically entered into long-term, fully amortized, constant-payment real estate mortgage loans. More recently we have witnessed the increased use of shorter-term, partially amortized, constant payment mortgage loans that are referred to as *balloon*

---

[3]Some authors prefer to use the term "present value of one-per-period" to identify PVIFA values for regular annuities.

COMPUTER SOFTWARE FOR CALCULATING FUTURE VALUES, PRESENT VALUES, AND LOAN AMORTIZATION SCHEDULES

The explosion in the development and use of financial calculators and personal computers during the 1980s has been accompanied by the development of software programs designed to make it easy to master time value of money and other real estate finance concepts. Consequently, while we believe that it is important to understand the concepts developed in this chapter, the tediousness of making many of the calculations can be substantially reduced.

Available for adopters of REAL ESTATE FINANCE is a basic *Decision Assistant* software package for use with IBM and IBM compatible personal computers. *Decision Assistant* contains software programs for computing future values and present values for problems involving a single cash flow (lump sum), as well as cash flow annuities.

Decision Assistant also contains a software program for a mortgage loan amortization schedule. Constant payments necessary to fully amortize a mortgage loan can be easily determined. Principal repayment amounts and remaining loan balances are also readily available throughout the life of the mortgage loan. In addition, sensitivity of loan amortization characteristics to changes in such factors as the interest rate can be easily examined once the basic problem has been set up.

This textbook does not directly refer to, or depend on, this available software. However, we encourage users of REAL ESTATE FINANCE to make use of the *Decision Assistant* in better understanding how time value of money concepts affect real estate financing and investment decisions.

loans because they require large principal repayments at maturity. Lender concern over rising interest rates also has led to the use of other alternative real estate financing methods such as graduated-payment mortgages (GPMs) and adjustable-rate mortgages (ARMs). It is important in real estate finance that we develop some understanding of the time value of money implications of these types of mortgage loans.

Fully Amortized Constant-Payment Mortgage Loans

Amortization involves the repayment of a mortgage loan's principal or amount over the life of the loan. A fully amortized loan is characterized by a zero loan balance at maturity. To illustrate this concept, let's assume that we borrow $40,000 for five years. The lender charges a 12 percent interest rate, requires annual constant payments, and the loan is to be fully amortized.

The first step is to determine the dollar amount of the constant payment by the borrower or the receipt to the lender. We do this by using the present value annuity equation to determine the periodic receipt as follows:

$$PR(\text{PVIFA, } 12\%, 5 \text{ yrs.}) = A_5$$
$$PR(3.605) = \$40,000$$
$$PR = \$40,000/3.605$$
$$PR = \$11,096 \text{ (rounded)}$$

The 3.605 PVIFA value can be determined from Table 8–2 or from Appendix B, Table 4, as we discussed above. We now know that the annual receipt to the lender or payment by the borrower to fully amortize the loan will be $11,096.

Each annual payment is comprised of both interest and principal repayment (or amortization) components. And, since interest is paid on the unpaid balance, the mix between interest and principal changes over the life of the loan. A loan amortization schedule is illustrated in Table 8–3 for our $40,000 loan. Notice that interest for the first year is $4,800 ($40,000 × .12) with the principal or amortization repayment being $6,296. Interest payments decline, while payments of principal increase, as the remaining loan balance declines toward zero. The loan is fully amortized since no loan balance remains at maturity.

Traditional long-term, fully amortized mortgage loans generally require constant monthly payments. Extensive real estate financial tables, including those provided in the *Realty Bluebook*,[4] provide monthly payment dollar amounts that are necessary to fully amortize various loan amounts over varying loan lives. Present value tables for annual interest rates with monthly discounting also are available to determine constant monthly payments needed to fully amortize a mortgage loan. Table 8–4 illustrates a monthly present value table for a 12 percent annual interest rate. Similar data for other interest rates are illustrated in Appendix B, Table 5.

Now we can see the impact of monthly discounting relative to annual discounting. Notice that at a 12 percent annual interest rate involving a cash flow at the end of five years that the present value of $1 interest factor involving monthly discounting is .550450 (Table 8–4). This contrasts with the

TABLE 8–3. Loan Amortization Schedule

Year	Annual Payment	Interest* (12% Rate)	Principal Repayment	Loan Balance
0	—	—	—	$40,000
1	$11,096	$4,800	$6,296	33,704
2	11,096	4,044	7,052	26,652
3	11.096	3,198	7,898	18,754
4	11,096	2,250	8,846	9,908
5	11,096	1,189	9,907**	0

*Interest for the first year is .12 × $40,000 = $4,800; for the second year, .12 × $33,704 = $4,044; and so on.

**The final principal repayment is off by one dollar due to rounding errors.

[4]Robert DeHeer, *Realty Bluebook* (San Rafael, California: Professional Publishing Corp., 1987).

TABLE 8–4. Monthly Present Value Table for a 12% Annual Interest Rate

Year	Months	Present Value of $1	Present Value Annuity of $1 Per Period	Loan Constant
1	12	.887449	11.255077	.088849
2	24	.787566	21.243387	.047073
3	36	.698925	30.107505	.033214
4	48	.620260	37.973959	.026334
5	60	.550450	44.955038	.022244
10	120	.302995	69.700522	.014347
15	180	.166783	83.321664	.012002
20	240	.091806	90.819416	.011011
25	300	.050534	94.946551	.010532
30	360	.027817	97.218331	.010286

12 percent, five-year PVIF in Table 8–2 of .567 reflecting the assumption of annual discounting. The PVIF value is smaller for more frequent intra-year discounting just as the PVIF value would be larger given more frequent compounding.

Also shown in Table 8–4 is the present value annuity of $1 per period at 12 percent for various years. Recall in Table 8–3 that we presented the loan amortization schedule for a 12 percent, five-year, $40,000 loan whereby annual lender receipts (or borrower payments) of $11,096 would be required to fully amortize the loan. Now let's assume that the lender requires monthly cash receipts. What monthly amount would be needed to fully amortize this mortgage loan? We determine the monthly cash flow by returning to the basic present value annuity equation as follows:

$$PR(\text{PVIFA}, 12\%, 60 \text{ months}) = A_{60}$$
$$PR(44.955038) = \$40,000$$
$$PR = \$40,000/44.955038$$
$$PR = \$889.78$$

The 44.955038 PVIFA value is taken from Table 8–4 and reflects a 12 percent annual interest rate and 60 monthly payments. We now know that the lender must receive $889.78 each month in order to fully amortize the mortgage loan by the end of five years. This could be verified by preparing a loan amortization schedule similar to the one illustrated in Table 8–3 except that we would have 60 monthly payments instead of five annual payments.

Most fully amortized, constant payment real estate loans traditionally have been for 25 or 30 years. For example, a $40,000, 12 percent, 30-year loan would require monthly payments of $411.45 ($40,000/97.218331). If, instead, the loan had been for $80,000, the monthly payment would have been determined as $80,000/97.218331 or $822.89, which is twice the required payment on the $40,000 loan.[5] As an alternative we might have been able to use "monthly payments necessary to amortize a loan" tables to directly find the required payments.

Loan Constants. The last column in Table 8–4 contains loan constant values[6] which are determined by dividing 1 by the appropriate PVIFA value. For example, 1/44.955038 produces a loan constant for a 12 percent, 60-month, fully amortized loan of .02224445 or .022244 rounded. Loan constants permit a simple multiplication (instead of the previously discussed division procedure) to determine monthly mortgage payments. Multiplying a $40,000 loan times .02224445 results in a monthly mortgage payment of $889.78, which is the same as we determined above for a mortgage loan with these characteristics.

Loan constants also are frequently annualized and are made available in table form. For example, the *annual loan constant* for a 12 percent, 60-month loan is .266928 (.022244 × 12) or about 26.693 percent when stated in percentage form. In more general terms, we can express an annual constant percentage as:

$$\text{Annual Constant} = (12 \times \text{Monthly Payment} \times 100)/\text{Loan Amount}$$

The 100 factor is used to express the annual constant in percentage form. For our example of a $40,000, 12 percent, 60-month mortgage loan, the annual constant would be:

$$\text{Annual Constant} = (12 \times \$889.78 \times 100)/\$40,000$$
$$= \$1,067,736/\$40,000$$
$$= .26693 \text{ or } 26.693\%$$

Knowing the annual constant percentage allows us to quickly assess the likelihood of our ability to service a mortgage loan. Our calculations indicate that we would need available cash inflow of 26.693 percent of $40,000 or $10,677 per year to meet our loan servicing obligations.

Now assume that you are offered a $200,000, 12 percent, 30-year (360 monthly payments) mortgage loan on an apartment building. What will be the annual cash payments that you would have to make in order to service the loan? We can use Table 8–4 to quickly determine the necessary amount.

---

[5]The unwillingness of some lenders during the early 1980s to enter into long-term, fully amortized, constant-payment loans because of concern over possible rising interest rates led to some offering of short-term, zero-interest, fully amortized loans. Such loans usually require substantial down payments of 30 percent or more and may have a life of five years. To illustrate, let's assume you purchase a house for $100,000, make a down payment of $30,000, and receive a $70,000 zero-interest loan that is to be fully amortized over five years (60 months). What would be your monthly payment? This is determined by dividing the $70,000 loan by 60 payments to arrive at a $1,166.67 monthly payment.

[6]Some authors prefer to refer to loan constant factors as principal *recovery* factors or as the *installment to amortize $1* factors.

First, the monthly loan constant of .010286 is annualized by multiplying by 12 to give .123432 or approximately 12.343 percent. Second, this annual constant percentage multiplied by the $200,000 loan indicates that $24,686 will be needed yearly to service the loan.

Remaining Loan Balances. Before leaving our discussion of fully amortized, constant-payment loans, we should recognize that it often is important to know the remaining balance on a loan that has been outstanding for a period of time. For example, the problem described in Table 8–3 requires an annual payment of interest and principal of $11,096 over five years to pay off a $40,000, 12 percent loan. At the end of one year the remaining loan balance is $33,704 after a principal repayment of $6,296. The remaining loan balance as a percentage of the original loan amount after one year is 84.26 percent ($33,074/$40,000). The percentage relationship at the end of two years is 66.63 percent ($26,652/$40,000). This greater drop in the remaining loan balance for the second year is due, of course, to the declining interest payments over the life of the loan.

Let's now return to our example of an $80,000, 12 percent, 30-year (360 monthly payments) loan. Recall that we previously found the monthly payment to be $822.89. What will be the remaining loan balance at the end of, say, 10 years? We can answer this question with the use of Table 8–4 by finding the PVIFA at 12 percent for 20 years or 240 months (the then remaining life of the loan) and multiplying this 90.819416 value by the $822.89 monthly payment as follows:

$$\text{Mortgage Balance} = \text{Monthly Payment(PVIFA, 12\%, 240 months)}$$
$$= \$822.89(90.819416)$$
$$= \$74,734.39$$

Alternatively, in more general terms, we could first find the ratio of the PVIFA for a 20-year loan over the PVIFA for the original 30-year loan to arrive at a percentage loan balance of 93.418 percent (90.819416/97.218331). Multiplying this percentage loan balance times the $80,000 loan results in a remaining loan amount of $74,734.39 at the end of 10 years. In lieu of having to make similar calculations for each new loan balance problem, standardized "percentage remaining loan balances" are available in the *Realty Bluebook* and from other sources.

Partially Amortized Constant-Payment Mortgage Loans

During the early 1980s, there occurred an increased use of balloon loans to finance real estate. Some lenders offered relatively short-term mortgage loans that carried long-term amortization provisions. Such loans are only partially amortized at maturity. An example would be a 12 percent, 30-year amortization mortgage loan with a five-year maturity and thus requiring a balloon payment at maturity. It is argued that this type of mortgage loan provides lenders with partial protection against the risk of rising interest rates because the loan matures and can be renegotiated in five years instead of the interest rate being fixed for 30 years. Of course, this shifts the risk to borrowers who possibly could ill afford payment of potentially higher interest rates at the end of five years. On a more positive note, the 30-year amortization schedule requires lower monthly loan payments (due to partial amortization) and thus makes it easier for prospective borrowers to meet loan qualifications.

Let's now illustrate the characteristics of this type of loan by returning to the previously discussed $80,000, 12 percent, 30-year mortgage loan example. However, while the loan is to be amortized over 30 years, it will have a five-year maturity. What will be the size of the balloon payment at the end of five years? It should be recognizable that this question is the same as the remaining loan balance question. Recall that we previously found the monthly payment to be $822.89 based on a 30-year amortization schedule. Using Table 8–4, we find the PVIFA at 12 percent for 25 years or 300 months (the time remaining on the 30-year amortization at the five-year maturity date) to be 94.946551. The size of the balloon payment then is estimated as:

$$
\begin{aligned}
\text{Balloon Payment} &= \text{Monthly Payment(PVIFA, 12\%, 300 months)} \\
&= \$822.89(94.946551) \\
&= \$78,130.57
\end{aligned}
$$

Thus the borrower will have reduced the original loan principal by only $1,869.43 ($80,000.00 − $78,130.57) and undoubtedly will need to refinance the loan at the end of the five-year period. Of course, the borrower absorbs the risk of tight funds availability and high interest rates at the time of the needed loan refinancing.

Adjustable-Rate and Graduated-Payment Mortgage Loans

In contrast with the standard fixed interest rate, fully amortized, constant-payment mortgage loan, the interest rate on an *adjustable-rate mortgage* (ARM) varies with changes in some predetermined index reflecting cost of funds. Recall that in a standard mortgage loan of $80,000 at 12 percent for 30 years the monthly payment would be $822.89 over the life of the loan. However, an adjustable-rate mortgage might start at 12 percent but increase to, say, 13 percent, at the end of one year. How would this affect the borrower? Actually one or a combination of two adjustments could take place: (1) the monthly mortgage payment could increase, and/or (2) the loan maturity could lengthen. We can illustrate adjustment alternatives using the partial monthly present value table for 12 percent and 13 percent annual interest rates at the top of the next page. More comprehensive data are shown in Appendix B, Table 5.

Let's begin by determining the increase in monthly mortgage payments that could occur under the first alternative. We start by calculating the loan balance at the end of one year, assuming the 12 percent rate held

		12 Percent		13 Percent	
Years	Months	PVIFA	Loan Constant	PVIFA	Loan Constant
29	348	96.865546	.010324	90.136227	.011094
30	360	97.218331	.010286	90.399605	.011062
35	420	98.468831	.010155	91.308095	.010952
40	480	99.157169	.010085	91.784030	.010895

throughout the year. Using the previously identified mortgage-balance equation we have:

$$\text{Mortgage Balance} = \text{Monthly Payment(PVIFA, 12\%, 348 months)}$$
$$= \$822.89(96.865546)$$
$$= \$79{,}709.69$$

The new monthly payment then would be determined as:

$$\text{Monthly Payment} = \text{Mortgage Balance(Loan Constant, 13\%, 348 months)}$$
$$= \$79{,}709.69(.011094)$$
$$= \$884.30$$

Thus the impact of an increase in the ARM from 12 percent to 13 percent with 29 years remaining on the loan would be $61.41 ($884.30 – $822.89) per month.

The second alternative involves increasing the loan maturity. If we wanted to keep the monthly payment at $822.89, how much would the loan maturity have to increase? We solve this by finding the new loan constant necessary to provide a 13 percent yield to the lender. The new loan constant would be determined as follows:

$$\text{New Loan Constant} = \text{Original Monthly Payment} \div \text{Mortgage Balance}$$
$$= \$822.89/\$79{,}709.69$$
$$= .0103235$$

However, examination of the partial monthly present value table at a 13 percent rate indicates that the new loan constant is not even close to being reached even if the loan maturity is extended to 40 years (480 months) where the loan constant is a much higher .010895. Since an even longer loan maturity extension would be unacceptable, some compromise between a higher monthly payment and a longer loan maturity would have to be reached.

For example, one possible compromise might be to extend the loan maturity to, say, 40 years, and accept a necessary increase in the monthly payment to provide the lender with a 13 percent yield. The required new monthly payment would be determined as follows:

New Monthly
   Payment   = Mortgage Balance(Loan Constant,
               13%, 480 months)
               = $79,709.69(.010895)
               = $868.44

Thus, instead of a monthly payment of $884.30 with no loan maturity extension, a lower payment of $868.44 monthly could be achieved if the loan maturity is extended from 29 years to 40 years. Many other combinations also could be examined.

Payment calculations for a renegotiable-rate mortgage (RRM) or "rollover" mortgage would be handled in a similar fashion as the ARM. However, interest rates or maturity periods are adjusted only at the end of each term loan period. For example, the rollover loan might consist of a series of renegotiable five-year term loans secured by a mortgage with a 30-year amortization. If interest rates were to rise, monthly payments and/or loan maturity extensions could first take place at the end of five years. The above example could be reworked to show the impact on the monthly payment associated with a rate increase from 12 percent to 13 percent at the end of five years.

The graduated-payment mortgage (GPM) plan was developed by the FHA under its Section 245 program. Through a complex computational process, initial payment levels are set below the monthly payment requirements for a standard constant-payment, fixed-rate, fully amortized mortgage loan. For example, the initial monthly payment during the first year for an $80,000, 12 percent, 30-year GPM with a 7.5 percent rate of graduation and a five-year graduation period would be $633.10.[7] Monthly payments during the second year would be $680.58 ($633.10 × 1.075) and would continue to increase by 7.5 percent per year through the sixth year at which time the payments would level off. Following is a comparison of monthly payments under this GPM loan and the previously discussed standard mortgage loan:

Year	Monthly Payments	
	GPM Loan	Standard Loan
1	$633.10	$822.89
2	680.58	822.89
3	731.63	822.89
4	786.50	822.89
5	845.49	822.89
6-30	908.90	822.89

---

[7]This initial monthly payment was calculated based on formulas presented in E. B. Greynolds, Jr., J. S. Aronofsky, and R. J. Frame, *Financial Analysis Using Calculators: Time Value of Money* (New York: McGraw-Hill Book Co., 1980), 417–420. For further discussion of GPM characteristics and terms, see: HUD *Handbook,* Graduated-Payment Mortgage Program, Section 245.

Notice that under the GPM the monthly payments during the first year are nearly $190 less than the payments on a standard mortgage loan. Monthly payments remain lower under the GPM until the fifth year and actually exceed the payments on the standard loan during years six through 30 by about $86 per month.

It is also important to understand that remaining loan balances will actually increase during the early years of a GPM (in our example the balance will rise above $80,000) in contrast with the continually decreasing loan balance under a standard mortgage. This occurs because of the initially lower payments under the GPM, and loan balances will continue to be higher under the GPM relative to the balances under a standard mortgage loan until the loans are paid off at maturity.

KEY TERMS

amortization
annuity
annuity due
compound interest

future value
present value
regular annuity
time value of money

QUESTIONS FOR REVIEW

1. Identify the meaning of "time value of money" and describe the process of compounding.
2. Describe the process involved with compounding more frequently than once a year.
3. The process of discounting is used to determine the present value or worth of an investment. Explain.
4. Define the concept of an annuity. Also differentiate between an "annuity due" and a "regular or ordinary annuity."
5. What is meant by a fully amortized constant-payment mortgage loan?
6. Describe the use of "loan constants" in conjunction with fully amortized constant-payment mortgage loans. How are remaining loan balances determined?
7. Explain the meaning of a partially amortized constant-payment mortgage loan.
8. Compare (a) adjustable-rate and (b) graduated-payment mortgage loans from the standpoint of monthly mortgage payments.

PROBLEMS

1. If you invest $1,000 now, what will be the future value of your investment if you can earn 12 percent per year for 8 years? What would be the value

after 12 years?

2. Assume you invest $1,000 now and can earn interest at a 12 percent annual rate for 12 years. If semiannual compounding takes place, what will be the future value of your investment? How will the future value change if quarterly compounding takes place?

3. Determine the present worth or value of a $10,000 amount to be received 10 years from now and given a required discount rate of 16 percent. What would be the present value if you had to wait 16 years before receiving your $10,000?

4. Based on an annual interest rate of 16 percent, what would be the present value of $10,000 to be received at the end of 10 years if semiannual discounting takes place? How would your answer change if you had to wait to the end of 16 years and there was quarterly discounting?

5. Rose Arapahoe is planning to build a "nest egg" by investing $3,000 per year for the next 6 years. Investments can earn 10 percent per year.
   a. How much money will Rose Arapahoe have at the end of 6 years if she makes her first investment one year from now and the remaining investments annually thereafter?
   b. How would Rose Arapahoe's future value be altered if she made her first investment now and the remaining investments at one-year intervals?

6. Fred Martinez wants to accumulate $25,000 at the end of 8 years from now. He can earn 14 percent annually on his investments. He will make annual contributions or payments starting one year from now.
   a. What would be the necessary size of Fred Martinez's annual payments?
   b. How would the size of the annual payments change if Fred Martinez were to make his first annual payment now rather than one year from now?

7. Julie Franklin is considering making an investment in rental property that will provide a cash inflow before depreciation and taxes of $15,000 a year for 15 years. Assume cash inflows will occur at the end of each year and that she requires a 20 percent rate of return on her investment. How much should she be willing to pay for the purchase of the rental property? What would be her maximum purchase price if she were to receive only $12,000 per year for 15 years?

8. Donna White requires a 14 percent rate of return on an investment in real property that will provide annual cash flow receipts. If her investment outlay or purchase price is $80,000, what cash flow amount will she have to receive at the end of each year if the cash flow stream is to last for 10 years? How will the necessary periodic receipt change if the cash flow stream is for 15 years?

9. Develop the loan amortization schedule for a $20,000, 14 percent, 4-year, fully amortized constant-payment mortgage loan requiring end-of-year annual payments. In working this problem, show the annual payment, the

annual interest amount, and the annual principal repayment amount.

10. Let's assume that you have requested a $20,000, 14 percent, 4-year, fully amortized constant-payment mortgage loan that will require monthly payments. Using present value tables, determine the monthly periodic receipt that the lender will require on the loan. If you could borrow for 15 years instead, what would the lender require in the way of a monthly periodic receipt?

11. Assume that you are offered a $300,000, 13 percent, 25-year mortgage loan on an apartment building that requires monthly mortgage payments. Determine the monthly loan constant. Next determine the annual constant percentage. What amount will be needed yearly to service the loan? How would your answer have changed if the interest rate had been 15 percent?

12. Assume that you have just borrowed $120,000 at 14 percent for 25 years and the mortgage loan requires monthly payments. What will be the required monthly payment? Now determine the remaining loan balance at the end of 5 years. How much will you still owe at the end of 15 years? How many years will it take before the remaining loan balance is less than one half of the initial amount borrowed?

13. The Smith-Jordans have been offered a $60,000, 14 percent, 30-year amortization mortgage loan requiring monthly payments and having a 5-year maturity. Determine the monthly payment that would be required on the loan. Next determine the size of the remaining balance or balloon payment that would be required at the end of five years. What would have been the size of the balloon payment if the maturity had been 10 years on the partially amortized constant-payment mortgage loan?

14. The Mattsons are interested in obtaining a $90,000, 25-year, standard mortgage loan. However, the current interest rate is 14 percent and they are unable to qualify for the loan because of the size of the monthly mortgage payments. An alternative adjustable-rate mortgage loan is available calling for a 12 percent rate the first five years before increasing to a 15 percent rate for the remaining 20 years.
   a. Determine the monthly mortgage payments for the standard 14 percent mortgage loan.
   b. For the adjustable-rate loan, determine the monthly mortgage payment for the first five years.
   c. Determine the monthly mortgage payment over the last 20 years of the adjustable-rate mortgage.
   d. What would be the monthly payment after five years if the mortgage at that time were extended to 30 years and the interest rate increased to 14 percent?

15. The monthly payment for the first year of an $80,000, 12 percent, 30-year graduated-payment mortgage with a five-year graduation period and a 7.5 percent rate of graduation is $633.10. Determine the monthly payments for years 3, 5, 10, and 20.

INVESTMENT RETURNS AND PRICE-RISK HEDGING

LEARNING OBJECTIVES

After studying this chapter, you should be able to do the following:

Describe how depreciation and tax rates affect after-tax cash flows.

Discuss how the Economic Recovery Tax Act of 1981 impacted on real estate financing and investment decisions.

Discuss how the Tax Reform Act of 1986 has altered the depreciation write-offs for real property.

Explain the application of the net present value (NPV) method for making investment decisions.

Describe how the internal rate of return (IRR) is used to determine an investment's yield.

Explain how lenders can make use of both liability and asset hedges.

Explain how mortgage bankers and builders can use financial futures to hedge against interest rate changes.

SOUND REAL ESTATE financing and investment decisions should include the consideration of relevant cash flows and required rates of return. Because of the volatile interest rates of the 1980s, many lenders, mortgage bankers, and builders also found it important to consider the possibility of hedging against price risk.

Since cash flows are heavily influenced by depreciation and taxes, the first section of this chapter discusses current real estate depreciation guidelines and tax implications. Our attention then focuses on measuring investment yields and returns. The final section examines price risk associated with changes in interest rates and explores possible hedging methods using financial futures.

REAL ESTATE DEPRECIATION AND TAX CONSIDERATIONS

The 1980s have been characterized by several major tax law changes which have impacted heavily on real estate finance and investment transactions. In this section, we first review how depreciation and tax rates affect cash flows. We then discuss some of the major tax and depreciation developments which occurred under the Economic Recovery Tax Act of 1981. Finally, we turn to a discussion of some of the major impacts on real estate decisions created by the Tax Reform Act of 1986.

Effects on After-Tax Cash Flows

Cash flows available to real estate investors are affected by two major factors in addition to the day-to-day operating revenues and expenses (including interest costs). These other factors are depreciation write-offs and income tax payments. For example, let's assume that rental property produces annual revenues of $100,000. Then, after subtracting annual operating expenses of $60,000 (excluding depreciation deductions), we have before-tax cash flow of $40,000. *Depreciation* is an accounting noncash write-off designed to provide for the recovery of the cost of assets as they are used up or wear out over time. Depending on the amount of depreciation (if any) and the applicable tax rate, we could proceed to estimate the after-tax cash flows.

Following are two scenarios, one with $20,000 of depreciation write-offs and the other with no depreciation to be taken. Assume the income tax rate is 40 percent in both cases.

	Scenario 1	*Scenario 2*
Revenues	$100,000	$100,000
Operating Expenses	−60,000	−60,000
Before-Tax Cash Flow	40,000	40,000
Depreciation	−20,000	—0—
Before-Tax Profit	20,000	40,000
Taxes @ 40%	−8,000	−16,000
After-Tax Profit	$ 12,000	$ 24,000
After-Tax Cash Flow (i.e., after-tax profit plus depreciation)	$ 32,000	$ 24,000

Although before-tax profit is larger for Scenario 2 because there is no depreciation write-off, income tax payments also are higher. Furthermore, while after-tax profit also is higher for Scenario 2, the after-tax cash flow is lower.

Since depreciation represents a noncash write-off, it serves to reduce taxable income but does not involve the outflow of cash. Consequently, depreciation charges are added back to after-tax profit to determine *after-tax cash flow.* For Scenario 1 the after-tax cash flow is the sum of the after-tax profit of $12,000 plus the depreciation write-off of $20,000 for a total of $32,000. The after-tax cash flow for Scenario 2 is $24,000 ($24,000 after-tax profit plus zero depreciation write-off). We now can see that larger depreciation write-offs are generally desirable because they serve to reduce tax payments and increase after-tax cash flows.

Changes in tax rates also affect after-tax cash flows. Following is a comparison of Scenario 1 versus a new Scenario 3 which is similar to Scenario 1 except that its tax rate is only 30 percent.

	Scenario 1	Scenario 3
Revenues	$100,000	$100,000
Operating Expenses	−60,000	−60,000
Before-Tax Cash Flow	40,000	40,000
Depreciation	−20,000	−20,000
Before-Tax Profit	20,000	20,000
Taxes (1 @ 40% and 3 @ 30%)	−8,000	−6,000
After-Tax Profit	$ 12,000	$ 14,000
After-Tax Cash Flow (i.e., after-tax profit plus depreciation)	$ 32,000	$ 34,000

As we would expect, if other things remain the same, lower tax rates result in higher after-tax cash flows.

To summarize, real estate investments become more attractive as depreciation write-offs increase and tax rates decrease. We now are ready to examine recent tax laws to assess their impact on depreciation write-offs and tax rates, and on real estate activity in general.

The Economic Recovery Tax Act of 1981

Major tax legislation was passed in 1981 in the form of the Economic Recovery Tax Act. Provision was made for cutting individual income taxes from the previous 14 to 70 percent range down to an 11 to 50 percent marginal tax rate range. The maximum capital gains tax rate on long-term investments likewise was reduced to 20 percent.

The 1981 Tax Act also lowered corporate tax rates to: 15 percent on the first $25,000 of taxable income, 18 percent on the second $25,000, 30 percent on the third $25,000, 40 percent on the fourth $25,000, and 46 percent on amounts in excess of $100,000. Prior to the 1981 legislation, the rates on the first two $25,000 increments of taxable corporate income were 17 percent and 20 percent, respectively. As might be expected, these tax cutting actions were designed to stimulate business investment activity.

In addition to tax-cut provisions, the Economic Recovery Tax Act of 1981 provided for a major overhauling of acceptable methods for depreciating personal and real property used for business purposes. The resulting depreciation schedules became known as the Accelerated Cost Recovery System (ACRS).

Straight-line depreciation provides for a constant dollar write-off annually. However, in an effort to provide for more rapid write-offs (and improved after-tax cash flows due to lower tax payments), tax laws have frequently permitted the use of various accelerated depreciation methods.

The Tax Act of 1981 provided for the use of the ACRS to depreciate recovery property (i.e., property held to produce income or used in a business that is tangible and depreciable). Most business assets were classified into three-year, five-year, and ten-year categories. Real property generally was allowed to be depreciated over 15 years which was a substantially shorter time period compared with past tax laws. No investment tax credit was allowed, as has been the case under prior tax laws, on real property.

Prior to 1981, the class-life depreciation guideline for apartment buildings was 40 years, while the depreciation guideline was 45 years for office buildings and factories. However, "component depreciation" was permitted so that roofs, plumbing, and depreciable contents could be written off over shorter time periods. Component depreciation was prohibited under the 1981 Tax Act.

These higher depreciation write-offs due to a much shorter investment recovery period, along with lower tax rates, resulted in a major increase in building activity and other real estate transactions during the first half of the 1980s. In fact in some sections of the country, "gluts" in office and apartment rental space developed. Although some of the overbuilding undoubtedly can be traced to the attractiveness of real estate investment created by the 1981 Tax Act, the collapse in the energy and related industries contributed to the excess real property problems.

The Tax Reform Act of 1986

The Tax Reform Act of 1986 provided for a substantial further reduction in both individual and corporate income tax rates. Personal income tax rates which had an 11 to 50 percent range (with 15 rate brackets) under the 1981 Tax Act were reduced to a three-bracket (15 percent, 28 percent, and 33 percent) system beginning in 1988. Likewise, the corporate tax rates were reduced to 15 percent on the first $50,000 of taxable income, 25 percent on the next $25,000, and 34 percent on amounts over $75,000.

However, in order to supposedly make the 1986 Tax Act revenue neutral (which was the stated objective), the reduction in tax rates was offset by several important changes. Depreciation schedules were made less attractive, the investment tax credit (which was permitted under the 1981 Tax Act) was repealed, long-term capital gains tax rates were eliminated, and alternative minimum tax rates were initiated.

The 1986 depreciation system relies on the Asset Depreciation Range (ADR) guidelines developed prior to 1981 for classifying assets. While the 1981 ACRS was designed to provide investment incentives, the 1986 tax law attempts to more evenly match class lives with economic lives. Depreciable personal property is assigned to one of six class lives. Most of the 1981 ACRS three-year and five-year property now falls into five-year or seven-year class lives. Depreciation on most personal property is handled using the 200 percent or double-declining balance method with a switch to the straight-line method when it becomes advantageous to do so.

The 1981 depreciation schedule for real property actually was first modified under the 1984 Tax Act. Instead of depreciating real property over a 15-year period, the depreciable life was extended to 19 years. Under the 1986 Tax Act, real property is classified into one of two classes for depreciation purposes and the straight-line depreciation method must be used. Residential rental property is to be depreciated over 27.5 years, whereas nonresidential real property must be written off over a 31.5-year period. Technically, certain special purpose buildings (e.g., telephone communications and agricultural facilities) can qualify for shorter depreciation class lives. The component method of depreciation continues to be prohibited.

The recent trend in the allowed depreciation of real property can be illustrated using a straight-line depreciation example.

	Annual Depreciation Rates
15-Year Life	6.67%
19-Year Life	5.26
27.5-Year Life	3.64
31.5-Year Life	3.17

Under a 15-year depreciation life, 6.67 percent of the investment could be written off annually. This drops to an annual depreciation of only 3.17 percent under a 31.5-year depreciation life. Of course, the use of ACRS under prior tax laws to depreciate 15-year and 19-year real property was even more favorable. Without question the depreciation of real property has moved from a very liberal schedule in 1981 to a much more stringent schedule under the 1986 Tax Act.

The Tax Reform Act of 1986 also impacted on real estate in a number of other ways. "At-risk" rules have been modified. Losses from real estate activities can be deducted only to the extent that an investor is at risk. Prior law exempted real estate activity from at-risk rules. The 1986 tax law also provided for changes in tax credits for low-income housing and for the rehabilitation of buildings.

RECENT COMMERCIAL PROPERTY DEVELOPMENTS

Many commercial real estate values plunged rapidly from their early 1980s highs. Commercial properties in early 1988 could be purchased at 75 percent of their cost in certain areas of the country. Distressed property often was selling below 50 percent of cost. Contributing factors have been the energy bust and overbuilding.

Thrifts' real estate loan losses over the most recent five-year period totaled nearly $23 billion and banks reported nearly $6 billion in real estate losses since 1984. In addition, as a result of declining commercial property values, lenders such as Gibraltar Financial Corporation of Beverly Hills, Allied Bancshares, Inc. of Houston, and First Republic Bank Corporation of Dallas, have written off millions of dollars in real estate investments during 1987.

However, declining commercial property values have been good news for tenants. Rents in Dallas have been cut in half, and concessions persist in Atlanta, Kansas City, and in many other cities throughout the U.S. For further discussion of recent commercial realty developments, see: Richard B. Schmitt, "Binge of Overbuilding Keeps Values Falling in Commercial Realty," *Wall Street Journal* (January 4, 1988) 1, 6.

INVESTMENT YIELDS AND RETURNS

The time value of money concepts discussed in Chapter 8 also may be used to determine rates of return or investment yields which, in turn, provide the basis for making real estate financing and investment decisions. We begin with a general discussion and then follow with consideration of the "net present value" method, which is used to determine whether a required rate of return is achieved on an investment, and conclude with the "internal rate of return" method designed to determine the explicit investment yield.

Single Receipts and Cash Flow Annuities

To illustrate, let's begin with an example involving a $1,000 investment now in raw land. Recall that earlier in the chapter we expected to be able to sell the property for $1,927 at the end of five years. What rate of return would we earn on this investment? We begin with the following expression which re-states the simple present value formula:

$$\text{Present Value} = \text{Future Value (PVIF, } i\%, n \text{ years)}$$
$$\$1,000 = \$1,927(\text{PVIF, } i\%, 5 \text{ years})$$
$$\$1,000/\$1,927 = (\text{PVIF, } i\%, 5 \text{ years})$$
$$.519 = (\text{PVIF, } i\%, 5 \text{ years})$$

Now that we know the PVIF is .519 and the time period between the investment and the cash receipt is five years, we can use Table 8–2 on page 140 to find the i percentage return or yield that equates the present and future values.

Reading across Table 8–2 at five years, we find that the .519 factor occurs in the 14 percent column indicating that this would be the investment return or yield.

Now let's assume that you have the opportunity of investing $100,000 in a piece of income-producing property that will provide you with a cash inflow at the end of each of five years amounting to $30,543.68. What rate of return would be provided by this investment? To begin with, you should recognize that this problem involves the present value of an annuity. Recall that we can express the present value of an annuity as:

$$A_n = PR(\text{PVIFA}, i\%, n \text{ years})$$

or in words

$$\text{Present Value Annuity} = \text{Periodic Receipt}(\text{PVIFA}, i\%, n \text{ years}).$$

To determine the rate of return we want to initially solve for the PVIFA as follows:

$$\$100,000 = \$30,543.68(\text{PVIFA}, i\%, 5 \text{ years})$$
$$\$100,000/\$30,543.68 = (\text{PVIFA}, i\%, 5 \text{ years})$$
$$3.274 = (\text{PVIFA}, i\%, 5 \text{ years})$$

Now that we know the PVIFA is 3.274 and that cash inflows will flow over a five-year period, we can use Appendix B, Table 4, to find the i percentage return or yield that equates the present value of an annuity and the stream of periodic receipts. Reading across the table at five years, we find that 3.274 occurs in the 16 percent column, which indicates that this is the rate of return. Alternatively, we could have added the PVIF values given in Table 8–2 for years one through five for various interest rates until we found a value of 3.274, which occurs, of course, at the 16 percent discount rate.

What if cash flows were to occur more frequently, such as once a month instead of once a year? For example, let's take the position of a lender who makes a $40,000, five-year mortgage loan and requires monthly payments of $889.78. What would be the lender's investment yield? Using the present value equation we have:

$$\$40,000 = \$889.78(\text{PVIFA}, i\%, 60 \text{ months})$$
$$\$40,000/\$889.78 = (\text{PVIFA}, i\%, 60 \text{ months})$$
$$44.955 = (\text{PVIFA}, i\%, 60 \text{ months})$$

Since cash flows occur monthly, we turn to Table 8–4 on page 147 (or the more detailed data in Appendix B, Table 5), and we find that the 44.955 PVIFA for 60 months is found at the 12 percent interest rate, which gives the lender's investment yield.

Let's take this rate of return analysis one step further by looking at a standard $80,000, 30-year mortgage loan requiring monthly payments of $822.89. What would be the rate of return to the lender or the percentage cost to the borrower? We would first determine the present value interest factor for the annuity (PVIFA) as follows:

$$\$80,000 = \$822.89(\text{PVIFA}, i\%, 360 \text{ months})$$
$$\$80,000/822.89 = (\text{PVIFA}, i\%, 360 \text{ months})$$
$$97.218 = (\text{PVIFA}, i\%, 360 \text{ months})$$

The 97.218 PVIFA is found in Table 8–4 for 360 months to provide the lender a yield, and the borrower a cost, of 12 percent.

In addition to monthly loan payments, the borrower may be faced with various prepaid finance charges, including loan application fees, loan commitment fees, and discount points. For our $80,000 mortgage loan example, let's assume that the lender charges two points (2 percent of $80,000), or $1,600, plus $400 in other prepayment fees, for a combined total of $2,000. This means that the borrower has use of only $78,000 ($80,000 – $2,000) but is required to pay back $80,000 plus 12 percent interest over the life of the mortgage loan. This raises the effective interest cost or *annual percentage rate* (APR) that must be reported under Truth in Lending requirements. The APR can be determined by substituting the $78,000 amount into the above present value annuity equation in place of $80,000 as follows:

$$\$78,000 = \$822.89(\text{PVIFA}, i\%, 360 \text{ months})$$
$$\$78,000/\$822.89 = (\text{PVIFA}, i\%, 360 \text{ months})$$
$$94.787881 = (\text{PVIFA}, i\%, 360 \text{ months})$$

This PVIFA falls between the 12 percent PVIFA (97.218331) and the 13 percent PVIFA (90.399605) and requires interpolation to arrive at the APR. We *interpolate* between two interest rates as follows:

$$
\begin{aligned}
(\text{PVIFA}, 12\%, 360 \text{ months}) &= 97.218331 \\
(\text{PVIFA}, 13\%, 360 \text{ months}) &= \underline{90.399605} \\
\text{Difference} &= 6.818726 \\
(\text{PVIFA}, 12\%, 360 \text{ months}) &= 97.218331 \\
\text{Actual PVIFA} &= \underline{94.787881} \\
\text{Difference} &= 2.430450
\end{aligned}
$$

$$(2.430450/6.818726) \times (13\% - 12\%) = .36 \times 1\% = .36\%$$

Adding the proportional .36 percent to the base (lower) interest rate of 12 percent gives an APR of 12.36 percent. APRs are typically rounded to the nearest one fourth of a percent, and thus the rate quoted to the borrower would be 12.25 in this example.

Net Present Value Method

Many real estate financing and investment decisions are made on the basis of whether a minimum rate of return or investment yield is anticipated. The *net present value method* involves the comparison of future cash benefits or inflows, adjusted for the time value of money, against the initial investment cost or outlay. A discount rate that reflects the minimum acceptable investment yield is applied to determine whether the present value of the stream of cash inflows is higher than the investment cost, a condition that would make the project acceptable.

Table 9–5 illustrates the use of a worksheet for calculating the net present value method. The initial property investment or cost outlay is $85,000, with the minimum required rate of return being set at 10 percent. Cash benefits or inflows will occur for five years. However, since the yearly cash inflows are uneven, annual discount factors are taken from a "present value of $1" table such as Table 8–2. The sum or total of the yearly cash flows discounted at a 10 percent rate equals $89,932 and is referred to as the present value of the cash inflows. Subtracting the investment or cost of $85,000 results in a difference or net present value of $4,932. A positive net present value implies that the rate of return is greater than 10 percent.

The net present value method does not usually permit the determination of investment yields or rates of return. In general, once a discount rate has been specified, this method allows us to say whether the rate of return is higher than the discount rate (a positive net present value) or lower than the discount rate (a negative net present value). Negative net present values occur when the investment or cost is greater than the present value of the cash inflows. Of course, if the cost is exactly equal to the present value of the cash flows, then the rate of return equals the discount rate.

TABLE 9–5. Net Present Value Method Worksheet

Date _____

Name _____ Property _____

Investment or Cost ____$85,000____ _____

End of Year	Cash Flow	Discount at _10_% PV of $1	Amount	Discount at ___% PV of $1	Amount	Discount at ___% PV of $1	Amount
1	$20,000	.909	$18,180				
2	$24,000	.826	19,824				
3	$24,000	.751	18,024				
4	$26,000	.683	17,758				
5	$26,000	.621	16,146				
6							
7							
8							
9							
10							
Total			$89,932				
Less Cost			−85,000				
Net PV			$ 4,932				

Internal Rate of Return Method

The *internal rate of return method* is directly related to the net present value method. However, instead of beginning with a specified discount rate, this method seeks to find the interest rate that makes the present value of cash inflows exactly equal to the initial investment or cost. That is, through a trial and error process we find the interest rate or discount rate that will result in a zero net present value.

The reader should recognize that this process of finding the internal rate of return (IRR) is comparable to our finding the interest rate that equates the present value or cost of an investment with a single future cash inflow or with a stream of constant periodic cash receipts. The only difference is that the trial and error process becomes more cumbersome when the cash receipts are not equal in amount.

The internal rate of return method can be illustrated by use of the same problem developed in Table 9–5. Assume that you can make an investment of $85,000 which will produce cash benefits or flows of $120,000 over the next five years. The individual end-of-year flows will be: year 1 ($20,000), year 2 ($24,000), year 3 ($24,000), year 4 ($26,000), and year 5 ($26,000). What yield or rate of return will you earn on the investment?

Table 9–6 illustrates the use of a worksheet for solving problems involving the use of the internal rate of return method. We begin by selecting what seems to be a reasonable discount rate. Let us assume that our first choice was 10 percent. This, of course, produces the same result as the net present value method since a 10 percent discount rate was specified in that example. We know that the interest rate or rate of return on the project is greater than 10 percent because of the $4,932 positive net present value. But how much greater?

In our trial and error process, we must now select a higher rate of discount. Assume that we decided to try 14 percent. The results for discounting at 14 percent, as shown in the middle of Table 9–6, indicate a *negative* net present value of $3,918. This indicates that the correct interest rate is between 10 percent and 14 percent. Working the problem with a 12 percent discount rate results in a net present value close to zero, indicating that the rate of return is slightly greater than 12 percent.

A more accurate measure of the internal rate of return can be determined by linear interpolation using the present value data. Table 9–6 shows that the return is between 12 and 14 percent and we interpolate as follows:

PV of Cash Inflows, 12% = $85,354
PV of Cash Inflows, 14% = 81,082

Difference = $ 4,272
PV of Cash Inflows, 12% = $85,354
Desired PV Cash Inflows = 85,000

Difference = $ 354
(354/$4,272) × (14% – 12%) = .083 × 2% = .17%
12% + .17% = 12.17% IRR

TABLE 9–6. Internal Rate of Return Method Worksheet

Date _____

Name _____ Property _____

Investment or Cost _____$85,000_____   _____

End of Year	Cash Flow	Discount at _10_%		Discount at ___%		Discount at _12_%	
		PV of $1	Amount	PV of	Amount	PV of	Amount
1	$20,000	.909	$18,180	.877	$17,540	.893	$17,860
2	$24,000	.826	19,824	.769	18,456	.797	19,128
3	$24,000	.751	18,024	.675	16,200	.712	17,088
4	$26,000	.683	17,758	.592	15,392	.636	16,536
5	$26,000	.621	16,146	.519	13,494	.567	14,742
6							
7							
8							
9							
10							
			$89,932		$81,082		$85,354
Less Cost			−85,000		−85,000		−85,000
___ Net PV ___			$ 4,932		$−3,918		$ 354

Thus you expect to earn a 12.17 percent rate of return on your $85,000 investment over the next five years.

HEDGING PRICE RISK WITH FINANCIAL FUTURES

During the 1970s and 1980s, changes in interest rates became increasingly more volatile—both in frequency and in magnitude. These interest role patterns and developments have, in turn, accounted for wide fluctuations in the earnings of financial institutions and business firms in general, and those involved in the housing and building industry in particular.

As a result, corporate managers and others have sought ways whereby they might reduce their exposure to *price risk* caused by fluctuations in interest rates. This risk exists because the prices of fixed-income securities or instruments move inversely with changes in associated "market" interest rates. Both lenders (or investors) and borrowers are exposed in the normal course of business to price risk, making it important to examine both sides or views.

A futures contract promises delivery of a specified amount of a particular commodity or financial instrument at a future point in time. *Hedging* is the process of buying or selling a futures contract to "lock-in" a current commodity price or a financial instrument price even though interest rates may change. The remainder of this chapter focuses on examples of possible interest rate hedging by lenders and by mortgage bankers and builders.

Interest Rate Hedging by Lenders

Characteristics of real estate and other business loans made by banks and by savings and loan associations have changed dramatically in recent years. These lenders have moved away from long-term fixed-rate real estate loans and even fixed-rate intermediate-term business loans and have tried to replace them with variable-rate loans. By doing so, these lenders are attempting to shift the risk of fluctuating interest rates to the borrowers, and this is, in turn, causing severe pressures on the building and housing markets.

Why have these lending patterns developed? Prudent financial management requires the application of the *principle of matching maturities,* which emphasizes the need to match the financial institution's average maturity of its assets with the average maturity of its liabilities. This has been shown to be particularly important in reducing liquidity pressures during periods of disintermediation. Commercial banks traditionally have been reasonably good practitioners of the hedging principle, whereas savings and loan associations have not because of their emphasis on long-term real estate mortgage loans financed by short-term savings deposits.

A second dimension of the matching principle has cropped up in recent years as interest rates have reached historically high levels. Thus, in

---

COMPUTER SOFTWARE FOR CALCULATING NET PRESENT VALUES AND INTERNAL RATES OF RETURN

Many financial calculators are available that have been pre-programmed to calculate the net present value (NPV) and the internal rate of return (IRR) for real estate and finance problems. Various computer software packages also have been developed to calculate NPVs and IRRs.

Available for adopters of REAL ESTATE FINANCE is a basic *Decision Assistant* software package to be used with IBM and IBM compatible personal computers. Software programs for determining present values, future values, and mortgage loan amortization schedules were mentioned in Chapter 8.

Decision Assistant also contains software programs for evaluating financing and investment decisions and for determining investment yields or rates of return. Once the timing of cash inflows and outflows are determined, both the net present value and internal rate of return can be easily calculated. Furthermore, the impact (sensitivity) of small changes in cash inflows or outflows on NPVs and IRRs can be easily examined.

REAL ESTATE FINANCE does not make use of, or depend on, this available software. However, we encourage users of this textbook to make use of the *Decision Assistant* in better understanding how the cost and timing of cash flows affect real estate financing and investment decisions.

addition to average maturities, lenders have discovered the need to also manage the amount of their outstanding *rate-sensitive assets* (consumer, business, and real estate loans) relative to their *rate-sensitive liabilities* (deposits, money market certificates, and certificates of deposit). When these liabilities exceed assets, rising interest rates result in the cost of money increasing more rapidly than the return on money, which leads to reduced profits or losses and, in severe cases, to possible failure.

Some lenders have opted to reduce their rate-sensitive risk by focusing on the asset side of their balance sheets. In essence, by switching from long-term fixed-rate real estate loans to shorter rate-sensitive loans, they have sought to achieve a better balance between their rate-sensitive liabilities and assets. The problem is that such lender activities serve to push the risk associated with changing interest rates on to the borrower. This, in turn, makes speculators out of home mortgage borrowers who can ill afford to assume the interest rate risk associated with variable-rate mortgages or short-term loans requiring large balloon payments. As a result, home mortgage borrowers are not always able to depend on lenders to provide traditional 30-year fixed-rate commitments, as has been the traditional common practice since the 1930s.

As an alternative to trying to shift interest rate risk to borrowers, federal regulatory bodies have relaxed restrictions on lenders' taking part in both asset and liability hedges. Actions were taken in early 1980 by the Federal Reserve Board (along with the Comptroller of the Currency and the Federal Deposit Insurance Corporation) concerning reporting requirements by commercial banks, and the Federal Home Loan Bank Board moved to broaden the opportunity for savings and loan associations to participate in financial futures in mid-1981. The result has been an increased interest in both liability and asset hedges.

Liability Hedges. One way of reducing interest rate risk is for the lender to reduce the sensitivity of lender's liabilities to interest rate changes by entering into a *liability hedge*. For example, the rates on money market certificates and certificates of deposit generally can be "locked-in" against future increases in short-term interest rates when the certificates come due and are to be "rolled-over" or replaced with new debt issues. Let's assume that it is early December and a bank has just issued $10 million in 3-month certificates at a 12 percent interest rate. However, management is concerned that interest rates will be substantially higher at the beginning of next March when the certificates are due and new ones are to be issued.

What can be done to offset the higher expected interest rates? One possibility is to sell short $10 million in U.S. Treasury bill futures. Each futures contract is for $1 million face amount of 90-day Treasury bills that are issued on a discount basis. Let's assume that a March contract is currently selling at an 11 percent discount rate or a price of 89.00 (100 − 11) as quoted by the International Monetary Market. Each .01 price change or 1 basis point (1/100 of 1 percent) is worth $25 per contract [$1 million × .0001 × (90/360)].

To provide protection against higher interest rates on its certificates in March, the bank would sell 10 March Treasury bill contracts in December. If interest rates increase to 14 percent on certificates and 13 percent (a price of 87.00) on Treasury bills by the beginning of March, the result of the hedging strategy could be shown as follows:

CASH MARKET	FUTURES MARKET
December	*December*
90-day certificate rate is 12%. Interest cost on $10 million is $300,000 ($10 million × .12 × ¹/₄ yr.).	Sell 10 March T-bill contracts at 11% or a price of 89 (100 −11).
March	*March*
Issue 90-day certificates at 14%. Interest cost on $10 million is $350,000 ($10 million × .12 × ¹/₄ yr.).	Purchase 10 March T-bill contracts at 13% or a price of 87 (100 − 13).

HEDGING TRANSACTION RESULTS

Added cost due to increase in interest rates:
$300,000 − $350,000 =   −$50,000
Gain on sale of Treasury bill futures:
(89 − 87) × 100 = 200 basis pts. gain
200 basis pts. × $25 × 10 contracts =   50,000
Net impact before transaction costs $0

This is an illustration of a so-called "perfect hedge" in that the higher interest costs are exactly offset (ignoring commissions) by the gain on the futures contract. The hedge was perfect because the "basis" or *spread* between the cash certificate rate and the March Treasury bill contract rate remained constant. Normally we state the basis as the cash price less the futures price. Here we are comparing differences in interest rates and thus will subtract the cash rate from the futures rate to determine the basis. Furthermore, since certificates generally have higher yields (because of greater default risk) than Treasury bills, the yield basis will be negative. In the above illustration, the basis of −100 basis points (11 percent − 12 percent) that existed in December when the hedge was initiated also existed at the beginning of March (13 percent − 14 percent) when the hedge position was closed out.[1]

In many instances, the basis between the cash and futures market will change between the date when the hedge is initiated and when the hedge is closed. This is often associated with a change in the *yield curve* in the case of financial futures. The yield curve graphically depicts the relationship be-

---

[1]This type of hedge is also referred to as a *cross hedge* because two different debt instruments are involved. The basis is often more volatile in a cross hedge than in a *straight hedge* involving the same financial instrument in both the cash and futures markets because supply and demand factors often differ across financial instruments.

tween interest rate levels and time to maturity. At any point in time, supply and demand factors might cause the yield curve to be flat, upward sloping, or downward sloping as expressed by the interest rates on short-term debt instruments relative to long-term instruments. Short-term interest rates are particularly volatile in response to changes in (1) Federal Reserve actions on the supply of money and credit, (2) federal government financing of budget deficits, and (3) the spending and savings patterns of businesses and individuals.

For example, the basis of –100 basis points (11 percent – 12 percent) that prevailed in December may have changed to a basis of, say –125 basis points (12.75 percent T-bill futures rate less 14 percent cash certificate rate) by early March. Such an outcome would produce only a partial hedge. Now we would have a selling price on the future's contract of 87.25 (100 – 12.75) for a profit of 175 basis points (89.00 – 87.25). This would then result in a total profit of $43,750 (175 × $25 × 10 contracts). Thus there would be a loss on the hedge of $6,250 due to an increase or widening in the interest rate basis of –25 basis points. We can confirm this loss as follows: (–25 basis pts. × $25 × 10 contracts) = –$6,250. Of course, had the interest rate basis narrowed to, say –75 basis points, then a profit on the hedge of $6,250 would have been realized. At this point it is important to recognize that hedging does not eliminate all risk but rather substitutes basis risk (volatility) for historically greater volatility risk in the cash or futures markets themselves.

What if a lender wanted to hedge for a longer time period such as might be the case with 6-month money market certificates? Ninety-day Treasury bill futures contracts are traded with a variety of delivery months. In December, for example, T-bill contracts will be available for delivery next year in March (as used in the above illustration), June, September, and so forth. Thus a June T-bill contract could be purchased in December to hedge against interest rate increases in money market rates between early December and the beginning of June.

Asset Hedges. The managements of savings and loan associations and other lenders know that rising interest rates can sharply reduce the values of the long-term fixed-rate real estate mortgage loans that they hold. One way of protecting asset values is to enter into an *asset hedge* when rising interest rates are expected. This can be accomplished by selling short futures contracts on U.S. Treasury notes or bonds which are traded on the Chicago Board of Trade and carry face values of $100,000 per contract.

The procedure would be the same as that described for liability hedges. If interest rates rise, the decline in the value of the mortgage loans being held will be offset (at least partially) by the gain on the futures contract.

Interest Rate Hedging by Mortgage Bankers and Builders

Besides real estate lenders, other participants in the housing and building industry might benefit from the use of financial futures to provide protection against the impact of changing interest rates. Hedging strategies could be very beneficial to both mortgage bankers and builder-developers.

Let's begin with a possible mortgage banking example. Mortgage bankers are in the business of originating real estate mortgage loans which are, in turn, resold to permanent investors. Since a period of time often is required to assemble a portfolio or pool of mortgages before delivery takes place, mortgage bankers are subjected to interest rate risk while they are "warehousing" these mortgage pools. It is this risk that can be reduced by hedging with financial futures.

Assume a mortgage banker is in the process of making commitments for several million dollars in new mortgages. U.S. Treasury note futures could be sold short to hedge against rising interest rates until the pool of mortgages is delivered. At delivery the short position would be closed. If interest rates increased between commitment and delivery, the loss on the mortgage pool would be offset, at least partially, by the gain on the T-note futures position.

Now let's consider the possibility of a hedge by a builder-developer who is interested in limiting the interest rate risk associated with the financing cost on construction loans. Interest rates on short-term construction loans frequently are tied to the prime rate that bank lenders offer to their highest quality business borrowers. For example, assume that it is the beginning of September and a builder-developer anticipates entering into a $1 million one-year construction loan in early December that will be fixed at two points above the prime rate. The builder-developer could protect against rising interest rates in the interim by selling one December Treasury bill contract now just as we illustrated earlier in our discussion of liability hedges by lenders. If interest rates actually rise between September and December, the builder-developer will pay, in effect, a higher interest rate on the construction loan, but this will be offset by a profit on the sale of the T-bill futures contract.

Furthermore, if the one-year construction loan "floats" at two points above the prime (instead of being fixed at the time of the loan), the builder-developer might want to hedge against further interest rate rises during the life of the loan. This could be accomplished by selling 90-day T-bill futures contracts having more distant delivery dates. As an alternative, if the floating-rate construction loan was for a period longer than one year, the builder-developer could sell short futures contracts in U.S. Treasury notes or bonds.

KEY TERMS

after-tax cash flow	net present value method
depreciation	price risk
hedging	principle of matching maturities
internal rate of return method	

QUESTIONS FOR REVIEW

1. Describe how cash flows are affected by the size of depreciation write-offs and tax rates.
2. How did the Economic Recovery Tax Act of 1981 affect real estate building activity?
3. Compare and contrast changes in depreciation of real property between the 1981 Tax Act and the Tax Reform Act of 1986.
4. Describe the use of the net present value method for making real estate investment decisions.
5. How is the internal rate of return method used in evaluating real estate investment alternatives?
6. What is the meaning of *price risk?*
7. What is meant by the *principle of matching maturities?*
8. Briefly define a *liability hedge* and describe how it might be used to offset the possibility of higher interest rates in the future.
9. What is an *asset hedge?* Describe how an asset hedge might be used by a real estate lender such as a savings and loan association.
10. Describe how mortgage bankers and builders might benefit from the use of financial futures.

PROBLEMS

1. The following information was available for the first year of an investment project. Revenues were projected to be $80,000 and operating expenses before both interest and depreciation were estimated at $40,000. Interest was expected to be $5,000 and depreciation $10,000. The effective tax rate was estimated to be 30 percent.
   a. Determine the after-tax cash flow for the project.
   b. What would have been the after-tax cash flow if no depreciation write-off had been allowed?
   c. Indicate what would have happened to the after-tax cash flow if passage of a new tax law had lowered the effective tax rate to 25 percent but had reduced the allowed depreciation write-off to $8,000.
2. Commercial property can be purchased for $250,000 now and a selling price of $650,000 is anticipated at the end of 12 years. Determine the rate of return on this investment. What would be the rate of return if the selling price could be obtained after 10 years? Interpolate if necessary in your answers.
3. Assume you have just invested $150,000 in an apartment building that will produce an annual cash inflow of $24,000 for a period of 15 years. What would be the rate of return on your investment? How would the rate of return change if the annual cash inflow had been only $21,000? Interpolate if necessary in your answers.

4. An $80,000, 30-year standard mortgage loan will require monthly payments of $947.90 and in addition the lender charges three points in the form of prepaid finance charges. Determine the effective interest cost or annual percentage rate on this loan. How would the APR change if the payments were $884.96 per month and prepaid finance charges were two points?

5. The Woodleys have just invested in a commercial property costing $400,000. After depreciation and tax, cash inflows are expected to be $90,000 per year for 15 years with no expected reversion or resale value.
   a. Determine the net present value if the required rate of return is 16 percent. Also calculate the internal rate of return.
   b. Now, if a reversion value of $300,000 is expected at the end of 15 years, what will be the net present value? Also calculate the internal rate of return.
   c. If instead of $90,000 per year, you received $7,500 per month, anticipated no reversion value, and required a 14 percent rate of return, what would be the net present value? Also determine the net present value if there is a $300,000 reversion value.
   d. Now assume that the net annual cash inflow (after depreciation, debt servicing costs, and taxes) is expected to be only $80,000 per year but the reversion value is anticipated to be $800,000 at the end of 15 years. Calculate the internal rate of return for this scenario.

6. As an investor in real estate you have an option to buy one of two properties. Property K costs $50,000 and expects to have cash inflows for the next five years of $15,000, $23,000, $15,000, $5,000, and $5,000. Property L also costs $50,000 and the expected five-year cash inflows are $5,000, $15,000, $15,000, $20,000, and $20,000, respectively. Assume a required rate of return of 10 percent.
   a. Based on the net present value method, which, if either, of the two properties would you choose to invest in?
   b. Calculate the internal rate of return for property K and also for property L. Which investment would be preferable?

7. The First National Bank regularly issues certificates of deposit (CDs) to obtain short-term funds. It is the beginning of June and the bank has just sold $30 million in 10 percent certificates that will come due at the beginning of September. Bank officers anticipate that when the certificates come due and are reissued, the interest rate will be substantially higher. Treasury bill futures contracts that call for delivery in late September are currently selling at a price of 88.
   a. Show the procedure and calculations for entering into a hedge of the $30 million in certificates now in early June.
   b. Assume that at the beginning of September the hedge is closed out when the new CD rate is 12 percent and T-bill futures are trading at 86. Show the appropriate hedging transaction results.
   c. Now assume that the T-bill futures price is actually 87 at the beginning

of September when the new CD rate is 12 percent. How are the hedging transaction results affected by this relationship?

d. Show the hedging transaction results if the hedge position is closed at the beginning of September when the new CD rate is 12.5 percent and the T-bill futures price is 85.

PART 4

REAL ESTATE
FINANCING
METHODS

CHAPTER 10
Seller Financing of Real Property

CHAPTER 11
Financing with Junior Liens

CHAPTER 12
Financing by Means of Long-Term Leases

10

SELLER FINANCING OF REAL PROPERTY

LEARNING OBJECTIVES

After studying this chapter, you should be able to do the following:

Define what is meant by a purchase money mortgage and explain how it works.

Describe how the purchase money mortgage is used in the seller financing of both residential real property and commercial property.

Define what is meant by a partial release and describe how it is used.

Explain the tax implications of purchase money financing.

Describe the installment land contract and explain how it is used.

Identify the common clauses contained in an installment land contract.

Explain the meaning of an "interest only" installment land contract.

Define what is meant by an option and describe how it is used in the financing of real property.

IN MANY CASES, it may not only be convenient for the seller to do the financing, but it may be necessary. The need for the seller to do the financing most often arises because financial institutions shy away from the deal due to a lack of good credit on the part of the buyer or because of a "tight" money situation. In addition, there may be legal restrictions placed on the institutions for that particular type of loan. Often a seller may decide to do the financing simply to earn the interest to be paid by the buyer.

THE PURCHASE MONEY MORTGAGE (OR DEED OF TRUST)

A *purchase money mortgage* is a mortgage that is given as part of the consideration for the sale of real property. The seller is really financing, or partially financing, the transaction. In a simple transaction, assume a seller agrees to sell property to a buyer for $50,000 with the buyer paying $10,000 down and the seller "taking back" a mortgage or deed of trust for $40,000. This is done by means of a purchase money mortgage (or purchase money deed of trust).

A mortgage becomes a purchase money mortgage by being created in the mortgage instrument. In other words, a statement spelling out that the instrument is a purchase money mortgage must be written into the mortgage. It is then sometimes colloquially referred to as a "P.M." mortgage.

The Purchase Money Clause

A clause spelling out the existence of the P.M. mortgage and the method of payment is added after the property description and may read as follows:

> Being the same premises which were conveyed by the mortgagor by deed dated March 13, 19-- and delivered and intended to be recorded simultaneously herewith, this mortgage being given to secure a portion of the purchase money or consideration for which the said conveyance was made.

Need for Delivery of Deed

In the clause above note that it states that the mortgage was given and a deed delivered *simultaneously.* The reason for this is that in order to effectuate a P.M. mortgage a crucial condition must be met; namely, that the mortgage be given at the same time the property is acquired and as a *part* of the entire transaction.

Priority of the P.M. Mortgage

The real reason for the simultaneous delivery of deed and the mortgaging is due to the P.M. mortgage's superiority in the priority of liens. Ordinarily it takes preference over all other existing and subsequent claims and liens against and through the borrower. This is because the mortgage is really a limitation on the borrower's title rather than a limitation on the land.

Many states provide for the P.M. mortgage's priority over liens by statute. In those states, it has priority over judgments, dower, and community property.[1]

Warrant of Title Clause in the P.M. Mortgage

All the forms of mortgage previously discussed contain a clause warranting title. This states in effect that the mortgagor warrants title to the premises and that the title is good. This means that the property is free from encumbrances according to the mortgagor's declarations. When the seller "takes back" the P.M. mortgage, the seller signs and delivers the deed to the purchaser, who is the mortgagor. The mortgagor delivers such cash as is being paid to the seller and at the same time signs and delivers the P.M. mortgage to the seller, who is the mortgagee. This exchange raises the question of what should be done with the "warrant of title clause" in the mortgage. Conceivably, the mortgagee (who is the seller in this case) may have a defective title which may be transferred over to the mortgagor (the purchaser); now the purchaser is placed in the position of the warrantor of title as a result of the clause in the mortgage. To avoid this situation, the warrant of title clause should be supplanted with a clause stating that the mortgagor warrants only such title as has been conveyed by the mortgagee. The net effect of this is that the burden of "good title" has been passed back to the seller "mortgagee," who is the logical defender of the title.

The P.M. Mortgage in Seller Financing

The P.M. mortgage is used, of course, in "seller" financing. Its use can be divided into two parts: residential seller financing, and the commercial- or investment-type financing.

Residential Seller Financing. There are three basic situations when this occurs: (1) when the seller owns the property free and clear, (2) when the seller is taking back a second P.M. mortgage (or deed of trust) and the buyer is assuming part of an existing mortgage, and (3) when the seller takes back a P.M. mortgage with a balloon.

For example, in the first case, assume an $80,000 purchase price, seller owning the property free and clear of all encumbrances. A buyer offers $8,000 cash and the seller offers to take back a P.M. mortgage. In this case, the mortgage is for $72,000. Generally, the seller does this if the market interest rate is high and the seller is willing to accept a lower-than-market rate of interest.

The second situation occurs when there is an assumable loan at a fairly low rate of interest with the seller willing to "take back" a second P.M. mortgage at a lower-than-market rate in order to expedite a sale. For example,

---

[1]In Arizona, California, Montana, North Carolina, and Oregon deficiency judgments against P.M. mortgages are prohibited.

assume the purchase price is $90,000 with an assumable loan of $60,000. A buyer has $10,000 in cash, assumes the $60,000 first mortgage, and the seller "takes back" a P.M. mortgage in the amount of $20,000. Often in these situations the pay-off period of the second mortgage is shorter than in the case of the first mortgage.

In the third situation, there is a balloon note payable in a relatively short time—five or seven years. It is often used when a buyer might not have a large enough cash down payment or otherwise qualify for an institutional loan. The thinking is that after, say, five years the buyer will qualify for an institutional loan. For example, the purchase price is $100,000, a buyer has $10,000 in cash, and there is an assumable loan of $70,000. The transaction might be arranged as follows: $10,000 is paid as the down payment, the $70,000 loan is assumed, and the seller takes back a second P.M. mortgage for $20,000 with relatively low monthly payments and a balloon at the end of five years, at which time the buyer will be required to refinance the entire transaction.

The P.M. Mortgage in Commercial Financing. One of the objectives of the "game" appears to be the desire of the builder-developers to obtain as much leverage as possible. One way this can be accomplished is with the P.M. mortgage or P.M. deed of trust.

If a builder-developer buys a parcel of raw or vacant land with a P.M. mortgage, the seller must be made aware of the fact that subsequent financing will be sought. Therefore, the first P.M. mortgage will have to be subordinated to subsequent financing. To induce the seller to do this, generally the following arguments are given by the builder-developer.

1. There will be *no* sale unless the seller's consent is secured.
2. The value of the property will rise after the development is in place.
3. A faster payout will be given to the seller than on an ordinary P.M. mortgage.

If the seller agrees, then a *self-executing* subordination clause is written into the mortgage. In short, if subsequent development financing is obtained, the first P.M. mortgage of the seller automatically becomes a second lien.

In return for this, the seller will generally insist on a clause to the effect that in the event of a sale of the property by the builder-developer, either all or part of the P.M. mortgage will be paid.

Suspension of Payment Clause in a P.M. Mortgage

In recent years a new clause has been added to the P.M. mortgage by builder-developers (mortgagors). This is done especially when the builder-developers plan a subdivision. In effect, the clause states that if a local governmental entity refuses to issue building permits because of the effects of the proposed subdivision on ecology, environment, or water facilities, or if building is prohibited because of governmental order, payments on principal will be suspended.

The Partial Release

The *partial release* is the instrument that is employed to release part of the mortgaged premises from the terms of the mortgage. It simply recites the mortgage, the amount paid for the release, and a description of the part of the mortgaged premises that has been released. The instrument is acknowledged and recorded in the office of the county clerk in the county in which the property is located.[2] The effect of this instrument is that part of the property is no longer subject to the mortgage. The owner may then, if desired, obtain a new mortgage on the parcel so released.

A partial release is shown in Figure 10–1.

Use of the P.M. Mortgage by Home Builders

Often a combination blanket P.M. mortgage containing a partial release clause is the favorite instrument of the home builder who operates with little cash and who can't afford to tie up capital in land. For example, A is a builder and B has 100 lots for sale. A arranges a transaction with B that requires very little cash down. After A has gone to a bank and has received a tentative commitment for a construction loan, A approaches B and offers $2,000 per lot. A proposes to B to pay $200 cash down for each of the lots and to give B a blanket P.M. mortgage covering $1,800 per lot for the balance due. This is accepted by B. A insists that the mortgage contain a partial release clause to the effect that upon the payment of $1,800, B will release from the terms of the mortgage any one of the lots that A desires. B agrees to all of this, and A pays out only 10 percent cash at this point, begins building, and obtains a commitment from a bank. When A has built enough of the house to satisfy the bank appraiser, B is paid for one lot (the $1,800 due), and A receives cash from the bank, finishes the building, and sells it for a profit.

This hypothetical problem is, of course, an oversimplification, but not completely. The only variations in the figures given would depend upon the bargaining position of the parties. A, the builder, might have to put down more than 10 percent cash, but, in the final analysis, this type of financing can be done with very little money.

The practitioner will recognize at once that there are "two sides to every coin." If the seller and the builder do make a deal as far as a price is concerned, should the seller draw up the partial release clause releasing one lot for the payment of the balance due on that one lot? It is thought that it might offer more protection to the seller to have A, the builder and mortgagee, pay off, let us say, $2,000 on each lot released, the extra $200 to be applied toward the payment of the principal on the balance of the mortgage. This would mean that the entire balance would be completely paid after the remainder of the lots had been released from the terms of the mortgage. It might be stated here that the seller should take another precautionary measure in the transaction outlined above.

---

[2]In Connecticut the instrument is recorded in the office of the town clerk.

RELEASE OF PART OF MORTGAGED PREMISES

THIS INDENTURE, made the   18th day of June   nineteen hundred and — ——

BETWEEN   Jenny C. Foster, residing at 361 First Street, Amityville, County of Suffolk, State of New York,

party of the first part, and   Denise Plant, residing at 1492 North 115th Street, Amityville, County of Suffolk, State of New York,

party of the second part,

WHEREAS, the party of the first part is the holder of the following mortgage   and of the bond—or note secured thereby:

Mortgage dated the 14th day of   July   , 19-- , made by Denise Plant

to   Jenny C. Foster

in the principal sum of $ 30,000   and recorded in (Liber) (Record Liber) (Reel)
   16   of section 8   of mortgages, page   in the office of the Clerk   of the County
of Suffolk

covering certain lands and tenements, of which the lands hereinafter described are part, and

WHEREAS, the party of the first part, at the request of the party of the second part, has agreed to give up and surrender the lands hereinafter described unto the party of the second part, and to hold and retain the residue of the mortgaged lands as security for the money remaining due on said mortgage   ,

NOW THIS INDENTURE WITNESSETH, that the party of the first part, in pursuance of said agreement and in consideration of   Fifteen Thousand and 00/100 ($15,000.00) --------------

-- Dollars,
lawful money of the United States,
paid by the party of the second part, does grant, release and quitclaim unto the party of the second part, all that part of said mortgaged lands described as follows:
Lots numbers 1 and 16 of the Map of Security Acres Development Company, surveyed by Rebecca Johnson, April 1, 19-- and recorded in the office of the Clerk of the County of Suffolk, August 7, 19--.

TOGETHER with all right, title and interest, if any, of the party of the first part in and to any streets and roads abutting the above described premises to the center lines thereof and in and to any fixtures and articles of personal property which are now contained in said premises and which may be covered by said mortgage.

TOGETHER with the hereditaments and appurtenances thereunto belonging, and all right, title and interest of the party of the first part, in and to the same, to the intent that the lands hereby released may be discharged from said   mortgage   , and that the rest of the lands in said
     mortgage   specified may remain mortgaged to the party of the first part as heretofore.

TO HAVE AND TO HOLD the lands and premises hereby released and quitclaimed to the party of the second part, and to the heirs, successors and assigns of the party of the second part forever, free, clear and discharged of and from all lien and claim under and by virtue of said   mortgage aforesaid.

IN WITNESS WHEREOF, the party of the first part has executed this release the day and year first above written.

IN PRESENCE OF:
/s/ Richard Roe   /s/ Jenny C. Foster

(Acknowledgment)
Standard Form of New York Board of Title Underwriters

FIGURE 10–1. Release of Part of Mortgaged Premises

As all practitioners know, different lots in a block have a different value as a general rule; hence, the partial release clause should be drawn in terms of at least two lots being paid for in full by the purchaser and released at the same time. One lot will be considered to be of greater value than the other. This will effectively avoid the seller's being "stuck" with the poorer lots in the event the builder becomes financially embarrassed before the mortgage has been completely paid.

Tax Implications of P.M. Financing

It is important in P.M. financing, or any other type of financing for that matter, to be aware of the new rules for depreciation under the 1986 Tax Reform Act. It is especially important in the P.M. mortgage because of the need to determine the adjusted basis of the property sold in order to calculate the profit from the sale.

Recovery Allowances for Depreciable Property. The 1986 Act has dictated the useful life of rental properties. Most rental properties are divided into two classes, residential property and nonresidential property, and the recovery allowances are as follows:

1. Recovery allowances for residential properties are calculated at a straight-line rate based on a recovery period of 27.5 years.
2. For nonresidential real estate, the cost recovery amount is determined by using a straight-line rate over a 31.5-year recovery period.

Using the Installment Method to Report Gain. A gain from the sale of residential property may be reported on the installment method. For example, if a property is sold for $120,000 with $20,000 down and an adjusted basis of $100,000, the profit is $20,000 ($120,000 − $100,000). When electing to *defer* the tax using the installment method, profit is 20 percent of the adjusted basis (i.e., $20,000/$100,000), so consequently 20 percent of each installment (the initial down payment and each subsequent payment) is considered taxable gain. Suppose there are to be four annual installments after the down payment the first year and each installment is $20,000, then:

Year 1	$ 20,000 down	× .20 =	$ 4,000 taxable gain
Year 2	20,000 payment	× .20 =	4,000 taxable gain
Year 3	20,000 payment	× .20 =	4,000 taxable gain
Year 4	20,000 payment	× .20 =	4,000 taxable gain
Year 5	20,000 payment	× .20 =	4,000 taxable gain
Adjusted Basis $100,000		Profit	$20,000

In general, the installment method outlined above may be used on the sale of real property used in a trade or business or rental income property sold for $150,000 or less.

THE REVENUE ACT OF 1987

Despite the name of the 1987 Act, it was actually a law passed by Congress to correct some of the mistakes and omissions of the 1986 Act. It contained a number of provisions relating to installment sales:

1. Dealers in both real and personal property were barred from using the installment method of reporting sales in the taxable years beginning after December 31, 1987. One exception to the ban on installment sales reporting by dealers applies to sellers of timeshares and residential lots who *elect* to pay interest on the amount of tax deferred by reason of installment selling.

2. The 1986 Act provided for what was called the "proportional disallowance rule." This rule was nearly incomprehensible and the 1987 Act repealed it.

3. Rules for nondealers of real property selling for over $150,000 were modified to include a special rule to (a) require nondealers to pay interest on the deferred tax resulting from installment reporting, and (b) treat as payment on an installment obligation (mortgage) the pledging of that obligation as security for an indebtedness. This rule applies *only* to installment obligations from sales of nonfarm real property used in the taxpayer's trade or business or held for the production of rental income where the selling price is over $150,000. Under the rule, nondealer sales of real property for less than $150,000 are reportable under the installment method and interest is not charged on the deferred tax. Even when the price exceeds $150,000, there is an interest charge *only* if the total face amount of the installment obligation arising during the year, and still outstanding at the end of the year, exceeds $5,000,000.

THE INSTALLMENT LAND CONTRACT

The *installment land contract* (or *contract for deed*) was historically used in the sale of vacant lots, generally with a small down payment and small monthly payments until the balance was paid. After the final payment a deed was delivered to the buyer. Under such an agreement the seller retains title to the property. In this sense it differs from the purchase money mortgage where title is delivered to the buyer at the time of the execution of the agreement.

Over time the installment land contract began to be used to finance homes, vacant land, and particularly farms and ranches. In practice the instrument began to be called "contract for deed," "land contract," and even "real estate contract." This sort of careless usage often confused it with the simple Contract for the Sale of Real Property or Purchase Agreement.

In a simple real estate transaction, a deed is delivered by a seller to a buyer. It is said that "legal title" passes to the buyer. *Title* is defined as the means whereby the owner of lands has the just possession of the property.

However, in a contract for deed legal title remains with the seller until the property is paid for. The buyer is said to have "equitable" title, which gives buyer the right of possession and an obligation to maintain the property and bear the risk of loss.

A simplified form of installment land contract is shown in Figure 10–2. It can, of course, be more complex than this illustration. In all cases an attorney should be consulted to actually prepare the contract.

The Installment Land Contract Must Be a Valid Contract

An installment land contract is governed by the law of contracts. It is an agreement resulting from an offer and acceptance. The parties must be identified and competent. There must be genuine assent (this means no fraud, duress, undue influence, or mistake). The subject matter must be identified and the terms definite and certain. There must be consideration. Because it is a contract for the sale of land, the Statute of Frauds must be satisfied.

The Statute of Frauds

The *Statute of Frauds* involves contracts which must be in writing to be enforceable. One section of the statute requires that contracts relating to real property must be in writing in order to be enforceable. If *A* agrees with *B* to purchase a lead pencil for the price of $1 and *A* agrees orally to deliver the pencil and then fails to do so, *B* may bring an action against *A* for any damages suffered.

If the same situation takes place, except that the oral agreement contemplates the transfer of *real property* rather than personal property, and *A* fails to keep the bargain, *B* will be unable to bring a successful action against *A,* for oral contracts concerning many real estate transactions are void under the Statute of Frauds.

For example, Section 259 of the New York Real Property Law is as follows:

> A contract for the leasing for a longer period than one year, or for the sale of any real property or an interest therein, is void unless the contract, or some note or memorandum thereof, expressing the consideration, is in writing, subscribed by the party to be charged, or by his lawful agent, thereunto authorized in writing.

The other states' statutes are substantially the same.

Of what then must this memorandum in writing consist to render a contract for the sale of real property enforceable? There are four things that must be done to bring the contract for the sale of real property into compliance with the Statute of Frauds. The memorandum must have a date, the terms of payment, a description of the property, and it must bear the signature of the party to be charged. The party to be *charged* is the person against whom the suit is brought. In practice both parties generally sign because no

CONTRACT FOR DEED

This contract for deed entered into this   3rd   day of   June   , 19--
by and between   Jane Doe   , residing at 1411 Mason Ct, Dayton, Ohio   ,
party of the first part, and   J.J. DeFoe , party of the second part residing at 501 Mary-
crest Lane, Dayton, Ohio

Witnesseth:

That for and in consideration of the payments hereinafter agreed to be made and the mutual covenants hereinafter set forth, the party of the first part agrees to sell and convey to the party of the second part, by good and sufficient warranty deed, the following described property to wit:

(Property description goes here).

The party of the second part agrees to purchase the above described property for the sum of   Fifty thousand dollars ($50,000)   , said amount to be paid in the following manner:

```
          The sum of Ten thousand dollars ($10,000) on signing of this agreement,
receipt of which is hereby acknowledged.
          The sum of Ten thousand dollars ($10,000) on or before November 1, 19--.
          The balance of Thirty thousand dollars ($30,000) to be paid in annual
installments of Three thousand dollars ($3,000) each, the first installment to
be paid on the 1st day of November, 19-- and the first day of November each
year thereafter.  It is agreed that the annual payment shall include interest
at 14 percent per annum.
```

It is agreed that the party of the second part is to have the privilege of prepaying any part of the unpaid balance at any time during the contract period without penalty.

It is agreed that the party of the second part shall have possession of the above described property from and after the date hereof.

It is agreed that the party of the second part is to pay all taxes levied upon said property prior to delinquency.

It is understood that the party of the first part has executed a good and sufficient Warranty Deed granting and conveying the above described property to the party of the second part and that said deed, a copy of this contract, and the Abstract of Title to the above premises, continued to date and showing merchantable title to the premises to be vested in the party of the first part free of encumbrances will be placed in escrow (name of escrow agent) and that said escrow agent acting as agent for both parties is instructed to deliver said deed and abstract to the party of the second part upon receipt of final payment as recited herein. It is further agreed that the second party shall have the right to examine said abstract at any time within ninety days after the date hereof and should said examination disclose any defect the first party shall take immediate steps to correct such defect or defects.

In the event the party of the second part shall default in the performance of any of the terms, covenants, conditions or obligations of this agreement assumed by the party of the second part, the parties agree that the party of the first part shall have the option to declare all deferred balances due and payable. Said option shall be exercisable by giving to the party of the second part at his address in   Dayton, Ohio   , by certified mail, thirty days written notice of the nature of such default. In the event of the failure of the party of the first part to cure such default within such thirty-day period, then all such deferred balances shall be due and payable at the end of such thirty-day period, the parties of the first part shall have the right to retake possession of the property described above and to retain all payments made by the party of the second part and all improvements made by them in the premises as liquidated damages for the breach of this agreement, accurate damages being incapable of ascertainment.

It is mutually agreed by and between the parties hereto that time of payment shall be an essential part of this agreement and that all the covenants and agreements herein contained shall be binding on the heirs, executors, administrators, and assigns of the respective parties.

FIGURE 10–2. Installment Land Contract

In witness whereof, both parties have hereunto set their hands and seals the day and year first above written.

_____ L.S.
/s/ Jane Doe

_____ L.S.
/s/ J.J. DeFoe

(Acknowledgment)

FIGURE 10–2. Installment Land Contract (concluded)

one knows ahead of time who is going to sue whom if it comes to that.

Uses of the Installment Land Contract

The installment land contract is used by builders in one of three ways: (1) to finance a subdivision; (2) to finance the sale of homes; and (3) for additional financing.

In the first instance, a builder will buy developed vacant lots from a subdivider under a blanket land contract. The down payment is generally minimal. The builder who has a line of credit with a commercial bank borrows most of the construction costs, builds the home, and then sells it. At the time of the sale the improved lot is paid for and is released from the terms of the contract. In this way the builder avoids having to have the money with which to buy the vacant land and the money necessary to put in roads, sewers, and so forth.

Builders and individual sellers often use the installment land contract to finance the sale of homes. For example, A desires to purchase a home and has insufficient funds for the down payment satisfactory to a financial institution. The builder or owner may enter into an installment contract with A providing that, when enough has been paid on the contract to satisfy a lending institution, the balance of the purchase price will be financed by an FHA loan or other suitable loan.

The question is, Why would a builder or individual seller do this? Obviously most builders would prefer to have the buyer pay the down payment and have an institution lend the buyer the balance. In the above case the builder would be "out" the money. If a builder has failed to arrange for permanent financing and a tight money situation arises, the builder may be unable to arrange for a financial institution loan. At the same time the builder has to pay interest on the construction loan on the property, and paying this sort of interest can be a disaster to a builder. The builder reasons that if sales cannot be made on a contract, at least the interest paid on the contract by the buyer will be enough to pay the interest on the construction loan.

In the last case, builders sometimes use contracts for additional financing. Although some builders have a strong line of credit with financial institutions, many do not. Thus, the installment land contract is used as collateral for personal notes; i.e., a builder may borrow additional sums by pledging installment land contracts in a portfolio.

Installment Contract Used in the Sale of Farms and Ranches

Financial institutions, for the most part, tend to shy away from farm and ranch financing. What little farm and ranch financing is done by institutions is hardly ever done with greater than a 60 percent loan-to-value ratio. For example, a 100-cow ranch, by a very rough rule-of-thumb appraisal, is worth $200,000. With a 60 percent loan-to-value ratio, this means institutions are reluctant to lend more than $120,000, requiring a substantial down payment of $80,000. This makes the property difficult to sell. Furthermore, many ranches on today's market were bought by "old timers" who would rather sell on an installment sale for tax purposes. This results in the extensive use of the installment land contract in farm and ranch sales with its smaller down payment, interest to the seller, and a tax advantage to the seller.

Common Clauses in an Installment Land Contract

The clauses in an installment land contract are much the same as in the mortgage. For example, the buyer promises to pay the indebtedness, taxes, and insurance; keep the premises in good repair; and not commit waste.

Furthermore, the buyer agrees that upon default all payments previously made are forfeited. Because of the severity of this penalty, many states prohibit strict forfeiture. This topic will be discussed in detail in Chapter 18.

The Mortgage Clause. This clause permits the seller to mortgage the property for an amount not to exceed the contract balance, in which case the mortgage is given priority over the contract. For example, the buyer owes the seller $50,000 on the contract. The seller may mortgage this for $50,000. If the seller defaults, the argument is that the buyer will not be hurt because the buyer can pay off the $50,000 due the seller on the mortgage.

Escrow Provision. Installment land contracts contain an escrow provision. *Escrow* may be defined as a scroll, writing, or deed delivered by the grantor into the hands of a third person to be held by the latter until the happening of a contingency or the performance of a condition, and then delivered by the third person to a grantee.[3]

The escrow clause in the contract states:

---

[3]Like the term "contract" or "agreement to purchase," the word *escrow* has many meanings. In California, Colorado, Idaho, Minnesota, Nevada, Oregon, and Washington, in addition to the escrow provision in an installment land contract, escrow means something quite different. In those states it is a step in a real estate transaction. Once a binding contract exists, the parties "open an escrow." The escrow agent has the transfer documents drawn, cash is impounded for future delivery, demands are made on existing loans, title is examined, and if necessary cleared, and prorations are calculated. Finally the deal is closed by transfer of title.

> The seller within . . . days from the date of this contract will deposit in
> escrow with . . . [the name of the escrowee is entered here], a good
> and sufficient deed together with an executed copy of this contract and
> such other documents including abstract of title or title insurance policy
> and fire insurance policies which shall pertain to this contract, to be by
> such escrow agent held in escrow until the terms of this contract shall be
> completely executed, or until default is made under the same. The terms
> of such deposit in escrow shall be given by separate escrow agreement
> to be at the same time executed.

The escrow agent, who is usually a bank or the escrow department of a
brokerage firm or title insurance firm, is paid a fee for holding the instruments
in escrow. The agent collects the monthly or annual payments on the contract
from the purchaser and turns the receipts over to the seller.

From the viewpoint of the buyer it is most important that the deed
signed by both husband and wife (if the sellers are married) be placed in
escrow. There are three main reasons for this: (1) in case of divorce either or
both parties may refuse to sign the deed, which can result in costly and time-
consuming litigation; (2) in the event of the death of the seller or sellers the
property can be tied up in an estate settlement; and (3) if one of the sellers is a
wife, she may refuse to release her dower interests, if any, after final payment
has been made.

Once an escrow agent is decided upon, the installment land contract, together with a deed, is sent to the escrow agent. This is done by means
of a Letter of Transmittal similar to the one shown in Figure 10–3 on the next
page.

Recording of Installment Land Contracts

An instrument affecting the title to land may be recorded in all states. In so
doing, notice is given to the "world" of the existence of the contract. In order
to record the contract it must be acknowledged; that is, the signature of the
seller and buyer must be witnessed by a notary public or other authorized
official.

From the viewpoint of the buyer it should be recorded because it
provides a greater degree of protection.

Effect of Judgments on Installment Land Contracts

Naturally any judgment of record against the seller prior to the contract is a
lien upon any land held by the seller. However, any judgment filed after the
contract does not become a lien on the buyer's real estate even though legal
title is still in the name of the seller. This is especially true after the contract
has been recorded.

The argument is that the judgment creditor can be paid through
court action as the buyer makes payments to the seller.

LETTER OF TRANSMITTAL

To _____   Date _____

_____   Net Escrow $ _____

_____

_____ as SELLERS,

whose address is _____ and

_____ as BUYERS,

whose address is _____

hereby employ the organization named above to act as Escrow Agent.

   We hand you herewith the following papers and documents as checked:

_____ Warranty Deed	_____ Mortgage
_____ Quit Claim Deed	_____ Release of Mortgage
_____ Contract for Deed	_____ Bill of Sale
_____ Abstract	_____ Insurance Policy
_____ Note	_____ Misc. Papers (Itemize Below)

_____

_____

Description of Property _____
(Full Legal Not Necessary)

_____

   Terms of Sale: Gross Sale Price $_____; Down Payment $_____;

Unpaid Balance $_____; Interest Starts: _____;

Manner of Payment: _____

_____

   Special Provisions: (If any) _____

_____

Proceeds to be _____

   BUYER and SELLER agree to pay herewith an Escrow Fee of $_____ and SELLER agrees to pay $_____ per payment thereafter until fully paid and authorize Escrow Agent to deduct this amount from proceeds.

   SELLER agrees that the escrow agent is authorized to affix revenue stamps in the sum of $_____ and deduct same from the last payment before delivery of deed.

   BUYER and SELLER agree that "The escrow agent's sole responsibilities hereunder are to keep safely the documents entrusted to it and to account for and remit moneys paid to it less its agreed fee. The escrow agent shall not be responsible for:

   (a) Payment of taxes;
   (b) Payment of liability or hazard insurance;
   (c) Giving notice of nonpayment to any party;
   (d) Safekeeping of abstract removed at request of either party;
   (e) Recording of contract."

BUYER_____   SELLER_____
BUYER_____   SELLER_____

   Receipt of above papers and escrow fee of $_____
acknowledged this _____ day of _____ 19_____.

_____

_____
Authorized Signature

FIGURE 10–3. Letter of Transmittal

"Interest Only" Land Contracts

Such a contract is often used in the sale of vacant land where the seller finances the transaction either with a land contract or a purchase money mortgage (deed of trust).

Suppose, for example, you have 20 acres of raw land and you are really not hurting for cash. You advertise the property, "no down payment, interest only." To begin with, because there is no down payment, you can probably charge an interest rate somewhat higher than the market rate. In addition, you may be able to charge somewhat higher than the going price for the land.

In these cases, most of the buyers are speculators who hope to sell to developers in the near future. Say you want $5,000 per acre and "interest only" for three years at 12 percent. Then the selling price is $100,000 covered by a mortgage and interest at $12,000 per year. Your buyer during the three-year period attempts to sell the land at a profit. If the buyer fails to do so, or fails to pay the interest, you may foreclose.

As a practical matter, this sort of buyer will probably give you a deed in lieu of foreclosure to avoid the additional expense of foreclosure.

THE OPTION AS A SELLER'S FINANCING METHOD

Simply put, an *option* is a contract to keep an offer open. Because an option is a contract, a seller cannot withdraw an offer until after the time stipulated in the contract. An option to purchase is shown in Figure 10–4.

Use of Option by Builders

Frequently a small builder will operate by means of an option taken on a relatively small number of lots. The builder will do this when uncertain whether the houses will sell readily and when the builder wishes or needs to remain in a financially liquid position. For example, if there are ten lots in which a builder is interested, one lot can be purchased outright and an option obtained from the seller on the other nine. After the first house is built and sold, the builder may, if the first house was profitable, exercise the option on the other nine lots.

In a situation of this type, the seller should, depending upon bargaining position, insist that the builder exercise the option on at least two lots at a time. If the lots vary in their price because some are more valuable than others, the owner might examine the possibility of the optionee's exercising the option on a high-priced lot and a low-priced lot at the same time. Otherwise, the builder might exercise the option on just the choice lots and leave the seller with the poorer ones. This is particularly applicable in a situation where there is a flat price per lot. If the purchaser exercised the option on the choice lots only, the seller would obviously be left in an unprofitable position if the builder discontinued the operation.

OPTION TO PURCHASE

THIS INDENTURE, made the   day of   , 19--, between
                              , residing at   , party of the first
part, and   , residing at
party of the second part,

WITNESSETH:

IN CONSIDERATION of the sum of   paid by the party of the second part
to the party of the first part, receipt whereof is hereby acknowledged, the party of the first part
hereby grants, bargains, and sells to the party of the second part   heirs, executors,
administrators, successors and assigns, the exclusive option to purchase the premises known as
                              , more particularly described in the form of agreement hereto an-
nexed and made a part hereof,[1]

UPON THE FOLLOWING TERMS AND CONDITIONS:

FIRST: This option and all rights and privileges shall expire on the   day of
                              , 19--, at

SECOND: This option is to be exercised by the party of the second part by written notice sub-
scribed by the party of the second part, sent by registered mail, within the time set herein for the
exercise of this option, to the address of the party of the first part above set forth.

THIRD: The total purchase price shall be the sum of   to be paid by the party
of the second part, if this option is exercised, as provided in the said annexed form of agreement
the sum paid for this option shall be credited on account of the cash payment to be made on closing title as provided in the said annexed form of agreement.

FOURTH: In the event that the party of the second part does not exercise this option as herein
provided the said sum of   shall be retained by the party of the first part free of
all claim of the party of the second part and neither party shall have any further rights or claims
against the other.

FIFTH: In the event that this option is exercised as herein provided, the party of the first part
and the party of the second part will respectively as Seller and Purchaser, perform the obligations
stated in the annexed form of agreement to be performed by the Seller and Purchaser therein.

SIXTH: This option and all rights hereunder shall be freely assignable, and if assigned by the
party of the second part, any and all acts performable by   hereunder (including the
execution and delivery of the purchase money bond and mortgage) may be performed by any
assignee, whether such assignment be before or after the exercise of this option.

IN WITNESS WHEREOF the party of the first part has signed and sealed this indenture the
day and year first above written.

L.S.

In the presence of

(ACKNOWLEDGMENT)

[1]A contract for sale of real property, complete except for execution, is annexed to the option.

FIGURE 10–4.   Option to Purchase

The Rolling Option

Many of the larger developers and subdividers use what they have labeled "the rolling option." It is simply a device to free capital and minimize risk. For example, a subdivider may have in mind to subdivide 150 acres. The subdivider may choose to purchase the 150 acres and subdivide it all at one time. However, if this is done, a large amount of capital is tied up and the subdivider faces a risk of loss in the event the project fails. Consequently, to avoid this risk the subdivider simply enters into an option agreement with the seller of the land which could be substantially as follows: 50 acres are purchased outright and an option is given to buy the second 50 within a stated time; then the subdivider has a further option to buy the third 50-acre tract within a stated time. Thus, if the subdivider fails on the first 50-acre tract project, there is no obligation to buy the second or third 50-acre tracts. If things go well, the whole tract will be subdivided, with options exercised as needed.

Use of Option by Speculators

Speculators frequently use an option. For example, suppose you see a property you believe to be underpriced. Say it's $20,000 and you really think you can resell it for $30,000. Instead of buying it for $20,000 and freezing that much capital, you can get an option on the property. If you succeed, you then may get a buyer for $30,000. In this case you simply assign the option to the buyer and the buyer exercises the option. The buyer pays you $10,000 and pays the optioner $20,000, or a total of $30,000, in return for a deed. Your profit is $10,000 minus the cost of the option.

　　As a general rule, the longer the option period the more you have to pay for it.

Lease with Option to Buy

Often, when a tenant erects a building upon the premises owned by the landlord, the lease contains an option giving the tenant the right to purchase the improvement and the land at the end of the term. The option may state a price to be paid for the property, or the option may provide that if the lessor and the lessee are unable to negotiate a price, then the lessor and the lessee shall each appoint an appraiser. The appraisers shall then appoint an umpire. Each of the appraisers and the umpire appraise the property. In general, the lease states that the decision of any two appraisers (one of whom is the umpire) as to the price shall be binding on the parties. In the event that the third party then refuses to accept the decision of the other two, it has been held in most states that the proper remedy for the enforcement of the option to purchase at an appraised valuation is by specific performance.

　　The lease with option to buy is sometimes used as a financing device in the purchase of a residence. For example, the price of the home is agreed upon at $75,000. The tenant moves in under a lease and is given an option to buy the home for $75,000, provided the option is exercised within a stated time. The tenant also agrees to pay rent. More often than not an agreed percentage of the rent is applied to the $75,000 purchase price.

KEY TERMS

escrow
installment land contract
option
partial release

purchase money mortgage
Statute of Frauds
title

QUESTIONS FOR REVIEW

1. What is a *purchase money mortgage?* Briefly describe some of the important characteristics of such a mortgage.
2. How is the P.M. mortgage used in seller financing? Give examples.
3. Describe how home builders make use of the P.M. mortgage.
4. Identify some of the tax implications associated with P.M. mortgage financing.
5. How does an installment land contract differ from a mortgage and from a deed of trust?
6. A number of clauses are contained in an installment land contract. Briefly explain (a) the mortgage clause, and (b) the escrow provision.
7. Briefly describe an "interest only" land contract.
8. Identify and describe how an option can be used by a seller of real property.

PROBLEMS

1. Assume that you own two residential properties. Property *M* has a selling price of $100,000 and property *O* has a $130,000 price. You own property *M* "free and clear" while you have a $60,000, 10 percent assumable first mortgage on property *O*. While the going mortgage interest rate is 14 percent, you are willing to "take-back" P.M. mortgages on each property at a 12 percent interest rate. A potential buyer for property *M* has $15,000 in cash for a down payment, while $20,000 is available from a potential buyer for property *O*.
   a. How could you prepare an acceptable seller financing arrangement for property *M?*
   b. Develop the financing scenario that would be necessary to complete the sale of property *O*. What might be negotiable in this type of P.M. mortgage?
2. A home owned for several years by Jane Williams is for sale at a price of

$120,000. There is an assumable first mortgage on the home amounting to $50,000. Ralph Richey is interested in purchasing the home but has only $20,000 for a down payment. Jane Williams is willing to "take back" a P.M. mortgage at a 10 percent interest rate. The adjusted cost basis of the home to Jane Williams is $80,000. The P.M. mortgage transaction will be treated as an installment sale for tax purposes. Installment payments are to be made over four years after the first year's down payment.

a. Determine Jane Williams' gross profit on the home sale. Also show the contract price.

b. What will be the taxable gain that Jane Williams will report in the year of the sale?

c. Determine the taxable gain that is to be reported each year by Jane Williams under the installment sale arrangement.

3. Farm and ranch financing is often difficult to obtain. In addition, loan-to-value ratios tend to be much lower than those for financing homes. If a loan-to-value ratio is set at 60 percent, how could a ranch appraised at $150,000 be purchased? Could you purchase the ranch with a $40,000 down payment? Why might the seller be interested in entering into an installment land contract?

11

FINANCING WITH JUNIOR LIENS

LEARNING OBJECTIVES

After studying this chapter, you should be able to do the following:

Define what is meant by a junior lien and describe how it is used in residential transactions and with commercial loans.

Describe the process of discounting loans.

Identify and describe how junior liens are used to increase leverage and to lower cash down payments.

Explain the purpose and use of a subordination agreement or clause.

Define what is meant by a call second mortgage and explain how it is used.

Identify residential and commercial sources of junior lien funds.

THE GENERAL RULE regarding the priority of liens is "first in time, first in right." This refers to time of recording the instrument, not the length of time of the instrument. For example, if A gives a mortgage to B today and another to C tomorrow, if C records prior to B, then C has the first lien. Subsequent recording by B gives B the second, or junior, lien. In the absence of fraud, C will win over B. B, of course, may have a legal cause of action against A.

THE JUNIOR LIEN AS A FINANCING DEVICE

A *junior mortgage* (second mortgage, second deed of trust, or second land contract) is a mortgage that is subordinate to another mortgage. It is used as a financing device in both residential and commercial real property transactions.

A *lien* is a legal claim that is placed against property as security for payment of a debt. A second purchase money mortgage, a second contract for deed, and a so-called wraparound mortgage all are examples of a *junior lien.*

Use in Residential Transactions

Where financing is difficult because of a tight money situation, the seller might take a second P.M. mortgage. In this sort of situation, interest rates have shot up and money is hard to obtain.

Suppose a seller purchased a home for $50,000 some years ago with a $7^3/4$ percent loan. The balance due on the loan has been reduced to $35,000. In the meantime, the home has increased in value to $87,500. This means a prospective buyer needs $52,500 ($87,500 purchase price – $35,000 indebtedness) *if* the first mortgage is assumable. Even if the buyer could obtain institutional financing, the interest rate could be as high as 15 percent in addition to, say, 10 percent down, or $8,750.

The seller could permit the buyer to make an $8,750 down payment (or more if possible) and take back a second P.M. mortgage for five years. This could be an "interest only" mortgage payable monthly or even annually, or it could involve payments of interest and part principal, with a balloon at the end of five years.

Another example where the P.M. mortgage is sometimes a junior land contract occurs when the property does not meet the requirements of financial institutions, e.g., some summer homes.

It would be naive not to realize that where a seller uses a junior lien, the price of the home frequently is "jacked up." For example, rather than sell the home in the example above at the $87,500 fair market value, the seller may price it at $90,000. The seller would argue that this is justified because the buyer is saving interest on the $7^3/4$ percent loan assumption rather than paying 15 percent on a new loan.

Use with Commercial Loans

With commercial loans, the time period of the secondary financing generally runs from one to ten years. In the shorter time periods, they consist, for the most part, of "interest only" loans with a balloon payment due at the end of the term. The longer loans, seven to ten years, may be fully amortized at the end of the term or may be partially amortized with a balloon at the end.

While a P.M. mortgage used in residential financing may call for a relatively low rate, often below the market rate, the rates on the commercial loans are quite high. Very often the interest rates for the commercial junior

TAX IMPLICATIONS

The profit on the sale can be converted into an installment sale and at a much lower rate than if it were "cashed out." *Cashed out* simply means that the seller receives all cash in a transaction. For example, assume a selling price of property at $170,000 that has a mortgage of $110,000 and a basis of $100,000. If the seller is a "dealer" for tax purposes and if the $110,000 mortgage is paid off at the time of the sale and the seller receives cash for the balance, then:

Selling price.......................................	$170,000
Minus basis of....................................	100,000
Amount Immediately Taxable as Ordinary Income to Seller	$ 70,000

However, if the purchaser pays the seller $20,000 at the time of the sale and assumes the $110,000 mortgage with the seller "taking back" a second P.M. mortgage in the amount of $40,000 ($170,000 purchase price - $110,000 first mortgage = $60,000 - $20,000 cash = $40,000), then under Internal Revenue Code, Section 453, the seller's tax obligations can be spread over the time in which the installment payments are received. See pages 182-183 for a detailed explanation of installment sales under the 1986 Tax Act.

liens are pegged at three to five points over the prime rate. In dollar amounts the sources of funds given at the end of this chapter under "Major Sources of Junior Lien Funds" generally restrict the amounts loaned within a range of $100,000 to $1.5 million, depending on the evaluation of the commercial project.

DISCOUNTING LOANS

In the real estate market of the eighties, homes and commercial properties are being sold with the P.M. mortgage or deed of trust and junior land contracts. In most cases, for a seller to "cash out," the loan must be discounted.

There are several meanings to the term "discounting." To avoid confusion, it would seem appropriate to discuss them here. In one sense a *discount* is an amount deducted in advance from a principal sum before the borrower is given the use of the principal. The problem arises from having a fixed rate of interest on some "paper" being offered investors in a market where "the" interest rate is over a fixed rate. For example, suppose the fixed rate on an FHA-insured mortgage is 14 percent and the market rate is 16 percent. Assume *A* has a home eligible for a $55,000 FHA mortgage. If the market rate is 16 percent, an institution will refuse to make a loan at 14 percent. Consequently, the seller, *A*, in order to sell the home, must be willing to discount the mortgage to obtain the FHA mortgage for *B*, the buyer. Assume the discount rate is three points or 3 percent. Then at the sale, (1) *A* receives $53,350 from the loan proceeds ($55,000 – $1,650 discount); (2) *B* pays back the entire $55,000 plus interest; and (3) the institution receives $1,650 it actually did not lend out, plus interest on the $1,650, plus $53,350 it did lend out, plus interest on the $53,350.

In the final analysis, this part of discount tends to equate the 14 percent fixed yield with the 16 percent market yield. And it is, in this situation, paid by the seller.

In dealing with second mortgages, the term "discount" can be thought of in the sense of discounting almost anything—a percentage "off the top" as it were. I own a bicycle worth $100. I offer it to you at a 10 percent discount or $90. And so it is with second mortgages.

For example, *A* is the owner of a second mortgage bearing a face value of $100,000 with interest at 12 percent for 10 years. *A* offers the mortgage for sale to *B* at $90,000. Put another way, it is offered for sale at a discount off the face value of 10 percent, more commonly referred to as a "ten-point" discount. If it were discounted at 5 percent, it would be called a "five-point" discount, and so forth.

Yields

This raises the question of the effective rate of interest or yield. In the case above, *A*'s mortgagor is paying $100,000 with interest at 12 percent for 10 years. *B*, upon buying the indebtedness, has paid only $90,000 for the instrument, but the mortgagor has to pay *B* back $100,000 with 12 percent figured on the $100,000.

The following formula is used to calculate an approximation of the effective rate of return or yield where discounts are involved:[1]

$$Y = \frac{Pr + \dfrac{d}{n}}{P - d}$$

where,

Y = yield or annual percentage rate
P = principal amount in dollars
r = the interest rate expressed decimally
d = discount or charge expressed in dollars
n = number of years or fraction thereof to maturity

Then, in the case above:

---

[1]The "true" annual percentage rate could be calculated using present value concepts as discussed in Chapter 9 under "Investment Yields and Returns."

$$Y = \frac{(\$100,000 \times .12) + \dfrac{\$10,000}{10}}{\$100,000 - \$10,000}$$

$$Y = \frac{\$13,000}{\$90,000}$$

$$Y = .144 \text{ or } 14.4 \text{ percent approximate effective rate of return}$$

Discounting a First Mortgage and Creating a Second Mortgage

Investors frequently buy first mortgages at a discount as well as second mortgages. Generally the amount of the discount is less on a first mortgage than on a second mortgage. However, the discount rate will vary with the money markets. Often to obtain cash, the purchaser of a first mortgage will create a junior or second position. For example, suppose A purchases a mortgage with a face value of $100,000 on a home valued at $200,000. Assume it bears a rate of 13 percent interest. A pays, say, $85,000 for the mortgage.

If and when the market rate falls to 13 percent, A arranges for a financial institution to participate as senior investor in the $100,000 face value mortgage. The institutional investor agrees to purchase a *senior* participation for, say, $70,000. A agrees to become a *junior* owner in the $100,000 mortgage for which A paid only $85,000. At this point A receives $70,000 cash from the savings bank and signs an ownership agreement agreeing to be in second place. A's equity in the $100,000 mortgage is $30,000 and the bank's first right is for $70,000. A now owns a $30,000 piece of the $100,000 mortgage for which $85,000 was paid, or at a 15 percent discount. Now A has "at risk" $15,000 for a return of $30,000, or what amounts to a 50 percent discount together with an increase in the effective yield.

For example, prior to A being placed in a junior position, A's income was $13,000 ($100,000 × .13), with a yield of 15.3 percent ($13,000 ÷ $85,000). After the participation A's income is $3,900 ($30,000 × .13). The yield on the $15,000 now at risk is 26 percent or $3,900 ÷ $15,000.

The specific clause creating the senior participation is written as follows:

> The ownership of the party of the second part (in this case the industrial bank or other investor) in said note and mortgage is $70,000 and interest thereon at the rate of thirteen percent per annum from July 1 . . . and the party of the first part (A in this case) is the owner of the balance of said debt amounting to $30,000; but the ownership of the party of the second part is superior to that of the party of the first part, as if the party of the second part held a first mortgage for said sum of $70,000 and interest thereon as aforesaid, and the party of the first part held a second and subordinate mortgage, to secure the interest of the party of the first part in said mortgage debt.

Participations are more fully discussed in Chapter 13.

USES OF JUNIOR LIENS

Use of the Second Mortgage by Home Builders

One reason home builders may use the second mortgage is to sell out subdivisions as fast as possible. This may be to their advantage even though the builders have to discount the mortgage.

Recall that home building is basically a two-step financing transaction. First is the construction loan (interim financing), which is to be replaced by a first mortgage (typically from an institution—the permanent financing). This is a simple case which may become more complex, as was pointed out in Chapter 6, Secondary Mortgage Market Activities and Procedures.

The thorn in the side of the builder is the interest or carrying charge that must be paid on the construction loan prior to the permanent loan. Suppose a builder's permanent financing commitment is for conventional mortgages with an 80 percent loan-to-value ratio. This means a home buyer must put down 20 percent. If there is a turndown in the economy, prospects with the necessary 20 percent decline. To increase the rate of sales, a builder might offer a home with 90 percent financing, 80 percent from the institution with the builder "taking" back a second P.M. mortgage for 10 percent of the purchase price. The builder will then discount these. This provides fast working capital for other prospects, as well as no further responsibility for carrying charges.

Use of Second Mortgage to Increase Leverage

Leverage is the use of borrowed money in an effort to increase gains. For example, suppose you have $20,000 to invest on which you can earn 10 percent or $2,000 per year. Suppose you can borrow another $20,000 at 8 percent. You then invest the $40,000 (your $20,000 plus the borrowed $20,000 at 10 percent). The gross income is $4,000 per year. Out of this you pay interest of $1,600, netting $2,400. The rate of return on your equity of $20,000 is then $2,400 ÷ $20,000, or 12 percent, a gain of 2 percent as a result of the leverage.

This sort of thing frequently arises in commercial or apartment-type ventures, the reason being that many institutional lenders will lend only between 60–75 percent of the appraised value. Assume the cost of a small apartment complex is $150,000 and a lender agrees to lend two thirds, or $100,000. Consequently, an investor may look to a second mortgage as a means of raising more money. Let's suppose a second mortgage can be obtained for $20,000. Then the amount of equity needed by the investor is reduced from $50,000 to $30,000, thereby increasing the leverage.

Furthermore, this could make the property easier to sell. If the owner of the property is a "builder-developer" rather than an "investor," in the sense of a person seeking income from the property, the "builder-developer" will attempt to sell to an "investor" for $150,000. Typically, it is easier to sell the property with $30,000 cash down as opposed to $50,000 cash down.

Use of Second P.M. Mortgage to Lower Cash Down

Often a second P.M. mortgage with an *increase* in the selling price and a *lower* down payment is used by a buyer to induce a seller to sell. For example, seller prices an income-producing property at $1 million with an assumable mortgage of $750,000, requiring $250,000 cash down. The property has a cash flow of $35,000. Then:

Selling price	$1,000,000	
Assumable mortgage	750,000	
Cash required	$ 250,000	
Cash flow		$35,000

If a buyer buys at this price:

$$\text{Return on Cash Down to Buyer} = \frac{\$35,000}{\$250,000} = 14\%$$

Suppose a buyer offers seller $1,050,000 or $50,000 more than the asking price. Buyer assumes the $750,000 mortgage and gives the seller $100,000 cash down, the seller to take back a second interest only P.M. mortgage of $200,000 at 10 percent for 10 years. Then:

Selling price	$1,050,000	
Assumable mortgage	750,000	
Balance	$ 300,000	
Less cash down	100,000	
Second P.M. mortgage	$ 200,000	
Cash flow		$35,000
Interest on second P.M. mortgage		20,000
Net Cash Flow		$15,000

$$\text{Return to Buyer on Cash Down} = \frac{\$15,000}{\$100,000} = 15\%$$

Why would a seller consent to this transaction?

1. The seller would receive $50,000 more for the property. The seller might negotiate for, say, 10.5 percent interest. This would still give the buyer a 14 percent yield on cash down (cash flow $35,000 – $21,000 = $14,000, or $14,000 ÷ $100,000 = 14 percent).
2. The buyer could make an argument to the seller that the seller's return on "true equity" is greater than 10.5 percent. The "true equity" is $150,000 ($100,000 cash down plus $50,000 added selling price) on which the seller is receiving $21,000 for a yield of $21,000 ÷ $150,000 = 14 percent.

Use of the Second P.M. Mortgage in Land Purchases

This is a device used by builder-developers in conjunction with a subordination clause in a mortgage. For example, A (a builder-developer) can buy 40 acres for a subdivision at $2,500 per acre. The seller agrees to sell it for 10 percent down or $10,000 cash down. The seller agrees to take back a first blanket P.M. mortgage containing partial release clauses as previously discussed.

The problem created is this: When a construction loan is sought, the builder-developer will be turned down. Why? Because there is an existing first mortgage held by the seller. Therefore the buyer-builder insists on a subordination clause in the seller's first mortgage. This states that the seller's first mortgage agrees to move into number two position in order for the buyer to obtain a *first* construction loan.

Briefly, the clause in the seller's first mortgage will state:

> The mortgagor shall have the right to substitute other mortgages for a prior mortgage or mortgages now in the mortgaged premises. Such substituted mortgage shall have the same priority with reference to this mortgage. The mortgagee hereby agrees to execute all necessary instruments to effectuate any substitution above described.

When the buyer is about to obtain the construction loan, the seller and the buyer enter into a subordination agreement. This is the instrument mentioned in the clause. The subordination agreement is recorded, at which time the seller's first P.M. mortgage is moved to a second. A subordination agreement is shown in Figure 11–1.

Very frequently the subordination clause in the P.M. mortgage calls for the subordination to become self-executing. That is, as soon as the builder-developer obtains a construction loan, the seller's first P.M. mortgage or deed of trust immediately becomes subordinated to the construction loan.

As a further protection, the subordinated mortgagee (now a junior lienor) frequently inserts a clause in the mortgage to the effect that the mortgagor cannot renew or increase the amount of the first mortgage without the consent of the junior lienor. In the event the builder-developer desires to increase the amount of the first, which can be done with the same lender by means of an extension agreement, the subordinated mortgagee will insist that all or part of the monies received go to pay off its indebtedness.

For example, suppose there is an $800,000 first lien and a $200,000 second or subordinated mortgage. Assume that over time the property has increased to $2 million. Rather than sell and pay taxes, the builder-developer decides to raise the first lien to $1.5 million. Assume the second mortgage is now paid down to $180,000. It becomes obvious that the "cushion" for the subordinate second lien has decreased. This is the reasoning of the junior lienor in insisting that the loan either be paid off or reduced when the first mortgage is increased.

Generally sellers of vacant land will go along with this sort of

SUBORDINATION AGREEMENT

AGREEMENT, made the 27th day of June nineteen hundred and ⁻⁻

BETWEEN William T. Harris, residing at 36 Trent Street, Rye, County of Westchester, State of New York,

party of the first part, and Faye L. Tracy, residing at 13753 Long Island Avenue, Medford, County of Suffolk, State of New York,

party of the second part,

WITNESSETH:

WHEREAS, the said party of the first part now owns and holds the following mortgage and the ~~bond~~

~~or~~ note secured thereby:

Mortgage dated the 4th day of July , 19⁻⁻ made by John Morrison

to Patrick Hayes

in the principal sum of $ 35,000.00 and recorded in the (Liber) ~~(Record Liber) (Reel)~~

of section 200 of Mortgages, page 42 in the office of the Clerk of the County of Suffolk, State of New York,

covering premises hereinafter mentioned or a part thereof, and

WHEREAS,

the present owner of the premises hereinafter mentioned is about to execute and deliver to said party of the second part, a mortgage to secure the principal sum of Eighty Thousand and 00/100 ($80,000.00)
-- dollars

and interest, covering premises

(here follows a complete legal description of the property)

and more fully described in said mortgage, and

WHEREAS, said party of the second part has refused to accept said mortgage unless said mortgage held by the party of the first part be subordinated in the manner hereinafter mentioned,

NOW THEREFORE, in consideration of the premises and to induce said party of the second part to accept said mortgage and also in consideration of one dollar paid to the party of the first part, the receipt whereof is hereby acknowledged, the said party of the first part hereby covenants and agrees with said party of the second part that said mortgage held by said party of the first part be and shall continue to be subject and subordinate in lien to the lien of said mortgage for Thirty-Five Thousand and 00/100 ($35,000.00)---
-- dollars and interest about to be delivered to the party of the second part hereto, and to all advances heretofore made or which hereafter may be made thereon (including but not limited to all sums advanced for the purpose of paying brokerage commissions, consideration paid for making the loan, mortgage recording tax, documentary stamps, fee for examination of title, surveys, and any other disbursements and charges in connection therewith) to the extent of the last mentioned amount and interest, and all such advances may be made without notice to the party of the first part, and to any extensions, renewals and modifications thereof.

FIGURE 11–1. Subordination Agreement

This agreement may not be changed or terminated orally. This agreement shall bind and enure to the benefit of the parties hereto, their respective heirs, personal representatives, successors and assigns. The word "party" shall be construed as if it read "parties" whenever the sense of this agreement so requires.

IN WITNESS WHEREOF, the said party of the first part has duly executed this agreement the day and year first above written.

IN PRESENCE OF :

                                        /s/ William T. Harris

/s/ Judith J. DeFore

(Acknowledgment)

Standard Form of New York Board of Title Underwriters

FIGURE 11–1. Subordination Agreement (concluded)

transaction because it is easier to sell the vacant land. In addition, it will increase the value of the land once the improvement is completed. Furthermore, the original mortgage generally contains a sliding interest rate. For example, the mortgage might state that so long as the mortgage is a first, the rate will be 10 percent; and once a subordination agreement, if any, is recorded, the rate shall be 12 percent as long as it is in second place.

The Call Second Mortgage

The *call second mortgage* is merely a second mortgage giving the lender the right to "call" it at a time prior to its termination date. At the time of the call, the borrower has to agree to refinance the entire loan into a first mortgage and to pay off the second mortgage.

For example, assume an institutional lender has committed an 80 percent loan-to-value ratio on a home development. In order to expedite sales, the builder-developer may offer the property with 10 percent down and agree to take back a second mortgage for 15 years with a call, at the developer's option, in 5 years.

Assume the sales price is	$34,000
An 80% first mortgage for 30 years at 8% is	27,200
	$ 6,800
Assume a $3,400 second mortgage with a 5-year call at 9% for 180 months (15 years)	3,400
The 10% down is	$ 3,400
Payments for principal and interest on the first mortgage ($7.34 per $1,000 × 27.2) are	$199.65 per month
Payments for principal and interest on the second mortgage ($10.14 per $1,000 × 3.4) are	34.48 per month
Total monthly payments are	$234.13 per month

The monthly payments were, of course, arrived at by using Table 6 in Appendix B. In addition, Table 8 in Appendix B is useful in determining the remaining loan balances.

At the end of the "call" period, five years in this case:

Balance due on first mortgage (95.1% × $27,200) is	$25,867
Balance due on second mortgage (80.1% × $3,400) is	2,723
Total due is	$28,590

The basic assumption is that the property will appreciate during the five-year period, thus making the "call" feasible. Assume a compound rate of growth or appreciation of 3 percent per year (i.e., a compound interest factor of 1.159 is obtained from Table 1 in Appendix B). Then, 1.159 × $34,000 = $39,406, the value of property at the end of five years. With a new 80 percent mortgage of $31,525 (.80 × $39,406), the original first and second mortgages could be retired for $28,590. This would result in a surplus to the owner less expenses of $2,935 ($31,525 − $28,590).

MAJOR SOURCES OF JUNIOR LIEN FUNDS

There are numerous sources of second mortgage funds available, both residential and commercial.

Residential Loan Sources

Under sanction of the Monetary Control Act of 1980, both savings and loan associations and commercial banks are permitted to make second mortgage loans. The restriction is that the sum of the first and second mortgages cannot be greater than a 90 percent loan-to-value ratio. For example, assume a home appraised at $100,000 with an existing mortgage of $80,000. These institutions are permitted to place a second mortgage on the property of no greater than $10,000.

Industrial banks have been a large source of funds for second mortgages for many years. Recently, they have purchased second P.M. mortgages from individuals who want to "cash out." These mortgages are generally bought at high discounts, thereby increasing the yield to the industrial banks over and above the stated rate on the face of the mortgage.

Second mortgage syndicates are also a source of funds. With the increase in seller financing, the number of second mortgage syndicates is increasing. The first such syndicate was Burlingame Mortgage Investors, a California limited partnership. It started in 1974 with assets of $64,000 and by 1983 had grown to over $7 million. The average loan is $28,000.

B.M.I. has strict guidelines to avoid being trapped by what might be an overinflated market:

1. The maximum loan-to-value ratio is 80 percent. Value is determined by an independent appraiser.
2. No one loan can be more than 5 percent of assets.

3. Mortgage insurance is necessary, but covers only 10 percent of the loan.
4. No balloon loans. The maximum loan is 10 years. No "interest only" loans. Debt service is paid monthly and fully amortized at the end of the term.

Commercial Loan Sources

These sources are used both for straight second mortgage financing and "gap" financing (temporary differences between construction loans and permanent loans) which will be discussed in Chapter 13.

In some cases commercial banks make second mortgage loans but only to customers with high ratings. For the most part the lenders consist of commercial finance companies (e.g., AIC Financial Corporation) or subsidiaries of industrial companies and life insurance companies (e.g., C.I.T. Corporation, Aetna Business Credit, Inc.).

Another source of funds which is rapidly increasing is foreign investors seeking U.S. investment or trying to escape rapid inflation in their own nations.

KEY TERMS

call second mortgage   junior mortgage
junior lien   lien

QUESTIONS FOR REVIEW

1. Under what conditions might a second mortgage be used to finance the purchase of a residential property? How is such an arrangement advantageous to the buyer? To the seller?
2. Why is it sometimes necessary to discount a mortgage in order to "cash out," and also to get financing for the buyer? Give an example.
3. Describe the procedure for discounting a first mortgage and creating a second. What are the respective advantages or gains for the senior and junior owners in such an arrangement?
4. How might a builder use a second mortgage to sell out a subdivision rapidly and provide fast working capital?
5. Explain the use of a second P.M. mortgage to increase leverage. How else might a second P.M. mortgage be used?
6. What is the purpose of a subordination agreement in a builder's P.M. mortgage with the seller?
7. What is a *call second mortgage* and what are its provisions?
8. What are the major sources of junior lien funds?

PROBLEMS

1. As an investor assume you hold a $60,000, 12 percent, 8-year mortgage loan. Now you are interested in selling the mortgage to a potential buyer.
   a. If the buyer offers you $55,000 for the mortgage, what will be the buyer's approximate effective yield?
   b. How would the buyer's approximate effective yield have changed if the mortgage still had 20 years until maturity and the buyer offered $55,000 for the mortgage?
   c. Based on the original mortgage terms, what purchase price could be offered by the buyer in order that buyer would receive a 16 percent approximate effective yield?

2. An institutional investor agrees to take a senior participation for $30,000 on a 10-year face value $45,000 mortgage paying 13 percent. The junior owner originally paid $39,000 for the mortgage. As a result of this arrangement, what does the junior owner have at risk, how much does the junior owner expect to receive in return, and what is the effective yield?

3. An institutional lender has committed an 80 percent loan-to-value ratio on the development of a home. The price of the home is $80,000, the interest rate on the lender's loan is 12 percent, and the mortgage is for 25 years. The developer offers to take 10 percent down and give you a 10-year second mortgage at 16 percent for the remainder with a call in 5 years. The property is expected to appreciate at 8 percent per year compounded. What is the owner's surplus, if any, after the call?

FINANCING BY MEANS OF LONG-TERM LEASES

LEARNING OBJECTIVES

After studying this chapter, you should be able to do the following:

Define what is meant by a lease and describe the parties involved in a typical lease arrangement.

Identify and describe various types of leases when they are classified by method of payment.

Identify and explain the major reasons for using leases as financing devices.

Describe what is meant by a ground lease and explain how the subordinated ground lease is used.

Name and describe several common terms included in the lease contract.

Describe what is meant by the sale of leaseholds.

A *LEASE* IS a contract creating a landlord and tenant relationship. The landlord is called the *lessor,* and the tenant, the *lessee.* The contract between the two parties conveys the right of possession of the leased premises to the tenant, in return for which the tenant pays the landlord rent. The term *rent* is defined as the compensation, whether money, provisions, chattels, or labor, received by the owner of the soil or buildings from the occupant thereof.

A lease may be thought of primarily as a contract; and as a general rule, the parties to a contract may agree to almost anything in a lease.[1] However, they cannot agree to things which are said to be against public policy.

As in all contracts, a lease must be entered into by persons having contractual ability. There must be a consideration, a delivery, and an acceptance. In addition, to validate a lease there must be a description that locates the premises with reasonable certainty. A lease should contain the term or the duration of the lease. The lease should also have a definite beginning and a certain ending. The following example illustrates a problem with a lease that is not properly executed:

> A written lease stating that the tenant's occupation was for the term of "one year, two years, three years" was sent to the landlord, who was to strike out all except one of the terms mentioned and then execute the lease. The landlord, however, executed the lease without striking out any of its terms. The court held there was no meeting of the minds, and consequently the lease was ruled invalid.[2]

A lease must also contain an agreement, technically called "an agreement to let and take," although the words "let and take" rarely appear in the lease. The lease generally will state that the lessor "grants, demises, and lets unto the lessee." This is considered to be the agreement to let and take. These words give the tenant the right of possession, and also, in the event that someone appears later who has a better title to the premises than the landlord, give the tenant the right to proceed against the landlord for damages.

Finally, the lease must be executed in accordance with the statute. Some statutes state that the lease must be acknowledged, while others do not contain this provision. As a practical matter, it is a good procedure to have the lease acknowledged in order to enable the lease to be recorded, if the occasion arises.

CLASSIFICATION OF LEASES

Leases are generally classified in one of two ways: (1) by method of payment, or (2) by term, which is by length of the lease.

Lease Classified by Method of Payment

In classifying by method of payment the most common lease is the gross, or flat, lease. Several other leases are also classified by this method and will be discussed in the following paragraphs.

---

[1]Actually the lease is both a contract and a conveyance.
[2]Sayles v Lienhardt, 119 Misc. 851, 198 NY Supp. 337.

The Gross Lease or Flat Lease. The *gross* (or *flat*) *lease* is a type of lease in which the premises are rented at a fixed rate. The rent is paid to the landlord by the tenant, and the landlord, in turn, agrees to pay the taxes, insurance, and any other expenses that might be incurred in the operation of the premises. The possible exception to this is that the tenant would pay ordinary repairs if they were called for under the terms of the lease.

The Semi-Gross Lease. Most of today's residential leases and some commercial leases have developed into what is commonly called the "semi-gross lease." This simply means that the lessee agrees to pay for electricity and other utilities in addition to paying a flat sum.

The Net Lease. The *net lease* is the type of lease in which the tenant pays the taxes, assessments, and all operating expenses in connection with the use of the premises. The landlord receives a net figure.

Most long-term leases are net leases. The net lease has become increasingly popular with owners of investment properties. Many owners do not wish to sell the property, but hope to obtain a steady income from the property without incurring any of the headaches of supervising the premises. The owner may lease the property and receive a flat rental from the lessee. The lease will provide that the lessee pay: (a) maintenance and costs; (b) real property taxes and assessments, except the landlord's income taxes and possible inheritance taxes; (c) insurance costs, including extended coverage plus insurance coverage for possible personal injury and property damage; and (d) costs of possible compliance with environmental protection laws.

The Bondable Lease. The *bondable lease* consists of two types of security to a lender: (a) the real estate; (b) the high credit rating of the tenant.

To be bondable, the lease must be noncancellable, which means the tenant cannot cancel for *any* default on the part of the landlord, with a large enough net rent to meet the debt service. The term of the lease must be long enough to amortize the loan or longer.

Because of the double security for the mortgage, lenders will often lend 100 percent of the appraised value of the property. The leases are immediately assigned to the lender because failure to assign would result in payment of the rent to a trustee in bankruptcy in the event the landlord becomes bankrupt.

Most of these loans are made by life insurance companies and high credit-rated tenants are involved, such as Sears, J. C. Penney, etc.

The Percentage Lease. The *percentage lease* is a type of lease in which the rental is based either on a flat fee plus a percentage of the gross or on the net income received by a tenant doing business on the premises.

There are several factors of importance that must be considered in the percentage lease. Suppose, for example, that the rental is based upon a

---

TAX IMPLICATIONS OF THE BONDABLE LEASE TO THE BUILDER—DEVELOPER

In order to obtain what amounts to a bondable lease from highly rated tenants, the cash flow is generally low. Yet the builder-developer often has a 100 percent loan and can take advantage of depreciation plus interest payments.

---

small flat fee plus a percentage of the gross. A goes into possession as the tenant and does a gross business that by far exceeds expectations; consequently, A's rent is high. Across the street from A there is a vacant property that is available for a flat or gross rental. A acquires this property and proceeds to open another store at that location. In effect, A enters into competition with the original store by drawing some of the patronage away from that store. This results in a reduction of A's gross receipts in the store where the percentage base is in effect. To guard against this, the landlord should insert in the percentage lease a clause to the effect that tenants may not enter into competition with themselves either in the city, if it is a small city, or within a stated number of blocks of the leased premises if it is a large city.

If the percentage lease is to be based upon a net profit, the definition of net profit must be made clear. Is the flat rental to be a deduction from the gross profit in determining net profit? Are repairs and alterations to be deducted? Who is to pay the taxes? These are but a few of the many questions that must be spelled out in the lease in order to avoid any later misunderstanding.

The lease should contain a clause giving the lessor the right at anytime during the demised term to examine all the books of account and any other records that might reflect the operations of the lessee.

The parties also might consider the feasibility of inserting a recapture clause. A *recapture clause* gives the right to the landlord to take back the demised premises in the event that the tenant's business does not reach a certain gross. The clause may also give the right to the tenant to surrender the premises in the event that business does not reach a stated gross.

Other Methods of Payment. There are other sorts of subclassification of leases as to payment, such as the escalator lease, the index lease, and the revaluation lease.

Escalator or step-up leases. In a long-term lease one of the problems to be considered by the landlord is changes in taxes, insurance, and operating costs over time. Although the precise changes in these amounts are at best a guess, rents are stepped up in long-term leases. A schedule is generally included in the *escalator* (or *step-up*) *lease* showing changes in rent over time.

Index leases.   The *index lease* provides for rental changes in accordance with changes in a price index. The index could be the consumer price index, the producer price index, or even the construction cost index. Obviously the purpose of the index lease is to guard against inflation and declines in the purchasing power of the dollar. Suppose, for example, the rents are linked with the consumer price index and the index rises 20 percent; the rents also must be raised 20 percent.

Revaluation leases.   A *revaluation lease* calls for the lessor to select an appraiser and the lessee to select an appraiser. The two appraisers then select a third appraiser and among them they re-evaluate the long-term lease. The three then set the rent for another time period, after which the rents may again be revalued.

Leases Classified by Term

Leases are generally referred to as short-term or long-term leases. Generally short-term leases are thought to be those of less than 21 years. Leases that are over 21 years are regarded as long-term leases.

THE STATUTE OF FRAUDS AND LEASES

The statute of frauds enters the picture regarding leases much in the same manner as it does in other types of real property contracts. Owners may lease their property for as long a period as they want, but in most states only a lease for less than one year's duration may be oral. Leases for over one year under the statute of frauds must be in writing.

If the state law requires a lease to be in writing and the parties have failed to comply with this, or if the lease fails for any reason to meet the statutory requirements, then the lease cannot be enforced. If the lease cannot be enforced and the tenant has not yet gone into possession, the landlord may refuse the tenant the possession. If the tenant is already in possession under a lease that should have been written, but was not, the lease may be terminated at any time by the landlord. On the other hand, the tenant may refuse to take possession, without any liability, under an unenforceable lease. If the possession has taken place, however, the tenant is liable for "use and occupancy" during the period of occupancy of the premises.

A written lease may be recorded. In New York, for example, a lease for more than three years may be recorded. This is not to imply that a lease must be recorded; it is merely better practice to record long-term leases. The recording gives notice to the world of the rights of the tenant in the property, although in many cases actual possession of the premises is sufficient to give such notice.

REASONS FOR USING LEASES FOR FINANCING

The major reasons leases are often used as financing devices are for tax purposes or as an alternative to mortgage financing which may tend to tie up needed capital.

Obtaining Financing Through a Lease

Suppose A, a small manufacturer, has the opportunity to increase business, but needs more factory space. Assume further that A can get a building built for $200,000. The land cost is $40,000 and the improvements $160,000. A has two alternatives: (1) obtain a mortgage and build the building, or (2) lease the building from an investor. Assume a mortgage can be acquired in the amount of $132,000. This means A has to put up $68,000 in cash. By doing this A will be strapped for working capital; thus, A is forced to lease the property. However, as a tenant the rent is a tax deduction for A. Perhaps more important, though, is the freeing of capital to increase the factory operation that is made possible if the property is leased.

Deferring Taxes Through Leasing

Suppose you own a parcel of land with a current value of $40,000. The property was originally purchased for $10,000. If sold, the property will be subject to a long-term capital gains tax. If developed and leased, the rental income will be taxable, but the long-term gain will be deferred.

Increasing Marketability Through Leasing

With a tenant of good reputation the marketability of the property may be enhanced. If there is a good cash flow and proper tax advantages, the property becomes more readily saleable.

THE COMMERCIAL GROUND LEASE

In the previous example the owner simply had a vacant land developed and rented it to a tenant. The ground lease situation is quite different. A *ground lease* is a device permitting the ground and the improvements to be owned by different persons. For example, in an oversimplified form, suppose A owns land and B rents the land and builds a home on it. A still owns the land, but B owns the home.

If B seeks and obtains a loan, the loan is on the improvement, not on the land. Actually the lender has a secondary lien, because the lease (or right to lease) is prior. A leasehold mortgage differs from the fee mortgage in the sense that the security for the leasehold mortgage is a defeasible estate (the lease).

However, in the commercial lease things can become quite complicated. Suppose an owner has property valued again at $40,000. *X,* a developer, borrows $160,000 from Acme Insurance Company, leases the $40,000 vacant land, and builds a small apartment complex. If the developer defaults on the leasehold mortgage (to be discussed in Chapter 16), the lender can take over the leasehold (thus winding up with the improvement), but must still pay rent to the owner. This type of situation is an *unsubordinated leasehold mortgage.* Note that in this case the owner has first claim to rents because they are due under the terms of the ground lease. As a result, it is difficult for a developer to get this rather shaky loan from a lender. Most lenders require that the ground lease be subordinated to the loan.

The Subordinated Ground Lease

Subordinated means to make inferior; consequently, in order for a developer to obtain a loan on a ground lease, the owner (lessor of the ground lease) must agree to subordinate to a mortgagee and thus create a **subordinated ground lease.** For example, assume again that an owner has land worth $40,000 and the developer borrows $160,000. The lender (mortgagee) then places the $160,000 mortgage on the fee plus improvements. Because it is a ground lease, the owner is fully aware that the developer will seek a loan. The owner also knows that the probabilities of the developer obtaining such a loan are slim if the developer's lease is unsubordinated. Consequently, a clause will be put in the ground lease similar to the following.

> The Lessor (the owner in our case) hereby agrees that his/her rights under this lease are subordinate to any and all mortgages hereafter placed from time to time on the said premises and if the Lessee (the developer in this case) or the mortgagee so desire, the Lessor agrees to execute any instruments or instrument to evidence such subordination.

At the time the loan is actually made the owner will execute a subordination agreement making the lease inferior to the mortgage. Figure 11–1 on pages 203 and 204 is an example of such a subordination agreement. This will be recorded, thus permitting the lender to move to a number one position. In short, as security for the $160,000 loan the lender has $200,000 worth of security after the improvement has been constructed. Furthermore, and this is most important, the property has been developed with 100 percent financing. In effect, the developer has used the owner-lessor's $40,000 piece of vacant land as a down payment.

Problems of the Subordinated Ground Lease

The subordinated ground lease is inferior to the first lien or the first mortgage. In most states, a lease is extinguished by a foreclosure. Consequently, as a practical matter, the following is demanded by a lender:

1. The subordinated ground lease must be used.
2. The ground lease must be equal to or greater than the length of the term of the mortgage.
3. The fee owner (lessor) who has leased to the builder-developer must sign the mortgage and put the fee subject to the mortgage.
4. All subtenants of the project, as well as any prime tenant, must attorn. This means that in the event of a foreclosure, the tenants will recognize the lender or any other purchaser at a foreclosure sale as the new landlord. For example, assume there is a loan on a shopping center. If a lender forecloses, in most states the leases would be extinguished and the tenants would be free to leave. Thus the reason for the attornment is to prevent the tenants from leaving in the event of foreclosure.

In the light of all this, the question is why would the fee owner of the ground get involved? The answer is that with the subordinated ground lease, the builder-developer can obtain a larger loan because the value of the ground is taken into account in the appraisal process. Presumably, with the larger loan the builder-developer can build a more expensive project and thus afford to pay a higher rent to the fee owner.

Fee Owner Protection under Subordinated Ground Lease

In a subordinated ground lease, graphically the situation looks like this: owner (lessor) leases to builder-developer (lessee); builder-developer obtains first mortgage from lender.

There are several things that might possibly take place which could be harmful to the owner-lessor:

1. The builder-developer may default on payments, causing the lender to foreclose.
2. The builder-developer may go bankrupt, which may give the lender the right to accelerate the loan as being "noncurable."
3. The building may be destroyed by fire or some other natural disaster.

The question is: How does the owner-lessor obtain protection from the above potential problems? Some possible answers are:

1. By inserting the following clauses in the lease or mortgage:
   (a) A clause in the lease to the effect that if the builder-developer defaults in payments, the lease between the builder-developer and the owner is automatically terminated.
   (b) A clause in the mortgage giving the owner-lessor the right to cure the mortgage and make future mortgage payments.
   (c) A clause in the lease permitting these mortgage payments to be construed as additional rent.
2. By insisting that the mortgagee remove the "noncurable" clause from the mortgage in the event of bankruptcy of the builder-developer and permit the owner-lessor to cure and take over.

3. By insisting that any insurance payments, fire, for example, go to restore the improvements rather than pay off the mortgage, and further that rent insurance be included in the policy to insure rent payments to the owner-lessor in the event of partial destruction of the premises.

TAX IMPLICATIONS OF THE GROUND LEASE

The ground rent paid by the lessee is deductible. More importantly, land cannot be depreciated. For example, a builder-developer leases land on which $20,000 is paid per year. A building is built for $1 million. The builder-developer (lessee) can deduct depreciation on the building plus the $20,000 per year ground rent paid to the owner-lessor. Had the builder-developer (lessee) purchased the land outright, the debt service might have been greater, yet depreciation could be deducted on the $1 million improvement only.

INSURED LEASES

One recent development has been the advent of private mortgage insurance companies. For the most part they insure conventional mortgages. However, they have recently begun insuring rents which facilitate financing. For example, if a builder is going to build a factory for a "triple A" rated tenant, the builder need only take the tentative lease to an institution and the financing will be readily available. However, if the prospective tenant is not rated triple A, a private mortgage insurance company must step in to insure the rent. If the private insurance mortgage company agrees to insure the rent, then the financial institution will lend the money knowing that if the tenant defaults it will be paid the money due under the terms of the mortgage.

SOME COMMON LEASE TERMS

Although real estate brokers are the prime negotiators of commercial leases, they should never attempt to draw the lease. This must be left to competent lawyers. However, one should be familiar with some of the more common aspects of the lease. Aside from such things as the rent payments, insurance provisions, and terms of length of the lease, some of the problems that arise are discussed in the following paragraphs.

Option to Purchase

Usually, when a tenant erects a building upon the premises of the landlord, the lease contains an option giving the tenant the right to purchase the improvement and the land at the end of the term. The option may state a price to be paid for the property, or the option may provide that if the lessor and the lessee are unable to negotiate a price, then the lessor and the lessee shall each appoint an appraiser. The appraisers shall then appoint an umpire. Each of the appraisers and the umpire appraise the property. In general, the lease states that the decision of any two appraisers (one of whom is the umpire) as to the price shall be binding on the parties. In the event that the third party then refuses to accept the decision of the other two, it has been held in most states that the proper remedy for the enforcement of the option to purchase at an appraised valuation is by specific performance. When such a clause exists, the proper procedure for its enforcement is by a suit for specific performance in a court of equity.

Often a lump sum for the option is paid to the lessor at the beginning of the lease. It sometimes is stipulated that this sum will be used as part of the purchase price if the option is exercised. Sometimes only part of this sum is applied to the purchase price. Frequently, all or part of the sum given for the option is applied to the last year's rent, if the option is not exercised.

The lease with option to buy is sometimes used as a financing device in the purchase of a residence. For example, the price of the home is agreed upon at $50,000. The tenant moves in under a lease and is given an option to buy the home at the $50,000, provided the option is exercised within a stated time. The tenant also agrees to pay rent. More often than not an agreed percentage of the rent is applied to the $50,000 purchase price.

Option to Renew

Often a lease contains an option to renew the lease. The option must usually be exercised within a stated time prior to the expiration of the lease. The right to renew may be either for a definite renewal period or for an automatic renewal. There may be included in this covenant granting the option to renew a different amount to be paid as rent for the renewal term.

In the first instance, the option gives a right to the lessee to notify the lessor within a stated time, prior to the end of the term of the lease, that the lessee desires to renew the lease for a stated period under the same terms and conditions as the old lease. The option to renew in the original lease states further that the old lease will be renewed as is, except for the deletion of the clause granting the option to renew. This suggests, then, that the lease may not be renewed under the option a second time.

The automatic renewal is slightly different in that it gives either party the right to notify the other within a stated period that a renewal is not wanted. In the ordinary option to renew, the right is given only to the lessee, but here both parties have the right to refuse to renew. It is different, too, from the option to renew for a definite period in that the option states that the renewal shall be in accordance with all of the provisions of the old lease "including this covenant." This suggests then that after the first renewal of the lease, the lease may again be renewed at the option of both parties to the original lease.

Covenant Not to Sublet or Assign

In the absence of a provision to the contrary, a tenant has a right to assign the lease or to sublet the premises. An *assignment* is the transfer of the entire term of the lease by the tenant; a *subletting* is, in effect, the making of a new lease in which the original tenant is the lessor and the subtenant the lessee. In the former case, the assignee steps into the shoes of the tenant and is generally liable for the payment of the rent to the original landlord. In the latter case, the subtenant is generally not liable for the rent or other obligations to the original landlord. However, the assignor may also be held for the failure of an assignee to live up to terms and conditions of the lease.

One distinction between a sublet and an assignment lies in the period of time involved. For example, if a lease was drawn for a term running from January 1 to July 15 and the tenant delivered the premises to another person until July 14, this would be a sublease. However, if the premises were occupied by another person from January 1 to July 15, which is the end of the term, then this would be construed as an assignment regardless of what the transaction was called. A second distinction is that a sublease may convey a portion of the premises.

To prevent the subletting or assignment of leased property, the landlord will usually insist that the lease contain a covenant in which the tenant agrees not to sublet or assign without the written consent of the land-lord.[3] The covenant will generally provide that the lease may be terminated if the tenant violates this covenant. Many landlords specifically insert a clause both to keep out undesirable tenants and to receive a bonus from the tenant in the event a tenant desires to sell a business opportunity.

Use of the Premises

When a property is leased, the landlord receives the right to the rent, and the tenant receives the right of possession. In a sense, the tenant is the owner of the premises during the period of the lease. The tenant may use this possession in any legal manner, in the absence of any covenants to the contrary, and the landlord may not prevent the tenant from so doing. There is, however, one restriction by implication on all tenants; that is, the tenant cannot do anything that will injure or diminish the value of the landlord's interest. Any improper use of the premises by the tenant that does injure or diminish the value of the landlord's reversion is known as waste. In the event the tenant does injure the value of the reversion, the landlord may bring an action for damages, or an injunction which may result in a court order restraining the tenant from committing waste, or both. The lease may also provide that such breach by the tenant gives the landlord the right to terminate the lease upon the occasion of such breach.

---

[3]In Texas, this clause is unnecessary because the Texas statutes prohibit subletting or assignment by tenants without the consent of the landlord.

It is customary in modern leases to limit the use of the premises. This is done by inserting a covenant in the lease stating what the premises are to be used for and including the words "only" or "no other." For example, the lease may state: "For use as a grocery store and for no other purpose." The words "only" or "no other" will limit the use of the premises to that which is specifically stated in the lease. The absence of these words may prevent the use of the premises from being effectively limited. In many states there are statutes providing for the termination of a lease if the lessee makes illegal use of the premises. A lease under these statutes is declared void.

Condemnation

Eminent domain is the right of the government or a governmental agency to take private property for public use, provided just compensation is paid to the owner. The legal proceeding to take property under eminent domain is called a "condemnation proceeding."

Ordinarily when leased property is condemned, the tenant has no right to condemnation awards paid to the lessor. Often, to ensure this, the lessor will insist on a clause stating that, in the event of a condemnation, ". . . the lessee shall not be entitled to any part of the award as damages, or otherwise, for such condemnation, and the lessor is to receive the full amount of such award."

An example of another situation that often arises is where X (lessor) leases a building to A (lessee) for a garage. Over a period of time, A builds up goodwill which gives value to the business over and above the fixtures and equipment. Assume that the equipment is worth $10,000, but that the business, because of the goodwill, is worth $50,000. A sells the business to B, assigning the lease with the consent of X (lessor), in return for which A receives $50,000. If the property is then condemned, the landlord (X) will receive compensation for the property, and B will be forced to move out of the premises taking only the $10,000 worth of equipment. B will thus suffer the loss of the $40,000 that was paid A for the goodwill of the business. If A had not sold the business, the value of the goodwill that had been developed would have been lost by A, the original lessee.

It is therefore important, from the viewpoint of the lessee, to insist upon a clause in the lease stipulating payment to the lessee in the event of condemnation. This clause generally states, in effect, that if the property is condemned before a certain date, the lessee is to receive a stated sum. Other dates are generally inserted with other sums stated, and the clause also contains a final date after which the tenant is not entitled to any part of the condemnation award.

For example, in the event of condemnation, the clause will state:

The lessee shall receive the following amounts and none other as the agreed share of the award for such condemnation when, as, and if it is paid:

If such final order of condemnation is entered before April 1, 1987, the sum of $40,000; if between April 1, 1987, and April 1, 1989, the sum of $30,000; if between April 1, 1989, and April 1, 1991, the sum of $20,000; if thereafter, no award or share whatsoever.

In the large commercial leases involving subordinated or unsubordinated ground leases, the situation becomes more complicated. There can be a total taking or a partial taking. Often there will be three concurrent parties involved: the lessor, the lessee, and the leasehold mortgagee. Consequently, the lease will provide that if there is a *total* taking, the lessor will receive the value of the land, the lessee will receive the value of the improvement, and the mortgage will provide that the leasehold mortgagee will receive from the lessee sufficient monies to pay the mortgage indebtedness.

Where there is a partial taking, the lessor receives a sum for the land taken and the mortgage will contain a provision permitting lessee's share of the proceeds to be used to restore the improvements.

THE SALE OF LEASEHOLDS

In one sense a lease consists of two parts: (1) a stream of income, and (2) the reversion, which is the right to the property after the termination of a lease.

The owner of a lease then has the stream of income, plus the reversion. If the owner has a need for money, both the income stream and the reversion could be sold; i.e., the fee subject to the lien of the mortgage could be sold in the case of a ground lease. The owner of the lease can also sell the stream of income. How much is it worth?

Suppose 10 years remain on the lease and the rental is $10,000 per year totaling $100,000 over the 10-year period. Clearly the income stream is not worth $100,000 because there is a 10-year waiting period. Assume that the "going rate is 9 percent." Then, using a 9 percent discount rate, the factor is 6.418 (the present worth of an annual income of $1 for 10 years discounted at 9 percent—see Table 4, Appendix B, Present Value of a $1 Annuity). Then $10,000 × 6.418 = $64,180, the present worth of the $100,000 stream of income.

Whether this can be sold for this sum is another matter considering bargaining power, risk factor of the tenant, and relative nonliquidity.

KEY TERMS

assignment (of a lease)	ground lease
bondable lease	index lease
eminent domain	lease
escalator lease	lessee
gross lease	lessor

net lease   revaluation lease
percentage lease   subletting (of a lease)
rent   subordinated ground lease

QUESTIONS FOR REVIEW

1. Briefly describe what a lease is.
2. Leases may be described by method of payment. Explain the differences among: (a) gross or flat lease, (b) semi-gross lease, (c) net lease, (d) bondable lease, and (e) percentage lease. Identify some additional methods relating to the payment of leases.
3. Discuss some of the reasons why leases are used for financing purposes.
4. What is meant by a *commercial ground lease*?
5. Describe a subordinated ground lease and indicate some problems associated with its use. How can fee owner protection be provided?
6. Leases are characterized by a number of common terms. Briefly describe the following terms: (a) option to purchase, (b) option to renew, (c) covenant not to sublet or assign, and (d) use of the premises.
7. The concept of condemnation is important to lease arrangements. Discuss.
8. In discussing the possible sale of leaseholds, what is meant by the reversion?

PROBLEMS

1. Assume that you have entered into an index lease and your rental payments are tied to the consumer price index. Recently, the consumer price index rose from 150 to 180. When the index was at 150 your monthly rent was $300. How much will your rent be raised? What percentage increase does this represent? What would have happened if the consumer price index had dropped from 150 to 120 instead of rising?
2. It is sometimes said that a tenant may obtain 100 percent financing from a lease. Explain this statement in terms of the following information. Assume that you want to expand your manufacturing plant capacity. Additional land requirements will cost $50,000 with plant costs amounting to $100,000. What factors would be important in deciding whether to obtain a mortgage and build the building or lease the building from an investor?
3. You have the opportunity to purchase an existing lease. The lease is for 7 remaining years and will produce a stream of income (i.e., cash inflows in the form of rental payments) of $15,000 per year.
   a. If you desire a 14 percent return on your investment, how much would you be willing to pay to own the lease? In other words, what is the present worth of this lease arrangement to you?

b. How much would you be willing to pay if instead of annual payments you received $1,250 per month?
c. How would a 16 percent required rate of return, a 10-year lease life, and lease payments of $15,000 per year affect the amount you would be willing to pay for the lease?

PART 5

CONSTRUCTION AND PERMANENT FINANCING PRACTICES

13

BUILDER-DEVELOPER FINANCING FUNDAMENTALS

LEARNING OBJECTIVES

After studying this chapter, you should be able to do the following:

Define the term limited partnership and describe its regulation and Internal Revenue Service qualification requirements.

Describe current tax implications for both typical limited partnerships and master limited partnerships.

Define an S Corporation and discuss the benefits of operating as an S Corporation.

Identify and describe the use of the joint venture.

Explain the meaning and use of both the convertible mortgage and the participation loan.

Define the term "gap financing" and explain its use.

Describe what is meant by both residential and commercial collateral loans or mortgages.

IT IS IMPORTANT to have a basic understanding of certain background fundamentals before topics pertaining to construction and permanent financing are addressed. Although usually organized as corporations, builder-developers often find themselves involved with limited partnerships and joint ventures. Other topics of potential interest to builder-developers include convertible mortgages, equity participations, the buy-sell agreement, gap financing, and collateral mortgages, all of which are discussed in this chapter.

BASIC FORMS OF BUSINESS ORGANIZATION

Corporate Form

Sooner or later, questions about the builder-developer's form of business organization will be raised. Is the builder a corporation, a partnership, or a single proprietorship? Most builder-developers are corporations. The reason for organizing as a *corporation* is to enable the builder-developer to hide behind the corporate veil, but only if the builder-developer is an exceedingly strong corporation financially will the lender permit the builder-developer to sign any legal document as a corporation only. The lender will insist that the builder-developer sign the documents both as the corporate entity and individually as a guarantor. This is to protect the lender in the event of bankruptcy by the corporation. If bankruptcy should occur, and if it is necessary, then the lender can possibly seize corporate assets as well as individual assets.

Builder-developers, although preferring to be organized as corporations, often find it advantageous to operate as general partners in limited partnership arrangements or to take part in other forms of equity participations. We will now discuss these other important considerations.

Limited Partnerships

The *limited partnership,* or syndicate, is both an investment vehicle for small investors and a source of funds for a builder-developer. The partnership consists of a general partner and limited partners who are the equity investors. The purchases and/or operations of the partnership can take many forms. For example, a broker may form a limited partnership for the purpose of buying and holding a piece of land for future resale. In this case it may be formed with contributions ranging upward from $1,000. Generally, the agreement incorporates a stipulation that the general partner will share any capital appreciation with the limited partners. This may be as high as 50 percent of the gain.

Often the limited partnership takes place where a builder-developer is involved. The builder-developer acts as the general partner, agreeing to sell the land to the partnership, build at a predetermined price, and manage the property. The agreement provides for sharing of profits, losses, and cash flow. In this case, the general partner usually receives 5 percent and the limited partners share 95 percent. There is also a provision for the sharing of any capital appreciation if the property is resold. Often the percentage of the capital appreciation is on a 50–50 basis after the limited partners have received the return of their equity investment.

Typically, if the project is an apartment house, or even a shopping center, the limited partners contribute one third on the signing of the agreement, one third on completion of construction, and one third when occupancy reaches 95 percent. The form of payment may vary with the agreement.

The Regulation of Limited Partnerships. The offerings of limited partnerships have been ruled as security offerings and subject to federal and state regulations. Unless the offering is "private," it must be registered under the Securities Act of 1933. Although never statutorily defined, a private offering has been presumed to be a sale to fewer than 25 persons. It should be noted, however, that even a private offering does not exempt the seller from the fraud provisions of the Act. There must be a full disclosure to proposed investors of all facts, circumstances, and risks involved in the investment. Furthermore, state laws have recently tightened up, which may affect the offering of limited partnership shares.

The Risks of Limited Partnerships. As in any investment, there are risks in the limited partnership which are listed as follows:

1. Rents may be lower than projected and operating expenses may be higher.
2. A partnership interest is not readily saleable; consequently, there is a high degree of liquidity risk.
3. It is conceivable that a future Congress may reduce, or even repeal, liberal depreciation allowances.

IRS Requirements for Limited Partnerships. Not only is the Securities and Exchange Commission interested in the limited partnerships, but the Internal Revenue Service also looks over the shoulder of the investors. Unless the agreement is properly drawn, the IRS will construe the limited partnership as a corporation. In this case, losses and other tax advantages cannot flow through to the investor. The IRS Code Section 7701 and its regulations provide that a partnership shall be classified as an association taxable as a corporation if its major characteristics more closely resemble those of a corporation than those of any other type of business organization.

The criteria used by the IRS to test for a corporation are as follows:

1. Is it an association?
2. Is there an intention to do business for a profit?
3. Does it have continuity of life?
4. Is there centralization of management?
5. Does it have free transferability of interests?
6. Is there limitation to the organization's property of liability for the organization's debts?

For a limited partnership to be classified as a corporation by the IRS, it must meet more than two of the above criteria. Since the first two criteria are common to all forms of business organization, they are excluded from consideration by the IRS in determining corporate form. Under the Uniform Partnership Act the general partner can dissolve the partnership at any time, or the partnership agreement may contain a terminal date. If the agreement is set up along these lines, the third criterion would not classify the limited partnership as a corporation. Most limited partnerships do have centralization of management, so criterion number four would apply. As to free transferability of interests, a properly drawn agreement would contain a clause requiring permission of the general partner or other partners before an interest could be transferred. Since the IRS regulations state that this interferes with free transferability, the fifth criterion would be eliminated. As for the sixth criterion, "limitation to the organization's property of liability for the organization's debts," the general partner has unlimited liability for the partnership debts, so this criterion also is eliminated. Thus, the limited partnership can be set up so that only one criterion, centralization of management, classifies it as a corpo-

---

TAX IMPLICATIONS OF LIMITED PARTNERSHIPS

The Tax Reform Act of 1986 placed severe limitations on real estate investment through limited partnerships as well as individuals. For example, prior law placed little or no limitations on the amount of income a taxpayer could "shelter" by using deductions and credits to offset income from other activities, e.g., wages and salaries. If a taxpayer could show a paper loss due to depreciation of a property in a limited partnership of $120,000, and his or her income from salary amounted to $120,000, then the taxable income for that individual was zero. All that has been changed under the 1986 Act. Depreciation must now be calculated on a straight-line basis, 27.5 years on residential income-producing property, or 3.63+ percent per year, and 31.5 years, or 3.17+ percent per year, for nonresidential (commercial) income-producing property. Even here there are limitations:

1. The use of "passive" activity losses against the income is limited. "Passive" gains or losses from a business activity are ones in which a taxpayer does not "materially participate." Thus, limited partners are not permitted to shelter other income. Other income includes salary, dividends, royalties, interest, or nonbusiness capital gains. This also applies to the S Corporation (discussed later in this chapter) where a shareholder does not "materially participate."
2. Rental activities, including net leases, are considered nonparticipatory business activities *even* if the taxpayer *does* materially participate. However, one who actively participates may take losses up to $25,000 against nonpassive income. For example, if a taxpayer has $20,000 in losses from a rental unit in which he or she actively participates and a salary of $50,000, then he or she is taxed on $30,000 ($50,000 - $20,000). The amount that can be taken as a loss, or $25,000, is phased out if the taxpayer's income exceeds $100,000.

ration for tax purposes. If necessary, the limited partnership agreement can even be drawn more loosely and permit free transfers.

Master Limited Partnerships (MLPs). A *master limited partnership* is a large partnership with interests (shares) that are sold on an established exchange; e.g., the New York Stock Exchange. MLPs originally started in 1980 and were used in the oil and gas industry. However since the passive tax rules were enacted in the Tax Reform Act of 1986, their use has multiplied rapidly. Touted as a means of "getting around" the rules, the MLP has many corporate characteristics such as limited liability, free transferability of interest, and centralized management. At the same time, the MLP has the favorable attributes of the limited partnership, passthrough of deductions (losses, etc.), and the avoidance of double taxation.

In the final analysis the MLP is a limited partnership, and it does generate what would be defined under the 1986 Act as passive income for its investors which can be used to offset any passive income generated by tax shelters.

Both the IRS and the Treasury Department indicated that the MLP should be taxed as a corporation. However, in December 1987 Congress voted that exchange-traded MLPs are to be grandfathered from federal tax treatment as corporations until 1998.

S CORPORATIONS

An *S Corporation* is simply a corporation wherein an application is made to the IRS to qualify under Subchapter S of the Internal Revenue Code. As a corporation under Subchapter S, there is still the limited liability of the corporation; however, the entity is taxed as a partnership. This means, of course, that (a) there is *no* corporate income tax and (b) the income, expense, and any losses are taxed to the shareholders.

In order to qualify as an S Corporation, there must be no more than 35 stockholders, who are either individuals or certain types of trusts, and furthermore the corporation cannot receive more than 25 percent of its income from "passive" income. Regular corporate tax rates will apply to amounts above 25 percent and if excesses occur for three consecutive years the Subchapter S election will be lost. *Passive income* includes rents, royalties, dividends, and interest. The "rents" category does not include payment for spaces where significant services are given the lessee, e.g., motels and hotels, but it does include rents from apartment buildings.

Oddly enough, the 1986 Act does not specifically mention the S Corporation stockholder, but common sense dictates that when an S Corporation shareholder/stockholder is an individual, the shareholder who claims deductions must show material participation on an "individual" basis. For example, if an individual owns 10 percent of the stock in an S Corporation located in New York State but lives in Georgia and does not participate in any of the corporation's activities or decisions, that individual obviously cannot claim deductions. If it were otherwise, a loophole would be provided which would be tantamount to opening the door to the limited partnerships that Congress worked so hard to close.

ADDITIONAL FORMS OF OWNERSHIP PARTICIPATION

The Joint Venture

Due to the inflation of the seventies and eighties, both the contributors of "entrepreneurial talent" and the contributors of money to a project want a share in the profits. This led to the formation of the joint venture. A *joint venture* is the coming together of a small number of persons for a particular transaction. The ownership can be a general partnership, limited partnership, or a tenancy in common. As far as the IRS is concerned, the "joint venture" is treated by the IRS as a partnership, unless it is clearly a corporation.[1]

In the joint venture, there are two players: (1) the builder-developer, and (2) the lender, who is usually a life insurance company.

In real life the joint venture may take several forms, three of which are described below:

The Limited Partnership. A limited partnership consists of one or more general partners who are liable for partnership debts and who carry out the partnership business. They operate with limited partners who contribute capital and who are not liable for the debts of the partnership beyond their capital contribution.

In this situation, the builder-developer organizes a partnership to own and operate the property. The lender organizes a subsidiary corporation, *lends* money on the property, and buys or receives an equity position with the builder-developer. At this point, the lender remains a silent limited partner with the builder-developer with *no* control over management.

The General Partnership. A general partnership is a partnership consisting of one or more partners to carry on a business with capital contributions either equal or unequal. All partners may be liable for the debts of the partnership.

Lenders appear to prefer this form of enterprise simply because in a strict limited partnership they have no control over management. Furthermore, in a limited partnership, the lenders may run into the section of the Uniform Limited Partnership Act which states, "No limited partner shall . . . receive or hold as collateral security for any partnership property." This is somewhat softened by the Official Comment of the Commissioners on Uniform State Laws stating that a limited partnership may lend to the partnership

---

[1]Internal Revenue Code, Section 7701(a)(2).

as a secured creditor if the partnership is solvent at the time the loan is made. However, this is only a comment and as yet has no binding legal effect.

In spite of the fact that a general partner may be liable for the debts of the partnership, this seems to be a preferred form of business enterprise.

Basket Loans. Many life insurance companies are involved both in sale-leasebacks (as will be discussed in Chapter 16) and in joint ventures. Much of the investment by life insurance companies in this type of venture has taken place since 1942. Prior to that time only five states permitted domiciled life insurance companies to buy real property for purposes other than their own use. It should be noted here that since 1942 life insurance companies have probably been the largest source of funds as "buyers" in sale-leaseback trans-actions and investors in joint ventures, the reason being that in 1942 the State of Virginia permitted insurance companies to invest up to 5 percent of their admitted assets in commercial real property. Other states followed Virginia's lead. Recently Connecticut permitted insurance companies to invest up to 5 percent of their admitted assets in loans or investments either not permitted by statute or by charter. Other states followed, with the percentage of permitted investment in income-producing real estate ranging from 3 percent to as high as 20 percent.

This type of investment by life insurance companies received the label of "basket loan." A *basket loan* is defined as a loan made as a result of a provision in the regulatory acts governing investments by insurance companies allowing for a percentage of total assets to be placed in otherwise unauthor-ized or illegal investments.

The Convertible Mortgage

The *convertible mortgage* is another form of equity participation, as discussed in Chapter 3, which, in effect, can turn into a form of joint venture at the option of a lender. It is an attempt by lenders to "cash in" on any capital appreciation by a builder-developer. For example, a lender lends 50 percent on a project—say $500,000 on a $1 million project. The loan is typically made at a lower-than-market rate. An agreement is made with the builder-developer enabling the lender to convert the loan into an equity position after five or ten years at the price in year one. Thus, the property may have appreciated to $1.5

TAX IMPLICATIONS OF THE CONVERTIBLE MORTGAGE

During the time of the loan, the builder-developer can deduct 100 percent of the interest, depreciation, and real property taxes. After the lender be-comes a 50 percent owner, the builder-developer can deduct 50 percent of the depreciation and real property taxes, but no longer has to pay principal and interest.

million at the end of five years, at which time the lender becomes a 50 percent owner with the builder-developer for the $500,000 original loan.

Participations in a Loan

The *participation* (or share) *loan* is a single loan made jointly by two or more lenders and is often called a "piggyback" mortgage.

Participation, or sharing, in the loan can be done either by an individual or an institution. For example, A and B agree to lend C $20,000 on a first mortgage. A is to put up $10,000 and B is to put up $10,000. In short, they will share equally. The borrower signs the note and mortgage in the amount of $20,000. The mortgage is then recorded. The two individuals (A and B) sign a participation agreement (in some states called an "ownership agreement").

A more common usage is to enable an institution to make a loan at higher than loan-to-value rates permitted by law. For example, suppose a lender cannot make a loan greater than a 75 percent loan-to-value ratio. Assume the borrower needs a 90 percent loan to purchase a $100,000 property. Legally the lender can lend only 75 percent, or $75,000. However, it can participate with an "approved lender."[2] The "lead" lender takes five sixths of $90,000 ($75,000 or 75 percent). The participant takes one sixth of $90,000 ($15,000 or 15 percent). Together, the loan equals $90,000 or a 90 percent loan-to-value ratio.

Often the loan is made with a private lender. However, this can only be done when the "lead" lender is the senior participant (first mortgagee) and the private investor is the junior participant (second mortgagee). Oddly, it has been ruled that this is not a participation.[3]

The participation agreement (illustrated in Figure 13–1) is the instrument used to define the ownership or shares that two or more persons may have in the same mortgage. It states the terms upon which the parties to the instrument agree to share in the mortgage. Generally, if both of the parties share equally in a single mortgage, they appear as co-owners on the face of the original mortgage. If they do not share equally in the mortgage, one of the parties will be junior to the other. The participation agreement indicates the extent to which one party is to hold a prior interest or position and the extent to which the other party is to hold a junior interest in the existing mortgage. It authorizes one of the parties to collect the mortgage interest and defines the method of distribution of principal and interest. It also recites the respective rights of the parties in the event of need to foreclose the mortgage.

The participation agreement is acknowledged but is generally not recorded. It may, however, be recorded in the event that it is subsequently necessary to bring an action under the terms of the instrument.

---

[2]These are federal- and state-chartered insured S&Ls and FHA-insured banks and government secondary market agencies.

[3]Opinion of the General Counsel, Federal Home Loan Bank Board, June 3, 1969.

SHARE OWNERSHIP AGREEMENT

AGREEMENT, made the   15th   day of   December   nineteen hundred and   --

BETWEEN   Arthur W. Johowitz, residing at 225 W. 55th Street, Borough of Manhattan, City and State of New York,

hereinafter designated as the party of the first part, and   Harriett A. Opperman, residing at 1892 Bleecher Street, Borough of Manhattan, City and State of New York,

hereinafter designated as the party of the second part,

WITNESSETH:—WHEREAS, the party of the second part is the holder of the following mortgage and of the bond   or note   secured thereby:

Mortgage dated the   5th   day of   September   , 19-- made by   Katherine Kline

to   David Rusher

in the principal sum of $ 50,000.00   and recorded in the (Liber) (Record Liber) (Reel) of section   28   of Mortgages, page   , in the office of the   Registra   of the   County of New York, September 6, 19--

hereinafter referred to together as the mortgage, which covers premises situate

(here follows a complete legal description of the property)

                                                                                                                                                                and

WHEREAS, there is unpaid on the mortgage the principal sum of   Forty Thousand and 00/100 ($40,000.00) ---
                                                                                                                                                                Dollars and interest, and the party of the first part has an interest therein to the extent only as hereinafter set forth, and

WHEREAS, the parties hereto desire to declare their respective interests in the mortgage, and the terms upon which the mortgage is held by the party of the second part,

NOW THEREFORE, the parties hereto mutually certify and agree:

First: The ownership of the party of the second part in the mortgage is now to the extent of Twenty Thousand and 00/100 ($20,000.00) --------------------------------------- Dollars.

FIGURE 13–1. Participation or Ownership Agreement

with interest thereon at the rate of 8-3/4 per centum per annum from December 15, 19 --,

and the party of the first part is now the owner of the balance of the mortgage; but the ownership of the party of the second part is superior to that of the party of the first part, as if the party of the second part held a first mortgage and the party of the first part held a second and subordinate mortgage to secure their respective shares of the mortgage.

SECOND: The party of the second part is authorized to collect all the interest due and to become due on the mortgage and to give proper receipts therefor, and after deducting the amount thereof due under this agreement to the party of the second part, shall remit any balance remaining to the party of the first part by mailing the same to the party of the first part at the address herein given.

THIRD: The party of the second part or any assignee of the interest of the party of the second part in the mortgage is authorized to accept payment of the mortgage and to execute the proper release, satisfaction or assignment therefor, and the holder so releasing, satisfying or assigning the mortgage shall account to the party of the first part for all money received in excess of the ownership in the mortgage of said party of the second part of such assignee.

FOURTH: The party of the second part shall have the exclusive right to foreclose the mortgage, to exercise all options therein contained and to receive the proceeds of the sale in the foreclosure action, but shall account to the party of the first part for any money received by the party of the second part in excess of the interest of the party of the second part in the mortgage. The party of the second part shall be under no obligation to protect the interests of the party of the first part in the foreclosure action or at the foreclosure sale, except that the party of the first part shall be made a party in the action. If the party of the second part is the highest bidder at the foreclosure sale the party of the second part may take absolute title to the mortgaged property and resell the same without accounting at any time to the party of the first part for the proceeds of the resale of the property.

FIFTH: The interest of the party of the first part in the mortgage is not assignable as against the party of the second part except by an instrument duly executed in the manner required for the execution of a deed of real property to entitle it to be recorded, and by delivering to and leaving with the party of the second part a duplicate original thereof; this provision shall apply to each assignment of such interest. Any assignee of the interest of the party of the first part in the mortgage shall have no rights under this agreement, nor be entitled to any payment thereunder until such duplicate original assignment shall have been delivered to and left with the party of the second part and the receipt of the same shall have been noted by the party of the second part on this agreement. Whenever the proceeds of the ownership of the party of the first part in the mortgage shall be paid to the holder thereof, this agreement and the original of all assignments thereof shall be surrendered to the party of the second part with a satisfaction piece or assignment to the party of the second part of the interest of the party of the first part in the mortgage in form satisfactory to the party of the second part, to whom the party of the first part shall also pay the fees for recording such documents. The interest of the party of the second part is assignable to any person or corporation, without liability on the part of the party of the second part, but the interest of any such assignee shall be subject to this agreement.

SIXTH: The party of the first part, for himself or itself, and his or its legal representatives, successors and assigns, hereby expressly waives any and all rights, claims and remedies under Section 1079-a of the Civil Practice Act as now enacted or as may hereafter be amended, and under any other law, State or Federal, now or hereafter enacted which in any manner is or may be inconsistent with the rights and remedies of the party of the second part as set forth in this agreement.

SEVENTH: All rights and authority given to the party of the second part under this agreement are irrevocable so long as the party of the second part or the assignee of the party of the second part has any interest in the mortgage, and shall pass to and apply to any assignee of the interest of the party of the second part in the mortgage.

This agreement may not be changed or terminated orally. This agreement shall bind and enure to the benefit of the parties hereto, their respective heirs, personal representatives, successors and assigns, provided, however, that assignment of the interest of the party of the first part shall become effectual only upon compliance with the provisions of Paragraph Fifth hereof. The word "party" shall be construed as if it read "parties" whenever the sense of this agreement so requires.

IN WITNESS WHEREOF, this agreement has been duly executed by the parties hereto the day and year first above written.

IN PRESENCE OF: /s/ Arthur W. Johowitz

/s/ D. D. Phillips   /s/ Harriett A. Opperman

(Acknowledgment)

Standard Form of New York Board of Title Underwriters

FIGURE 13–1. Participation or Ownership Agreement (concluded)

The Buy-Sell Agreement

In most financing requiring large sums of money, a builder-developer obtains a commitment from a permanent lender who requires that both of the following criteria be met:

1. The developer must obtain a construction lender satisfactory to the permanent lender.
2. A buy-sell agreement must be entered into with the interim lender.

Prior to the closing of the construction loan, a three-party agreement is entered into by (a) the borrower, (b) the construction lender, and (c) the permanent lender.

Basically, the borrower and construction lender agree not to find another permanent lender. In return for this, the permanent lender agrees to buy the loan. This prevents the borrower from seeking out another permanent lender in the event interest rates fall.

GAP FINANCING

Gap financing, sometimes called "bridge" or "swing" financing, is in effect a second or junior lien which is paid off when a permanent lender pays the full amount of the money due under a first mortgage.

For example, assume there is a construction loan of $1 million to be taken over by a permanent lender upon the completion of the construction. There is an agreement between the borrower and permanent lender that if, by the date of completion, the "rent roll" (tenant rental commitments) does not equal X amount of dollars, the permanent lender will take only $800,000 (called a floor amount), leaving a gap of $200,000. Further, the agreement states that the permanent lender will fund the gap if the rent rolls meet a specified amount by a specified date.

The question is: How is the $200,000 gap financed? The answer is: Either from a private investor or the construction lender. The procedures for each method are as follows:

1. The private investor lends the $200,000 at a relatively high rate of interest. In return, the investor receives a second mortgage for a period of between four and five years. The document also contains a clause that the permanent lender can pay off the gap loan at any time. Generally, this second mortgage is an interest-only mortgage.
2. The construction lender fills the gap. This is arranged for by the parties prior to construction and is incorporated into the buy-sell agreement. The construction lender then receives a second mortgage for the amount of the gap.

It should be noted that under the terms of some limited partnerships involving construction, particularly where there are cost overruns, the limited partners are required to cover the gap at the time the permanent loan is closed.

Mortgaging Out

The amount of the construction loan is tied to the commitment of the permanent lender. Many permanent commitments have two provisions in terms of the amount of the permanent loan: (a) a "floor" amount upon completion of construction; and (b) a "ceiling" amount when the project is fully rented. For example, say $800,000 when completed and $1 million when fully rented.

Construction lenders often will not lend more than the floor amount ($800,000 in this case) because they don't want to get involved in gap financing if they can avoid it. The floor amount consists of what the construction lenders regard as "hard costs" and "soft costs." *Hard costs* consist of materials and labor, while *soft costs* include such things as interest on the loan, the land, legal fees, etc.

Another group of construction lenders takes a different view and will permit what is called **mortgaging out.** Assume that the $200,000 difference here consists of profit to the builder-developer. These lenders will lend the floor, plus the ceiling proposed by the permanent lender, or the entire $1 million in our example.

However, when the construction lender is adamant and will lend only the floor, then the builder-developer has several choices until the permanent lender comes up with an additional $200,000 when the project is fully rented:

1. To use $200,000 in equity capital.
2. To obtain a letter of credit guaranteeing the extra $200,000.
3. To obtain a third-party guarantee.
4. To use collateral.

In the last three instances, the construction lender will then be willing to make the loan of $1 million rather than the $800,000 floor.

COLLATERALIZED MORTGAGES

This type of loan is used in both residential and commercial real estate loans, but somewhat differently in each.

The Residential Collateral Loan

Although used infrequently, the **residential collateral loan** is sometimes employed when the buyer is "assuming" or taking "subject to" a mortgage and doesn't have enough cash to pay the difference between the selling price and the mortgage. An additional prerequisite for its use is that the seller does not need the cash and does not want to get involved in a second mortgage.

The seller and lender enter into an agreement whereby the seller agrees to put a certain sum from the proceeds of the sale into a savings account. The existing first mortgage is then increased by this amount. When the new buyer reduces the mortgage to the amount approved by the lender, the savings account is released. It should be noted that the savings account carries with it a rate of interest which is paid to the seller.

For example, the seller has a parcel of property priced at $25,000 and there is an assumable mortgage of $15,000. A buyer comes up with $5,000 cash down. Thus, $5,000 cash plus the $15,000 mortgage equals $20,000, or $5,000 short of the purchase price. The seller puts the $5,000 received over the mortgage from the buyer into a savings account. The lender raises the mortgage from $15,000 to $20,000. When the buyer reduces the mortgage to $15,000, the savings account, plus the additional $5,000 paid by the lender into the account, is released to the seller. Therefore, the seller receives $10,000—the $5,000 cash down plus the $5,000 paid by the lender into the account at the time the mortgage was raised from $15,000 to $20,000.

A variation of this is to have a private investor, instead of the seller, deposit the money required by the lender into the savings account. This sum will then be held by the lender until the mortgage is reduced.

The Commercial Collateral Loan

In the *commercial collateral loan* or mortgage, the purchase basically is to enable institutions to make higher loan-to-value loans than permitted either by policy or law. For example, assume a borrower needs $100,000 and an institution can lend only 75 percent, or $75,000. The "excess" amount of the loan is $25,000. The institution can make a loan of the additional $25,000 if the loan is collateralized, or secured by something other than the real property. Consequently either (a) the deposits of the borrower are put up for collateral, or (b) another institution guarantees the loan, normally a national bank which can legally make such a loan.

The Backup Contract Loan

One of the most difficult loans to obtain is one for a special-purpose building; for example, a racquet club with a swimming pool. Lenders are apprehensive because if the lender has to foreclose, the property may prove unmarketable. Consequently, lenders will look not only to the real estate as security for the loan, but often require a *backup contract loan.* A mortgage loan is given by a lender and, in addition, a contract is entered into with a corporation or individual possessing a high credit rating, wherein monthly payments on that mortgage are guaranteed by the corporation or individual. Thus, if the borrower is unable to meet the monthly mortgage payments, the lender looks to the guarantor for payment. The term of the contract and the term of the mortgage are equal.

KEY TERMS

backup contract loan

basket loan

commercial collateral loan

convertible mortgage

corporation

gap financing

joint venture

limited partnership

master limited partnership

mortgaging out

participation loan

residential collateral loan

S Corporation

QUESTIONS FOR REVIEW

1. Builder-developers generally are organized as corporations. Why?
2. Why are limited partnerships used in real estate investments? How are they regulated?
3. Briefly describe the tax implications of a limited partnership.
4. Identify and briefly describe an S Corporation.
5. Define a *joint venture* and indicate the several different forms that might be used.
6. What is a *convertible mortgage* and how is it used?
7. How and why are participation loans used?
8. Identify and briefly describe "gap" financing and indicate how it is used in real estate financing.
9. What are *residential* and *commercial collateralized mortgages?*

PROBLEMS

1. Assume depreciation per $1,000 of property investment is $36.36 ($1,000/ 27.5 years) per year and the property is placed in service at the beginning of the first year.
   a. Show the first year's tax implications of a property valued at $800,000, net operating income of $100,000, and debt service of $75,000 (interest of $70,000 and amortization of principal of $5,000).
   b. Now assume depreciation occurs over 31.5 years and will be $31.75 annually per $1,000 of property investment. Using the information in Part a, indicate the first year's tax implications.
2. Assume a borrower is seeking a $108,000 loan on property valued at $120,000. However, a lender is restricted to a maximum 75 percent loan-to-value ratio. Describe how a participation arrangement might be used to provide the borrower with adequate mortgage funds.

14

CONSTRUCTION FINANCING

LEARNING OBJECTIVES

After studying this chapter, you should be able to do the following:

Discuss the preliminary lending procedures used in construction financing.

Define the term take-out commitment and describe the three types of take-out commitments.

Identify the three costs of "buying" construction funds.

Discuss how a construction loan is finalized.

Define the term mechanic's lien and describe the priorities between liens and mortgages.

Discuss how a builder-developer protects himself or herself against a mechanic's lien.

CONSTRUCTION FINANCING IS a two-stage procedure consisting of interim financing and permanent financing. *Interim financing* is relatively short-term financing involving a loan designed to finance the building during the construction period. *Permanent financing* takes place after the building is completed and is designed to cover the long term. The construction loan is paid off by the permanent loan and the buyer of the house or improvement pays off the permanent loan. For example, suppose a house is sold for $50,000, the construction loan is $40,000, and a buyer puts $5,000 down and obtains a long-term mortgage for $45,000. The long-term lender pays off the construction loan of $40,000 and gives the builder $5,000, which, together with the $5,000 down payment, presumably is the builder's profit.

Although not always, the construction loan and the permanent financing are generally handled by two different financial institutions. For example, a commercial bank may make the construction loan while a savings and loan association places the so-called permanent loan. There may be many variations of this, as shown in Table 14–1.

Construction loans can be used for three types of site improvements:

1. One- to four-family residential dwellings.
2. Multifamily residential dwellings.
3. Other commercial improvements; e.g., a shopping center.

TABLE 14–1. Variations in Construction Financing

Construction Loan (Interim)	Permanent (Long-Term Mortgage/Deed of Trust)
1. Commercial bank	Mortgage banker, who may intend to sell the mortgage at a later date.[1]
2. Savings and loan association	Savings and loan association, which may hold the mortgage or sell it at a later date to the Federal Home Loan Mortgage Corporation or another participating savings and loan association.[2]
3. Commercial bank	Mortgage banker with an advance commitment from the Federal National Mortgage Association.[3]
4. Commercial bank	Savings and loan association, which may either hold the mortgage or sell it.
5. Commercial bank	Mortgage banker with an advance commitment from either a life insurance company or a mutual savings bank.
6. Mortgage banker (who is in effect a subsidiary of a commercial bank)	Commercial bank, which may keep the mortgage or, most likely, sell it to another institution. The mortgage banker may sell directly to another institution such as a savings and loan association.

[1]A mortgage banker is defined as any person, firm, or corporation engaged in the business of lending money on the security of improved real estate or who is an investor in real estate securities or is the recognized agent of an insurance company or the direct purchaser of first mortgage real estate securities for investment only. The mortgage banker's activities are discussed in further detail in Chapter 6.

[2]The Federal Home Loan Mortgage Corporation's activities are outlined in Chapter 6.

[3]The Federal National Mortgage Association is discussed in Chapter 6. The term "advance commitment," as used above, means that the Federal National Mortgage Association has agreed to buy the mortgages when the builder has sold the homes. To obtain the "advance commitment" the mortgage banker has to pay a sum of money. The mortgage banker is then said to have "bought" money. These costs are, in turn, paid for by the builder-developer. The idea of "buying" money is discussed later in this chapter.

While the basic principles are the same in all these instances, there are some slight differences with regard to the institutions employed.

PRELIMINARY LENDING PROCEDURES

Assume a builder-developer who develops one- to four-family residential houses makes a decision to approach a mortgage banker for financing and that the mortgage banker is a subsidiary (or, as they prefer to be called, a separate entity) of a commercial bank. The builder-developer hopes to obtain construction financing from the mortgage banker and permanent financing from the parent bank.

In essence, what the builder-developer is doing is "buying" money, or seeking an advance commitment. Of course, like buying anything else, the money has its price, as will be pointed out later.

Assume further that the builder-developer has the necessary zoning, water tap permits, and any other necessary permissions. In addition, the builder-developer has land or an option on land for, say, 100 homes and asks for a commitment for a construction loan for this number of homes. Unless the builder-developer has an absolute triple A credit rating, this proposal will be rejected.

In most cases, the construction lender will insist that off-site improvements be made on a maximum of 20 lots. Then, and only then, will the mortgage banker make a commitment for a construction loan. In all probability, the commitment will be made on four units at a time. Four is the chosen number because both the builder-developer and the mortgage banker know that the construction costs for building four homes at a time are much less than building one home at a time. For example, if a backhoe or bulldozer is being used to dig basements, it's less expensive to have four basements done at one time than one at a time, and so on with other costs.

TAKE-OUT COMMITMENTS

Under normal conditions, a construction lender will not lend unless a builder-developer has a permanent *take-out commitment* from a permanent lender. In short, no permanent financing—no construction loan. Sometimes savings and loan associations permit small builders to go "naked" when granting construction loans with the knowledge that they can take the permanent loans. This is particularly true if the builder is engaged in building single-family homes on a relatively small scale.

The situation is quite different if a *national* commercial bank becomes involved. At the outset, it should be recognized that there is a distinction between a national bank and a state bank. A national bank is chartered and regulated by the Comptroller of the Currency while a state bank is chartered and regulated by state banking authorities. The Federal Reserve Act (as amended in 1974) provides that loans can be made by national banks up to the following limits:

1. 66^2/$_3$ percent of the appraised value of unimproved property
2. 75 percent of the appraised value if property has off-site improvements, e.g., streets, sewers, etc., or if it is in the process of being improved by buildings
3. 90 percent of the appraised value if such property is improved by a building

On the surface, this appears pretty cut and dried. The problem is this: If a builder-developer has land and needs $1 million to build, an examination of the above would appear to limit the construction loan to $750,000, meaning the builder-developer is coming up $250,000 short. However, construction loans of five years or less made on residential, farm, industrial, and commercial construction can be treated as *commercial* loans (up to 100 percent of the appraised value) by *national* banks *provided* the builder-developer has a firm commitment of permanent financing from a responsible lender[1] even though the loan is secured by a first mortgage.

This is the reasoning behind the need for the take-out commitments when the builder-developer is unable to immediately inform the construction lender of a permanent commitment. These commitments are of three types: (1) the forward take-out commitment, (2) the standby commitment, (3) the fundable standby.

Forward Commitment (Permanent Commitment)

This is an agreement by a permanent lender to pay off the construction lender when the project is completed. Forward commitments can generally be broken down into two categories by types of lenders into (a) residential construction and (b) commercial construction.

Residential Construction. In residential construction, the lenders are savings and loan associations, mortgage bankers, and commercial banks.

Lenders agree to finance buyers of homes or condominiums when sold. The terms of the commitments vary considerably. They may be at fixed rates. For example, the agreed financing rate may be 13 percent. If rates go up, loans are still made at 13 percent. If they fall, say to 11 percent, the builder-developer tries to get an 11 percent loan, losing whatever advance fees may have been paid for the commitment.

Second, the commitment may be made with an "upside only" fixed rate. For example, the commitment may be made with a top rate of, say, 14 percent. That is, at time of funding, the rate cannot go over 14 percent, but if the market rate at that time is lower, the loan will fund at a lower rate.

Third, the commitment may call for the builder-developer to pay whatever the lender is charging at the time of the take-out. This is sometimes called an "over-the-counter" commitment.

---

[1]12 United States Code Annotated, Section 371(c) (Supp. 1980).

Commercial Construction. Institutions making most of the permanent loans in large projects are the life insurance companies and, more increasingly, pension funds. The pension funds rarely deal directly with a builder-developer, but work through agents (frequently savings and loan associations) who process and service the loans.

The Standby Commitment

This situation arises when a builder-developer is unable to obtain permanent financing immediately, without which it will be impossible to obtain a construction loan. The typical lender is a national commercial bank.

The builder-developer may then obtain from another lender a "standby" commitment. Basically, the lender is assuring the construction lender that the "standby" lender will take the permanent loan, if the builder-developer is unable to find a permanent lender by the time construction is completed.

The interest rate on the standby is very high, often several points over the market rate, and the builder-developer has to pay a substantial up-front fee to obtain the commitment.

Because of these high interest rates, the builder-developer is motivated during the period of construction to obtain a permanent lender at a lower rate of interest.

The Fundable Standby

This is a standby of comparatively recent origin. A builder will obtain a "fundable," sometimes called "bankable," standby to satisfy a construction lender.

The interest rates are high—three or more points higher than might have been obtained from a "normal" permanent lender.

The annual constant payments are relatively low because the term of the loan is based on a 25- to 30-year term with a balloon note on the end. This means, of course, that the borrower can meet the annual payments on the loan.

The loans are locked in, generally, for two years. This means that the borrower must pay the very high interest rates for at least a two-year period. However, the borrower generally is unable to complete the project and fully rent the project during this time period. At this point, the project becomes more attractive to an institutional lender, who pays off the fundable loan and takes over the permanent financing at a more reasonable interest rate.[2]

---

[2]In the past the sources of funds for these loans have been: Aetna Business Corporation, CIT Corporation, General Electric Credit Corporation, and U.S. Life Real Estate Services Corporation.

COST OF MONEY

If a builder-developer decides to go along with the building of four homes at a time, the discussion will turn to the cost of money.

There are three "costs" of buying money:

1. The cost of the construction commitment
2. The cost of the advance commitment (permanent financing)
3. The cost of the construction loan itself

The Cost of the Construction Commitment and the Advance Commitment

Both the initial cost of the construction commitment and the permanent commitment are expressed in "points"—one point being equal to one percent of the face amount of the loan. Suppose, for example, that both loans are to be $200,000. The commitment fee on the construction loan is 2 points, and on the permanent financing, 3 points. The cost, then, is $4,000 for the construction financing ($200,000 × .02 = $4,000), plus $6,000 for the permanent financing ($200,000 × .03 = $6,000), or a total of $10,000. This amount ($10,000) cannot be borrowed as part of the loan but must be paid by the borrower at the time the loan is made.

Admittedly, 2 points and 3 points are high rates. The range is from 1 to 3 points. The amount depends on the availability of money: if money is "easy," the lower figure will prevail; if money is "tight," the higher figure will prevail.

The Cost of the Construction Loan

The cost of the construction loan is the interest that must be paid on the construction loan during the time of building or until the property is sold. This rate is either a "fixed" or a "floating" rate.

The Fixed Rate. By definition, this rate is a stated rate that does not vary during the period of the loan. In short, the rate is set by contract in the construction loan agreement (called a "building loan agreement" in some states). For example, the agreement may state that 8 percent interest will be paid on the amount of money advanced for the construction loan.

The Floating Rate. The floating rate amounts to a variable interest rate. For example, the agreement may read to the effect that the builder-developer must pay interest of, say, two points above the prime rate. The *prime rate* is the rate of interest charged by large banks to their most credit-worthy customers. The prime rate of a particular bank is chosen as a reference point. Assume their prime rate at the time of signing the agreement is 9 percent. Then initially the borrower must pay 9 + 2, or 11 percent. The rate "floats" because it is adjusted either monthly or quarterly—depending on the agreement. If the prime rate goes to, say, 10 percent, then the builder-developer pays 10 percent until the next adjustment period. If at the following adjustment period the prime rate has risen to 14 percent, then the builder-developer pays 16 percent.

In general, builders dislike floating rates because they cannot easily calculate their costs, and because the cost of money is a rather large portion of the total cost of construction.

Why are floating rates used? Lenders will insist on floating rates, particularly in a market where interest rates are rising rapidly. When interest rates are firm or thought to be firm, fixed rates are most likely to be used.

THE PROPOSED SITE

At this point, the lender of the construction money will raise the question as to whether or not the four (or perhaps more) lots are encumbered. The construction loan, after all, is a mortgage or deed of trust and the lender will insist on having a first lien against the property. If the land is free and clear, there is no problem. However, if the builder-developer purchased the land and gave the seller a blanket purchase money mortgage, then one of two things must be done:

1. If the blanket purchase money mortgage or deed of trust contained a partial release clause, then the four (or more) lots must be paid off. A partial release of the lots proposed for development is obtained from the mortgagee. The partial release is then recorded, thereby rendering the lots free and clear.
2. Any mortgage or deed of trust in existence on the proposed building sites must be made subordinate to the construction loan. In order for this to be done, a clause to this effect must have been included in the blanket purchase money mortgage or deed of trust that had been entered into by the builder-developer and the seller. In this case, the seller enters into a subordination agreement, such as that shown in Chapter 11, making the purchase money mortgage or deed of trust subordinate to the proposed construction loan. This subordination agreement will contain a clause to the effect that the builder-developer's seller will be paid a certain amount as each home is sold.

Many builder-developers prefer the subordination agreement to a partial release. The reason for this is that it enables the builder-developer to operate using less out-of-pocket cash.

FINALIZING THE LOAN

There are many steps to be taken before the loan is finally approved. After the preliminary discussions, as outlined above, the builder-developer must submit an application for the construction loan. This will be discussed in Chapter 17. In essence, the application contains a list of assets and liabilities to reveal the builder-developer's net worth. At this point, unless the builder-developer is well known, a credit check is made to ascertain credit-worthiness. Next, a title insurance policy, or abstract of title, is ordered to determine if the title to the proposed development site is clear.

The builder-developer may have to submit a feasibility study to determine the marketability of the proposed project. In any event, the lender, if familiar with the location of the project, will attempt to analyze the marketability of the proposed project.

Assuming the builder-developer's credit rating is satisfactory and the homes appear to be marketable, then a number of other steps are taken:

1. Plans, specifications, and cost estimates are submitted to the lender. The plans and specifications must be complete, clear, and accurate. Costs must be accurately estimated. This sounds like a truism. However, an experienced lender will check subcontractors' bids when analyzing the overall builder's cost estimates. Subcontractors' bids which are either "too low" or "too high" in the lender's opinion constitute a red flag to the lender. For example, if the subcontractors' bid is "too low" under local conditions, it may mean that the builder cannot complete the job without obtaining additional funds. If the subcontractors' bid is "too high," this may cause the price of the home to be out of the market.
2. An appraisal is made by the lender on the basis of the lot, plans, and specifications. Assume, for the purposes of illustration, that the proposed construction loan is to be $40,000 and the builder-developer has placed an exaggerated selling price of $85,000 on the proposed home. Obviously, the construction lender won't go along with this because the home won't appraise out to this amount and consequently won't sell under current market conditions.
3. At this point, the Construction Loan Agreement will be entered into. In those states using the mortgage, it will be in the form of a blanket mortgage on, say, four lots. In those states using the deed of trust, the agreement will take the form of a blanket deed of trust. An example of a construction loan agreement is shown in Figure 14–1.

CONSTRUCTION LOAN CONTRACT

THIS AGREEMENT, made the   day of
nineteen hundred and

BETWEEN

hereinafter referred to as the borrower, and

hereinafter referred to as the lender.

FIGURE 14–1. Construction Loan Agreement

WHEREAS, the borrower has applied to the lender for a loan of
Dollars to be advanced as
hereinafter provided and to be evidenced by the note of the borrower for the payment of said sum, or so much thereof as shall at any time be advanced thereon, on the day of
nineteen hundred and with interest upon each amount so
advanced from the date of such advance at the rate of per centum per annum to
be paid on the day of and quarter annually thereafter;
said note to be secured by a
on the premises described as follows:

(here follows complete legal description)

TOGETHER with all fixtures and articles of personal property now or hereafter attached to, or contained in and used in connection with said premises, including but not limited to all apparatus, machinery, fittings, gas ranges, ice boxes, mechanical refrigerators, awnings, shades, screens, storm sashes, plants and shrubbery.

WHEREAS the lender agrees to make said loan upon the terms, covenants and conditions hereinafter set forth and the borrower agrees to take said loan and expressly covenants to comply with and perform all of the terms, covenants and conditions of this agreement.

NOW, THEREFORE, it is agreed between the parties as follows:

1. The borrower expressly covenants to make on said premises the improvement described below in accordance with the plans and specifications therefor, which, before the making of the first advance hereunder, the borrower agrees to file with all governmental authorities having jurisdiction and to obtain all necessary approvals of said plans and specifications and all necessary building permits from said authorities. The said plans and specifications shall first be submitted to and approved by the lender in writing; and no changes or amendments thereto shall be made without first obtaining the written approval of the lender. The said improvements to be made shall be as follows:

(here follow plans and specifications)

2. Said loan is to be advanced at such times and in such amounts as the lender may approve, but substantially in accordance with the following schedule:

(a schedule of payments follows here)

(Corporate Seal)	/s/ Ace Realty Corporation, Inc., by George Ace, President
(Corporate Seal)	/s/ Fourth National Bank of Mineola, N.Y. by Frances Jones, Cashier

FIGURE 14–1. Construction Loan Agreement (continued)

Acknowledgment
STATE OF NEW YORK, COUNTY OF   s.s.:

                                                    being dully sworn, deposes and says:
I am at No.   . I am the   , the borrower mentioned in the
within building loan contract. The consideration paid or to be paid by the borrower to the lender
for the loan described therein is   Dollars ($), and that all other
expenses incurred, or to be incurred, in connection with said loan are as follows:*

Broker's commission $ _____

Examination and insurance of title and recording fees $ _____

Mortgage tax $ _____

Architect's, engineer's, and surveyor's fees $ _____

Inspections $ _____

Appraisals $ _____

Conveyancing $ _____

Building loan service fees $ _____

Sums paid to take by assignment prior existing mortgages which are consolidated with building loan mortgages and also the interest charges on
such mortgages $ _____

Sums paid to discharge or reduce the indebtedness under mortgages
and accrued interest thereon and other prior existing encumbrances $ _____

Sums paid to discharge building loan mortgages whenever recorded $ _____

Taxes, assessments, water rents and sewer rents paid (existing prior to
the commencement of improvement) $ _____

and that the net sum available to the said borrower for the improvement is
          Dollars ($) less such amounts as may become due or payable for insurance
premiums, interest on building loan mortgages, ground rent, taxes, assessments, water rents and
sewer rents accruing during the making of the improvement.

SWORN TO before me this   day of   , 19   .

/s/ _____   /s/ _____
     Notary Public
     (Seal)

*This is the statement regarding the fee for the loan commitment. For example, assume the
total loan is to be $160,000 and the borrower is to pay one point, or 1 percent. This equals $1,600
and is mentioned here and paid immediately.

FIGURE 14-1.   Construction Loan Agreement (concluded)

The schedule of payments mentioned in the preceding loan agreement can be
made substantially in accordance with the building loan inspection report
shown in Figure 14-2. This payment schedule can be set up in five, four, or
any number of payments. Sometimes the schedule is set up in percentages

BUILDING LOAN INSPECTION REPORT

Inspected for Payment No.	Date Inspected	Approved By	Rejected By

REMARKS:

*Check Box to indicate applicable payment plan ⟶

Standard Requirements for Four Payment Plan
Standard Requirements for Five Payment Plan

1
- Building dimensions and set-back
- Foundation complete
- Mud sills set and treated
- Ground Story studs creosoted
- Joists set—properly spaced and blocked
- Joists doubled under partitions
- Sub-flooring laid diagonally
- Framing lumber on site

2
- Room lay-out according to plans
- Fireblocking and bracing
- Rough framing complete
- Exterior sheathing complete
- Roof complete
- Shower stall backframed and pan in place

3
- Fireplace complete except for mantel
- Flashings at doors, windows, chimney, etc.
- Door and window frames complete
- Bathtub set and properly blocked
- Plumbing roughed in
- Clean-out plug accessible
- Wiring roughed in

INTERIOR WALLS
- If plaster—complete, quality, texture, thickness
- If sheetrock—completely nailed and ready to tape

EXTERIOR WALLS
- If stucco—brown coat complete and primed
- If wood—wood finish shall have prime coat of paint

4
- Standard finish stock lumber items on site
- Windows and doors fit properly—move easily
- Interior painting complete
- Exterior painting or stucco complete
- Floors completely finished
- Finish trim, molds, etc. complete
- All plumbing fixtures completely installed
- Gutters, downspouts, diversions complete
- Chimney contact caulking
- Mantel of fireplace installed
- All electrical fixtures installed
- Water heater, laundry trays, furnace ready to use
- Yard facilities according to plan
- Structure is ready to occupy

5
- Final Disbursement

*Unchecked items indicate reasons for rejection.

FIGURE 14–2.   Building Loan Inspection Report

which are spelled out in the agreement. The percentages may be substantially as shown in Table 14–2.

TABLE 14–2. Schedule of Payments Using Percentages

	Six Payouts	Five Payouts	Four Payouts	Three Payouts	Three Payouts
Foundation and rough grading / First floor laid	15%	25%	25%	50%	30%
Framing complete and sub-flooring / Roof sheathing and chimney / Window frames set	15%				
Rough plumbing, heating, wiring	10%	15%	25%		
Exterior finish / Lath and plaster or dry wall	20%	20%		25%	30%
Basement floor and heating plant / Interior finish, except flooring	20%	20%	25%		
All finish flooring / Ready for occupancy	20%	20%	25%	25%	40%

MECHANIC'S LIENS

The *mechanic's lien,* created solely by statute, gives the right of lien to those persons who have furnished work or materials for the improvement of real property. The persons who are entitled to the lien include contractors, subcontractors, laborers, material suppliers, engineers, and architects.

The underlying basis of the right of lien lies in the fact that, as a result of the work done or materials furnished, the property is improved. *Improvement* means generally the erection, alteration, or repair of any structure upon, connected with, or beneath the surface of any real property. It also includes any work done or materials furnished for the structure's permanent improvements.

Because the lien is based on the idea of improvement, it can be placed only against the property. For example, A owns two parcels of property. B works on one of them and is not paid. B's right to a lien exists only against the property on which B has actually worked. The right of lien does not exist against both parcels of property.

Time in Which to File the Mechanic's Lien

The lien laws contain a statement regarding the time in which to file. Generally it states "that four months have not elapsed dating from the last item of work performed and dating from the last items of materials furnished. . . ."

The purpose of this statement is to show compliance with the statute when, for example, the statute states that the notice must be filed within four months after the last work or last items of material are furnished. Although most state statutes require that the lien be filed within four months, the requirements vary among states. They may also vary with regard to the time in which the material supplier has a right to file, and the time in which the laborer has a right to file. For example, in Idaho and Oregon the material supplier must file within sixty days after the last items of materials are furnished; the laborer must file within ninety days after the completion of the work.

Priorities Between Liens and Mortgages

In the larger construction projects the problem of the mechanic's lien arises with the construction lender and not the permanent lender because the permanent lender will not "take out" a construction loan with prior liens.

Construction loans are paid out over time. It is conceivable, then, that another lien might take precedence, placing the construction lender in the position of a second lienor. Therefore, in those states, e.g., Pennsylvania and Minnesota, where the lien relates back to "commencement of construction," construction lenders make certain the site was vacant at the time the mortgage was recorded.[3] "Commencement of construction" has been interpreted by the courts to mean that the work must be conspicuous and substantial and apparent to all that the owner is constructing improvements on the site. This is done by affidavits both from the borrower and the contractor that no work has been done nor have materials been delivered to the site. In addition, construction lenders often require photographs of the site.

In some states the mortgage of the construction lender is given the first lien over a mechanic's lien,[4] but only as to funds paid out by the construction lender prior to the filing of the mechanic's lien. For example, suppose the construction loan is for $1 million and has been recorded prior to "commencement of construction." Assume that under the terms of the building loan agreement $200,000 has been handed over to the builder. After this, $150,000 in mechanic's liens is placed against the project. The $150,000

---

[3]The following states and the District of Columbia gave priority to mortgages recorded *prior* to "commencement of construction": Arizona, Arkansas, California, Connecticut, Delaware, Florida, Georgia, Hawaii, Idaho, Iowa, Kansas, Kentucky, Louisiana, Maryland, Massachusetts, Minnesota, Mississippi, Nebraska, Nevada, New Hampshire, New Jersey, New Mexico, New York, North Carolina, Pennsylvania, Tennessee, Utah, Vermont, Washington, West Virginia, and Wisconsin.

[4]District of Columbia, Kentucky, New Jersey, North Dakota, South Dakota, and South Carolina.

would in effect come after the $200,000 disbursed and thus ahead of the $800,000 not yet disbursed by the lender.

The "Contract" Priority States.[5] Simply put, the "contract" priority states will give priority to mechanic's liens on the date the owner contracted for improvements. For example, suppose an owner or contractor enters into a contract for material on June 15 and the supplier of the materials files a lien dated October 2. Assume a mortgage is recorded on September 15. Who has priority between the mortgagee and the lienor? In the contract states, it is the lienor.

The Obligatory Construction Loan. Some construction loans (mortgages) are obligatory, which becomes relevant to mechanic's lien priorities. For example, suppose an obligatory construction loan of $500,000 wherein the lender is obligated to make five disbursements of $100,000 each. Assume a $100,000 disbursement is made and four are due. The loan is recorded. The general rule is that the recorded mortgage has priority over subsequent liens. This is true of all states listed in footnote 3, except Delaware, Louisiana, and Maryland.

The "Optional" Construction Loan. This type of loan is sometimes called an "open" end mortgage. In short, a construction loan is made payable for $500,000 with a provision that at the option of the *lender* another $100,000 will be forthcoming, if necessary. The construction loan (mortgage) is recorded. Assume $500,000 is advanced and an extra $100,000 is paid, and then a mechanic's lien is filed for $45,000. Who has priority? In general, the rule is the lienor has priority of $45,000 over the last $100,000 loan, which the lender was not obligated to make.

Mechanic's Liens and Cost Overruns. Another problem facing construction lenders with regard to mechanic's liens arises when there is a cost overrun. For example, a construction lender has a first lien of $1 million under the terms of a building loan agreement. Assume a cost overrun of $100,000. A subcontractor files a mechanic's lien for $50,000. The construction lender advances $100,000, but the $50,000 lien remains unpaid. The construction lender adds the $100,000 to the original mortgage or deed of trust of $1 million. Does the construction lender have a priority over the $50,000 lien?

Generally, the excess ($100,000 here) becomes subordinate to the mechanic's lien ($50,000 in our example). However, some states (Florida, for example) will permit the construction lender to retain the priority of the first lien if the original building loan agreement provides for "future advances." This is a clause in the building loan agreement that calls for, say, a $1 million

---

[5]The states are Alabama, Alaska, Colorado, Illinois, Indiana, Maine, Michigan, Missouri, Montana, Oregon, Texas, Virginia, and Wyoming.

loan with possible future advances up to 125 percent. In this case, the construction lender could lend up to $1,250,000 and still be protected by the first lien.

Mechanic's Liens and Foreclosures. If a construction loan is foreclosed on, as will be discussed in Chapter 18, liens junior to the first mortgage are extinguished. On the other hand, if a construction lender receives a Deed in Lieu of Foreclosure, the title from the borrower to the construction lender is conveyed subject to the mechanic's liens, and these must be paid off by the construction lender prior to the sale of the property to a permanent investor.

Protection Against Liens

The basic methods of protection against liens are outlined below.

Title Insurance. In many cases, construction lenders will insist that they receive full-coverage mortgage title insurance from an approved title insurance company. In addition, the lenders require that prior to each advance to the builder-developer the insurance be extended by endorsement to cover the advance of funds.

In the so-called nonpriority states listed in footnote 3, because of recent large losses companies require such things from the builder-developer as receipts from material suppliers and contractors and waivers of liens before they will add an endorsement to the policy.

Waiver of Lien. This instrument waives the right of subcontractors to file any liens against the premises. Sometimes this is signed by the subcontractors when final payment is made or the instrument may be executed prior to beginning work on the premises. In the event the subcontractors enter into this type of agreement, they are bound by its terms not to file liens. However, in some states, although the subcontractor cannot file a lien in the event of nonpayment, the subcontractor may still obtain a personal judgment against the builder-developer.

When final disbursements are made, construction lenders require waivers of lien from all contractors, subcontractors, and suppliers of materials. They also require a certificate of occupancy from local governments, and, more importantly, a written statement from the permanent lender that the permanent lender is satisfied with the construction of the improvement and that the loan will be taken out in accordance with the take-out commitment.

Completion Bond. Another means of protection against liens is to have the contractor obtain a *completion bond,* a type of surety bond, prior to commencing a job. In the event that any parties remain unpaid, they will be taken care of under the terms of the bond and no liens will be attached to the property.

In the larger projects, the performance bond may even go a step further. The bond will provide that the bonding company will, if the contractor defaults, complete the project according to the terms of the contract between the builder-developer and the contractor.

The major problem is that small contractors often don't have the financial strength to obtain a completion bond.

Holding Funds. Holding funds can be utilized effectively to thwart mechanic's liens. The construction lender merely holds back part of the contract price until the period for the filing of the mechanic's liens has passed. After this period, the balance due to the contractor is paid.

In those states where the lien relates back to the commencement of the job, another method of holding back funds is employed. The construction loan agreement is executed by the builder-developer and is recorded. After the recording the contractor starts the job. In this case no actual cash is delivered to the builder-developer at the time of execution of the mortgage but is turned over as the job progresses. The construction loan agreement is recorded prior to the beginning of the job and thus is prior in right to any subsequent mechanic's liens.

To further make certain of this, a lot inspection is done by the construction lender. The lot is physically inspected to determine that no work has been done or material delivered to the job. A report is made attesting to this fact. Often, in addition to the written report, photos are taken of the lot as additional substantiation.

Another way a lending institution may attempt to protect itself against liens is to pay the contractors' bills itself. The contractors list monies owed on the form shown in Figure 14–3 on page 254 and the institution pays the bills and charges such payments against the construction loan.

Some institutions will also insist upon a preconstruction *affidavit,* which is a sworn statement. To swear falsely puts the affiant in a position subject to criminal penalties. A preconstruction affidavit is shown in Figure 14–4 on page 255.

KEY TERMS

affidavit	mechanic's lien
completion bond	permanent financing
construction financing	prime rate
interim financing	take-out commitment

QUESTIONS FOR REVIEW

1. What is meant by the statement that construction financing is a two-stage

CONSTRUCTION LOAN DRAW REQUEST

TO SAVINGS BUILDING AND LOAN ASSOCIATION

LOAN NO._____   DATE_____

LOAN IN NAME OF:_____

PROPERTY ADDRESS:_____

LEGAL DESCRIPTION: _____

PLEASE PAY THE FOLLOWING BILLS:

NAME OF PERSON, SUPPLIER, OR SUB-CONTRACTOR	FOR	NET AMOUNT (AFTER DISCOUNT)	
		$	
(Paid bills and/or invoices and/or labor list for the above are enclosed herewith)		Total $	

_____
Authorized Signature

Remarks:

FIGURE 14–3. Construction Loan Draw Request

procedure? Also indicate some variations in construction financing arrangements.

2. Identify and briefly describe the three types of take-out commitments.
3. List and explain the three costs in "buying" construction money.
4. What is a floating rate on a construction loan?
5. Discuss general differences in priorities between liens and mortgages according to state laws.
6. Identify and briefly describe the basic methods for protecting against liens.
7. What does the preconstruction affidavit attempt to do?

STATE OF   )
)ss
COUNTY OF   )

The undersigned, first being duly sworn, deposes and says that your affiant is about to commence construction on the premises known as _____ which has been mortgaged to (the interim lender) _____ to secure a construction loan for the erection of _____ buildings on said premises. Affiant further states that a true itemization of said construction costs is furnished at this time, said to be used for labor and materials on said premises.

Affiant further states that no labor or materials, prefabricated or otherwise, have been used or prepared for use on said premises to this date.

Further affiant sayeth naught.

_____
                                        Contractor

SWORN TO before me this _____ day of _____, 19_____.

                                /s/ _____
                                        Notary Public

FIGURE 14–4. Preconstruction Affidavit

PROBLEMS

1. Assume that a construction loan for $65,000 is obtained from a commercial bank with permanent financing to be provided by a savings and loan association. The builder sells the house for $90,000 and the savings and loan will make a mortgage loan for 80 percent of the purchase price. Explain what will happen.

2. Money has a "cost" or "price." For example, a builder often is faced with costs for a construction loan commitment and the advance commitment or permanent financing. The builder also must pay interest on the construction loan itself. Using the data in problem 1 above, calculate the builder's cost of money if 2 points are charged on each of the construction and advance commitments. Also, the interest cost on the construction loan is 14 percent with the building time expected to last 6 months. What is the total cost of buying the construction money?

3. The Third National City Bank holds a first lien of $2 million on a construction loan agreement. There has been a $250,000 cost overrun on the building construction costs. A subcontractor also has filed a mechanic's lien for $75,000. In order to complete the construction, the Third National City Bank advances the additional $250,000 and adds this amount to the original mortgage for a total of $2,250,000.

   a. If the $75,000 mechanic's lien remains unpaid, does the construction lender have priority over the lien?

   b. What would happen in the event that foreclosure took place and the $75,000 mechanic's lien had remained unpaid?

15

TRACT AND SPECIAL PURPOSE FINANCING

LEARNING OBJECTIVES

After studying this chapter, you should be able to do the following:

Describe the basic requirements of the Interstate Land Sales Full Disclosure Act.

Discuss how a tract or land development loan is used by a developer or subdivider.

Define the term cooperative dwelling and describe how cooperatives are financed.

Define the term condominium and describe how condominiums are financed.

Indicate what is meant by a condominium conversion and discuss how these conversions are financed.

Indicate what is meant by timesharing and discuss how time-shares are financed.

MOST REAL ESTATE development begins with the land or tract, as it is sometimes called. This chapter focuses on tract financing before turning to several special-purpose financing topics, including the financing of cooperatives, condominiums, and time-shares.

INTERSTATE LAND SALES FULL DISCLOSURE ACT

Lenders financing subdividers or tract developers must make certain that borrowers using lots as security for loans comply with the Interstate Land Sales Full Disclosure Act. The Act protects the buyer against fraudulent and deceptive sales practices by providing civil and criminal remedies against the land developer and the sales agent for willful violations of the Act.

Requirements of the Act

Basically, the Act requires the seller of subdivided property to make a full, complete, and accurate disclosure of all relevant information about the property *prior* to the consummation of the sale to the buyer of the land. Land developers are required to file a statement of record with the Office of Interstate Land Sales Registration (OILSR), Department of Housing and Urban Development. The statement of record details information which is summarized in a document called the "property report," which must be given to the prospective purchaser prior to a sale. It contains such things as name and location of developer and subdivision; effective date of the report; road distances to nearby communities; financial terms and refund policies, if any; mortgages and liens; protection, if any, afforded the buyer in case of financial default of the developer; leasing arrangements; taxes and special assessments to be paid by the buyer; escrow and title arrangements, plus any restrictions, easements, covenants, and their effects on the buyer; recreational facilities available and expected dates of completion of proposed ones; availability or lack of utilities and services, such as trash collection, sewers, water supply; any need for drainage and fill before the land can be used for building; presence of schools, medical facilities, shopping and transportation or proposed dates of availability of such services; number of homes now occupied; and accessibility of lots by roads. Developers' financial statements are also required, as well as any other data HUD may require.

Problems of the Lenders

Many subdivisions are sold by means of an installment land contract or a contract for deed or simply a promissory note. Frequently these are "sold" to a lender. The problem arises if the subdivider violates the Act or any part thereof. If so, the sale on which the lender is basing security may be suspended by HUD. In addition, the subdivider may have the contract rescinded and be required to repay the purchaser.

Furthermore, if a lender forecloses against the entire subdivision, the lender may find itself in the position of the developer and hence subject to the Act. If the lender seeks to escape the "developer" role and sell the entire subdivision to another developer, permission has to be obtained from HUD to exempt that sale from the Act. Failure of the lender to do so is a violation of the Interstate Land Sales Full Disclosure Act.

TRACT OR LAND DEVELOPMENT LOANS

A *tract* (or *land*) *development loan* is a loan given to a developer or subdivider to put in streets and utilities after the acquisition of raw land. Most land development loans by institutions are made on land to be used for residential purposes.

The amount of the loan can be as much as 75 to 80 percent of the appraised valuation of the finished lots. Sometimes due to inaccurate appraisals or even accurate appraisals (in a rapidly rising market) the subdivider with an 80 percent loan frequently winds up with a sum greater than the cost of the land plus the site improvements.

A financial institution, as security for the development loan, places a blanket mortgage containing a partial release clause on the lots. The loan is, of course, a lump sum loan on the tract, but for purposes of the partial release a part of the total amount loaned is attributed to each lot.

Let's now illustrate the procedures involved in a land development loan. Assume a developer can purchase a tract of land for $200,000 and subdivide it into 100 lots. An off-site improvement of storm sewers requires an expense of $100,000, while on-site improvement costs for grading, streets, and miscellaneous expenses will be $250,000. The developer will make a down payment of $50,000 on the land so that a $500,000 loan will be necessary as follows:

Land costs	$200,000	
Less: Down payment	50,000	$150,000
Off-site expenses		100,000
On-site expenses		250,000
Total Loan Needs		$500,000

An appraisal of the property (based on the indicated improvements) indicates a value of $7,500 per lot for a total of $750,000 ($7,500 × 100 lots). Thus a $500,000 loan would be equal to two thirds or $66^2/3$ percent of the appraised value. While each lot has a retail value of $7,500, the loan-related value per lot would be $5,000 ($7,500 × .6667). Of course, a wide range of prices could exist for the different lots. Lot #20 might have an appraised value of $15,000 and a loan-related value of $10,000 ($15,000 × .6667), while lot #5 might be appraised at $3,000 with a $2,000 loan-related value. However, for our purposes, let's continue with the level or equal value lot example.

The developer decides to pursue the land development project and borrows the $500,000 at a 12 percent interest rate under a blanket mortgage containing a partial release clause. At a minimum the lender would require payment of a *release price* of $5,000 per lot so that the loan would be repaid when all 100 lots were sold (100 × $5,000 = $500,000). In practice, a 15 to 20 percent premium is included in the release price to protect the lender against potential developer problems associated with slow sales and/or being "stuck" with undesirable lots after the best lots have been sold. Thus the lender might require a release price of $6,000 ($5,000 × 1.20) per lot.

If the developer sells 30 lots during the first year, 45 lots the second year, and the remaining 25 lots the third year, the following loan repayments would occur under the partial release clause:

Year	Lot Sales	Payment to Lender	Remaining Loan Balance
0	—	—	$500,000
1	30 × $6,000	$180,000	320,000
2	45 × $6,000	270,000	50,000
3	8 × $6,000 plus $2,000 on 9th lot	50,000	0

Notice that in the first and second years the developer will have a margin of only $1,500 ($7,500 selling price less $6,000 release price) per lot to cover interest payments on the loan, other operating expenses, and possibly some profit. The opportunity for much of the profit comes in the third year if the remaining lots are sold. The first eight lots sold also will have a margin of only $1,500, while the ninth lot requires a final $2,000 loan repayment out of the $7,500 selling price. Much of the developer's return comes from the sale of the remaining 16 lots in the amount of $120,000 ($7,500 × 16).

In instances where lots in a land development sell more slowly than anticipated, the additional interest costs could substantially reduce the attractiveness of the development land project and might even force the developer into bankruptcy. For example, the annual interest payments on a $500,000 loan at 12 percent would be $60,000. The failure to sell any lots during the first year would result in no release prices being applied to reduce the existing loan balance. In this worst case scenario there would be no sales revenues but a $60,000 interest payment obligation the first year. Likewise, the failure to fully sell out the land development could result in financial ruin for the developer and might leave the lending institution holding a loan with an unpaid balance.

Purchase Money Financing

Much of subdivision financing starts with a builder-developer who intends to build houses. This individual buys land and gives the seller a P.M. mortgage containing a partial release clause.

However, in addition to the partial release clause, a builder-developer who intends to obtain a construction loan must negotiate a clause whereby the holder of the P.M. mortgage agrees to become subordinate to the construction lender. In return for this, the seller generally insists on another clause in the mortgage in effect stating that any monies obtained in the form of a first mortgage on the property must be used *only* for the purpose of improving the property.

Sometimes the seller who is holding a P.M. mortgage will insist on what is termed a "rollover" provision. For example, suppose there are 20 lots. However, the agreement by the seller to take a subordinate or junior position behind an institutional lender might be on only 10 of the lots. Under a roll-over provision, when those 10 lots are developed and sold with the seller being paid in full, the P.M. mortgage is then placed in a subordinate position to the construction loan on the remaining 10 lots.

COOPERATIVES, CONDOMINIUMS, AND TIME-SHARES

A *cooperative dwelling* is one in which a tenant purchases stock in the corporation that owns the building rather than renting an individual unit in the building. Thus, tenant-stockholders own a portion of the building's equity. Tenants pay rent, which includes a portion of the cost of operation, plus interest and amortization of the mortgage, if any.

In such a building, 100 percent of the ownership of the building is allocated to the various units. For example, if there are 100 identical units in the project, then each shareholder owns one one-hundredth of the building. When tenant-stockholders purchase stock, it covers their proportionate share of the equity over and above the amount of the outstanding mortgage. As the mortgage is amortized, the equity in the tenant-stockholder's unit increases. In addition to stock, a tenant-stockholder is given a *proprietary lease,* which is a long-term lease. The lease also gives a tenant-stockholder a restricted right to sell to a third party during the term of the lease. Under the lease restriction a tenant-stockholder often must obtain the consent of a majority of the other stockholders to sell a unit. In some cases the tenant-stockholder must obtain the consent of the Board of Directors of the corporation in order to sell the unit.

Sometimes this method of tenant-ownership is in the form of a trust. In these cases a certificate of beneficial interest is given the tenant instead of a stock certificate.

Financing the Cooperative

The financing of the cooperative is similar to the financing of any commercial property. First the developer obtains a construction loan and a commitment for permanent conventional financing. Like most commercial financing the loan maximum is about 75 percent of the appraised value. The corporate mortgage covers all of the apartments. Stock is then sold and the proprietary lease executed. For example, suppose a particular apartment is valued at $60,000. Assume the pro rata share of the mortgage is $40,000. The stock is then sold for $20,000 with the purchasers liable for their share of the payments on $40,000 plus maintenance costs, a pro rata share of the taxes, and so forth.

Because of the initial low loan-to-value ratio ($66^2/3$ percent in this example) the buyer of the cooperative must put down a substantial down payment. This makes the units difficult to sell. Furthermore, a lender cannot take a second mortgage on an "individual" apartment. The reason obviously is that there is no way in the cooperative building for a holder of a second mortgage to foreclose against a single unit. Any borrowing done by a prospective purchaser of a unit must be done on a personal basis; for example, a prospect with only $15,000 in cash who needs a total of $20,000 must borrow the additional $5,000 on a personal note. This means it will probably have to be paid off at a faster rate than the underlying mortgage.

This leads to another difficulty with the cooperative. Suppose that A buys a cooperative apartment for $40,000 and it appreciates to $60,000. There is no way that A's individual unit can be refinanced because of the underlying blanket corporation mortgage. In addition, suppose A purchased a single-family home for $40,000 and its value is now $60,000. If A needs money for family responsibilities such as a child's education, the loan can be entirely refinanced or a second mortgage placed on the property. This cannot be done with the cooperative apartment.

Another problem arises when a prospective tenant wishes to pay all cash for a unit. In this case the unit still bears a pro rata share of the entire blanket corporate mortgage. If the neighbors fail to make their payments, and a foreclosure takes place, the individual's apartment is lost with the rest. In some parts of the country, title companies have issued policies against this sort of loss.

Cooperative Loan Procedure.   The cooperative loan procedure is not unlike any other loan. There are, however, a few minor variations within the mortgage instrument. For example, any subsequent transaction is subject to the terms of the executed mortgage. If A owns a unit and sells it to B, the executed mortgage is made a part of the conveyance. Further, in case of default the lender is immediately given the power of attorney to collect all rents and profits of the mortgaged property. In addition the mortgage contains a clause specifically stating that no individual unit will be released to an individual cooperative owner until the underlying mortgage is paid in full.

FHA Cooperative Financing.   The FHA cooperative insurance program provides for two basic types: (1) the sales-type project and (2) the management-type project.

The sales-type project.   Here a cooperative corporation is organized, and each individual member is a stockholder. It should be noted that the sales-type cooperative involves new construction. Consequently, an FHA-insured blanket mortgage is placed by the lender on the project while it is being built. After the sale of the individual units an FHA mortgage is given to the individual purchasers with the proceeds going to pay off the blanket mortgage. Title to common spaces remains in the name of the cooperative.

The management-type cooperative.   Here a nonprofit cooperative corporation or trust is organized. The purpose is to build permanent cooperative housing for its stockholders. The management-type project is covered by a blanket mortgage. The shareholders do not receive title to their individual units, but have the right to occupy individual units. They do, however, both share in the management of the project and have a share interest in the entire project. The interest paid is the FHA maximum rate plus one half of one percent on the unpaid balance of the mortgage as the insurance premium.

Condominium Financing

Some housing authorities predict that by the year 2025 over 50 percent of the nation's population will be housed in condominiums. What is a condominium? *Webster's Third New International Dictionary* defines a **condominium** as:

> Common ownership by two or more persons holding undivided fractional shares in the same property and having the right to alienate their shares resembling tenancy in common in Anglo-American law rather than joint tenancy with its right of survivorship.

Briefly, the condominium is an ownership in fee simple by an individual of a single unit in a multi-unit structure, coupled with ownership of an undivided interest in the land and other elements of the structure held in common with other unit owners of the building. The fee simple ownership of the single unit generally applies to the airspace between the walls and between the floors and ceilings. If the walls are for the support of the building or are in common with another unit, they belong in the category called "common elements." Generally, the common elements consist of the land beneath the buildings, yards, service installations, and community entrances and exits. In the final analysis, individuals own their own units in fee simple and are co-owners with others in the common elements.

Most condominiums are found in the area of residential housing. However, the condominium form of ownership is growing in the area of office buildings, industrial property, and even shopping centers.

There are four basic documents to establish a condominium:

1. The declaration (sometimes called a master deed). The declaration places the property under the condominium statutes.
2. The plot plan or architect's drawing showing the division into apartments.
3. The by-laws which control and govern the internal organization of the condominium.
4. The deed conveying the apartment and rights in common areas to purchasers.

Why the Condominium? Logically the question arises as to the reason why condominiums have taken over from the cooperatives. There are a number of reasons:

1. The cooperative tenant does not own an individual apartment. The cooperative corporation owns it. The shareholder-tenant merely has a proprietary lease.
2. The cooperative building has a *single* mortgage on the entire structure. Shareholders are responsible not only for their individual pay-

ments on interest and taxes, but also are collectively responsible if one shareholder fails to meet the payments.

3. In the condominium, each person has an individual mortgage and is responsible for taxes on that unit and is thus personally liable.
4. In the cooperative, an individual shareholder can increase equity through amortization of the loan, through appreciation in the value of the unit, or both. However, if the shareholder wants to sell, the buyer must be able to put down a large amount in cash. In the case of the condominium, the individual unit can be refinanced or the owner can take back a second mortgage.

The FHA and Condominiums. Although there has been a form of condominium ownership in Puerto Rico since 1958, the major impetus for this form of ownership is to be found in Section 234 of the Housing Act of 1961. This Act provided for FHA financing and insurance. Two conditions had to be met by the individual states:

1. Historically, assessors levied taxes on the value of the land plus the structure as a single unit. Basically they were limited to a two-dimensional concept. Because FHA financing was and is available only if the states permitted taxes to be levied on a three-dimensional concept, the states hurried to comply. Thus, taxes are now levied on the individual apartment plus a proportion of the value of the common spaces.
2. One other requirement was necessary which follows from the above FHA requirement. That is, the states also had to provide for the recording of title to the condominium as a three-dimensional unit. This, too, the states have done.

Condominium Conventional Financing. Although the availability of FHA financing gave impetus to condominiums through expediting the state statutes providing for real property taxes on individual units, relatively little FHA financing is done. Most of the condominiums are built with conventional financing.

First, a construction loan is obtained. Typically in connection with condominium loans the interim lender agrees to place the permanent financing. The length of the construction loan ranges from 1 to 3 years with the loan maturity matched with the expected time of completion of the project.

Second, each unit is financed by means of a permanent loan. It is here that it becomes conventional financing with a difference. The reason is that many state statutes provide that the individual unit cannot be sold subject to the construction loan. Consequently the developer must pre-sell enough units to pay off the construction loan. In cases like this, the developer retains the right to call off the condominium if an insufficient number of units are pre-sold. In this case the project will revert to a unit rental situation.

The Construction Lender and the Master Deed. Like any other loan, the construction loan is recorded to give the construction lender a first mortgage.

However, in most states the construction loan is recorded before the Declaration or Master Deed is filed. The reason for this is that once the Master Deed is filed establishing a condominium, the property remains a condominium. Consequently, if the construction lender is forced to foreclose, the foreclosure is against a condominium with the result that the construction lender must recoup the loan by selling condominiums rather than regarding the property as a rental unit. By recording the mortgage first, the lender can choose either to rent the units or sell them as condominiums if foreclosure is necessary.

In some states, even where the Master Deed is filed first, the courts have held that a subsequent foreclose of the construction mortgage wipes out the condominium regime, as it is called.

Condominiums and the Partial Release. The construction mortgage is a blanket mortgage with a partial release clause similar to most blanket mortgages. However, there is a slight difference. For example, in the case of a blanket mortgage covering a number of lots where a stipulated sum is paid to the lender, the lot is simply released. In the case of a construction loan on a condominium, not only must the partial release clause provide for a release of the unit itself, but also it must release a proportionate interest in the common elements.

Division of Proceeds Between the Builder-Developer and the Construction Lender Upon Release. The division of monies between the builder-developer and the construction lender in condominium lending is quite different from the case of a subdivision containing single-family homes. For example, assume a builder-developer wants to build 100 single-family homes costing $100,000 each to be priced to sell at $110,000 (or at a profit of $10,000 each). Assume a 100 percent construction loan. The total amount to be loaned is $10 million with a maximum profit of $1 million to the builder-developer. There's *no* way the construction lender will lend the builder-developer the $10 million immediately. The loan agreement might call for an initial loan on, say, 10 homes or $1 million. When the homes are built and sold, the construction lender is paid by the permanent lender, and the builder-developer has a profit of $100,000.

If sales come to a halt with the builder-developer selling only five of the homes, the construction lender will be forced to foreclose on the remaining $500,000 of the loan. The builder-developer still owns 90 lots and has a profit of $50,000.

In the case of a 100-unit condominium, the construction lender is forced to loan the entire $10 million. Assume the same facts as above, but five units are sold. In this case, the construction lender will have to foreclose on a $9.5 million loan which may be difficult to liquidate.

In the case of the single-family home construction loan, if sales are slow after, say, 50 homes have been sold and the builder-developer decides to abandon the project, the construction lender has been paid $5 million and the builder-developer has made a profit of $500,000.

Builder-developers have been known to "walk away" from condominium projects when sales are slow. Suppose 50 units are sold, the builder-developer has made $500,000, but the construction lender has to foreclose on the $5 million remaining on the loan.

To prevent this, construction lenders either:

1. Require 100 percent of the proceeds to pay down the loan. Often this has resulted in bankruptcies of builder-developers because of the lack of cash flow to pay overhead and selling expenses.
2. Require between 85 and 90 percent of the proceeds to prevent the bankruptcy situation from developing.

The Interstate Land Sales Full Disclosure Act and the Condominium. As previously described in this chapter, the purpose of the Interstate Land Sales Full Disclosure Act is to require the seller to make a full disclosure of all relevant information to a prospective buyer by means of a property report if the sale is to be made through the mail or other means of interstate commerce. Consequently, if this is to be done with a condominium, a property report must be submitted to a prospective buyer. The argument supporting this is that in the case of a condominium the "airspace" *lot* is being sold rather than a structure (e.g., a house where the Act does not apply).

A condominium is exempt from the I.L.S.F.D.A. if (a) the unit is completed before it is sold, or (b) there is a sale under a contract where the developer must complete the structure within two years after the signing of the sales contract.

The so-called townhouse, sometimes called a "patio house," is also exempt from the Act. Although the townhouse has many features of the condominium, it is distinguished from the condominium in that the townhouse cannot be "stacked." In short, the owner of the townhouse owns the fee simple in the land underneath it, as distinguished from the condominium owner who owns the land beneath as a tenant in common and has a fee simple in the airspace only.

State Regulations. With regard to condominiums, some states have statutes similar to the I.L.S.F.D.A. with regard to full disclosure.[1] The statutes require that a registration statement be filed with the Real Estate Commission before the condominium project may be sold.

State Regulation of Earnest Money. In the past there have been numerous instances where a prospective buyer gave a builder-developer a down payment on a condominium to be built, and the builder-developer either defaulted on the construction loan or went bankrupt. Thus the buyer lost the down payment.

---

[1]Florida Stat. Ann. Sec. 718.504; Virginia Code Ann. Sec. 57–79.88(a).

A few states have statutes to protect the innocent buyers.[2] In both Maryland and Virginia, the law provides that deposits on condominium units must be placed in escrow. In Virginia, the statute also provides that the escrow account cannot be attached by creditors of the builder-developer. In this way, even if the builder-developer goes bankrupt, the innocent buyer is able to recoup the earnest money.

Condominium Conversions

Condominium conversion means converting an existing rental unit into condominiums. An apartment owner will either personally engage in the conversion or sell the project to a converter. There are a number of reasons owners engage in conversions: (a) operating expenses have risen faster than rents; (b) tax shelter benefits have declined—in short, an owner has fully depreciated the property; (c) rent controls have resulted in a low or nonexistent cash flow; and (d) the opportunity has arisen to realize a large gain from the conversion.

There are several rules of thumb followed by most successful converters:

1. At least 25 percent of existing tenants must indicate a willingness to purchase their units.
2. New units should sell for at least 30 percent over the proceeds if the building were sold as one unit. For example, if an apartment complex sold as a unit would bring $1 million, the individual units should sell for a total of $1.3 million after conversion.
3. The condominiums should sell for about 25 percent lower than comparable single-family homes.
4. The debt service to buyers must be lower than the debt service to single-family home buyers.

Problems With Local Governments. Prior to engaging in a conversion, an apartment owner must check local statutes for such things as moratoriums, zoning regulations, and ground leases.

Moratorium statutes. Many communities have enacted moratorium statutes to discourage conversions. Most of these statutes are based on the police power of the municipality. For example, in Brookline, Massachusetts, the conversion statute was amended to provide that a tenant in a converted unit could be evicted only by the *purchaser* of the converted unit, *not* the developer. Further, if the tenant did not vacate voluntarily, the tenant had a mandatory stay of six months from the issuance of the eviction notice, which could be extended for six months in case of hardship. In addition, the town imposed a general six-month moratorium on the issuance of certificates of eviction against all tenants in possession of apartments at the time of purchase

---

[2]Florida Stat. Ann. Sec. 18.201; Maryland Real Property Code Ann. Sec. 10–31; Virginia Code Ann. Sec. 55–79.95.

for conversion.

In a subsequent suit, the plaintiffs argued that the statute constituted a taking without just compensation. The court upheld the statute stating (a) the housing crisis in Brookline justified the exercise of police power; (b) the amendments, while causing a transfer of rights incident to ownership, were no more severe than caused by general rent or eviction control; and (c) a mere period of delay before conversion was not confiscatory.[3]

Zoning regulations. Normally conversion from a rental unit to a condominium is not a change in use. However, if the converter intends to put part of the building to commercial use (for example, retail shops on the first floor), there may be problems.

Ground leases. The apartment to be converted may be on leased land, in which case lenders may refuse to lend unless the land is purchased.

Financing the Conversion. Since most buildings to be converted have an existing mortgage, it must be paid off. This is done by means of "gap" or "bridge" financing, as previously discussed. Basically, the converter approaches a lender willing to pay off the underlying mortgage, plus any sums necessary for upgrading. Often the same lender agrees to place the permanent financing as units are sold.

The Wraparound Bridge. This type of financing often occurs when the existing mortgage carries a low rate of interest. For example, suppose the converter has an apartment complex with a $1 million first mortgage at 7 percent interest or at a cost of $70,000 per year. Assume the conversion costs are $250,000 and the conversion time is one year.

A "bridge" loan of $1,250,000 might be obtained at 15 percent, the interest costs being $187,500. If a wraparound bridge is obtained at a rate even as high as 20 percent on $250,000, then the total costs would be $50,000 on the wrap, plus $70,000 interest on the first mortgage, or $120,000, which would result in a substantial savings.

Another way of obtaining the same result would be to obtain a second mortgage of $250,000.

In both cases the condos are sold on contract for deed. When all the units are sold, the contracts are sold to a permanent lender, who then pays off the underlying mortgage plus the wraparound bridge or second mortgage.

Owner-Converter Checklist. The checklist on pages 268 and 269 has been developed by the Mortgage Guaranty Insurance Corporation to help an owner-converter decide whether to become the permanent lender on a particular condominium project.

---

[3]Grace v Town of Brookline, 399 N.W. 2nd 1038 (Mass. 1979).

OWNER-CONVERTER CHECKLIST:

PHYSICAL CHARACTERISTICS OF PROJECT AND NEIGHBORHOOD

____ Parking ratio? Adequate?

____ Is parking owned? Rented? Assigned? Uncontrolled?

____ Are balconies of adequate size? One or more for each unit?

____ Do balconies permit owners to clean own windows?

____ Any design elements that increase maintenance cost?

____ Is maintenance of common areas good?

____ Is exterior design acceptable to market?

____ Are floor plans acceptable to market?

____ Is there proper mix of one-, two-, or three-bedroom units?

____ Are streets public or private?

____ Who provides police and fire protection?

____ How is trash pickup handled? At whose expense?

____ Are utilities public or private?

____ Is unit price and quality comparable to neighborhood?

____ What is density of dwelling units per acre?

____ Is project large enough for efficient management?

____ Is ethnic mix appropriate?

COMMON AREAS

____ Are common areas defined?

____ Are limited common areas defined? Who maintains?

____ Are there restrictions on use of common and limited common areas?

____ Are common facilities rented or owned?

____ Are common areas encumbered?

____ Is common-area ownership equal or proportioned?

____ Are recreational facilities adequate? Superadequate?

____ Are there any club membership privileges or requirements?

____ What does common-area maintenance charge include? Taxes? Insurance? Common-area maintenance? Central heat and/or air conditioning? Window cleaning?

____ Is monthly maintenance charge reasonable?

____ When does developer control expire?

____ Can common areas or facilities be enlarged later?

____ Are there TV and parking restrictions?

OWNERS ASSOCIATION

____ Is association empowered to collect monthly maintenance fees?

____ What is penalty for nonpayment? How enforced?

____ Is association required to notify lender of default in common-area charge payments?

____ Is association solvent?

____ Is association balance sheet and operating statement data available?

____ Is provision being made for reserve funds for major maintenance items?

____ Does association provide professional management? Review management contracts?

____ When does builder turn over control to owners?

____ Is insurance adequate?

____ Does association approve new owners?

____ Is time allowed for owner approval reasonable?

____ Must association advise lenders of maintenance payment default?

CONDOMINIUM DECLARATION

____ Is declaration recorded?

____ What are occupancy restrictions? Children? Pets? Renters? Family members? Guests?

____ Can units be rented on long-term basis?

____ Is a rental pool permitted?

____ Are resales restricted?

____ What are unit owners' voting rights?

____ Provisions for amendments?

____ When does builder's control terminate?

____ What percentage of units must be sold before the condominium declaration is filed?

____ Any restrictions on owners' mortgage financing?

____ What are rights of mortgagee-in-possession?

____ How are insurance proceeds applied?

____ Is there an obligation to repair and rebuild?

____ What insurance coverage is required?

____ Is there provision for construction of additional living units?

____ Are unit air-lot surveys recorded?

____ Are there any unusual provisions?

____ Is the declaration silent on typical matters?

____ Are powers and duties of officers defined?

Time-Sharing

Time-sharing is a method of providing multiple use and/or use of vacation and recreational properties. Originally the term "time-share" developed around the fact that many mid-size businesses during the 1950s and 1960s were unable to afford to buy expensive computers; as a result, a group of these smaller businesses would buy a computer and share computer time. Compared to an outright purchase of a property, an individual may purchase the ownership of, or the right to use, a property for a fraction of the time during the year for a fraction of the cost of purchasing the entire unit.

It should be added that most time-share resorts are affiliated with an exchange network. This enables the owners of the time-share units to swap the time in their resort unit with an equal time at another resort.

Types of Time-Share Interests. There are two types of time-share interests: (1) the time-share estate, and (2) the right to use (RTU).

The time-share estate. In this type of ownership, after making the final payment, the buyer is given a deed granting a fee simple interest in the time purchased. One problem which might arise is the possibility that liens might be filed against the buyer's property before the final payment is made. Generally this possibility can be avoided by the execution of an agreement between the builder-developer and a bank, whereby the bank actually takes title to the property under a trust agreement. This will cut off liens against the developer from attaching to the property, and when the final payment is made, the bank will convey the property to the buyer.

The right to use (RTU). In this type of arrangement, a contract is signed giving the purchaser the right to use the property for a stated number of years. After this time, the property reverts to the builder-developer.

Financing the Time-Share. The financing for a time-share, like most condominium developments, is done in two steps. First, the builder-developer must obtain construction financing. This is easier than obtaining funds for many other types of commercial construction or apartment complexes because (a) sales are often made prior to completion and these funds are turned over to the construction lender, and (b) in a period of rising interest rates, the time-share builder-developer is less affected than other types of developers since the loans to buyers are smaller and are for shorter time periods.

After a sale and the repayment of the construction loan, a builder-developer generally does her/his own financing. There is no mortgage. There is simply a promissory note and a retail sales contract ranging from three to seven years. It is much like a consumer loan. The builder-developer may or may not sell the note to a financial institution.

Because of the way financing is done for time-shares, the builder-developer comes under Regulation Z with regard to the Truth-in-Lending Act. This means that the annual percentage rate of interest must be spelled out when advertising the units to be sold.

KEY TERMS

condominium   proprietary lease
condominium conversion   time-sharing
cooperative dwelling   tract development loans

QUESTIONS FOR REVIEW

1. Briefly describe the major provisions of the Interstate Land Sales Full Disclosure Act.
2. What is a land development loan? How is it secured?
3. How is a land development loan generally paid off?
4. Why is the tenant of a cooperative actually a tenant-stockholder? What privileges, responsibilities, and relations exist for tenant-stockholders?
5. What are the financing difficulties and disadvantages of a tenant in a cooperative?
6. Explain the difference between the sales-type cooperative project and the management-type cooperative.
7. What are the advantages of a condominium over a cooperative?
8. How did the availability of FHA financing pave the way for the condominium boom? Also describe the process of obtaining conventional financing of condominiums.
9. Why do condominium conversions take place? What are some rules of thumb used by successful converters?
10. How are condominium conversions usually financed?

PROBLEMS

1. The Reilly Land Development Company has the opportunity to purchase a $350,000 tract of land to be used for a residential subdivision. Management is interested in subdividing the land into 40 parcels. Off-site improvement costs will be $100,000. Grading of the land and street paving are estimated at $300,000, while other on-site costs will be $125,000. Reilly Land Development has $75,000 in equity to be put in the project in the form of a down payment on the land. The appraised value for the completed land development is $1.2 million and a loan is available from a lending institution at a 12 percent interest rate.
   a. Determine the size of loan that is needed by Reilly. What is the average loan-related value of each land parcel? If the appraised value is used to set selling prices, what will be the average selling price for each land parcel?
   b. Assume that the loan is in the form of a blanket mortgage which contains a partial release clause. If the lender requires a 20 percent pre-

      mium, what will be the average release price for each parcel of land?

  c. Reilly Land Development expects to sell 10 parcels during the first year of operation, 20 parcels the second year, and the remaining 10 during the third year. Show the payments to the lender under the partial release clause requirements for each year. Also calculate the remaining loan balance at the end of each year.

  d. How would your answers in Part C change if 20 lots had selling prices of $40,000 each, the other 20 were priced at $20,000 each, and the first 20 lots sold were the higher priced ones?

2. Calculate the "value" on which an FHA condominium construction loan would be based given the following conditions. Assume a 30-unit condominium complex is to be constructed with a selling price of $20,000 per unit. Twenty units are pre-sold. Costs associated with selling the additional units are expected to be $30,000. It is estimated that the additional units will require, on the average, one year to sell. The cost of funds or discount factor will be 10 percent. How would your answer change if the cost of funds were 14 percent?

3. The Rightway Construction Company is planning two builder-developer projects. One project will consist of a 50-unit condominium at a proposed construction cost of $4 million, while the second project will consist of 50 single-family homes costing $80,000 each to build, or a total of $4 million. Rightway expects to sell each single-family home and each condominium unit at a price of $100,000.

  a. What size loan would the construction lender likely enter into on each of the two projects?

  b. In the event of foreclosure or a builder-developer "walk away," what would be the implications in terms of each of the two projects?

HIGH RATIO OR LEVERAGE FINANCING

LEARNING OBJECTIVES

After studying this chapter, you should be able to do the following:

Define what is meant by leverage and describe how leverage works.

Describe what is meant by a sale-leaseback and discuss how it is used in high ratio financing.

Describe the sale-buyback arrangement.

Indicate what is meant by front money deals or financing.

Describe the use of both the fee mortgage and the leasehold mortgage in obtaining maximum leverage.

HIGH RATIO FINANCING involves a higher-than-normal loan-to-value ratio. This results in low or no-cash equity by a builder-developer.

Most of the high ratio financing, both in joint venturing and the sale-leaseback, is done by life insurance companies. The statutes of most states prohibit life insurance loans with a greater than 75 percent loan-to-value ratio, prohibit junior mortgages, and are restricted to first mortgage loans on property that is both improved and unencumbered. Thus, life insurance companies are not permitted to make construction loans.

In the light of all these restrictions, how are the insurance companies able to engage in high ratio financing? In 1942, the State of Virginia passed what is termed a "leeway" statute which permitted Virginia-domiciled insurance companies to invest up to 5 percent of their admitted assets in nonconforming mortgage loans. In short, loans could be made with that percentage limitation in mortgages that the statute specifically prohibited.

Other states followed Virginia's lead, with the percentage of permitted assets that can be placed in nonconforming mortgages ranging from 3 percent to as high as 20 percent of admitted assets.

The more conservative lenders regarded these loans as "basket cases," and very shortly the loans were referred to as "basket loans."

LEVERAGE

All high ratio financing involves the use of leverage.

Leverage is the use of borrowed money—hopefully to increase gains. It is based on the assumption that the borrower can earn more from the borrowed money than the amount paid in interest for the use of the borrowed money.

For example, *A* borrows money at 7 percent and lends the money out at 11 percent for a gross gain of 4 percent. Basically this is what the small loan companies do. The problem comes when *A* borrows at 7 percent, but can lend at only 5 percent, thereby losing 2 percent.

How Leverage Works

Assume an investor has $100,000 equity capital to invest. It is estimated that a 12 percent return is feasible, or $12,000 per year. Assume further that $100,000 can be borrowed at 10 percent and invested at 12 percent, together with the original $100,000. Then,

Amount borrowed	$100,000
	.10
Cost at 10%	$ 10,000
Total investment	$200,000
	.12
Earnings at 12%	$ 24,000

The effect of the leverage is as follows:

Gross income	$24,000
Less cost of borrowing	10,000
Net Earnings	$14,000

As a result of the leverage, $14,000, or 14 percent, has been earned on the equity capital of $100,000. In short, the ratio of earnings to equity is $14,000 ÷ $100,000, or 14 percent on the $100,000 equity.

The preceding example is of a one-to-one ratio. The ratio can be one to two, one to three, or whatever. Assume that on a one-to-four ratio (which is not at all unusual) you borrow four times the equity, or $400,000, at 10 percent hoping to earn 12 percent. Then,

Amount borrowed	$400,000
	.10
Cost at 10%	$ 40,000
Total investment	$500,000
	.12
Earnings at 12%	$ 60,000

The effect of leverage is as follows:

Gross income	$60,000
Less cost of borrowing	40,000
Net Earnings	$20,000

The ratio of earnings to equity is $20,000 ÷ $100,000, or 20 percent on the $100,000 equity.

Reverse Effect of Leverage

In high ratio financing, the ratio can be as high as one to 50 percent or even 100 percent borrowed money. However, the problem in high ratio financing is that the leverage may work in reverse. For example, assume a one-to-fifty ratio where $5,000,000 is borrowed at 10 percent. Assume further that as a result of a miscalculation or economic recession, only 9 percent is earned on the $5,000,000. Then,

Amount borrowed	$5,000,000
	.10
Cost at 10%	$ 500,000
Total investment	$5,100,000
	.09
Earnings at 9%	$ 459,000

The effect of leverage is as follows:

Gross income	$459,000
Less cost of borrowing	500,000
Net Loss	($ 41,000)

SALE-LEASEBACK AS HIGH RATIO FINANCING

A *sale-leaseback* is a transaction in which a seller sells real property to a buyer who, as part of the transaction, leases the property back to the seller, usually for a long period of time.

Originally the sale-leaseback was termed a "purchase-leaseback" deal. As far back as 1882 a sale-leaseback was reported in England, but very little was known of the technique in the United States until the advent of the basket loan.

Types of Sale-Leaseback

There are a number of types of sale-leasebacks. The earliest type, still in use, is simply an institutional investor assuming the role of buyer-lessor with, more often than not, a supermarket assuming the role of seller-lessee. Both the terms of the sale and the lease are designed to fit the parties' requirements, particularly the lessee's credit rating. The leases are for an initial fixed term at a net rental designed to give the buyer an adequate return on the investment, plus a rate designed to retire the investment over the term of the lease. For example, a seller-lessee builds a building for $100,000. The building is sold to an investor, the buyer-lessor. It is leased back to the seller-lessee for 20 years. The rent is calculated to net out at 10 percent over the 20 years or $10,000 per year. Five percent is used to amortize the loan over the 20-year period, or $5,000 per year ($5,000 × 20 years = $100,000 cost of investment). The other 5 percent per year, or $5,000 per year, is considered an adequate return on the investment of the buyer-lessor of $100,000.

Since its early beginnings many other forms of sale-leaseback have been created. Many of these forms are based on fragmenting interests, such as in the sale and leaseback of land and partial financing by sale-leaseback.

Sale-Leaseback of Land. This agreement provides that the tenant is to erect a building financed by a leasehold mortgage. An example of a *leasehold mortgage* or what is also called a mortgage on a lease is shown in Figure 16–1.

For example, A paid $100,000 for land now valued at $300,000 and sells it to B with a leaseback of $50,000 rent per year for 20 years. A, now the tenant, builds an office building for $1 million financed by a life insurance company, C. C obtains the mortgage on the lease, which makes the lease of A subordinate to the mortgage. A rents the offices and pays B $50,000 rent per year. A pays on the mortgage and presumably has money left over as profit. In the event of default, C (the life insurance company) forecloses on the lease, pays B the $50,000 per year, and rents out the building.

The property is thus 100 percent financed as far as A is concerned. It was sold to B at $300,000 for a $200,000 profit to A. B has a $300,000 equity position in the land, the life insurance company a $1 million mortgage on the building, and A has invested the $300,000 in land proceeds elsewhere. The label put on this sort of transaction is "land-sale-leaseback and leasehold mortgage." It should be noted that lenders will often require a participation in the income.

In addition to the profit from rents, A has a tax shelter through the use of depreciation, as well as the rental payments to B, greater than if A had

MORTGAGE ON A LEASE

This indenture made this   day of   , One thousand nine
hundred and   , by and between
                    , party of the first part and   , party of the
second part.

WHEREAS   , did, by a certain indenture of lease, bearing date the
            day of   , in the year One thousand nine hundred and
                    , demise, lease, and farm-let unto   , and to its
successors and assigns, all and singular the premises hereinafter mentioned and described together
with their appurtenances;

TO HAVE AND TO HOLD THE SAME unto said   , and its successors and
assigns, for and during and until the full end and term of   years, from the
                    day of   One thousand nine hundred and
                    , fully to be completed and ended, yielding and paying therefor unto the
said   , and to its heirs, successors and assigns, the yearly rent or sum of
                                    ; and

WHEREAS the said party of the first part is justly indebted to the said party of the
part in the sum of   secured to be paid by a certain note
bearing even date herewith conditioned for the payment of the said sum of
on the   day of   , One thousand nine hundred and
                                (   ), and the interest thereon to be computed
from (the date thereof) at the rate of 10 per centum per annum and to be paid monthly on the
                    day of   and monthly thereafter on the first day
of each and every month thereafter.

IT BEING THEREBY EXPRESSLY AGREED that the whole of the said principal sum shall
become due at the option of the mortgagee after default in the payment of interest, taxes or
assessments of rents as hereinafter provided.

NOW THIS INDENTURE WITNESSETH that the said party of the second part, for the better
securing the payment of the said sum of money mentioned in the condition of the said note, with
interest thereon, and also for and in consideration of the sum of *one dollar,* paid by the said party
of the first part, the receipt whereof is hereby acknowledged, doth grant and release, assign, transfer
and set over unto said party of the second part, and to its heirs and assigns forever:

(Description of the Lease)

TOGETHER with the appurtenances and all the estate and rights of the party of the first part of
and in and to said premises under and by virtue of the aforesaid indenture of lease.

TO HAVE AND TO HOLD the said indenture of lease and renewal thereof, if any, and the
above granted premises, unto said party of the second part, its heirs, and assigns for and during
all of the rest, residue and remainder of said term of years yet to come and unexpired in said indenture of lease and in the renewals therein provided for; subject, nevertheless, to the rents,
covenants, conditions and provisions in the said indenture of lease above mentioned.

FIGURE 16–1. Mortgage on a Lease

Provided always that if the said party of the first part shall pay unto the said party of the second part, the said sum of money mentioned in the condition of the said note and all the interest thereon, at the time and in the manner mentioned in the said condition, that then these presents and the estate hereby granted shall cease, determine and be void.

And the said party of the first part covenant(s) with the said party of the part as follows:

FIRST: That the party of the first part will pay the indebtedness hereinbefore provided. And if default shall be made in the payment of any part thereof, the said party of the second part shall have power to sell the premises therein described according to law.

SECOND: That the said premises now are free and clear of all incumbrances whatsoever, and that the party of the first part has good right and lawful authority to convey the same in manner and form hereby conveyed.

THIRD: That the party of the first part will keep the building on the said premises insured against loss by fire, for the benefit of the mortgagee.

FOURTH: And it is hereby expressly agreed that the whole of the said principal sum shall become due at the option of the said mortgagee after default in the payment of any install-ment of principal, or after default in the payment of interest for (20) days, or after default in the payment of any rent or other charge made payable by said indenture for (40) days or after default in the payment of any tax or assessment for (20) days after notice and demand.

AND THAT IN CASE OF ANY DEFAULT, Whereby the right of foreclosure occurs hereunder, the said party of the second part or the holder of said note shall at once become entitled to the possession, use and enjoyment of the property aforesaid, and to the rents, issues and profits thereof, from the accruing of such right and during the pendency of foreclosure proceedings and the period of redemption, if any there be; and such possession shall at once be delivered to the said party of the second part or the holder of said note on request and on refusal, the delivery of such possession may be enforced by the said party of the second part or the holder of said note by any appropriate civil suit or proceeding, and the said party of the second part, or the holder of said note, or any thereof, shall be entitled to a Receiver for said property, and of the rents, issues and profits thereof, after such default, including the time covered by foreclosure proceedings and the period of redemp-tion, if any there be, and shall be entitled thereto as a matter of right without regard to the solvency or insolvency of the party of the second part, without regard to the value thereof, and such Receiver may be appointed by any court of competent jurisdiction upon ex parte application and without notice—notice being hereby expressly waived—and all rents, issues and profits, income and revenue therefrom shall be applied by such Receiver to the payment of the indebtedness hereby secured, according to law and the orders and directions of the court.

IN WITNESS WHEREOF, the said party of the first part to these presents has hereunto set hand and seal the day and year first above written.

Sealed and delivered in the presence of   /s/ A Inc., (L.S.)

(JOHN DOE)

(Acknowledgment)

FIGURE 16–1. Mortgage on a Lease (concluded)

had a straight mortgage.

Partial Financing by Sale-Leaseback. In this situation the object is to reduce the amount of equity which would be obtained through "normal" or conventional financing.

   For example, A (or a syndicate) buys an existing building and land (typically an office building) for $1,500,000. Simultaneously the property is sold to a life insurance company for $1,350,000, or 10 percent off the purchase price. Then the property is leased back to the group under a very long-term lease at a rental of $200,000 per year. Space is leased out by group A, which hopes to receive more than the $200,000 rental per year.

1. A has $150,000 invested ($1,500,000 purchase price – $1,350,000 selling price = $150,000).
2. If A had used conventional financing on this older building, the best loan-to-value ratio it could hope for would be a 75 percent loan, or in this case .75 × $1,500,000 = $1,125,000. This means that A would have to put down $375,000 in cash. Thus, A reduced the needed cash by $225,000: $375,000 cash by conventional financing – $150,000 cash by the sale-leaseback = $225,000 less cash than needed by conventional mortgage financing.

Advantages and Disadvantages of the Sale-Leaseback

Before becoming involved in a sale-leaseback, both the buyer-lessor and the seller-lessee should analyze the advantages and disadvantages of such a transaction.

Advantages to the Buyer-Lessor. The advantages to the buyer-lessor are:

1. The rents would probably yield a higher rate of return than would a mortgage investment.
2. The buyer-lessor is the owner and thus has direct control rather than the indirect control of a mortgagee.
3. The transaction is set up so that much of the cost is amortized over the term of the first lease. Consequently, the buyer-lessor can cash in on the sale or lease of the remainder.
4. While rental income is taxable as income, depreciation is permitted within IRS limitations, thereby reducing the taxable income of the buyer-lessor.

Disadvantages to the Buyer-Lessor. The disadvantages to the buyer-lessor are:

1. The risk is greater than it would be if the investment were a mortgage because presumably there would be a down payment which would serve as a "cushion" in a mortgage.
2. The buyer-lessor becomes tied to both the management and the credit of the seller-lessee. In case of bankruptcy, the Chandler Act limits the

TAX IMPLICATIONS OF THE SALE-LEASEBACK

Many tax problems can, and do, arise in connection with a sale-leaseback. Suppose a chain store sells the property to investors and leases it back:

1. If the chain seller-lessee is considered a "dealer," any gain is considered "ordinary income" and taxable as such.
2. Generally the sale-leaseback agreement contains an option to repurchase by the seller-lessee. If the repurchase price is considered "too low," the IRS could argue that the agreement was in reality a mortgage and not a sale and this could defeat any tax advantages of a true sale-leaseback. To avoid this, the sale-leaseback agreement should contain a provision providing for repurchase at the "fair market" value.

buyer-lessor's claim to one year's rent in case of general bankruptcy, but three years' rent in case of reorganization.

3. Because a portion of the rent is set aside to amortize the investment, the actual net income is lowest in the early years when the investment is the highest and the risk is the greatest.

In some states statutes require that the "basket" loan made by insurance companies be amortized according to statute. For example, in New York the cost must be amortized at not less than two percent per annum and all income over four percent must be used to amortize the cost. In Pennsylvania improvements, not the cost of the land, must be amortized at two percent per year.

Advantages to the Seller-Lessee. Advantages to the seller-lessee are:

1. The seller-lessee frees up cash.
2. The financing constitutes 100 percent financing.
3. Rent is deductible for tax purposes.

Disadvantages to the Seller-Lessee. The disadvantages to the seller-lessee are:

1. Rents are higher than mortgage payments because the property is being amortized. Furthermore, mortgage payments stop after the debt is repaid, while the rent continues in the event the lease is renewed.
2. The remainder value is lost to the seller-lessee.
3. The seller-lessee is not permitted to take any depreciation.

SALE-BUYBACK

The basic idea of the *sale-buyback* is quite simple. A lending institution buys the property and sells it back to the builder-developer. The instrument used is a contract for deed (discussed in Chapter 10).

While the concept of a sale-buyback is simple, the contract executing it may be rather complex. An institution such as an insurance company will agree to pay between 80 and 90 percent of the market value of the project, which is designed to equal 100 percent of the developer's cost. For example, assume the market value of a proposed apartment project is $1,000,000 ($100,000 for land and $900,000 for buildings), which the lender-institution buys for $850,000. The builder-developer receives a contract for deed to buy it back in installments at the $850,000 price. At this point legal title is in the lending institution and equitable title is with the developer.

The developer-purchaser is entitled to a tax shelter income by depreciating the property because the developer has equitable title. In this example, the $900,000 value for the buildings could be depreciated and the developer-buyer has received 100 percent financing. Let's also assume that the sale-buyback contract will be for 30 years. This contract may provide for a "lock-in" period of several years prohibiting the developer-buyer from paying off the contract early. After the lock-in period has passed, the terms of the contract might call for termination options at several year intervals.

The question arises at this time as to why an insurance company or other institution would get involved in this type of transaction. The answer is more money for the lender. This is achieved by increasing the effective interest cost to the developer-purchaser. For example, the current interest rate on a fully-amortized 30-year mortgage loan requiring annual payments might be 12 percent. Using the present value interest factor for an annuity at 12 percent for 30 years from Appendix B, Table 4, of 8.055, we can determine the annual payments for the $850,000 loan as follows:

$$\text{Annual Payments} = \frac{\$850,000}{8.055} = \$105,525$$

To increase the return in a sale-buyback, the lender might use a 12 percent, 20-year amortization schedule but require the annual payments to be made for 30 years. The present value interest factor at 12 percent for 20 years would be 7.469. This would result in annual payments of:

$$\text{Annual Payments} = \frac{\$850,000}{7.469} = \$113,804$$

However, instead of 20 payments, the lender would require 30 annual payments of $113,804. Thus, the last ten payments would increase the lender's return to about 13 percent annually. A present value interest factor of 7.469 at 12 percent for 30 years is found in Appendix B, Table 4, approximately midway between the 12 percent and 14 percent factors. Of course, if monthly payments were required, the above example could be redone using Appendix B, Table 5.

Another method for increasing the rate of return would be for the lender to treat the $850,000 loan as an installment loan using the add-on interest method. In this case, the annual interest charge might be 12 percent of $850,000 or $102,000. Multiplying the $102,000 times 30 years would result in total interest payments of $3,060,000. Adding the principal of $850,000 plus the $3,060,000 interest will result in a total repayment of $3,910,000. The annual payments over 30 years are then determined as follows:

$$\text{Annual Payments} = \frac{\$3,910,000}{30} = \$130,333$$

These payments are, of course, substantially higher than payments required to amortize a conventional 12 percent, 30-year mortgage loan. Dividing $850,000 by $130,333 gives a 30-year present value annuity interest factor of 6.522. Turning to Appendix B, Table 4, and reading across at 30 years, we find that the factor falls about midway between 14 percent and 16 percent for roughly a 15 percent annual return to the lender. Of course, Appendix B, Table 5, could be used if the installment loan using the add-on interest method had required monthly payments.

FRONT MONEY DEALS

Front money financing is another form of high ratio real estate financing. It takes the form of a joint venture with the lender supplying the money and the developer supplying land plus development skills. Because the lender becomes a participant in the project, the lender cannot be charged with *usury,* which is charging interest in an amount greater than the legal rate. Furthermore, the risk of losing equity capital is shared between the lender and the developer, which brings up the old adage, "where risk is shared there's a partnership." By giving the lender a share of the profits, the developer can reduce the risk involved and is further able to increase the size of the project.

The Organizational Form

Assume a lender and a developer agree to enter into a joint venture. Generally the first step is for the lender and the developer to form subsidiary corporations in order to limit their liability. If the lender is an insurance company or a mutual savings bank, it is legally required to form a corporation. After having formed the corporation, it must then be approved by the state insurance commissioner or another regulatory body.

The second step is for the two corporations to enter into either a general partnership or a limited partnership (see Chapter 13).

The typical arrangement may be shown as follows:

a. Ace Insurance Company, Inc.   b.   J. Developer
              forms   forms

        Earth Movers, Inc. (lender)   Fantastic Builders, Inc.
           (Limited Partner)   (General Partner)

                        Limited Partnership

Typically Ace Insurance Company will provide both the interim and permanent financing for the project with the money being filtered through its subsidiary, Earth Movers, Inc., allowing Ace Insurance Company to receive interest on both type loans. Furthermore, Earth Movers, Inc., and Fantastic Builders agree that Earth Movers, Inc., will participate in the net income (usually 50–50), with this money filtering upward to Ace Insurance Company from Earth Movers, Inc.

For example, suppose J. Developer, through its subsidiary Fantastic Builders, Inc., purchases a piece of land for $125,000. J. Developer approaches Ace Insurance Company with a proposal for a $5,000,000 project on which the development cost is $4,875,000. Ace agrees to the deal and forms Earth Movers Inc., which enters into the limited partnership. Then the project financing may appear as follows:

Lender provides 100% of development cost	$4,875,000
Developer provides land cost	125,000
Total Cost	$5,000,000

It is projected that the cash flow will be 10 percent of cost per year, or $500,000. Each corporation is to receive an 8 percent return on its cash outlay or investment. Thus, Earth Movers, Inc., receives 8 percent of $4,875,000, or $390,000 per year. Fantastic Builders receives 8 percent of $125,000, or $10,000 per year. Since the 8 percent return to each partner amounts to $400,000, the balance of the cash flow ($100,000) is split 50–50, with Earth Movers, Inc., receiving $50,000 and Fantastic Builders receiving $50,000. The total return for each corporation is then

Earth Movers	$390,000
	50,000
	$440,000 per year
Fantastic Builders	$ 10,000
	50,000
	$ 60,000 per year

Fantastic Builders thus receives a return on the money paid down of 48% ($60,000 ÷ $125,000 = 48%), which is an excellent rate of return.

Other Variations

There are other variations of this type of financing. For example, a developer wants to build a project costing $1,000,000, of which the land is to cost $100,000. Construction financing will be at an 80 percent loan-to-value ratio, or $800,000. It is estimated that on completion the project will sell for $1,225,000. The developer approaches an investor who agrees to put up $100,000 and the developer puts up $100,000 to make up the difference between the $800,000 loan and the $1,000,000 project cost. For tax purposes the investor and the developer form a limited partnership. Assume a 10 percent loan is obtained on the $800,000 construction cost. The interest is

$80,000 (in real life this would be less because the $800,000 is not all borrowed at once). The results are as follows:

Sale price	$1,225,000
Less construction loan plus interest	880,000
	$ 345,000
Less investor loan plus 10% interest	110,000
	$ 235,000
Less developer's investment	100,000
	$ 135,000

The balance of $135,000 is divided 50–50, so the developer has earned on the cash paid down:

$$\frac{\$67,500}{\$100,000} = 67.5 \text{ percent, again a high rate of return}$$

Another variation is where the investor puts up the entire $200,000 with the net proceeds being split 50–50. Ownership of the land prior to the sale is in the name of the investor. When the project is sold, the $1,225,000 is divided as follows:

Sale price	$1,225,000
Less construction loan plus interest	880,000
	$ 345,000
Less investor's loan plus 10% interest	220,000
	$ 125,000

The balance of $125,000 is split 50–50 with the developer receiving $62,500 without having to pay any money down.

FEE MORTGAGE AND LEASEHOLD MORTGAGE

Suppose a builder-developer has a piece of raw land for which $100,000 was paid and it is now worth $500,000. If the builder-developer becomes involved in a sale-leaseback, the resultant $400,000 profit will result in a long-term capital gains tax. The builder-developer wishes to build a $1 million building on the land, after which the combined value of the land and building will be $1.5 million.

The builder-developer is faced with several choices, as follows:

1. Entering into a sale-leaseback arrangement which would necessitate payment of taxes on the sale and the execution of a ground lease subordinated to the first mortgage of a permanent investor.
2. Entering into a $1.5 million project with a mortgage on the land given by a lender and improvements when built owned by the builder-developer. In this case, the builder-developer would probably

receive a 75 percent loan-to-value ratio, amounting to $1.5 million × .75 or $1,125,000.

The object of the game is to obtain as much leverage as possible. Therefore:

1. The builder-developer forms a corporation called "Business, Inc." which the builder-developer owns and controls.
2. The $500,000 parcel of property is leased to Business, Inc. This lease is recorded first.
3. Builder-developer owns the fee simple in the land now leased to Business, Inc. In short, the real estate has been split into a fee interest and a leasehold interest. Each part will be mortgaged separately. Thus there will be both a *fee mortgage* and a leasehold mortgage.
4. Builder-developer is owner-lessor and Business, Inc. is the lessee.
5. Builder-developer arranges for two separate mortgages:
   (a) An unsubordinated mortgage on the fee for a 90 percent loan-to-value ratio, or $500,000 × .90 = $450,000. The lease, having been recorded first, is superior to the mortgage.
   (b) A mortgage on the lease from Business, Inc. on the building for a 75 percent loan-to-value ratio, or $1 million × .75 = $750,000.
   The total amount is $1,200,000 ($450,000 mortgage on unsubordinated fee, plus $750,000 mortgage on the lease).

Why will lenders lend in this situation? It should be understood at the outset that this type of loan is permitted by insurance companies under the "basket loan" statutes pointed out earlier in this chapter. They justify this sort of loan because:

1. The 90 percent unsubordinated mortgage on the fee is secured by both the $500,000 value of the land and the rents paid by Business, Inc. to the builder-developer.
2. The fee mortgage is *unsubordinated;* therefore, if the mortgage on the lease is foreclosed, title to the fee still remains in the builder-developer subject to the unsubordinated mortgage.
3. If the mortgagee has to foreclose on the fee, the mortgagee receives the land, *but* because the lease has been recorded first, the mortgagee has the land subject to the leasehold rent and the leasehold mortgage.

The lenders are generally insurance companies lending under the "basket loan" statutes, and loans are generally made with very high interest rates. Typically a builder-developer will refinance these loans on a more normal basis once the value of the property has appreciated.

KEY TERMS

fee mortgage	sale-buyback
leasehold mortgage	sale-leaseback
leverage	usury

QUESTIONS FOR REVIEW

1. What is "high ratio" financing and to what extent are life insurance companies involved in this type of financing?
2. Define "leverage" and illustrate how it works positively and in reverse.
3. What is a sale-leaseback? Also indicate some types of sale-leasebacks.
4. Discuss some of the advantages and disadvantages of the sale-leaseback to the (a) buyer-lessor, and the (b) seller-lessee.
5. Differentiate between a sale-leaseback and a sale-buyback.
6. What are the steps involved in establishing front money financing?
7. How is risk divided in front money deals?
8. Briefly describe how a builder-developer might make use of both a fee mortgage and a leasehold mortgage to obtain maximum leverage.

PROBLEMS

1. What is the return on a 1 to 5 ratio with the equity portion being $1,000,000? The cost of the borrowed money is 10 percent and the expected return is 12 percent.
2. Syndicate A buys a building for $1,000,000 and immediately sells it to an insurance company for $900,000. The property is then rented back to the syndicate at $50,000 per year. What is the syndicate's reduction of equity financing if the best loan-to-value ratio they could obtain is 75 percent?
3. Using examples, explain how and where leverage manifests itself in the sale-leaseback, sale-buyback, and front money deals.
4. Assume a 20-year loan for $500,000 is being negotiated that will require annual payments or amortization. The loan will carry a 14 percent annual interest rate if it is to be a fully amortized mortgage loan. An alternative arrangement would be to enter into a sale-buyback arrangement with a lending institution whereby the $500,000 represents a 14 percent, 20-year installment loan using the add-on interest method and requiring annual payments.
   a. Determine the annual mortgage payment under the 14 percent mortgage loan alternative.
   b. Under the sale-buyback alternative, determine the annual interest amount, and the annual total payment amount.
   c. Estimate the approximate effective annual interest rate on the sale-buyback loan.

REAL ESTATE PRACTICES AND SETTLEMENT PROCEDURES

CHAPTER 17
Loan Application, Analysis, and Closing

CHAPTER 18
Mortgage Default and Foreclosure

17

LOAN APPLICATION, ANALYSIS, AND CLOSING

LEARNING OBJECTIVES

After studying this chapter, you should be able to do the following:

Describe the basic factors considered in the analysis of a residential loan application.

Discuss the roles of the Equal Credit Opportunity Act and the Consumer Credit Protection Act in terms of prohibiting discrimination against credit applicants.

Identify and briefly describe the documents that the lender must obtain in support of the residential loan application.

Describe the cost-to-replace, market-data, and income approaches used in the appraisal of real property.

Briefly discuss the major provisions contained in the Real Estate Settlement Procedures Act.

Identify the two major parts of the Truth in Lending Act and describe the documents that a lender must furnish to assure compliance with the Act.

Discuss the use of pro-forma financial projections when assessing whether to make income-producing real estate loans.

Briefly explain the meaning and use of a Loan Closing Statement.

THE SUBJECT MATTER of loan applications, loan analysis, and loan closings can be broken down into two broad categories: (1) residential real estate, and (2) income-producing, or commercial, real estate. As will be pointed out later in the chapter, there are different problems involved with each category, depending upon the type of property involved.

RESIDENTIAL LOANS

The residential or home loan can be utilized where property is sold with new financing or where an existing mortgage is assumed.

New Financing

Regardless of whether the loan is to be FHA, VA, conventional, or conventional with mortgage insurance, the loan begins with a loan application. The application form shown in Figure 17–1 is a standard Federal Home Loan Mortgage Corporation, Federal National Mortgage Association form. It can, however, be used by the institution for a straight conventional mortgage or a conventional mortgage insured by a private mortgage insurance company by simply checking the proper box.

Analysis of the Loan Application

Each loan application is considered on a "case by case" basis. The security of the mortgage rests not only on the value of the property but also upon the borrower's ability and willingness to meet obligations. To this end the Federal Home Loan Mortgage Corporation has created guidelines in reviewing the creditworthiness of borrowers. In general, lenders follow these guidelines regardless of the type of residential mortgage involved. The guidelines, monthly housing expense-to-income ratio and monthly debt payments-to-income ratio, are discussed in the following paragraphs.

Monthly Housing Expense-to-Income Ratio. Normally, monthly housing expense (first and second mortgage payments, less escrows, impounds for taxes, insurance premiums, leasehold payments) and other expenses required to be paid under the mortgage must not exceed approximately 25 percent of the borrower's "stable monthly income." *Stable monthly income* is gross monthly income from primary base earnings plus recognizable secondary income. Secondary income of the borrower, such as bonuses, commissions, and income from overtime or part-time employment, is only recognized as stable monthly income if such items of secondary income are typical for the occupation.

The FHLMC strongly suggests that items such as age, education, training, technical skills, occupation, and past employment be taken into account on a case-by-case basis in determining stable monthly income. If the income of the applicant-borrower is from self-employment, then the lender must examine both the previous year's profit and loss statements and the tax

RESIDENTIAL LOAN APPLICATION

MORTGAGE APPLIED FOR	Type	Amount	Interest Rate	No. of Months	Monthly Payment Principal & Interest	Escrow/Impounds (to be collected monthly)
	☐ Conv. ☐ FHA ☐ VA	$	%		$	☐ Taxes ☐ Hazard Ins. ☐ MI ☐

Prepayment Option

In accordance with Regulatory Agencies

SUBJECT PROPERTY

Property Street Address	City	County	State	Zip	No. Units

Legal Description (Attach description if necessary)	Year Built	Property is: ☐ Fee ☐ Leasehold ☐ Condo ☐ PUD ☐ DeMinimis PUD

Purpose of Loan: ☐ Purchase ☐ Construction-Perm. ☐ Construction ☐ Refinance ☐ Other (Explain)

Complete this line if Construction-Perm. or Construction Loan	Lot Value Data	Original Cost	Present Value (a)	Cost of Imps. (b)	Total (a+b)	ENTER TOTAL AS PURCHASE PRICE IN DETAILS OF PURCHASE
Year Acquired	$	$	$	$		

Complete this line if a Refinance Loan			Purpose of Refinance	Describe Improvement [ ] made [ ] to be made
Year Acquired	Original Cost	Amt. Existing Liens		
	$	$		Cost: $

Title Will Vest in What Names?	How Will Title Be Held? (Tenancy)

Note Will Be Signed By?	Source of Down Payment and Settlement Charges?

BORROWER				**CO-BORROWER***			
Name	Age	Sex**	School Yrs	Name	Age	Sex**	School Yrs
Present Address No. Years ___ ☐ Own ☐ Rent				Present Address No. Years ___ ☐ Own ☐ Rent			
Street				Street			
City/State/Zip				City/State/Zip			
Former address if less than 2 years at present address				Former address if less than 2 years at present address			
Street				Street			
City/State/Zip				City/State/Zip			
Years at former address ☐ Own ☐ Rent				Years at former address ☐ Own ☐ Rent			

Marital Status	☐ Married Yrs. ___ ☐ Unmarried ☐ Separated	(Check One)** ☐ American Indian ☐ Negro/Black ☐ Oriental ☐ Spanish American ☐ Other Minority ☐ White (Non-minority)	Marital Status	☐ Married Yrs. ___ ☐ Unmarried ☐ Separated	(Check One)** ☐ American Indian ☐ Negro/Black ☐ Oriental ☐ Spanish American ☐ Other Minority ☐ White (Non-minority)
Dependents other than Co-Borrower			Dependents other than listed by Borrower		
Number	Ages		Number	Ages	

Name and Address of Employer	Years employed in this line of work or profession? ___ years Years on this job ___ ☐ Self Employed***	Name and Address of Employer	Years employed in this line of work or profession? ___ years Years on this job ___ ☐ Self Employed***
Position/Title Type of Business		Position/Title Type of Business	

GROSS MONTHLY INCOME				**MONTHLY HOUSING EXPENSE**			**DETAILS OF PURCHASE**	
Item	Borrower	Co-Borrower	Total	Rent	PREVIOUS	PROPOSED		
Base Income	$	$	$	First Mortgage (P&I)	$		a. Purchase Price	$
Overtime				Other Financing (P&I)			b. Total Closing Costs	
Bonuses				Hazard Insurance			c. Pre Paid Escrows	
Commissions				Taxes (Real Estate)			d. Total (a + b + c)	$
Dividends/Interest				Assesments			e. Amt. This Mortgage	( )
Net Rental Income				Mortgage Insurance			f. Other Financing	( )
Other (SEE SCHEDULE BELOW)				Homeowner Assn. Dues			g. Present Equity in Lot	( )
				Total Monthly Pmt	$	$	h. Amt. of Deposit	( )
				Utilities			i. Closing costs paid by Seller	( )
Total	$	$	$	Total	$	$	j. Cash required for closing	$

DESCRIBE OTHER INCOME	
▷ B—Borrower C—Co-Borrower NOTE: ALIMONY/CHILD SUPPORT PAYMENTS NEED NOT BE LISTED UNLESS THEIR CONSIDERATION IS DESIRED	Monthly Amt. $

IF EMPLOYED IN CURRENT POSITION FOR LESS THAN TWO YEARS COMPLETE THE FOLLOWING						
B/C	Previous Employer/School	City/State	Type of Business	Position/Title	Dates From/To	Monthly Salary $

QUESTIONS APPLY TO BOTH BORROWERS

If Yes, explain on attached sheet	Borrower Yes or No	Co-Borrower Yes or No		Borrower Yes or No	Co-Borrower Yes or No
Have you any outstanding judgments, ever taken bankruptcy, had property foreclosed upon, or given deed in lieu thereof?			Do you have health and accident insurance?		
Co-Maker or endorser on any notes?			Do you have major medical coverage?		
Defendant/Participant in a Law Suit?			Do you intend to occupy property?		
Obligated for child support/alimony payments?			Will this property be your primary residence?		
Any portion of the down payment borrowed?			Have you previously owned a home?		
			Value of previously owned home	$	$

*Complete this section and all other co-borrower questions about spouse if the spouse will be jointly obligated with the borrower on the loan or if the borrower is relying on the spouse's income or on community property in obtaining the loan.
**This information is requested only for statistical purposes in accordance with the intent of fair housing law. Furnishing this information is voluntary, but borrowers are urged to do so. No lending decision will be made on the basis of this information or on whether or not it is furnished.
***FHLMC requires self employed to furnish signed copies of one or more most recent Federal Tax Returns or audited Profit and Loss Statements. FNMA requires business credit report, signed Federal Income Tax returns for last two years, and, if available, audited P/L plus balance sheet for same period.

FIGURE 17–1.   Residential Loan Application

This Statement and any applicable supporting schedules may be completed jointly by both married and unmarried co-borrowers if their assets and liabilities are sufficiently joined so that the Statement can be meaningfully and fairly presented on a combined basis; otherwise separate Statements and Schedules are required (FHLMC 65A/FNMA 1003A). If the co-borrower section was completed about spouse, complete this statement and supporting schedules about spouse also.

☐ Completed Jointly ☐ Not Completed Jointly

ASSETS		LIABILITIES AND PLEDGED ASSETS		
Description	Cash or Market Value	Owed To (Name, Address and Account Number)	Mo. Pmt. and Mos. left to pay	Unpaid Balance
Cash Toward Purchase held by		* Indicate by (*) which will be satisfied upon sale or upon refinancing of subject property.		
		Installment Debt (include "revolving" charge accounts)	$ Pmt./Mos. /	$
Checking and Savings Accounts (Indicate names of Institutions/Acct. Nos.)			/	
			/	
			/	
Stocks and Bonds (No./description)			/	
Life Insurance Net Cash Value			/	
Face Amount ($		Automobile Loan	/	
SUBTOTAL LIQUID ASSETS				
Real Estate Owned (Enter Total Market Value from Real Estate Schedule)		Real Estate Loans (Itemize and Identify Lender)	/	
Vested Interest in Retirement Fund				
Net Worth of Business Owned (ATTACH FINANCIAL STATEMENT)				
Auto (Make and Year)		Other Debt Including Stock Pledges (Itemize)	/	
Furniture and Personal Property		Alimony and Child Support Payments	/	
Other Assets (Itemize)				
		TOTAL MONTHLY PAYMENTS	$	
TOTAL ASSETS	A. $	NET WORTH (A.–B.) $	TOTAL LIABILITIES	B. $

STATEMENT OF ASSETS AND LIABILITIES

SCHEDULE OF REAL ESTATE OWNED (If Additional Properties Owned Attach Separate Schedule)								
Address of Property (Indicate S if Sold, PS if Pending Sale or R if Rental being held for income)		Type of Property	Present Market Value	Amount of Mortgages & Liens	Gross Rental Income	Mortgage Payments	Taxes, Ins. Maintenance and Misc.	Net Rental Income
TOTALS →								

LIST PREVIOUS CREDIT REFERENCES					
B—Borrower C—Co-Borrower	Owed To (Name and Address)	Account Number	Purpose	Highest Balance	Date Paid
				$	

AGREEMENT: The undersigned hereby applies for the loan described herein to be secured by a first mortgage or trust deed on the property described herein and represents that no part of said premises will be used for any purpose forbidden by law or restriction and that all statements made in this application are true and made for the purpose of obtaining the loan. Verification may be obtained from any source named herein. The original or a copy of this application will be retained by the lender even if the loan is not granted.

I fully understand that it is a federal crime punishable by fine or imprisonment or both to knowingly make any false statements concerning any of the above facts, as applicable under the provisions of Title 18, United States Code, Section 1014.

Signature (Borrower) .... Date .... Signature (Co-Borrower) .... Date ....

Home Phone .... Business Phone .... Home Phone .... Business Phone ....

The Federal Equal Credit Opportunity Act prohibits creditors from discriminating against credit applicants on the basis of sex or marital status. The Federal Agency which administers compliance with this law concerning this federal savings and loan association is Federal Home Loan Bank Board, Washington, D.C.

Additionally the Federal Fair Housing Act also prohibits discrimination on the basis of race, color, religion, sex or national origin.

BORROWER	CO-BORROWER
Social Security #....................	Social Security #....................
Employee or Badge #....................	Employee or Badge #....................

Applicant's Attorney	Real Estate Agent or Builder
Name .... Tel. No.	Name .... Tel. No. ....
Address	Address ....

Name Present Owner ....

Property now Mortgaged to ....   Occupant ....

If vacant, key at ....   Tel. No. ....

Annual Real Estate Taxes $....................   BRANCH ....

It is understood and agreed there are no conditions under which this application fee of $.................... will be refunded in whole or in part.

FIGURE 17–1. Residential Loan Application (concluded)

returns to verify the income.

Monthly Debt Payments-to-Income Ratio. The FHLMC normally requires that monthly housing expense, plus all other monthly payments on all installment debts having reversionary terms of more than seven months, not exceed approximately 33¹/₃ percent of the borrower's stable monthly income. Alimony and/or child support payments are considered long-term monthly obligations unless there is evidence of a court-approved reduction or termination.

For example, assume that the stable monthly income is $3,000. The home loan payment is $600 and the debt payments amount to $300, or a total of $900. Assuming no other problems, then in all probability the loan will be made. However, if the loan payment is $600 and debt payments are $1,200, then there is a strong chance the loan will be denied.

Without being specific the FHLMC guidelines state that higher percentages may be appropriate with respect to lower income borrowers, "depending on conditions prevalent in the area in which the mortgaged property is located and a review of the borrower's recent ratio of monthly housing expense and total debt payments to income." (The "conditions" are not spelled out in the guidelines.)

Also, FHLMC declares higher ratios may be offset by a demonstrated ability of the borrower to accumulate wealth and by histories of good debt service. Such ratios may also be offset by larger down payments and net worth to assure that the borrower has enough to repay the loan regardless of debt-to-income ratios.

The FNMA Lending Guidelines

Effective October 15, 1985, the Federal National Mortgage Association laid down stricter residential guidelines than had been previously required.

FNMA is the nation's largest single buyer of mortgages from lenders. In a single 18-month period from January 1, 1984, to July 1, 1985, it had suffered losses from delinquent mortgages amounting to $134.3 million. Blame for these losses ranged from dishonest appraisers to what was called by many "new creative" financing (which was actually neither new nor creative). As a result the following guidelines were issued:

1. FNMA would no longer purchase adjustable-rate mortgages (ARMs) with negative amortization.
2. FNMA would no longer purchase graduated-payment plans combined with ARMs.
3. The minimum down payment for an ARM would be 10 percent.
4. In fixed-rate mortgages if a borrower wants a loan of over 90 percent, the mortgage payment cannot be greater than 25 percent of applicant's income, and this added to other monthly obligations cannot exceed 33 percent of gross income.

Because Fannie Mae purchases 10 percent of all home mortgages, all lenders have tightened their lending procedures and are following the FNMA rules. FHA and VA programs are not affected.

Credit Report

Regardless of the type of mortgage a borrower is seeking, a credit report will be required by the lender. Specifically, if the lender is thinking of doing business with the FHLMC, the FHLMC requires a credit report.

Furthermore, if the property is located within a standard metropolitan statistical area, the report must verify current employment, salary, and all debts listed on the credit application including terms, balances, and ratings; and list all other debts discovered and all legal information, such as suits, judgments, foreclosures, garnishments, bankruptcies, and divorce actions. In the case of a change in employment within the past two years, the report must also contain information as to the borrower's previous employment, location, and salary.

Borrower's Credit Reputation

In addition to the above information, a lender will look at the borrower's credit reputation, considering such things as:

1. *Bankruptcy.* If the borrower has been bankrupt, the lender will try to verify that at the moment the borrower evidences sufficient credit-worthiness.
2. *Job Tenure/Change of Residence.* Three or more changes in occupation by the borrower within the previous five years, or four or more changes of residence within the previous six years, must be satisfactorily explained.
3. *Slow Payments on Credit Report.* If the borrower has a recent history of slow payments on a previous mortgage or mortgages, the FHLMC requires a detailed written explanation.

Furthermore, slow payment of other debts, constituting a pattern which appears to indicate slow payments on debts related to basic needs while prompt payments were made on debts related to less important needs of the borrower and the borrower's family, must also be satisfactorily explained.

Nondiscrimination

The Equal Credit Opportunity Act, 15 USC 1691, prohibits discrimination against credit applicants on the basis of sex and marital status. Furthermore, an amendment to the Act (beginning March 23, 1977) extends this to race, color, religion, national origin, age, whether all or part of the applicant's income is derived from any public assistance program, or if the applicant has in good faith exercised any right under the Consumer Credit Protection Act. The lender must provide the notice of the agency administering the Act either on the application or some other separate sheet of paper. In addition, the notice must provide the name of the lender's supervising agency. This is done on the application form shown in Figure 17–1.

There have been numerous attempts to circumvent this law. For example, Amoco Oil Company rejected applications based on its "credit experience in the immediate geographical area." The courts held this to be racially discriminatory.[1]

Verification of Employment

At the time an application for a loan is made the applicant will be asked to sign an "Employment Verification Authorization" such as that shown in Figure 17–2.

Having been granted permission, the lender will then send a form to the applicant's employer. The form will request information regarding the employee such as job tenure and salary.

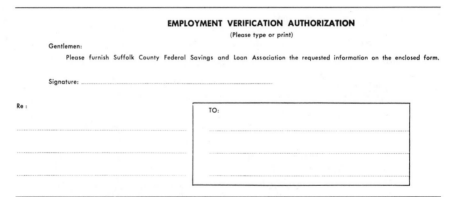

EMPLOYMENT VERIFICATION AUTHORIZATION
(Please type or print)

Gentlemen:

Please furnish Suffolk County Federal Savings and Loan Association the requested information on the enclosed form.

Signature: ....

Re :

TO:

FIGURE 17–2.   Verification of Employment

Deposit Verification

As a general rule, if the loan-to-value ratio is 80 percent or more, the lending institution will want to verify that the borrower has the down payment. Put another way, if the down payment is going to be 20 percent or less, the lender will demand verification that the potential borrower has the necessary cash on deposit with a financial institution. Consequently, the applicant will give the proposed lender consent to obtain this information from the financial institution. The lender then uses the form or a modification of the form shown in Figure 17–3 to obtain this information.

---

[1]Chevy v Amoco Oil Co., 481 FSupp 727 (N.D. Ga. 1979). In another matter, Amoco agreed to pay a civil penalty to settle charges that it illegally discriminated against blacks, Hispanics and women: United States v Amoco Oil Co., U.S. District Court D.D.C. No. 792–3088 (Apr. 29, 1980).

VETERANS ADMINISTRATION
AND
U. S. DEPARTMENT OF HOUSING AND URBAN DEVELOPMENT
FEDERAL HOUSING ADMINISTRATION

REQUEST FOR VERIFICATION OF DEPOSIT

INSTRUCTIONS: LENDER – Complete Items 1 thru 7. Have applicant complete Items 8 and 9. Forward directly to bank or other depository named in Item 1.
ADDRESSEE – Please complete Items 10 thru 13. Return directly to Lender named in Item 2.

PART I – REQUEST

1. TO (Name and Address of Bank or other Depository)	2. FROM (Name and address of lender)

3. SIGNATURE OF LENDER	4. TITLE	5. DATE	6. FHA OR VA NUMBER

7. STATEMENT OF APPLICANT

A. NAME AND ADDRESS OF APPLICANT	B. TYPE OF ACCOUNT	BALANCE	ACCOUNT NUMBER
	CHECKING	$	
	SAVINGS	$	

I have applied for a mortgage loan and stated that I maintain account(s) with the bank or depository named in Item 1. My signature below authorizes that bank or other depository to furnish the lender named in Item 2 the information set forth below in Part II. Your response is solely a matter of courtesy for which no responsibility is attached to your institution or any of your officers.

8. SIGNATURE OF APPLICANT	9. DATE

PART II – VERIFICATION

10A. DOES APPLICANT HAVE ANY OUTSTANDING LOANS?			CURRENT STATUS OF ACCOUNTS		
☐ YES ☐ NO (If "Yes," enter total in Item 10B)				CHECKING	SAVINGS
10B. TYPE OF LOAN	MONTHLY PAYMENT	PRESENT BALANCE	11A. IS ACCOUNT LESS THAN TWO MONTHS OLD? (If "Yes," give date opened in Item 11B)	☐ YES ☐ NO	☐ YES ☐ NO
SECURED	$	$	11B. DATE ACCOUNT OPENED		
UNSECURED	$	$			
10C. PAYMENT EXPERIENCE			11C. CURRENT BALANCE		
☐ FAVORABLE ☐ UNFAVORABLE (If unfavorable, explain in Remarks)			11D. IS ACCOUNT OTHER THAN INDIVIDUAL, E.G., JOINT OR TRUST? (If "Yes," explain in remarks)	☐ YES ☐ NO	☐ YES ☐ NO
12. REMARKS					

The above information is provided in strict confidence in response to your request.

13A. SIGNATURE OF OFFICIAL OF BANK OR OTHER DEPOSITORY	13B. TITLE	13C. DATE

THE INFORMATION ON THIS FORM IS CONFIDENTIAL. IT IS TO BE TRANSMITTED DIRECTLY, WITHOUT PASSING THROUGH THE HANDS OF THE APPLICANT OR ANY OTHER PARTY.

FIGURE 17–3.   Request for Verification of Deposit

Sellers' Discounts

Sellers' discounts are not difficult to understand. Most of the time, though not always, they apply to FHA and VA loans. There are two basic reasons for this:

(1) legally a buyer cannot pay discounts on FHA and VA loans—the discounts, if any, must be paid by the seller; and (2) there are interest rate ceilings imposed on both FHA and VA loans. However, it should be remembered that these interest rate ceilings change from time to time.

It should also be remembered that institutions are not compelled to make either FHA or VA loans. Consequently, a lending institution has alternatives. For example, suppose the institution has the opportunity to make a conventional mortgage at 13.5 percent or an FHA mortgage with the rate frozen at 11.5 percent. Obviously, not being compelled to make the FHA loan, the institution would make the loan at 13.5 percent. However, with sellers' discounts available to the institution, the interest rates between the two types of loans can be equated. The discount, expressed in points, is the amount deducted from the face value of the loan to increase the effective yield.

For example, assume an FHA mortgage is to be $50,000. The institution determines that two points are necessary for the FHA loan to equate to the market yield on a conventional loan. What this means is that at the closing the seller will receive the down payment made by the purchaser plus $50,000 minus $1,000 ($50,000 × .02 = $1,000), or $49,000. The purchaser signs a note and mortgage (or deed of trust) agreeing to pay the institution $50,000 plus interest. The yield is greater because the institution put out only $49,000 but will receive from the purchaser $50,000 plus interest. Put another way, the institution is receiving $1,000 plus interest which it never loaned out.

Generally, to a lender each point is worth $1/8$ of 1 percent in interest on a 30-year mortgage. For example, assume that the $50,000 loan with a two-point discount is at $13 1/2$ percent: in reality, the yield to the lender is $13 3/4$ percent.

One question remains. Why would a seller insist on an FHA or VA loan knowing that the face value of the loan would not be received? The answer is that it frequently broadens the market for the seller. Furthermore, the seller may attempt to compensate for the loss by increasing the price of the home. If the seller is a builder, corners may sometimes be cut to make up the difference in the discount, thereby reducing construction costs.

THE PROPERTY AS SECURITY

So far the discussion has centered on the individual as a credit risk; however, it is the real property which is the basis of the loan. Consequently, prior to approving the loan, a lending institution will require an appraisal of the property. If a VA or FHA loan is to be made, the VA or FHA is requested to make the appraisal. If the loan is to be a conventional loan, the institution makes its own appraisal.

The appraisal of real property requires specialized knowledge and skill. Because of its complexity, only the basics can be discussed here. Essentially, the appraiser uses three approaches to value and attempts to correlate the three approaches into the final estimate of value.

The Cost-to-Replace Approach

Generally with the *cost-to-replace approach* the replacement cost of the building minus depreciation plus the value of the land equals the estimated value of the property.

Cost is generally obtained by multiplying the cost to replace per square foot times the number of square feet, which equals the replacement cost.

The depreciation estimated by the appraiser can consist of three possible types:

1. *Physical deterioration.* This is the decay and natural wear and tear on a building. For example, the shingles on a home may be rotted.
2. *Functional obsolescence.* This is an impairment of desirability and usefulness brought about by changes in design or in the arts. For example, bathroom fixtures may be outdated. The homeowner has little or no control over this.
3. *Economic obsolescence.* This is the impairment of desirability or useful life of the property arising from economic forces. Here again, an owner has no control as it is an external factor causing a loss of value. For example, a flight pattern from a nearby airport may be changed, causing a loss of value due to a shift in demand for property in that particular neighborhood.

The Market-Data Approach

The *market-data approach* is sometimes called the "sales-comparison approach," which involves a comparison of sales prices that have been obtained for like properties. Because similar properties are not usually sold on the same date and because "similar" properties are not exactly similar, adjustments have to be made. These adjustments include such things as time, number of square feet in the building, number of baths, types of construction, garage, and even the number of stories.

The Income Approach

The rationale for the *income approach* is simply that value is equal to the present worth of future income. Consequently, the income is "capitalized" to give the property value. Thus, if the income from a piece of real property were $12,000 and the capitalization rate were, say, 10 percent, then:

$$\text{Value} = \frac{\text{Annual Net Income}}{\text{Capitalization Rate}}$$

or

$$\text{Value} = \frac{12,000}{.10}$$

$$= \$120,000$$

However, in residential properties a "gross rent multiplier" is used. In essence, the appraiser again goes to the "market." Here, the appraiser finds the sales prices of similar homes and their gross monthly rents. For example, a $40,000 home rents for $350 per month. The $350 is divided into $40,000 to obtain the gross rent multiplier. Thus, $40,000 ÷ $350 = $114 (rounded off). In practice, five or six similar homes and their sales prices and rentals are obtained and a gross rent multiplier is obtained, say 118. Then an estimate of rent is made on the house under appraisement, say $400 per month, and this is multiplied by the multiplier to obtain the estimate of value (118 × $400 = $47,200).

The form shown in Figure 17–4 is an FHA appraisal or underwriting form. The application for the FHA appraisal is made at the same time the loan application is made. It should be noted that VA and conventional mortgage appraisals are done on what amounts to a variation of this form.

THE REAL ESTATE SETTLEMENT PROCEDURES ACT

The Real Estate Settlement Procedures Act (RESPA) was first passed by Congress in 1975. The result was chaos—within six months its provisions were suspended.

In June, 1976, the Act was amended. Its purpose is to protect the consumer from paying exorbitant closing costs and kickbacks, often hidden in the closing statement. It must be complied with by all *federally regulated lenders*. In this way the Act has clout, because most real estate loans are made by federally regulated lenders. It covers all federally regulated mortgages secured by single-family dwellings, condominiums, and cooperatives occupied by one to four families. Exempt from the Act are properties in excess of 25 acres, construction loans, and loans on vacant lots.

More specifically, the Act attempts to bring about changes that result in:

1. More effective *advance* disclosure of settlement costs
2. Elimination of kickbacks, or unearned fees
3. A reduction in the amount of escrow funds placed in accounts by homeowners
4. Modernization of local land title records and information

Regarding loan origination fees, Paragraph 801 of the Act states that:

> This fee covers the lender's administration costs in processing the loan. Often expressed as a percentage of the loan, the fee will vary among lenders from locality to locality. Generally, the buyer pays the fee unless another arrangement has been made with the seller and written into the sales contract.

The statement, "This fee covers the lender's administrative costs in processing the loan," is a bit misleading. The cost of processing a $50,000 loan is the same as the cost of processing a $500,000 loan. However, if the cost is 1

1. FHA MORTGAGEE NO.	FHA UNDERWRITING REPORT	2. FHA CASE ▲ NO.

3. NEIGHBORHOOD CODE
▲1.☐ Core City 2.☐ Other City 4.☐ Sub-urban ▲1.☐ Model City 2.☐ Peri. of MC 4.☐ Rural ▲1.☐ URA 2.☐ Code Enf. 4.☐ Bligh-ted

4. ▲ PROPERTY ADDRESS

MORTGAGE TO BE INSURED UNDER
☐ SEC. 203(b) ☐ SEC._____

3

LEGAL-LOT _____ BLK. _____ TR./SUBD. _____

5. MORTGAGEE

6. ESTIMATE OF VALUE AND CLOSING COSTS
VALUE OF PROPERTY $_____
Closing Costs . . . $_____
TOTAL (For Mortgage Insurance Purposes) . . $_____

7. MONTHLY EXPENSE ESTIMATE
Fire Ins. . . . . $_____
Taxes . . . . . $_____
Main. & Repairs $_____
Heat & Utilities $_____

8. APPROVED FOR COMMITMENT

9. COMMITMENT
Issued: _____ 19__
Expires: _____ 19__

10. COMMITMENT TERMS MAX. MORT. AMT. $_____ NO. MOS. _____ MAX. INTEREST _____ %

11. ☐ EXISTING ☐ PROPOSED

12. ▲ EXISTING HOUSE 4.☐ Name of Occupant (or person to call if unoccupied) _____ Tel. No. _____ Key Encl. ☐ (If unfurnished)
Mon. & Yr. Completed ▲ _____ ☐ Never Occup. ☐ Vacant Occupied by ☐ Owner ☐ Tenant at $ _____ Per Mo. ☐ Furn. ☐ Unfurn

13. ▲ PROPOSED 1.☐ SUBSTAN. REHAB. 2.☐ UNDER CONSTR. 3.☐ Builder's Name & Address Including ZIP Code _____ Tel. No. _____ Model Identification
Plans: ☐ First Subm. Prob. Repeat Cases ☐ Yes ☐ No ☐ Prev. Proc. as FHA Case No.

14. DESCRIPTION
▲1.☐ Wood siding 2.☐ Wood shingle 3.☐ Asb. shingle 4.☐ Fiber board
▲1.☐ Detached 2.☐ Semi-det. 3.☐ Row
▲1.☐ Frame 2.☐ Masonry 3.☐ Concrete
Factory Fabricated ▲1.☐ Yes 2.☐ No
▲1.☐ Stories ▲ Liv. room ▲ Din. room Kitchen ▲ No. rms. ▲ Baths ▲ ½ Baths % Non-res.
7.☐ Split Foyer 8.☐ Bi-Level 9.☐ Split Level
▲1.☐ Full Basement 2.___% Basement 3.☐ Slab on Gr. 4.☐ Crawl Space
5.☐ Brick or stone 6.☐ Stuc. or c.blk. 7.☐ Aluminum 8.☐ Asph. siding 9.☐
_____ Bedrooms ☐ Store Rm ☐ Util. Rm.
▲1.☐ Garage 9.☐ Carport No cars
2.☐ Attached 3.☐ Detached
Mineral Rights Reserved ☐ No ☐ Yes (Explain)
Util-ities: Public Comm. Individual Water ▲1.☐ 2.☐ 3.☐ Gas ☐ ☐ ☐ Elect. ☐ ☐ ☐ ▲1.☐ Underground Wiring Sanitary: Sewer ▲1.☐ 2.☐ 3.☐ 4.☐
▲ Type of Heating ▲1.☐ Cent. Air Cond. 2.☐ Wall Air Cond.
Type of Paving (Str.) ☐ None
☐ Curb & Gutter Sept. Cess tank Pool ☐ Sidewalk ☐ Storm Sewer

EXTRA FEATURES ▲1.☐ Fireplace 2.☐ Rec. Room 4.☐ Sw. Pool ▲1.☐ Enclosed Porch 2.☐ Breezeway 4.☐ Fence
▲1.☐ Extra Fire Pl. 2.☐ Expand Attic 4.☐ Fin. Attic ▲1.☐ Open Porch 2.☐ 4.☐

15 SPEC. ASSESS. Prepayable $_____ Non-Prepay. $_____ Int.___% Ann. Pay. $_____ Unpd. Bal. $_____ Rem. Term___ Yrs.
16. ▲ LOT _____ × _____ 1.☐ Irr. 2.☐ Acres _____ Sq. Ft.
17. GENERAL LOCATION:

18. ANN. R. EST. TAXES $ _____ **19. ANN. FIRE INS $** _____ **20. ▲ SALE PRICE $** _____

21. EQUIPMENT IN VALUE: ▲1.☐ Range or Counter cook unit & oven 2.☐ Refrig. 4.☐ Dishwasher
▲1.☐ Auto. washer 2.☐ Dryer 4.☐ ___ ▲1.☐ Garb. Disp. 2.☐ Vent. fan 4.☐ Carpet

22. ▲ LOC. CODE
23. BASIC CASE
24. SUB FILE NO.
25. REM. LIFE ☐ ECON. ☐ PHYS. _____ YRS.
26. CONDITION AS APPRAISED ▲1.☐ Excellent 2.☐ Good 3.☐ Fair 4.☐ Poor
27. NEIGHBORHOOD DATA
Pres. Land Use _____
Anticip. Land Use _____
Owner Occp. Appeal _____
Demand for Amenity Inc. Prop. _____
___% Blt. up ___% own. ___% Ten. ___% Vac.
Age Typ. Bldg. _____ to _____
Typ. Mo. Rent $_____ to $_____
▲ Price Range $_____ to $_____
28. ▲ Location ☐ Acceptable ☐ Reject ☐ 223e
Property ☐ Acceptable ☐ Reject
29. IMPROVED ▲ LIVING AREA _____ Sq. Ft.

30. COST DATA: 2800-3 for _____ ☐ Integ.
2014-d _____ ☐ 2014
Cost @ $_____ Per Sq. Ft. = $_____
31. BLDG. DESC/VARS. — +
Fdns. _____ Frpl. _____
Ext. Wall _____
Shtg. _____
Sub. Fl. _____ Fin. Fl. _____
Rfg. _____ Int. Wall _____
Plg. _____
Htg. _____ Insul. _____
Equip. _____
Total Variations _____ $

Net variations - - - - - - - - $ _____
Basic cost - - - - - - - - - $ _____
Main Bldg. (Subtotal) - - - $ _____
Gar./Carport - - - - - - - - $ _____
Porches/Terraces - - - - - $ _____
Walks/Drives - - - - - - - - $ _____
Ldsp./Pltg./Fin. Gr. - - - - $ _____
Other on-site imp. - - - - - $ _____
On-site imp. unadj. (Total) $ _____
2511 Comb. ___% × wkmp. ___% = ___%
On-site imp. adj. - - - - - - $ _____
Arch. services - - - - - - - $ _____
Water/sewer tap charges - - $ _____
EST. REPL. COST IMP. - $ _____
32. REPL. COST Review
▲ Repl. cost imp. $ _____
▲ Mkt. Price Eq. site $ _____
Misc. Allow Costs $ _____
Mktg. Expense - - $ _____
▲ Repl. Cost - - - $ _____
33. COST OF REPAIRS/IMPROVEMENTS Prop. $ _____ Req. $ _____

34. COMPARABLE PROPERTIES

	Sq. Ft. Imp. Area	Sto-ries	Rms.	Bed Rms.	Bath	Const.	Gar.	Yr./cond.	Price	Date	L	S Date Inspec.	+/=	Variations
SUBJECT PROPERTY														
(1)														
(2)														
(3)														

35. CAP. INCOME: Mon. Rent $_____ − Excess exp. $_____ = $_____ × Rent multiplier of _____ = CAP. INCOME $_____
36. APPRAISAL SUMMARY: Capitalized Income $_____ Cost $_____ Market ▲ $_____
VALUE: Vol. (Excl. Cl. Costs) $_____ Closing Costs $_____ Total ▲ $_____
37. LEASE: ANN. GRD. RENT $_____ CAP. AT _____% = ▲ $_____ Val. of Leased Fee. Val. of Leasehold Est. $_____
38. (1) Remarks (2) Spec. Cond. (3) Rej. Reasons (4) Neigh. Charac. (5) Land excl. From Val. (6) Items Excl. From Repl. Cost.

39. INSPECTIONS: ☐ Repair
☐ Proposed Construction
☐ Mortgagee's Certificate
☐ Appr. Arch. Proc. _____ Date
☐ Reject
Review
☐ Commit. Staff Val. ☐ Other
☐ Reject
Review _____ Date

WARNING: All persons by signing this report certify that they have no interest present or future, in the property, application or mortgage.

FIGURE 17-4. FHA Underwriting Report

percent, then on the $50,000 loan, the buyer pays $500; on the $500,000 loan, the fee is $5,000. The difference goes to the lender and may cover any loss when the mortgage is sold in a secondary market.

Income-Producing Loan Fees

An income-producing, or commercial, borrower is faced with a number of "up-front" fees. Two of them are described below.

The Application Fee. This is a percentage of the loan and is paid with the submission of the application for the loan. It is the consideration paid for processing the loan and for retaining sufficient funds available to fund the loan.

"Good Faith" Deposits. Sometimes this is called a "security deposit." In periods of normal interest, it is about 2 percent of the loan. The amount is refundable *except* if the borrower seeks out another lender when interest rates decline, or if the borrower defaults. The amount on deposit is regarded as liquidated damages, if reasonable. *Liquidated damages* are damages decided

---

TAX IMPLICATIONS

Residential Application Fees. Although for many years the IRS permitted this fee as a deduction in the year paid, the Act of 1986 did make some changes. In 1987, a ruling made by the IRS provided that (a) points (a point being 1 percent of the mortgage charged by lenders and paid by buyers) could be fully deducted in the year paid *only* if the proceeds of the mortgage are used to buy or improve a principal residence, and (b) when the proceeds of a mortgage are used to pay off an old mortgage or to finance an education, points must be deducted over the life of the loan.

For example, a borrower borrows $80,000 to refinance a mortgage and is charged $2,400 in points. There are 240 monthly payments; therefore, the borrower can deduct $10 for each monthly payment made during the year.

Income-Producing Loans. Fees paid on a commercial mortgage must be written off over the life of the loan. Even if the mortgage is prepaid by refinancing, the fees must be written off over the life of the original loan.

For example, suppose a borrower has taken out a commercial loan for five years and the fees are $25,000. At the end of the first year, the borrower writes off $5,000, leaving a balance of $20,000. Then the borrower decides to refinance and pay off the loan. The $20,000 cannot be written off at that time, but must be written off at the rate of $5,000 per year for the remaining four years even though the original loan has been paid off.

on beforehand in the event of a breach of the agreement. The deposit is forfeited to the lender.

The borrower, rather than tie up money in the deposit, generally uses a certificate of deposit or a letter of credit. A letter of credit is a letter from the borrower's bank, giving credit to the borrower and agreeing to pay the good faith amount in the event of a breach of the agreement.

TRUTH IN LENDING

The Truth in Lending Act, effective July 1, 1969, can be broken down into two major parts with regard to real estate: (1) the right of rescission, and (2) disclosure.

The Right of Rescission

A borrower has the right to rescind a loan contract within three business days after having agreed to the contract. But, if the loan contract is a new or assumed first mortgage, deed of trust, or contract for deed, the borrower *cannot* rescind the loan contract. It will apply where an interest in real estate occupied by the borrower as a residence is issued as security for the loan. Thus the refinancing of an existing first mortgage, loans for home improvements, and second mortgages are all subject to the right of cancellation.

The lender involved must give the borrower a written notice of the right to rescind. Failure to do so may result in the borrower's suing for double the amount of the finance charge up to $1,000 plus court costs and attorneys' fees.

Disclosure

Under the law, the terms and conditions of the loan must be declared in writing to the borrower. The disclosures consist of:

1. The total finance charges
2. The date finance charges begin
3. Number of payments
4. Due dates of payments
5. Prepayment penalties
6. Total of all payments
7. The annual percentage rate (APR) (This is most important.)

The APR is *not* just the stated interest rate. It is a combination of the interest rate plus the other charges outlined above, and is designed to reveal the true costs to the borrower. Assume, for example, you borrow $10,000 for a year at an interest rate of 12 percent plus two points or $200 ($10,000 × .02) as an origination fee. At the end of the year you pay back $11,200. The effective rate is not 12 percent because you had the use of only $9,800 ($10,000 –

$200) for the year because of the two-point origination fee. You paid $1,400 for the use of $9,800 ($11,200 – $9,800 = $1,400). Thus you paid an effective interest rate of 14.29 percent ($1,400 ÷ $9,800 = .1429). This rounded off to the nearest $1/4$ percent, is $14^1/4$ percent.

Tables have been prepared by the Board of Governors of the Federal Reserve System to make it easy to find the actual percentage rates on various types of loans. For example, assume that the finance charges on a $30,000 loan are $5,000, the contract rate is 15 percent, and the number of monthly payments is 25 (with an adjustable-rate mortgage or a renegotiable-rate mortgage, this is not unique—available tables are designed for many more months than this).

The formula for finding the APR is:

$$\frac{\text{Total Finance Charges}}{\text{Amount Financed}} = \text{Ratio} \times \$100 = \frac{\text{Amount Per}}{\$100 \text{ Financed}}$$

For the $30,000 loan involving monthly payments, we have:

$$\frac{\$5,000}{\$30,000} = .1667 \times \$100 = \$16.67$$

Table 17–1 now can be used to obtain the APR. Follow the left-hand column of the table down to the line for 25 months. Read across until you find the number nearest to 16.67; in this example, 16.76. Reading up the column shows an annual percentage rate of 14.75 percent.

As a result of the Monetary Control Act of 1980, effective March 31, 1982, the disclosure of the annual percentage rate (APR) is deemed accurate if the rate is within a tolerance not greater than $1/8$ of 1 percent more or less than the actual rate, or rounded to the nearest $1/4$ of 1 percent.

To assure compliance with the Truth in Lending Act:

1. The lender is required to furnish the borrower a copy of a HUD-approved information booklet at the time application is made for the loan or within three days. This booklet entitled *Settlement Procedures Special Information Booklet* specifies the main procedures cited by the Act and lists unfair practices prohibited under the Act.

2. The lender must furnish a "good faith" estimate of settlement costs to the loan applicant within three days of the written loan application. The standard "good faith" estimate is shown in Figure 17–5 on page 304.

3. The lender must furnish the borrower a standard form to be used in all regulated settlements (or closings). If the borrower requests it, the settlement costs, to the extent known, must be made available to the borrower 24 hours before settlement. This settlement form is shown in Figure 17–6 on pages 305 and 306.

TABLE 17-1. Sample Page from Table for Computing Annual Percentage Rate for Level Monthly Payment Plans

Number—Annual Percentage Rate of

(Finance Charge Per $100 of Amount Financed)

Payments	14.00%	14.25%	14.50%	14.75%	15.00%	15.25%	15.50%	15.75%	16.00%	16.25%	16.50%	16.75%	17.00%	17.25%	17.50%	17.75%
1	1.17	1.19	1.21	1.23	1.25	1.27	1.29	1.31	1.33	1.35	1.37	1.40	1.42	1.44	1.46	1.48
2	1.75	1.78	1.82	1.85	1.88	1.91	1.94	1.97	2.00	2.04	2.07	2.10	2.13	2.16	2.19	2.22
3	2.34	2.38	2.43	2.47	2.51	2.55	2.59	2.64	2.68	2.72	2.76	2.80	2.85	2.89	2.93	2.97
4	2.93	2.99	3.04	3.09	3.14	3.20	3.25	3.30	3.36	3.41	3.46	3.51	3.57	3.62	3.67	3.73
5	3.53	3.59	3.65	3.72	3.78	3.84	3.91	3.97	4.04	4.10	4.16	4.23	4.29	4.35	4.42	4.48
6	4.12	4.20	4.27	4.35	4.42	4.49	4.57	4.64	4.72	4.79	4.87	4.94	5.02	5.09	5.17	5.24
7	4.72	4.81	4.89	4.98	5.06	5.15	5.23	5.32	5.40	5.49	5.58	5.66	5.75	5.83	5.92	6.00
8	5.32	5.42	5.51	5.61	5.71	5.80	5.90	6.00	6.09	6.19	6.29	6.38	6.48	6.58	6.67	6.77
9	5.92	6.03	6.14	6.25	6.35	6.46	6.57	6.68	6.78	6.89	7.00	7.11	7.22	7.32	7.43	7.54
10	6.53	6.65	6.77	6.88	7.00	7.12	7.24	7.36	7.48	7.60	7.72	7.84	7.96	8.08	8.19	8.31
11	7.14	7.27	7.40	7.53	7.66	7.79	7.92	8.05	8.18	8.31	8.44	8.57	8.70	8.83	8.96	9.09
12	7.74	7.89	8.03	8.17	8.31	8.45	8.59	8.74	8.88	9.02	9.16	9.30	9.45	9.59	9.73	9.87
13	8.36	8.51	8.66	8.81	8.97	9.12	9.27	9.43	9.58	9.73	9.89	10.04	10.20	10.35	10.50	10.66
14	8.97	9.13	9.30	9.46	9.63	9.79	9.96	10.12	10.29	10.45	10.62	10.78	10.95	11.11	11.28	11.45
15	9.59	9.76	9.94	10.11	10.29	10.47	10.64	10.82	11.00	11.17	11.35	11.53	11.71	11.88	12.06	12.24
16	10.20	10.39	10.58	10.77	10.95	11.14	11.33	11.52	11.71	11.90	12.09	12.28	12.46	12.65	12.84	13.03
17	10.82	11.02	11.22	11.42	11.62	11.82	12.02	12.22	12.42	12.62	12.83	13.03	13.23	13.43	13.63	13.83
18	11.45	11.66	11.87	12.08	12.29	12.50	12.72	12.93	13.14	13.35	13.57	13.78	13.99	14.21	14.42	14.64
19	12.07	12.30	12.52	12.74	12.97	13.19	13.41	13.64	13.86	14.09	14.31	14.54	14.76	14.99	15.22	15.44
20	12.70	12.93	13.17	13.41	13.64	13.88	14.11	14.35	14.59	14.82	15.06	15.30	15.54	15.77	16.01	16.25
21	13.33	13.58	13.82	14.07	14.32	14.57	14.82	15.06	15.31	15.56	15.81	16.06	16.31	16.56	16.81	17.07
22	13.96	14.22	14.48	14.74	15.00	15.26	15.52	15.78	16.04	16.30	16.57	16.83	17.09	17.36	17.62	17.88
23	14.59	14.87	15.14	15.41	15.68	15.96	16.23	16.50	16.78	17.05	17.32	17.60	17.88	18.15	18.43	18.70
24	15.23	15.51	15.80	16.08	16.37	16.65	16.94	17.22	17.51	17.80	18.09	18.37	18.66	18.95	19.24	19.53
25	15.87	16.17	16.46	16.76	17.06	17.35	17.65	17.95	18.25	18.55	18.85	19.15	19.45	19.75	20.05	20.36

Source: Board of Governors of the Federal Reserve System, Exhibit G—"Truth in Lending—Consumer Credit Cost Disclosure."

ESTIMATED CLOSING COSTS

The following are estimates of the amount of costs for certain services which Borrowers are likely to purchase in connection with the settlement on the purchase of real property.

These estimated amounts reflect charges experienced in the locality, but may be substantially different from the actual costs you will incur.

This is not a loan commitment.

ESTIMATED CLOSING COSTS BASED ON A LOAN AMOUNT OF $ _____ .
RATE _____ TERM _____ RATIO _____

**NO. ON
UNIFORM
SETTLEMENT
STATEMENT**

No.	Item	Amount
801	LOAN ORIGINATION FEE	_____
804	CREDIT REPORT	_____
805	INSPECTION (APPRAISAL) FEE	_____
806	PRIVATE MTG. INS. APPLICATION REVIEW FEE	_____
807	ASSUMPTION FEE	_____
808	COMMITMENT FEE _____ %	_____
901	INTEREST____ days	_____
902	PRIVATE MTG. INS. PREMIUM	_____
903	MORTGAGEES HAZARD INSURANCE PREMIUM*	_____
1001	INSURANCE RESERVE	_____
1002	PRIVATE MTG. INS. RESERVE **	_____
1102	ABSTRACT OR TITLE SEARCH	_____
1103	TITLE EXAMINATION	_____
1107	ATTORNEYS CERTIFICATE OF TITLE	_____
1108	TITLE INSURANCE-LENDER'S COVERAGE	_____
1111	TAX SERVICE	_____
1201	RECORDING FEES	_____
1203	DOCUMENTARY FEE	_____
1301	SURVEY	_____
____	TAX CERTIFICATE	_____
____	FHA INSURANCE RESERVE	_____
____	OTHER	_____

APPROXIMATE LOAN PAYMENT
P&I = _____
TAX = _____
INS = _____
MTG
INS = _____
TOTAL = _____

APPROXIMATE SETTLEMENT AMOUNT:

A. PURCHASE PRICE _____
B. REPAIRS AND IMPROVEMENTS _____
C. TOTAL CLOSING COSTS _____
D. PREPAID ESCROWS _____
E. TOTAL _____
F. AMT. THIS LOAN _____
G. OTHER FINANCING _____
H. DEPOSIT TO DATE _____
I. CLOSING COSTS PAID BY SELLER _____
J. CASH REQUIRED FOR CLOSING _____

* Hazard insurance is required. You may purchase insurance from any person or organization you choose.
** Mortgage insurance, if required, is paid from the interest charged.

An attorneys certificate of title will be provided to the lender at an estimated cost of $_____ ,

by (name)_____

(address)_____ (phone) _____ .
This provider has a business relationship with Midland Federal Savings.

THIS FORM DOES NOT COVER ALL ITEMS YOU WILL BE REQUIRED TO PAY IN CASH AT SETTLEMENT, FOR EXAMPLE, DEPOSIT IN ESCROW FOR REAL ESTATE TAXES. YOU MAY WISH TO INQUIRE AS TO THE AMOUNT OF SUCH OTHER ITEMS.

Date: _____

_____   _____
BORROWER   LOAN COUNSELOR

_____
BORROWER

FIGURE 17–5. Estimated Closing Costs

A. U.S. DEPARTMENT OF HOUSING AND URBAN DEVELOPMENT	B. TYPE OF LOAN
	1. ☐ FHA 2. ☐ FMHA 3. ☐ CONV. UNINS.
	4. ☐ VA 5. ☐ CONV. INS.
DISCLOSURE/SETTLEMENT STATEMENT	6. FILE NUMBER 7. LOAN NUMBER
If the Truth-in-Lending Act applies to this transaction, a Truth-in-Lending statement is attached as page 3 of this form.	8. MORTG. INS. CASE NO.

C. **NOTE:** This form is furnished to you prior to settlement to give you information about your settlement costs, and again after settlement to show the actual costs you have paid. The present copy of the form is:

☐ ADVANCE DISCLOSURE OF COSTS. Some items are estimated, and are marked "(e)." Some amounts may change if the settlement is held on a date other than the date estimated below. The preparer of this form is not responsible for errors or changes in amounts furnished by others.

☐ STATEMENT OF ACTUAL COSTS. Amounts paid to and by the settlement agent are shown. Items marked "(p.o.c.)" were paid outside the closing; they are shown here for informational purposes and are not included in totals.

D. NAME OF BORROWER	E. SELLER	F. LENDER

G. PROPERTY LOCATION	H. SETTLEMENT AGENT	I. DATES	
		LOAN COMMITMENT	ADVANCE DISCLOSURE
	PLACE OF SETTLEMENT	SETTLEMENT	DATE OF PRORATIONS IF DIFFERENT FROM SETTLEMENT

J. SUMMARY OF BORROWER'S TRANSACTION		K. SUMMARY OF SELLER'S TRANSACTION	
100. **GROSS AMOUNT DUE FROM BORROWER:**		400. **GROSS AMOUNT DUE TO SELLER:**	
101. Contract sales price		401. Contract sales price	
102. Personal property		402. Personal property	
103. Settlement charges to borrower *(from line 1400, Section L)*		403.	
		404.	
104.		Adjustments for items paid by seller in advance:	
105.		405. City/town taxes to	
Adjustments for items paid by seller in advance:		406. County taxes to	
		407. Assessments to	
106. City/town taxes to		408. to	
107. County taxes to		409. to	
108. Assessments to		410. to	
109. to		411. to	
110. to		420. **GROSS AMOUNT DUE TO SELLER**	
111. to			
112. to			
120. **GROSS AMOUNT DUE FROM BORROWER:**		*NOTE: The following 500 and 600 series section are not required to be completed when this form is used for advance disclosure of settlement costs prior to settlement.*	
200. **AMOUNTS PAID BY OR IN BEHALF OF BORROWER:**		500. **REDUCTIONS IN AMOUNT DUE TO SELLER:**	
201. Deposit or earnest money		501. Payoff of first mortgage loan	
202. Principal amount of new loan(s)		502. Payoff of second mortgage loan	
203. Existing loan(s) taken subject to		503. Settlement charges to seller *(from line 1400, Section L)*	
204.		504. Existing loan(s) taken subject to	
205.		505.	
Credits to borrower for items unpaid by seller:		506.	
		507.	
206. City/town taxes to		508.	
207. County taxes to		509.	
208. Assessments to		Credits to borrower for items unpaid by seller:	
209. to		510. City/town taxes to	
210. to		511. County taxes to	
211. to		512. Assessments to	
212. to		513. to	
220. **TOTAL AMOUNTS PAID BY OR IN BEHALF OF BORROWER**		514. to	
		515. to	
300. **CASH AT SETTLEMENT REQUIRED FROM OR PAYABLE TO BORROWER:**		520. **TOTAL REDUCTIONS IN AMOUNT DUE TO SELLER**	
301. Gross amount due from borrower *(from line 120)*		600. **CASH TO SELLER FROM SETTLEMENT:**	
302. Less amounts paid by or in behalf of borrower *(from line 220)*		601. Gross amount due to seller *(from line 420)*	
303. CASH ☐ REQUIRED FROM OR ☐ PAYABLE TO BORROWER:		602. Less total reductions in amount due to seller *(from line 520)*	
		603. **CASH TO SELLER FROM SETTLEMENT**	

HUD-1A (6-75) AS & AS (1323)

LENDER'S COPY

FIGURE 17–6. Disclosure/Settlement Statement

L. SETTLEMENT CHARGES		PAID FROM BORROWER'S FUNDS	PAID FROM SELLER'S FUNDS
700.	SALES/BROKER'S COMMISSION based on price $ @ %		
701.	Total commission paid by seller		
	Division of commission as follows:		
702.	$ to		
703.	$ to		
704.			
800.	**ITEMS PAYABLE IN CONNECTION WITH LOAN.**		
801.	Loan Origination fee %		
802.	Loan Discount %		
803.	Appraisal Fee to		
804.	Credit Report to		
805.	Lender's inspection fee		
806.	Mortgage Insurance application fee to		
807.	Assumption/refinancing fee		
808.			
809.			
810.			
811.			
900.	**ITEMS REQUIRED BY LENDER TO BE PAID IN ADVANCE.**		
901.	Interest from to @ $ /day		
902.	Mortgage insurance premium for mo. to		
903.	Hazard insurance premium for yrs. to		
904.	yrs. to		
905.			
1000.	**RESERVES DEPOSITED WITH LENDER FOR:**		
1001.	Hazard insurance mo. @ $ /mo.		
1002.	Mortgage insurance mo. @ $ /mo.		
1003.	City property taxes mo. @ $ /mo.		
1004.	County property taxes mo. @ $ /mo.		
1005.	Annual assessments mo. @ $ /mo.		
1006.	mo. @ $ /mo.		
1007.	mo. @ $ /mo.		
1008.	mo. @ $ /mo.		
1100.	**TITLE CHARGES:**		
1101.	Settlement or closing fee to		
1102.	Abstract or title search to		
1103.	Title examination to		
1104.	Title insurance binder to		
1105.	Document preparation to		
1106.	Notary fees to		
1107.	Attorney's Fees to		
	(includes above items No.:)		
1108.	Title insurance to		
	(includes above items No.:)		
1109.	Lender's coverage $		
1110.	Owner's coverage $		
1111.			
1112.			
1113.			
1200.	**GOVERNMENT RECORDING AND TRANSFER CHARGES**		
1201.	Recording fees: Deed $; Mortgage $ Releases $		
1202.	City/county tax/stamps: Deed $; Mortgage $		
1203.	State tax/stamps: Deed $; Mortage $		
1204.			
1300.	**ADDITIONAL SETTLEMENT CHARGES**		
1301.	Survey to		
1302.	Pest inspection to		
1303.			
1304.			
1305.			
1400.	**TOTAL SETTLEMENT CHARGES** (entered on lines 103 and 503, Sections J and K)		

The Undersigned Acknowledges Receipt of This Disclosure Settlement Statement and Agrees to the Correctness Thereof.

_____   _____
Buyer or Agent   Seller or Agent

NOTE: Under certain circumstances the borrower and seller may be permitted to waive the 12-day period which must normally occur between advance disclosure and settlement. In the event such a waiver is made, copies of the statements of waiver, executed as provided in the regulations of the Department of Housing and Urban Development, shall be attached to and made a part of this form when the form is used as a settlement statement.

HUD-1B (6-75) AS & AS (1323)

LENDER'S COPY

FIGURE 17–6.   Disclosure/Settlement Statement (concluded)

TAX IMPLICATIONS OF RESIDENTIAL SALES

1. When a personal residence is sold at a profit, the seller can buy or build another one within 24 months *before* or *after* the sale. The gain is recognized and currently taxed only to the extent that the sales price, minus fixing-up expenses, exceeds the cost of purchasing or building the new residence.

2. There is a once-in-a-lifetime exclusion of gain from the sale of a principal residence by a taxpayer aged 55 or over amounting to $125,000, provided it has been the taxpayer's principal place of residence three out of five prior years. The exclusion is $62,500 in case of a separate return by a married taxpayer.

3. The Tax Reform Act of 1986 left the two above provisions of the previous law intact. However, there is an additional provision which applies not only to residential real estate but to commercial real estate sales as well; that is, the closing agent is required to submit a Form 1099-B to the IRS. This form must include the gross proceeds *received*. For example, if the selling price is $100,000 and the seller, after commissions and other costs, receives $12,226, it is that figure which is sent to the IRS on the form shown in Figure 17-7 on page 308.

INCOME-PRODUCING REAL ESTATE LOANS

Income-producing real estate loans are always a two-step proposition, often by two different lenders, and the two steps go hand in hand. These loans are the construction loan (interim financing) and the permanent loan. The former is a short-term loan and the latter, a long-term loan.

In the area of relatively small loans, both the borrower's financial status and the property are carefully scrutinized. With larger loans most of the emphasis is placed on the property itself. The main question from the viewpoint of the lender is whether or not the property itself will support the loan. Consequently, most lenders in this situation will require a feasibility study, or as it is sometimes called, an economic feasibility study. For the most part, these studies are prepared by professional consultants. In general, the format is the same, but with varying emphasis, depending on the purpose of the study. For example, a developer might want to build a condominium with 300 units to sell at $85,000 per unit. The lender might want to know whether the area chosen for the proposed project can absorb 300 units and, more important, whether it can absorb 300 units at $85,000 per unit. The feasibility study might conclude that the area can absorb 300 units priced perhaps at $50,000, but not at $85,000.

In general, then, a study might cover the following minimum topics:

INFORMATION FOR REAL ESTATE 1099-B REPORT FILING
as required by the Internal Revenue Service

This is important tax information and is being furnished to the Internal Revenue Service. If you are required to file a return, a negligence penalty or other sanction will be imposed on you if this item is required to be reported and the IRS determines that it has not been reported.

File Number _____ (10)   Taxpayer ID No. _____ (9)

Taxpayer type _____ (1)   1=business   2=individual

INDIVIDUAL SELLER NAME

Last _____ (20) First & Middle _____ (20)

BUSINESS SELLER NAME

_____ (40)

MAILING ADDRESS

Street _____ (40)

City _____ (20) State _____ (2)

Zip Code _____ (9)

TRANSACTION INFORMATION

Closing Date _____ (6) Gross Proceeds _____ (11)

Description of Property _____ (26)

Was the property the personal residence of the Seller? _____ (yes or no)

Has the Seller received (or will receive) property or services other than the gross proceeds set out above? _____ (yes or no)

You are required by law to provide the Closing Agent with your correct taxpayer identification number. If you do not provide the Closing Agent with your correct taxpayer identification number, you may be subject to civil or criminal penalties imposed by law.

Under penalty of perjury, I certify that the Tax ID No. shown on this statement is my correct taxpayer identification number. I further certify that the above information is true and correct and acknowledge receipt of a copy of this statement.

Date _____   _____

CLOSING AGENT INFORMATION

Name _____

Address _____

City _____ State _____ Zip Code _____

Taxpayer ID Number _____

FIGURE 17–7. Real Estate 1099-B Report Filing Statement

1. How many people live in the area? What is the population trend? What is the average family size? (In general, condominium units sell to families of small size.) What is the size breakdown of the popula-

tion? This is very relevant in trying to forecast the demand for rental units. People below the age of 30 and over the age of 65 are more likely to rent apartment units than the 30-to-65 age group.

2. What is the income of the population in the area?
3. What sort of employment is in the area? Is it a "one industry" town, or is it well balanced? Is employment fairly stable?
4. What sort of transportation is available?
5. What is the real estate market in terms of number of projects, dollar volume, average prices?
6. How many dwelling units or commercial units are being constructed? What is the nature of these units (i.e., single family, multifamily, or shopping centers, for example)?
7. How is land being used within the area? What are the planned areas? What is the average market value by type of use?
8. What sort of zoning regulations and land-use restrictions are there?
9. What are current rents in the area of the proposed project?
10. What are current vacancy rates in similar projects?
11. What are current interest rates? Is the project feasible, given current rates?
12. Is the area growing? What is the rate of land absorption by type of use? What is the direction of growth?
13. What is the competition?

The preceding list is by no means complete. A real estate professional will go into much more detail, for more detail will be demanded by a financial institution before the loan is granted.

PRO FORMA FINANCIAL PROJECTIONS

In addition to a feasibility study, lenders are interested in pro forma financial projections. Both are analyzed by lenders and must certainly be as realistic as possible.

For example, if a project totaling $1 million has land costs of $200,000 and improvement costs of $800,000, with a proposed 30-year loan at 9.8 percent, the pro forma financial projections would be as follows:

Capital Costs:

Building construction costs (include nonconstruction items such as legal, architectural, engineering)	$ 800,000
Land	200,000
Total	$1,000,000

Estimated Income and Expenses:

Rents	$ 200,000
Less 5% for vacancy	10,000
Expected gross income	$ 190,000

Operating Expenses:

Real estate taxes	$15,000	
Fuel and energy	25,000	
Maintenance	15,000	
Management	15,000	
Insurance	3,000	
Miscellaneous	17,000	
Total		90,000
Net Operating Income		$ 100,000

Economic Value and Mortgage:

Net operating income	$ 100,000
Project economic value capitalized at 10%	1,000,000
Assume a 75% loan-to-value ratio; loan is	750,000

Debt Service and Cash Flow:

Net operating income	$ 100,000
Less debt service: $750,000 × 10.352% constant (9.8% for 30 years)	77,640
Cash Flow Before Taxes	$ 22,360

Equity and Yield:

Total costs	$1,000,000
Mortgage	750,000
Cash Down Payment	$ 250,000

$$\text{Yield on Cash Paid Down} = \frac{\text{Cash Flow}}{\text{Cash Down}} = \frac{\$\ 22,360}{\$250,000} = 8.94\%$$

Debt Service

In order to be able to analyze a *pro forma* balance sheet, it is first necessary to understand the meaning of the term "debt service." **Debt service** is the dollar amount of periodic payments needed to pay off the mortgage or mortgages. With a second mortgage there must be enough income to pay the first mortgage as well as the second mortgage and other operating expenses. Most loans are of the *direct reduction* type. This means that the debt service consists of fixed periodic payments of principal and interest during the term of the loan. The interest is paid on the reduced principal balance. Consequently, as each payment is made, the interest paid declines while the amount of principal due is reduced. Put another way, as the interest paid declines, the amount paid on the principal increases.

There are two basic ways that the debt service is expressed: by a monthly amortization amount or by an annual constant.

The Monthly Amortization. This simply indicates the amount of monthly payments necessary to amortize a loan of $1,000 at a given rate for a given period of time. Thus, given a $10,000 loan at 12 percent for 25 years, the payback is $10.53 per thousand per month. Then for a $100,000 loan, monthly payment is $1,053 ($100 × $10.53), or $12,636 annually. (See Table 6 in Appendix B for the monthly amortization schedule for a $1,000 loan.)

The Annual Constant. The mortgage constant is a way to estimate how much money it takes on an annual basis to amortize a mortgage. The annual constant is calculated by multiplying the monthly payments, including principal and interest, by 12.

For example, assume a 20-year mortgage of $100,000 at 12 percent interest. From Table 6 in Appendix B, it takes a monthly payment of $11.01 to amortize a $1,000 loan at 12 percent over 20 years. This means it takes $132.12 annually to pay off $1,000 over 20 years. To pay off $100,000 over 20 years at $11.01 monthly per $1,000, it takes $1,101 per month, or $13,212 annually.

The annual constant as a ratio of annual payment to the original mortgage is expressed as a percentage. Thus:

$$\text{Annual Constant Percentage} = \frac{\$13,212}{\$100,000} = .13212 \text{ or } 13.212\%$$

In this case, the annual constant is equal to $132.12 per $1,000 borrowed. What difference does it make? It's a rapid method of calculating the amount needed to pay off the loan annually. For example, if the property nets $12,500 per year, it can be quickly calculated that $13,212 ($100,000 × .13212) is needed annually to pay off the loan. You'd be coming up short. In this case, it might be feasible to lengthen the loan and lower the constant. For example, if the length were increased to 30 years, it would take $10.29 per $1,000 per month, or $1,029 per month for the $100,000 loan, or $12,348 per year. The annual constant would then be 12.348 percent ($12,348 ÷ $100,000). Then, with an income of $12,500, the project would be feasible, the payment being $12,348 ($100,000 × .12348) annually. (Table 7 in Appendix B contains some selected annual constant percentages to two decimal places.)

Analyzing the Financial Projections

The starting point for lenders in analyzing the financial projections is the effective gross income. The *effective gross income* is simply the projected rental income minus the vacancy costs. From the preceding figures:

Effective gross income	$190,000
Less operating expenses including taxes	90,000
Net Income	$100,000

Now assume a 10 percent decrease in the effective gross income ($190,000 − $19,000 = $171,000). Then:

Effective gross income	$171,000
Less operating expenses and taxes	90,000
Net Income	$ 81,000

You can see by this example that a 10 percent decrease in effective gross income results in a 19 percent reduction in net income, or $100,000 − $81,000 = $19,000 ÷ $100,000 = 19% drop.

The seriousness of a miscalculation of effective gross income is readily seen when comparing it with a miscalculation in operating expenses. For example, if a 10 percent error in operating expenses occurs, then:

Effective gross income	$190,000
Less operating expenses and taxes now of	99,000
Net Income	$ 91,000 (instead of $100,000)

Thus, while net income is reduced from $100,000 to $91,000 because of an error of 10 percent in the operating expenses, the percentage change in net income amounts to $100,000 − $91,000 = $9,000. The $9,000 ÷ $100,000 = 9% drop.

Margin and Break Even. Margin can best be thought of as a cushion. It is the difference between 100 percent occupancy and the point at which either operating expenses and debt service must be met out of pocket or the property is threatened by foreclosure. In simple formula form, the break-even point as a percentage is first found as follows:

$$\text{Break-Even Point} = \frac{\text{Debt Service} + \text{Operating Expenses}}{\text{Gross Potential Income}}$$

This break-even point, then, is subtracted from 100 percent to find the *margin,* which indicates the allowable vacancy before there is a need for out-of-pocket payments.

For example, looking at the preceding problem:

Potential gross before vacancy	$200,000
Less operating expenses	90,000
Potential net	$110,000
Less debt service (interest plus principal)	77,640
	$ 32,360

Assume: Debt service	$ 77,640
Operating expenses	90,000
Total Charges	$167,640

Thus: $\dfrac{\$167,640}{\$200,000} = 83.8\%$ break-even point

Then: $100\% - 83.8\% = 16.2\%$ margin (allowable vacancy or rental decrease before out-of-pocket funds are necessary)

The concept of margin is very important where a second mortgage is to be used in financing. The payments on the first as well as the second mortgage must be met, and the payments become a part of the debt service. In this case, the margin, or cushion, can disappear rapidly. For example, in the case preceding assume that the builder-developer decides to use a second mortgage to finance part of the loan. The debt service on the second mortgage is $17,000 per year. Then:

Debt service on first mortgage	$ 77,640
Debt service on second mortgage	17,000
Operating expenses	90,000
	$184,640

Thus, $\dfrac{\$184,640}{\$200,000} = 92.3\%$ break-even. Then, $100\% - 92.3\% = 7.7\%$ margin (allowable vacancy)

Thus, with the addition of a second mortgage with debt service of $17,000 per annum, a vacancy rate of over 7.7 percent means out-of-pocket payments, which would probably bring about a refusal of the loan by the lender.

Debt-Service-Coverage Ratio. An analysis of debt service coverage is of prime concern to a lender. The debt-service-coverage ratio is:

$$\text{Debt Service Coverage} = \frac{\text{Net Operating Income}}{\text{Total Mortgage Payment per Year}}$$

Thus in our case above:

$$\frac{\$100,000}{\$77,640} = 1.29$$

This means that its net operating income (NOI) can meet the annual mortgage payment 1.29 times. The borrower, in our case here, is seeking a 75 percent loan in the amount of $750,000. The margin of safety to the lender is $100,000 - $77,640 = $22,360. Therefore, the cushion to the lender is $22,360 and the NOI must fall by this amount before the loan is threatened.

What does the lender do with these figures? The lender compares them with past loan experience. They are compared with the ratios in loans that have gone into default. For example, suppose that, based on past experience, most of the borrowers have gone into default with a debt-service ratio of 1.15. Then clearly, if this were our case here, if the debt-service ratio were 1.15 or lower, the $750,000 or 75 percent loan would not be granted. It might be that a loan of only $500,000, or a 50 percent loan-to-value ratio, will be made, with the borrower having to have cash down of $500,000 instead of $250,000. Lenders use several rules of thumb regarding the debt-service-coverage ratio:

1. On top-rated tenants in office buildings or shopping centers, the NOI coverage should be 1.1 more times the sum of the debt service on a first and possible second mortgage.
2. On apartments or motels, the lender considers a range of between 1.2 and 1.5 times the debt-service-coverage ratio.

Operating-Expense Ratio. Another point of analysis used by lenders to determine the feasibility of a loan is the operating-expense ratio. It is simply:

$$\text{Operating Expense Ratio} = \frac{\text{Operating Expenses}}{\text{Effective Gross Income}}$$

In the case outlined above, it is:

$$\frac{\$90,000}{\$110,000} = 81.8\%$$

The lender then compares this with ratios of comparable properties to determine any deviations from the comparables. If the deviation from the standard is great, this would suggest that the borrower might be unable to meet the debt service.

Return-on-Investment Ratio. Lenders worry about an income property deteriorating from lack of proper management and maintenance; therefore, they have developed a "return-on-investment" ratio. This shows how much income *before* debt service is earned on the total investment which, in turn, relates to the current profitability of the investment. Reduced to a formula:

$$\text{Return on Investment} = \frac{\text{Net Operating Income}}{\text{Total Invested Capital}}$$

Using the figures in our case above:

$$\frac{\$100,000}{\$1,000,000} = 10\%$$

After having arrived at the 10 percent, lenders will then compare this figure to the return on investment of comparable properties at the *moment*. In short, the rates on all properties fluctuate over time due to such things as inflation and interest rates. However, this is regarded in the same sense as a balance sheet—changing from time period to time period.

Five-Times-the-Bottom-Line Rule. This is another rule of thumb used by lenders in setting the limit on loan-to-value ratios of second mortgages. For example, assume a property has a net operating income of $110,000 and that the debt service on the first mortgage is $60,000, resulting in a cash flow before taxes of $50,000. Using this rule of thumb, the maximum second mortgage given by lenders would be $250,000 ($50,000 × 5).

THE LOAN CLOSING STATEMENT

The *Loan Closing Statement* is not a seller's or buyer's closing statement; it is simply a statement by a financial institution or title insurance company concerning the disbursement of borrowed funds. For example, assume a loan of $200,000 (the sales price may have been $300,000 or whatever) has a loan fee of one percent. For purposes of simplification, assume no other disbursements by the institution; then the net proceeds to the borrower would be $200,000 – $2,000 = $198,000.

A form commonly used for the loan closing statement is shown in Figure 17–8 on page 316.

In the very large projects, involving several millions of dollars, construction lenders require much more by way of documentation when a construction loan is closed.

For example, the builder-developer is required to assign all construction contracts to the construction *lender*. The reason for this is to prevent the builder-developer from making any deviations from the plans and specifications without the consent of the construction lender.

In addition, evidence of compliance with municipal regulations, such as building permits and licenses, must be submitted, as well as liability and workers' compensation insurance policies.

KEY TERMS

cost-to-replace approach
    (to appraisal)
debt service
income approach (to appraisal)

Loan Closing Statement
market-data approach
    (to appraisal)

QUESTIONS FOR REVIEW

1. How does the Federal Home Loan Mortgage Corporation define stable monthly income?
2. What are the three items that lenders examine closely in terms of a borrower's credit reputation?
3. The Equal Credit Opportunity Act as amended beginning March 23, 1977, prohibits discrimination against credit applicants. What sort of discrimination does the Act prohibit?
4. Explain what is meant by sellers' discount points. Include the reasons why they exist.

LOAN CLOSING STATEMENT

Borrower .... Date ....

Seller .... Agent ....

Address of Property ....

  The following costs are based on information available at this time. This association is not a party to the sale of the property and figures related to sale are included hereon only as an accomodation.

Loan Charges {	Loan Fee	$ _____
	Attorney's Opinion	
	Credit Report	
	Documentary Fee	
	Appraisal Fee	
	....	
	....	
Recording {	Release—Deed of Trust	
	Warranty Deed	
	Deed of Trust	
	....	
	....	
Abstracting {	Abstracting To Date	
	Release—Deed of Trust	
	Warranty Deed	
	Deed of Trust	
	....	
	....	
	Abstract Certificate	
Title Insurance {	Owner's Policy	
	Mortgagee's Policy	
Survey		
Taxes {	Tax Certificate	
	(General Taxes 19 ....)	
	Tax Reserve to 1st Payment (...........)	
	Special Assessments	
	....	
Insurance {	$ .... Expires .... Prem.	
	....	
	Additional	
	Insurance Reserve to 1st Payment (...)	
Encumbrances {	....	
	....	
	....	
.... Interest on $ .... to 1st Payment (........)		
Total		$

Loan Amount $ _____

Total Costs _____

Net Proceeds $ _____

Approved and Copy Received

_____   _____

_____   _____

FIGURE 17–8.   Loan Closing Statement

5. Three basic approaches are used to appraise the value of real property. Identify them and provide brief explanations.
6. Identify and briefly describe the Real Estate Settlement Procedures Act.
7. What is the purpose of the Truth in Lending Act? How does the Act impact on real estate transactions?
8. Explain the concept of margin and break-even in commercial real estate lending. How is it useful?
9. What is a "loan closing" statement?

PROBLEMS

1. A request is made for a residential mortgage loan. The potential borrower has a gross monthly income from primary base earnings of $2,000, and a secondary income, which is typical for the borrower's occupation, of $400 per month. Payments on the home mortgage loan are expected to be $600 per month. The borrower has additional installment loan commitments of $400 per month. Is the loan likely to be granted? What would be the situation if the installment loan commitments were $200 per month? Finally, would the loan be granted if the monthly housing expenses were $650 and there were no additional installment loan commitments?
2. A prospective home buyer wants an FHA insured mortgage loan for $55,000. If the conventional loan rate is higher than the FHA rate, then "points" will be used to equate the two rates. Assume the equating rate is three points. How much will the seller receive?
3. Determine the annual percentage rate using Table 17-1 in the chapter for each of the following loans:
   a. A two-year, $20,000 loan requires monthly payments. Total interest expenses will be $2,800 plus there are $300 in loan fees.
   b. Finance charges are $2,000 on a $15,000, 18-month loan. Monthly payments are required.
   c. A 15-month, $10,000 loan requires monthly payments and the associated interest and loan origination finance charges are $1,200.
4. Assume that you consider building a commercial real estate project. Land acquisition costs will be $350,000 with building construction costs estimated at $900,000. Rental income is expected to be $300,000 if fully occupied. Operating expenses are estimated at $120,000. A $1,000,000 mortgage loan is available on the project. The loan will be for 30 years at 12 percent interest.
   a. Indicate the total capital costs for the project.
   b. Determine the monthly amortization amount using Table 6 in Appendix B. What will be the annual payment on the mortgage loan?
   c. Use Table 7 in Appendix B to determine the annual constant percentage and the annual mortgage payment.
   d. What is the percentage break-even point on the project? What flexibility, in terms of margin or allowable vacancy, is available?
   e. Calculate the debt-service-coverage ratio, the operating-expense ratio, and the return-on-investment ratio for the project.

18

MORTGAGE DEFAULT AND FORECLOSURE

LEARNING OBJECTIVES

After studying this chapter, you should be able to do the following:

Describe the foreclosure process.

Identify and describe the four types or methods of foreclosure.

Describe what has been happening to mortgage foreclosure rates by type of loan during the 1980s.

Identify what is meant by deficiency judgments and indicate recent developments in terms of deficiency judgments.

Discuss the proceedings involved when a buyer defaults on an installment land contract.

Describe the extension agreement, the consolidation and extension agreement, and the spreading agreement as they are used as alternatives to foreclosure.

Briefly explain the use of a deed in lieu of foreclosure as a means of avoiding going through a mortgage foreclosure.

DURING THE EIGHTIES, the number of mortgages and deeds of trust that entered into default was staggering. Although default on a loan occurs when the borrower has failed to fulfill one or a number of the contractual obligations agreed to in the mortgage instrument, there was one breach most frequently leading to foreclosure—failure on the part of the mortgagor to make timely payments. Both lenders and borrowers sought alternatives to foreclosure, with foreclosure as a last resort.

FORECLOSURE AND REDEMPTION

Historically the English law simply held that there was no need for foreclosure. The courts enforced the strict written terms of the mortgage. Debts had to be paid if the borrower wished to retain rights in the land; failure to pay debts resulted in the termination of land rights.

About the middle of the 17th century, there developed a right of a borrower to redeem the land at a future date. This right was known as the *equity of redemption.* This concept worked a hardship on the borrower's creditor because the creditor might never receive the money owed. Consequently, a time limit was placed on the equity of redemption by a decree of foreclosure issued by a court. By virtue of the decree of foreclosure, the right to redeem was cut off unless the debt was paid by the time named in the decree. Today the time limit for redeeming the property is set by statute in the various states.

The Foreclosure Process

While the methods of foreclosure may vary from state to state, the meaning of *foreclosure,* "to shut out, exclude, or bar," is still the same in all states. The actions beginning and ending the foreclosure process are discussed in the following paragraphs.

Commencing the Action. The summons and the complaint begin the foreclosure action. A copy of the summons and a copy of the complaint are served on the mortgagor and on any of the lienors determined from the title search. If the mortgagor has a defense against the foreclosure, the mortgagor answers the complaint, thus raising an issue that is triable by jury. In some states a "master in chancery" hears the matter without a jury. In the event that the mortgagor defaults (fails to answer the summons and complaint), the foreclosure proceeds to its conclusion.

At the time of the filing of the summons and the complaint, a *lis pendens* (notice of pendency of action) is filed with the clerk of the county in which the property is located. The *lis pendens* is a warning to anyone concerned with, or about to be concerned with, the mortgaged property that there is an action pending on it.

Completing the Action. If a default is made by the mortgagor, the mortgagee is entitled to a judgment which is filed with the court. This judgment directs that the property be sold at public auction, either by a referee appointed by the court or by the sheriff, or in states using a deed of trust by the public trustee. Notice of the sale is given to all defendants, and it is published in such newspapers as the judge or statute directs for the number of times required by law. At the sale bids are made on the property. If the mortgagee does not think the bids are high enough, the mortgagee may also bid on the property.

Mortgage Foreclosure Under The Bankruptcy Act. Under Section 362(a) of The Bankruptcy Act there is an automatic stay of the foreclosure proceeding or any action to obtain possession of the property upon the filing of a bankruptcy petition by the borrower. There is one exception: the stay does not apply to an action by the Secretary of HUD to foreclose on an FHA-insured mortgage and if the property consists of five or more living units.

Types of Foreclosure

Basically, there are four methods of foreclosure; some states use one or a combination of several. The methods are: (1) strict foreclosure, (2) foreclosure by sale in a judicial process, (3) foreclosure by exercise of power of sale, and (4) foreclosure by entry and possession.

Strict Foreclosure.[1] The procedure in a strict foreclosure is the same as that outlined in the preceding discussion on the foreclosure process. If there has been a default, the court determines if the mortgagee has a right to foreclose. In the absence of a valid defense, a judgment is entered setting out the amount due. Generally the judgment will specify that the borrower has from two to six months within which to redeem by paying the amount due. Further, the judicial decree states that if the borrower fails to pay, then all persons claiming under this action shall be forever barred and foreclosed. The mortgagee becomes the sole owner of the property and there is no sale.

Because of the lack of sale and the value of the property not being taken into account, the courts regard the strict foreclosure as a harsh remedy.

Foreclosure by Sale in a Judicial Process.[2] The procedure used here is identical with that of a strict foreclosure *except* that in the judicial sale the land is sold at public auction. The theory behind this process is that the property may bring more than the indebtedness. If so, this excess is turned over to the borrower.

One of the basic steps taken by the mortgagee in pursuing this foreclosure action is to have a title search or abstract of title prepared. The *abstract of title* is a brief history of the particular property with which the action is concerned. The reason for having the abstract prepared is that pre-

---

[1]In theory the strict foreclosure can be used in many states; however, it is used only in Vermont and Connecticut.

[2]In Arizona, California, Florida, Idaho, Illinois, Iowa, Kansas, Montana, New Jersey, New Mexico, North Dakota, Oklahoma, and Oregon a foreclosure suit is the *only* method of foreclosing on a mortgage.

sumably the mortgagee has the first lien on the property; in addition, it is necessary to bring in all other parties in interest, who generally are lienors junior to the mortgagee's lien. There may be a good possibility of the foreclosure cutting off the rights of the other lienors, and consequently they must have notice of this action. Otherwise, they will be deprived of their day in court. This violates the 14th Amendment of the Constitution; namely, a deprivation of property without due process. Furthermore, if any surplus monies result from a foreclosure sale, the junior lienors then have the requisite notice to commence a surplus money proceeding in order to establish their rights to the surplus monies.

Foreclosure by Exercise of Power of Sale. This method of foreclosure constitutes a foreclosure without recourse to the courts. Here the mortgage instrument provides for the remedy in case of default. The instrument spells out what shall be considered a default and confers power on the mortgagee (or public trustee in case of a trust deed) to sell the property after public notice at public auction.

Power of sale is the customary method in 21 states. All formalities and requirements must be meticulously observed; otherwise, the sale may be set aside by the courts.

Foreclosure by Entry and Possession. In four states (Maine, Massachusetts, New Hampshire, and Rhode Island) the mortgagee may foreclose by taking peaceful possession of the mortgaged premises and by remaining in possession for a specified time. The entry is made in the presence of witnesses and a certificate of that fact is filed. The mortgagor has a period in which to redeem the property. If the mortgagor does not redeem the property, the mortgagee receives good title to the premises. In a real sense this procedure comes fairly close to being a strict foreclosure.[3]

Other Aspects of Foreclosure

In addition to the preceding types of foreclosure methods, there are various other actions that may be taken in relation to a foreclosure.

Deficiency Judgments. The idea behind the deficiency judgment is quite simple. For example, suppose A owes a lender $20,000 on a mortgage. If the foreclosure sale of the property brings only $19,000, then A still owes the lender $1,000. Depending on the state, the lender either obtains a personal judgment against A at the time of the sale or the lender obtains a judgment for

---

[3]Foreclosure in Maine is quite unique. It is called foreclosure by advertisement and the property concerned is described and a statement made that the conditions of the mortgage were broken. Foreclosure is made by serving an attached copy of this notice on the borrower and recording the service. The mortgagor has one year within which to redeem, the period dating from the first publication.

MORTGAGE FORECLOSURE RATES BY TYPE OF LOAN

Mortgage foreclosures as a percentage of total loans have increased dramatically during the 1980s. This much higher foreclosure rate has severely affected the operating performances of many lenders and has caused members of housing-related government agencies to voice concern about the record high levels of consumer debt and the debt repaying capabilities of consumers. Following are recent mortgage foreclosure rates as reported in the U.S. League of Savings Institutions annual *Sourcebook.*

MORTGAGE FORECLOSURE RATES

YEAR-END	ALL MORTGAGE LOANS	CONVEN-TIONAL LOANS	FHA LOANS	VA LOANS
1980	.38%	.17%	.53	.46
1981	.44	.24	.57	.55
1982	.67	.39	.88	.76
1983	.67	.46	.84	.76
1984	.73	.47	.98	.82
1985	.81	.61	1.01	.88
1986	.98	.69	1.22	1.14

Notice that the mortgage foreclosure rate for all loans had increased to nearly one percent by 1986. This represents an increase greater than two and one-half times the 1980 level of .38 percent. Of particular interest are the increases in foreclosure rates by type of loan. For example, conventional mortgage loans had a foreclosure rate of only .17 percent as of the end of 1980. However, the foreclosure rate increased fourfold by the end of 1986 to the .69 percent level.

The increase in foreclosure rates was less for FHA and VA mortgage loans relative to conventional mortgage loans. However, both the FHA and VA loans started the 1980s with much higher rates which were at about the .5 percent level. Of increasing concern is the fact that by the end of 1985 the foreclosure rate had surpassed the one percent level for FHA loans. Furthermore, the one percent foreclosure rate level for VA loans also had been surpassed by the end of 1986.

These recent foreclosure rate trends certainly are of concern to lenders, homeowners, and governmental agencies and need to be closely monitored in the future.

$1,000 after the sale.

The deficiency judgment came under attack during the depression of the 1930s. Many states passed legislation providing that the deficiency judgment be limited to the difference between the mortgage debt and the "fair market value." The fair market value is determined by qualified appraisers. Thus, in the preceding example, if the fair market value was $20,000, then there was no deficiency judgment. In addition, some states outlawed the deficiency judgment (Nebraska and South Dakota) completely. Further, California, North Carolina, Oregon, and Montana outlawed deficiency judgments on purchase money mortgages.

If there is a surplus, or monies resulting from the sale, other lienors divide it according to the amount of surplus money which establishes their priorities.

Recent Developments in Deficiency Judgments. In late 1987, HUD announced, and the VA began actively pursuing, deficiency judgments even in states that ordinarily protect borrowers against deficiency liability—California, for example. The reason for this action was that many FHA and VA borrowers had particularly abused the FHA program with multiple defaults. Such individuals had simply paid small down payments, and, after having lived in the home for a year or so, "walked away" without further payment, in effect inviting foreclosure.

In addition, FHA is now publishing a "credit alert." This is a list of mortgagors who have defaulted within the past three years. It is now necessary for lenders to check all applicants for FHA loans against this list. At the same time, the FHA declared that for owner-occupied homes, extenuating circumstances will be considered, such as illness, unemployment, or death of the principal owner, in its decision to approve or deny an application for a new loan.

Foreclosure and Junior Lienors. As was previously pointed out, one of the reasons interest rates on second mortgages are normally higher than on first mortgages is that the risk is greater. The foreclosure proceeding is the proof of the high-risk pudding.

In the event of foreclosure, there is either (1) a surplus over the amount owed to the first mortgagee, or (2) no surplus. If there happens to be a surplus, then after the indebtedness and costs are paid to the senior lienor the surplus is distributed according to the priority rights of the junior lienors. (Junior lienors, may, in addition to second mortgagees, consist of mechanic's lienors, judgment creditors, and so forth.)

What happens if the surplus is insufficient to entirely satisfy the junior lienor? For example, suppose the property is sold for $150,000 and the first mortgage is $100,000. There is also a second mortgage of $80,000. The first mortgagee is paid $100,000 and the $50,000 is paid to the second mortgagee who may then sue the mortgagor for the $30,000 owed on the note that was signed in conjunction with the second mortgage.

Suppose there is no surplus. In this case the second mortgagee and any other junior lienors may sue on their claims, obtain a judgment, and hope to satisfy their debts out of the mortgagor's other assets, if any.

Sometimes junior lienors will pay off senior lienors and foreclose themselves, hoping again to recoup their funds.

Some states permit second mortgagees to "marshall assets" to protect themselves in the event of foreclosure. Assume, for example, that A is given a blanket mortgage by B (senior mortgagee) on two parcels, Lot 1 worth $30,000 and Lot 2 worth $10,000. The total amount of the blanket is

$40,000. Suppose that later *C* loans *A* $5,000 secured by Lot 1. *C* is now a second mortgagee. Suppose *B* forecloses on Lot 1 without foreclosing on Lot 2. Is *C* wiped out? In some states *C* can force *B* to foreclose on Lot 2 worth $10,000, and then on Lot 1 worth $30,000, and presumably thereby protect *C*'s $5,000 second mortgage.

Appointment of a Receiver. In Chapter 2 it was pointed out that many mortgages provide for the appointment of a receiver in the event of foreclosure. The purpose of the receiver is to protect the property from the time of the commencement of the foreclosure to its conclusion. For example, borrowers will frequently abandon the property once the foreclosure proceeding begins. In this case, the receiver will rent the property and apply this rent to the reduction of the mortgage debt. Often, too, there is a business involved in the foreclosure proceeding. In this case, the receiver will run the business during the foreclosure process. The receiver's function is to keep a disgruntled mortgagor from running the business into the ground or from committing waste.

Priority of Tax Liens. Even though a first mortgage is senior to other recorded liens, the real property tax takes precedence. Consequently, in the event of foreclosure the real property taxes are generally paid by the lender and added to the amount due in the foreclosure proceeding.

PROCEEDINGS ON A DEFAULTED LAND CONTRACT

When a buyer defaults on an installment land contract,[4] the first step to the seller regaining possession of the property is to send the defaulting buyer a so-called "30-day notice." Technically, this notice is entitled "Notice of Default and Intent to Declare Whole Obligation Due and Payable Under Contract." In essence, the property is described, the contract recited, and the buyer is given 30 days within which to "cure" the default.[5]

The land contract usually contains a liquidated damages clause. *Liquidated damages* are damages decided upon before a breach under the terms of the contract takes place. It has long been held that liquidated damages must be reasonable, otherwise it is possible that a forfeiture will be declared which will be upheld by the courts. For example, suppose a buyer enters into a contract to buy a home and agrees to take possession on June 18th. In the contract there is a liquidated damages clause providing that if the seller fails to give the buyer possession on that date, seller will pay liquidated damages of $25 per day for every day purchaser does not have possession.

---

[4]The installment land contract was discussed more fully in Chapter 10. It is a contract used instead of a mortgage in the sale of property. Title remains with the seller until the final payment takes place.

[5]This 30-day "grace" period applies to Colorado, Iowa, Minnesota, and South Dakota, among others. In North Dakota it is one year, and in Arizona the time depends upon the amount of the buyer's equity.

Clearly, in light of today's prices, this is reasonable. But supposing the contract called for $1,000 per day in liquidated damages. Clearly the courts would say this is unreasonable and therefore a forfeiture would follow.

Briefly, in a land contract (also known as a *contract for deed*), the liquidated damages clause provides that if the purchaser under a contract fails to make a payment, the seller who has retained title is entitled to possession. In addition to possession, the contract provides that the seller is entitled to all funds previously paid by the buyer.

Some states by statute prohibit a forfeiture. In other states, the courts will prevent a forfeiture at a point. But at what point is often unclear. For example, suppose a parcel of property is sold under a $40,000 land contract and $1,000 is paid when the default occurs. Probably the courts will permit the seller to regain possession of the property and keep the $1,000. But suppose the buyer has paid $39,000 and then defaults. Obviously it would be unfair to permit the seller to keep the $39,000 and regain possession of a piece of property presumably worth $40,000 when only $1,000 is owed on it.

In Ohio, by statute, the seller must foreclose on the contract if the buyer has an equity of 40 percent. Consequently, as in cases where forfeitures are prohibited by statute, the seller must foreclose on the contract. Basically, the procedure is the same as in the mortgage foreclosure.

The question of liquidated damages versus forfeiture has been raised in some states as the result of inflation. For example, supposing *A* sells *B* a home on a contract for deed at $100,000 with $10,000 down. Assume the value of the home rises to $200,000 and *B* has made no further payments. Should *A* be able to repossess and reap the $100,000 gain as liquidated damages, or should the home be put up for sale at public auction for $200,000, *A* receiving $90,000 and *B* receiving the equity of $110,000? This precise question was raised but not decided in Alaska.[6]

ALTERNATIVES TO FORECLOSURE

In many instances it is possible to work out an arrangement with the mortgagee if the mortgagor cannot meet the payments on a loan. Examples of such arrangements are the *extension agreement,* the *consolidation and extension agreement,* and the *spreading agreement.*

Extending the Mortgage

The situation may arise when a mortgage payment is soon to come due and the mortgagor cannot make the payment. If the payment is not made, the mortgage will either be foreclosed or remain open. In the latter case the mortgagee has the right to foreclose at any time. The mortgagee may, however, be willing to extend the time in which the mortgagor must pay off the mortgage

---

[6]See Curry v Tucker, 616 P2d 8 (Alaska 1980).

indebtedness. This is done by means of an extension agreement.

The *extension agreement* is a device employed to extend the due date of the mortgage, and in some cases to modify the original note and mortgage. This modification may take the form of a different interest rate, a different method of amortization, or both.

The instrument recites the parties, the old mortgage, and the amount presently due and payable. It also states that the mortgagor covenants to pay a certain rate of interest, which may or may not be the same rate as that called for by the original mortgage. If the mortgagor cannot make the payments due, this rate will probably be higher than the rate called for in the mortgage instrument itself. All of the covenants of the original mortgage instrument (the covenant to pay taxes, the warrant of title, etc.) are contained in the extension agreement. This instrument should also contain substantially the following clause:

> (The mortgagor) is now the owner and holder of the premises upon which said mortgage is a valid lien for the amount above specified, with interest at the rate above set forth, and there are no defenses or offsets to said mortgage, or the debt which it secures.

This clause will prevent the mortgagor from later asserting any defenses that might have been valid prior to the date of the extension agreement.

A question arises concerning the position of the original signer of the note in the event that the property is sold. The signer's liability depends upon what happens to property values. Before the signing of the extension agreement, the original mortgagor on the note can demand that the mortgage be foreclosed. If property values are high, the mortgagor will know that a foreclosure will not result in a deficiency judgment. However, after an extension agreement is executed, the original mortgagor, or maker of the note, is not liable for any value that the property might lose after the signing of the extension agreement because the mortgagor is no longer a surety. For example, A obtains a mortgage from B in the amount of $30,000 on a parcel of property valued at $40,000. A sells the property to X, who takes it subject to the mortgage. Later the time for payment becomes due and the mortgage is open. The property has risen in value to $60,000. A can demand that B foreclose on the mortgage. B does not foreclose, but gives X an extension. Thus, B cannot foreclose. Later the value of the property declines to $20,000 and X defaults. B cannot collect the difference between $20,000 and $30,000 from A under the original note signed by A.

Consolidation and Extension

A mortgagee, either by having a first and second mortgage on a single piece of property or by having purchased two mortgages on one piece of property, may desire to create a single mortgage. This may be done by means of a *consolidation and extension agreement*. This arrangement would relieve the mortgagor of the burden of high amortization payments because the length of time for payment is usually extended, meaning that the monthly payments decline.

The instrument converts both of the mortgages into a single mortgage which becomes a first mortgage. It describes the property and recites the interest and payments to be made, and also the date when the final payment shall become due. The due date is included because, generally speaking, second mortgages have a due date prior to that of first mortgages; by this means the monies due under the previously existing mortgages become due and payable at the same time.

TAX IMPLICATIONS OF FORECLOSURE

As the result of a foreclosure, there may be taxable gains or losses to either the mortgagor or mortgagee.

If the proceeds from the sale are greater than the mortgagor's adjusted basis, the mortgagor is subject to a taxable gain. If the proceeds are less than the mortgagor's adjusted basis, there will be a loss.

For example, assume an income property with a purchase price of $200,000; $180,000 is financed by an institutional lender. Assume that in five years the borrower has paid off $60,000 on the loan and has taken depreciation of $66,600. At a foreclosure, let's first assume the property is sold for $150,000, or $30,000 more than the then remaining unpaid mortgage balance of $120,000. The tax implications would be:

Amount received at foreclosure sale		$150,000
Purchase price	$200,000	
Minus depreciation	66,600	
Less adjusted cost basis		133,400
Taxable Gain to Borrower		$ 16,600

If an amount equal to or less than the mortgage debt is received at the foreclosure sale, then for tax purposes the $120,000 unpaid debt amount would be substituted in place of the actual amount received. The tax implications for the borrower based on a $120,000 selling price would be:

Amount of unpaid mortgage debt		$120,000
Purchase price	$200,000	
Minus depreciation	66,600	
Less adjusted cost basis		133,400
Taxable Loss to Borrower		($ 13,400)

Now let's assume that the actual amount received at the foreclosure sale was only $100,000. The initial tax implication would be to show a $13,400 loss for the borrower, as we have just calculated when the sales price is equal to the $120,000 unpaid mortgage amount. However, in the event of a deficiency judgment, there will be additional tax implications if the $20,000 ($120,000 - $100,000) that is deficient is subsequently paid. The $20,000 amount would be added to the $13,400 loss, for a total taxable loss of $33,400 to the borrower.

The form shown in Figure 18–1 is a standard FNMA, FHLMC consolidation/extension agreement. It can be used as either a consolidation agreement, an extension agreement, or both. It is designed to become a part of a mortgage to be sold to either FNMA or FHLMC.

Spreading Mortgages

The *spreading agreement* is used by a mortgagee to incorporate other lands owned by the mortgagor under the terms of an existing mortgage. The situation usually arises when the mortgagor requests an extension of a mortgage that is about to become an open mortgage or go into default. The mortgagee may feel that additional security is needed in order to extend the mortgage. If this is the case, the mortgagor will be asked to allow the mortgagee to cover with the existing mortgage additional lands owned by the mortgagor. This is done by means of the spreading agreement, which is acknowledged and recorded. In effect, it becomes a blanket mortgage.

The same form used for the consolidation and extension agreement may be quite readily adapted for the spreading agreement.

Deed in Lieu of Foreclosure

Often, rather than go through a mortgage foreclosure, a mortgagor will give the lender a *deed in lieu of foreclosure.*

There are several concerns about which the lender ought to be aware:

1. When a mortgagee accepts a deed, the mortgagee's first mortgage is extinguished. However, any second liens, such as a second mortgage or mechanic's lien, moves into first place and the mortgagee does not receive the property free and clear of encumbrances.

2. If the mortgagor goes bankrupt within four months after giving the deed to the mortgagee and there is a substantial equity in the property, the transaction may be regarded as a "preference." A *preference* is payment to one creditor by an insolvent debtor, to the exclusion of other creditors, or of a larger amount than the creditor would be entitled to receive on a *pro rata* distribution. Therefore, the courts may declare the deed void.

3. Where a deed is given in lieu of foreclosure to a mortgagee, it must clearly be shown that the existing note and mortgage are cancelled. Otherwise the courts might construe the deed as a deed absolute (like a deed of trust) given as security for the debt: in short, simply another mortgage.

CONSOLIDATION/EXTENSION AGREEMENT

THIS AGREEMENT is made this .... day of .... , 19 ....
between ....
.... (herein "Borrower") and ....
.... , a corporation organized and existing under the laws of ....
.... , whose address is ....
.... (herein "Lender").

WHEREAS, Lender is the holder of a mortgage made by ....
.... as Mortgagor, to ....
....
as Mortgagee, in the principal sum of ....
.... Dollars (U.S. $ ....), dated ....
19 .... , and recorded in the Office of .... of the County of ....
.... , State of New York, in Liber .... , of Section .... of Mortgages,
page .... , which mortgage is a lien on the property located in the County of ....
.... , State of New York (herein "Property"), which has the address of ....
....

[*and is more particularly described in Schedule "A" attached hereto and made a part hereof*]*, and was given to secure a note
dated .... , 19 .... , on which there is now due, without defense or offset of any
kind, the principal sum of ....
Dollars (U.S. $ ....), with interest thereon.

[*Whereas, Lender is also the holder of a mortgage made by* ....
.... *as Mortgagor, to* ....
....
as Mortgagee, in the principal sum of ....
.... *Dollars (U.S.$* .... *), dated* ....
19 .... , *intended to be recorded herewith, which mortgage is also a lien on the Property, and was given to secure
a note dated* .... , *19* .... , *on which there is now due, without defense or offset of any kind,
the principal sum of* ....
.... , *Dollars (U.S. $* .... *), with interest thereon.*]**

[*Whereas, Lender, the holder of the aforesaid mortgages and notes secured thereby, and Borrower, the owner of* [*the fee
interest*]**[*a leasehold estate*]** *in the Property, desire to consolidate the aforesaid notes and consolidate and coordinate the
liens of the aforesaid mortgages and modify the terms therein in the following manner; and*]**

Whereas, Lender, the holder of the aforesaid mortgage(s) and note(s) secured thereby, and Borrower, the owner of [*the fee
interest*]**[*a leasehold estate*]** in the Property, desire to extend and modify the terms of payment of the principal sum, with
interest thereon, in the following manner;

NOW, THEREFORE, in consideration of the mutual promises of the parties and other valuable consideration, the
parties hereto mutually covenant and agree as follows:

[*1. The liens of the aforesaid mortgages be and the same are consolidated and coordinated so that together   they will
constitute in law but one first mortgage and a single lien on the Property, securing the principal sum of* ....
Dollars (U.S. $ .... *), with interest thereon.*]**

2. The time of payment of said principal sum evidenced by the aforesaid note(s) secured by the aforesaid mortgage(s)
[, *as consolidated,*]** is hereby extended until the .... day of
.... , 19 .... , and Borrower promise(s) to pay ....
.... , or order, said principal
sum of .... Dollars (U.S. $ ....
...............), with interest on the unpaid principal balance from the date of this agreement, until paid, at the rate of
............percent per annum. Principal and interest shall be payable at ....
or such other place as Lender may designate, in consecutive monthly installments of ....
.... Dollars (U.S. $ ....),
on the .... day of each month beginning
.... , 19 .... Such monthly installments shall continue until the entire
indebtedness evidenced by this Agreement is fully paid, except that any remaining indebtness, if not sooner   paid, shall
be due and payable on .... , 19 ....

3. Borrower shall pay to Lender a late charge of .... percent of any
monthly installment not received by Lender within .... days after the installment is due.

4. Any prepayment privilege heretofore reserved or granted is hereby cancelled, and the following shall be the sole
rights of prepayment of the aforesaid note(s): Borrower may prepay the principal amount outstanding in whole or in part.
Lender may require that any partial prepayments (i) be made on the date monthly installments are due and (ii) be in
the amount of that part of one or more monthly installments which would be applicable to principal. Any partial
prepayment shall be applied against the principal amount outstanding and shall not postpone the due date of any
subsequent monthly installments or change the amount of such installments, unless Lender shall otherwise agree in

FIGURE 18–1. Consolidation/Extension Agreement

writing. If within twelve months from the date of this Agreement, Borrower make(s) any prepayments with money lent to Borrower by a lender other than the Lender hereof, Borrower shall pay Lender .... percent of the amount by which the sum of prepayments made in such twelve month period exceeds twenty percent of the original principal amount of this Agreement.

5. Borrower covenants and warrants that Borrower is the owner of [*the fee interest*]**[*a leasehold estate*]** in the Property.

6. Borrower hereby assumes all obligations of the obligor and mortgagor, respectively, under the aforesaid mortgage(s) and note(s), as herein modified, and covenants to perform and comply with all of the terms, provisions, conditions and covenants of the aforesaid mortgage(s) and note(s), as herein modified. Except as herein modified, the terms, provisions, covenants and conditions of the aforesaid mortgage(s) and note(s) are hereby ratified and confirmed, with the same force and effect as if herein incorporated and set forth in full. [*If there should be any ambiguity or conflict between the terms, provisions, conditions and covenants if the aforesaid mortgages or notes, the terms, provisions, conditions and covenants off the mortgage and note most recently executed by Borrower shall govern.*]**

7. No termination, alteration or amendment of this Agreement shall be effective unless in writing and signed by the party sought to be charged or bound thereby, and this Agreement shall be binding upon the heirs, executors, administrators, successors and assigns of the parties hereto.

IN WITNESS WHEREOF, this Agreement has been duly executed by the parties hereto the day and year first above written.

....
—Borrower

....
—Borrower

....
—Lender

* Delete bracketed material if not necessary for recordation.
** Delete bracketed material if not applicable.

FIGURE 18–1.   Consolidation/Extension Agreement (concluded)

KEY TERMS

abstract of title	equity of redemption
consolidation and extension agreement	extension agreement
deed in lieu of foreclosure	foreclosure
	spreading agreement

QUESTIONS FOR REVIEW

1. What is the right of equity of redemption?
2. Describe the foreclosure process.
3. What is the rationale behind the judicial sale of land as opposed to strict foreclosure? Or, vice versa, what is the legal limitation of a strict foreclosure?
4. What is the difference between foreclosure by a judicial sale and foreclosure by exercise of power of sale?
5. What is a *deficiency judgment* and what is its current status?
6. Describe the process undertaken when there is default on a land contract.

7. How is an extension agreement used? What are its usual provisions? How does it affect a seller of a home purchased subject to the existing mortgage?
8. Why might a lender request a spreading agreement?
9. Describe the use of a "deed in lieu of foreclosure."

PROBLEMS

1. Assume that foreclosure proceedings take place on a piece of property carrying a $50,000 first mortgage and a $10,000 second mortgage. If the property is sold for $55,000, what will happen to the claims of the first and second mortgagees?
2. Assume that two parcels of property are sold for $30,000 each under a land contract agreement. The purchaser of one parcel pays $1,000 per year for 2 years before defaulting on the land contract. The second purchaser pays $1,000 per year for 20 years before defaulting. What is likely to happen in these two situations?
3. The Sikeston partnership purchased a piece of income-producing property several years ago for $300,000. A $60,000 down payment was initially made and a $240,000 first mortgage loan was obtained from the Frankfort Savings and Loan Association. The property has since then been depreciated by $90,000 and the remaining mortgage loan amount is $190,000. At this time the property is being sold at a foreclosure sale.
   a. Show the lender's tax implications associated with the foreclosure if the property is sold for $215,000. What will be the foreclosure sale impact on the Sikeston partnership?
   b. What if, instead, the foreclosure sale brought in only $175,000? Indicate the impact on the Frankfort Savings and Loan Association and the impact on the Sikeston partnership. Also indicate the impact of any subsequent deficiency judgment and its payment on the lender.

APPENDIX A

Standard Residential Mortgage and Deed of Trust

OPEN-END MORTGAGE

THIS MORTGAGE is made this........16th................day of.....June.................., 19--.., between the Mortgagors. John M. Wilks and Elizabeth S. Wilks....................... ....(herein "Borrower"), and the Mortgagee,...The First...... ....Savings and Loan Association........................., a corporation organized and existing under the laws of........Ohio........................, whose address is. 203 Indianola Avenue, ...Columbus, Ohio...(herein "Lender").

WHEREAS, Borrower is indebted to Lender in the principal sum of. Forty-Seven Thousand and 00/100 .....($47,000,00). ------------------------Dollars, which indebtedness is evidenced by Borrower's note dated. June 16, 19--...........(herein "Note"), providing for monthly installments of principal and interest, with the balance of the indebtedness, if not sooner paid, due and payable on....July 1, 20--............. ....;

To SECURE to Lender (a) the repayment of the indebtedness evidenced by the Note, with interest thereon, the payment of all other sums, with interest thereon, advanced in accordance herewith to protect the security of this Mortgage, and the performance of the covenants and agreements of Borrower herein contained, and (b) the repayment of any future advances, with interest thereon, made to Borrower by Lender pursuant to paragraph 21 hereof (herein "Future Advances"), Borrower does hereby mortgage, grant and convey to Lender the following described property located in the County of..........Franklin...................., State of Ohio:

(here follows a complete legal description of the property)

which has the address of. 14 "E" Avenue, Columbus, ..., ...,
[Street]   [City]

Ohio 43207 ....(herein "Property Address");
[State and Zip Code]

TOGETHER with all the improvements now or hereafter erected on the property, and all easements, rights, appurtenances, rents, royalties, mineral, oil and gas rights and profits, water, water rights, and water stock, and all fixtures now or hereafter attached to the property, all of which, including replacements and additions thereto, shall be deemed to be and remain a part of the property covered by this Mortgage; and all of the foregoing, together with said property (or the leasehold estate if this Mortgage is on a leasehold) are herein referred to as the "Property".

Borrower covenants that Borrower is lawfully seised of the estate hereby conveyed and has the right to mortgage, grant and convey the Property, that the Property is unencumbered, and that Borrower will warrant and defend generally the title to the Property against all claims and demands, subject to any declarations, easements or restrictions listed in a schedule of exceptions to coverage in any title insurance policy insuring Lender's interest in the Property.

OHIO—1 to 4 Family—6/75—FNMA/FHLMC UNIFORM INSTRUMENT

Standard Residential Mortgage

UNIFORM COVENANTS. Borrower and Lender covenant and agree as follows:

1. Payment of Principal and Interest. Borrower shall promptly pay when due the principal of and interest on the indebtedness evidenced by the Note, prepayment and late charges as provided in the Note, and the principal of and interest on any Future Advances secured by this Mortgage.

2. Funds for Taxes and Insurance. Subject to applicable law or to a written waiver by Lender, Borrower shall pay to Lender on the day monthly installments of principal and interest are payable under the Note, until the Note is paid in full, a sum (herein "Funds") equal to one-twelfth of the yearly taxes and assessments which may attain priority over this Mortgage, and ground rents on the Property, if any, plus one-twelfth of yearly premium installments for hazard insurance, plus one-twelfth of yearly premium installments for mortgage insurance, if any, all as reasonably estimated initially and from time to time by Lender on the basis of assessments and bills and reasonable estimates thereof.

The Funds shall be held in an institution the deposits or accounts of which are insured or guaranteed by a Federal or state agency (including Lender if Lender is such an institution). Lender shall apply the Funds to pay said taxes, assessments, insurance premiums and ground rents. Lender may not charge for so holding and applying the Funds, analyzing said account, or verifying and compiling said assessments and bills, unless Lender pays Borrower interest on the Funds and applicable law permits Lender to make such a charge. Borrower and Lender may agree in writing at the time of execution of this Mortgage that interest on the Funds shall be paid to Borrower, and unless such agreement is made or applicable law requires such interest to be paid, Lender shall not be required to pay Borrower any interest or earnings on the Funds. Lender shall give to Borrower, without charge, an annual accounting of the Funds showing credits and debits to the Funds and the purpose for which each debit to the Funds was made. The Funds are pledged as additional security for the sums secured by this Mortgage.

If the amount of the Funds held by Lender, together with the future monthly installments of Funds payable prior to the due dates of taxes, assessments, insurance premiums and ground rents, shall exceed the amount required to pay said taxes, assessments, insurance premiums and ground rents as they fall due, such excess shall be, at Borrower's option, either promptly repaid to Borrower or credited to Borrower on monthly installments of Funds. If the amount of the Funds held by Lender shall not be sufficient to pay taxes, assessments, insurance premiums and ground rents as they fall due, Borrower shall pay to Lender any amount necessary to make up the deficiency within 30 days from the date notice is mailed by Lender to Borrower requesting payment thereof.

Upon payment in full of all sums secured by this Mortgage, Lender shall promptly refund to Borrower any Funds held by Lender. If under paragraph 18 hereof the Property is sold or the Property is otherwise acquired by Lender, Lender shall apply, no later than immediately prior to the sale of the Property or its acquisition by Lender, any Funds held by Lender at the time of application as a credit against the sums secured by this Mortgage.

3. Application of Payments. Unless applicable law provides otherwise, all payments received by Lender under the Note and paragraphs 1 and 2 hereof shall be applied by Lender first in payment of amounts payable to Lender by Borrower under paragraph 2 hereof, then to interest payable on the Note, then to the principal of the Note, and then to interest and principal on any Future Advances.

4. Charges; Liens. Borrower shall pay all taxes, assessments and other charges, fines and impositions attributable to the Property which may attain a priority over this Mortgage, and leasehold payments or ground rents, if any, in the manner provided under paragraph 2 hereof or, if not paid in such manner, by Borrower making payment, when due, directly to the payee thereof. Borrower shall promptly furnish to Lender all notices of amounts due under this paragraph, and in the event Borrower shall make payment directly, Borrower shall promptly furnish to Lender receipts evidencing such payments. Borrower shall promptly discharge any lien which has priority over this Mortgage; provided, that Borrower shall not be required to discharge any such lien so long as Borrower shall agree in writing to the payment of the obligation secured by such lien in a manner acceptable to Lender, or shall in good faith contest such lien by, or defend enforcement of such lien in, legal proceedings which operate to prevent the enforcement of the lien or forfeiture of the Property or any part thereof.

5. Hazard Insurance. Borrower shall keep the improvements now existing or hereafter erected on the Property insured against loss by fire, hazards included within the term "extended coverage", and such other hazards as Lender may require and in such amounts and for such periods as Lender may require; provided, that Lender shall not require that the amount of such coverage exceed that amount of coverage required to pay the sums secured by this Mortgage.

The insurance carrier providing the insurance shall be chosen by Borrower subject to approval by Lender; provided, that such approval shall not be unreasonably withheld. All premiums on insurance policies shall be paid in the manner provided under paragraph 2 hereof or, if not paid in such manner, by Borrower making payment, when due, directly to the insurance carrier.

All insurance policies and renewals thereof shall be in form acceptable to Lender and shall include a standard mortgage clause in favor of and in form acceptable to Lender. Lender shall have the right to hold the policies and renewals thereof, and Borrower shall promptly furnish to Lender all renewal notices and all receipts of paid premiums. In the event of loss, Borrower shall give prompt notice to the insurance carrier and Lender. Lender may make proof of loss if not made promptly by Borrower.

Unless Lender and Borrower otherwise agree in writing, insurance proceeds shall be applied to restoration or repair of the Property damaged, provided such restoration or repair is economically feasible and the security of this Mortgage is not thereby impaired. If such restoration or repair is not economically feasible or if the security of this Mortgage would be impaired, the insurance proceeds shall be applied to the sums secured by this Mortgage, with the excess, if any, paid to Borrower. If the Property is abandoned by Borrower, or if Borrower fails to respond to Lender within 30 days from the date notice is mailed by Lender to Borrower that the insurance carrier offers to settle a claim for insurance benefits, Lender is authorized to collect and apply the insurance proceeds at Lender's option either to restoration or repair of the Property or to the sums secured by this Mortgage.

Unless Lender and Borrower otherwise agree in writing, any such application of proceeds to principal shall not extend or postpone the due date of the monthly installments referred to in paragraphs 1 and 2 hereof or change the amount of such installments. If under paragraph 18 hereof the Property is acquired by Lender, all right, title and interest of Borrower in and to any insurance policies and in and to the proceeds thereof resulting from damage to the Property prior to the sale or acquisition shall pass to Lender to the extent of the sums secured by this Mortgage immediately prior to such sale or acquisition.

6. Preservation and Maintenance of Property; Leaseholds; Condominiums; Planned Unit Developments. Borrower shall keep the Property in good repair and shall not commit waste or permit impairment or deterioration of the Property and shall comply with the provisions of any lease if this Mortgage is on a leasehold. If this Mortgage is on a unit in a condominium or a planned unit development, Borrower shall perform all of Borrower's obligations under the declaration or covenants creating or governing the condominium or planned unit development, the by-laws and regulations of the condominium or planned unit development, and constituent documents. If a condominium or planned unit development rider is executed by Borrower and recorded together with this Mortgage, the covenants and agreements of such rider

Standard Residential Mortgage (continued)

shall be incorporated into and shall amend and supplement the covenants and agreements of this Mortgage as if the rider were a part hereof.

7. Protection of Lender's Security. If Borrower fails to perform the covenants and agreements contained in this Mortgage, or if any action or proceeding is commenced which materially affects Lender's interest in the Property, including, but not limited to, eminent domain, insolvency, code enforcement, or arrangements or proceedings involving a bankrupt or decedent, then Lender at Lender's option, upon notice to Borrower, may make such appearances, disburse such sums and take such action as is necessary to protect Lender's interest, including, but not limited to, disbursement of reasonable attorney's fees and entry upon the Property to make repairs. If Lender required mortgage insurance as a condition of making the loan secured by this Mortgage, Borrower shall pay the premiums required to maintain such insurance in effect until such time as the requirement for such insurance terminates in accordance with Borrower's and Lender's written agreement or applicable law. Borrower shall pay the amount of all mortgage insurance premiums in the manner provided under paragraph 2 hereof.

Any amounts disbursed by Lender pursuant to this paragraph 7, with interest thereon, shall become additional indebtedness of Borrower secured by this Mortgage. Unless Borrower and Lender agree to other terms of payment, such amounts shall be payable upon notice from Lender to Borrower requesting payment thereof, and shall bear interest from the date of disbursement at the rate payable from time to time on outstanding principal under the Note unless payment of interest at such rate would be contrary to applicable law, in which event such amounts shall bear interest at the highest rate permissible under applicable law. Nothing contained in this paragraph 7 shall require Lender to incur any expense or take any action hereunder.

8. Inspection. Lender may make or cause to be made reasonable entries upon and inspections of the Property, provided that Lender shall give Borrower notice prior to any such inspection specifying reasonable cause therefor related to Lender's interest in the Property.

9. Condemnation. The proceeds of any award or claim for damages, direct or consequential, in connection with any condemnation or other taking of the Property, or part thereof, or for conveyance in lieu of condemnation, are hereby assigned and shall be paid to Lender.

In the event of a total taking of the Property, the proceeds shall be applied to the sums secured by this Mortgage, with the excess, if any, paid to Borrower. In the event of a partial taking of the Property, unless Borrower and Lender otherwise agree in writing, there shall be applied to the sums secured by this Mortgage such proportion of the proceeds as is equal to that proportion which the amount of the sums secured by this Mortgage immediately prior to the date of taking bears to the fair market value of the Property immediately prior to the date of taking, with the balance of the proceeds paid to Borrower.

If the Property is abandoned by Borrower, or if, after notice by Lender to Borrower that the condemnor offers to make an award or settle a claim for damages, Borrower fails to respond to Lender within 30 days after the date such notice is mailed, Lender is authorized to collect and apply the proceeds, at Lender's option, either to restoration or repair of the Property or to the sums secured by this Mortgage.

Unless Lender and Borrower otherwise agree in writing, any such application of proceeds to principal shall not extend or postpone the due date of the monthly installments referred to in paragraphs 1 and 2 hereof or change the amount of such installments.

10. Borrower Not Released. Extension of the time for payment or modification of amortization of the sums secured by this Mortgage granted by Lender to any successor in interest of Borrower shall not operate to release, in any manner, the liability of the original Borrower and Borrower's successors in interest. Lender shall not be required to commence proceedings against such successor or refuse to extend time for payment or otherwise modify amortization of the sums secured by this Mortgage by reason of any demand made by the original Borrower and Borrower's successors in interest.

11. Forbearance by Lender Not a Waiver. Any forbearance by Lender in exercising any right or remedy hereunder, or otherwise afforded by applicable law, shall not be a waiver of or preclude the exercise of any such right or remedy. The procurement of insurance or the payment of taxes or other liens or charges by Lender shall not be a waiver of Lender's right to accelerate the maturity of the indebtedness secured by this Mortgage.

12. Remedies Cumulative. All remedies provided in this Mortgage are distinct and cumulative to any other right or remedy under this Mortgage or afforded by law or equity, and may be exercised concurrently, independently or successively.

13. Successors and Assigns Bound; Joint and Several Liability; Captions. The covenants and agreements herein contained shall bind, and the rights hereunder shall inure to, the respective successors and assigns of Lender and Borrower, subject to the provisions of paragraph 17 hereof. All covenants and agreements of Borrower shall be joint and several. The captions and headings of the paragraphs of this Mortgage are for convenience only and are not to be used to interpret or define the provisions hereof.

14. Notice. Except for any notice required under applicable law to be given in another manner, (a) any notice to Borrower provided for in this Mortgage shall be given by mailing such notice by certified mail addressed to Borrower at the Property Address or at such other address as Borrower may designate by notice to Lender as provided herein, and (b) any notice to Lender shall be given by certified mail, return receipt requested, to Lender's address stated herein or to such other address as Lender may designate by notice to Borrower as provided herein. Any notice provided for in this Mortgage shall be deemed to have been given to Borrower or Lender when given in the manner designated herein.

15. Uniform Mortgage; Governing Law; Severability. This form of mortgage combines uniform covenants for national use and non-uniform covenants with limited variations by jurisdiction to constitute a uniform security instrument covering real property. This Mortgage shall be governed by the law of the jurisdiction in which the Property is located. In the event that any provision or clause of this Mortgage or the Note conflicts with applicable law, such conflict shall not affect other provisions of this Mortgage or the Note which can be given effect without the conflicting provision, and to this end the provisions of the Mortgage and the Note are declared to be severable.

16. Borrower's Copy. Borrower shall be furnished a conformed copy of the Note and of this Mortgage at the time of execution or after recordation hereof.

17. Transfer of the Property; Assumption. If all or any part of the Property or an interest therein is sold or transferred by Borrower without Lender's prior written consent, excluding (a) the creation of a lien or encumbrance subordinate to this Mortgage, (b) the creation of a purchase money security interest for household appliances, (c) a transfer by devise, descent or by operation of law upon the death of a joint tenant or (d) the grant of any leasehold interest of three years or less not containing an option to purchase, Lender may, at Lender's option, declare all the sums secured by this Mortgage to be immediately due and payable. Lender shall have waived such option to accelerate if, prior to the sale or transfer, Lender and the person to whom the Property is to be sold or transferred reach agreement in writing that the credit of such person is satisfactory to Lender and that the interest payable on the sums secured by this Mortgage shall be at such rate as Lender shall request. If Lender has waived the option to accelerate provided in this paragraph 17, and if Borrower's successor in interest has executed a written assumption agreement accepted in writing by Lender, Lender shall release Borrower from all obligations under this Mortgage and the Note.

Standard Residential Mortgage (continued)

If Lender exercises such option to accelerate, Lender shall mail Borrower notice of acceleration in accordance with paragraph 14 hereof. Such notice shall provide a period of not less than 30 days from the date the notice is mailed within which Borrower may pay the sums declared due. If Borrower fails to pay such sums prior to the expiration of such period, Lender may, without further notice or demand on Borrower, invoke any remedies permitted by paragraph 18 hereof.

NON-UNIFORM COVENANTS. Borrower and Lender further covenant and agree as follows:

18. Acceleration; Remedies. Except as provided in paragraph 17 hereof, upon Borrower's breach of any covenant or agreement of Borrower in this Mortgage, including the covenants to pay when due any sums secured by this Mortgage, Lender prior to acceleration shall mail notice to Borrower as provided in paragraph 14 hereof specifying: (1) the breach; (2) the action required to cure such breach; (3) a date, not less than 30 days from the date the notice is mailed to Borrower, by which such breach must be cured; and (4) that failure to cure such breach on or before the date specified in the notice may result in acceleration of the sums secured by this Mortgage, foreclosure by judicial proceeding and sale of the Property. The notice shall further inform Borrower of the right to reinstate after acceleration and the right to assert in the foreclosure proceeding the non-existence of a default or any other defense of Borrower to acceleration and foreclosure. If the breach is not cured on or before the date specified in the notice, Lender at Lender's option may declare all of the sums secured by this Mortgage to be immediately due and payable without further demand and may foreclose this Mortgage by judicial proceeding. Lender shall be entitled to collect in such proceeding all expenses of foreclosure, including, but not limited to, costs of documentary evidence, abstracts and title reports.

19. Borrower's Right to Reinstate. Notwithstanding Lender's acceleration of the sums secured by this Mortgage, Borrower shall have the right to have any proceedings begun by Lender to enforce this Mortgage discontinued at any time prior to entry of a judgment enforcing this Mortgage if: (a) Borrower pays Lender all sums which would be then due under this Mortgage, the Note and notes securing Future Advances, if any, had no acceleration occurred; (b) Borrower cures all breaches of any other covenants or agreements of Borrower contained in this Mortgage; (c) Borrower pays all reasonable expenses incurred by Lender in enforcing the covenants and agreements of Borrower contained in this Mortgage and in enforcing Lender's remedies as provided in paragraph 18 hereof, including, but not limited to, reasonable attorney's fees; and (d) Borrower takes such action as Lender may reasonably require to assure that the lien of this Mortgage, Lender's interest in the Property and Borrower's obligation to pay the sums secured by this Mortgage shall continue unimpaired. Upon such payment and cure by Borrower, this Mortgage and the obligations secured hereby shall remain in full force and effect as if no acceleration had occurred.

20. Assignment of Rents; Appointment of Receiver. As additional security hereunder, Borrower hereby assigns to Lender the rents of the Property, provided that Borrower shall, prior to acceleration under paragraph 18 hereof or abandonment of the Property, have the right to collect and retain such rents as they become due and payable.

Upon acceleration under paragraph 18 hereof or abandonment of the Property, Lender shall be entitled to have a receiver appointed by a court to enter upon, take possession of and manage the Property and to collect the rents of the Property, including those past due. All rents collected by the receiver shall be applied first to payment of the costs of management of the Property and collection of rents, including, but not limited to, receiver's fees, premiums on receiver's bonds and reasonable attorney's fees, and then to the sums secured by this Mortgage. The receiver shall be liable to account only for those rents actually received.

21. Future Advances. Upon request of Borrower, Lender, at Lender's option prior to release of this Mortgage, may make Future Advances to Borrower. Such Future Advances, with interest thereon, shall be secured by this Mortgage when evidenced by promissory notes stating that said notes are secured hereby. At no time shall the principal amount of the indebtedness secured by this Mortgage, not including sums advanced in accordance herewith to protect the security of this Mortgage, exceed the original amount of the Note plus US $. . . . .

22. Release. Upon payment of all sums secured by this Mortgage, Lender shall discharge this Mortgage, without charge to Borrower. Borrower shall pay all costs of recordation, if any.

IN WITNESS WHEREOF, Borrower has executed this Mortgage.

Witnesses:

/s/Bonita C. Greene	/s/John M. Wilks
	—Borrower
	/s/Elizabeth S. Wilks
	—Borrower

STATE OF OHIO, ... Franklin . . . . County ss:

On this . . . . . 16th . . . . day of . . . . . June . . . . 19 - - , before me, a Notary Public in and for said County and State, personally appeared John M. Wilks and Elizabeth S. Wilks . . . ., the individual(s) who executed the foregoing instrument and acknowledged that .they. did examine and read the same and did sign the foregoing instrument, and that the same is . . their . . . . . free act and deed.

IN WITNESS WHEREOF, I have hereunto set my hand and official seal.

[Seal]

My Commission expires:

/s/Leroy P. Starkey
. . . .
Notary Public

———————————— (Space Below This Line Reserved For Lender and Recorder) ————————————

Standard Residential Mortgage (concluded)

DEED OF TRUST

THIS DEED OF TRUST is made this. . . . . 18th . . . . .day of . . June . . . .,
19.. . ., among the Grantor, . Marvin. J.. Miller. and. Cynthia. Miller. . . . .
. . . . (herein ''Borrower''), the Public Trustee of
. . . . Denver. . . . . .County (herein ''Trustee''), and the Beneficiary, MIDLAND
FEDERAL SAVINGS AND LOAN ASSOCIATION, whose address is 444 17th Street, Denver, Colorado 80202 (herein
''Lender'').

BORROWER, in consideration of the indebtedness herein recited and the trust herein created, irrevocably grants
and conveys to Trustee, in trust, with power of sale, the following described property located in the County of
. . . . Denver. . . . ., State of Colorado:

Lot 6, Block 8, of the Map of Security Acres Subdivision recorded in
the office of the Recorder of the County of Denver, May 1, 1953.

which has the address of . 318 Stout Street . . . ., ... Denver . . . .,
                                            [Street]   [City]
Colorado   80208 . . . . (herein ''Property Address'');
   [State and Zip Code]

TOGETHER with all the improvements now or hereafter erected on the property, and all easements, rights,
appurtenances, rents (subject however to the rights and authorities given herein to Lender to collect and apply such
rents), royalties, mineral, oil and gas rights and profits, water, water rights, and water stock, and all fixtures now or
hereafter attached to the property, all of which, including replacements and additions thereto, shall be deemed to be
and remain a part of the property covered by this Deed of Trust; and all of the foregoing, together with said property
(or the leasehold estate if this Deed of Trust is on a leasehold) are herein referred to as the ''Property'';

To SECURE to Lender (a) the repayment of the indebtedness evidenced by Borrower's note dated . June 18,,
. 19--. . . . .(herein ''Note''), in the principal sum of . Forty-Two Thousand Five . . . . . .
Hundred and 00/100 ($42,500.00)------------.Dollars, with interest thereon, providing for monthly
installments of principal and interest, with the balance of the indebtedness, if not sooner paid, due and payable on
. . . . . . July 5, 20--. . . . .; the payment of all other sums, with interest thereon, advanced
in accordance herewith to protect the security of this Deed of Trust; and the performance of the covenants and
agreements of Borrower herein contained; and (b) the repayment of any future advances, with interest thereon, made
to Borrower by Lender pursuant to paragraph 21 hereof (herein ''Future Advances'').

Borrower covenants that Borrower is lawfully seised of the estate hereby conveyed and has the right to grant and
convey the Property, that the Property is unencumbered, and that Borrower will warrant and defend generally the title
to the Property against all claims and demands, subject to any declarations, easements or restrictions listed in a
schedule of exceptions to coverage in any title insurance policy insuring Lender's interest in the Property.

COLORADO—1 to 4 Family—6/75—**FNMA/FHLMC UNIFORM INSTRUMENT**

M-504 L

Deed of Trust

UNIFORM COVENANTS. Borrower and Lender covenant and agree as follows:

1. Payment of Principal and Interest. Borrower shall promptly pay when due the principal of and interest on the indebtedness evidenced by the Note, prepayment and late charges as provided in the Note, and the principal of and interest on any Future Advances secured by this Deed of Trust.

2. Funds for Taxes and Insurance. Subject to applicable law or to a written waiver by Lender, Borrower shall pay to Lender on the day monthly installments of principal and interest are payable under the Note, until the Note is paid in full, a sum (herein "Funds") equal to one-twelfth of the yearly taxes and assessments which may attain priority over this Deed of Trust, and ground rents on the Property, if any, plus one-twelfth of yearly premium installments for hazard insurance, plus one-twelfth of yearly premium installments for mortgage insurance, if any, all as reasonably estimated initially and from time to time by Lender on the basis of assessments and bills and reasonable estimates thereof.

The Funds shall be held in an institution the deposits or accounts of which are insured or guaranteed by a Federal or state agency (including Lender if Lender is such an institution). Lender shall apply the Funds to pay said taxes, assessments, insurance premiums and ground rents. Lender may not charge for so holding and applying the Funds, analyzing said account or verifying and compiling said assessments and bills, unless Lender pays Borrower interest on the Funds and applicable law permits Lender to make such a charge. Borrower and Lender may agree in writing at the time of execution of this Deed of Trust that interest on the Funds shall be paid to Borrower, and unless such agreement is made or applicable law requires such interest to be paid, Lender shall not be required to pay Borrower any interest or earnings on the Funds. Lender shall give to Borrower, without charge, an annual accounting of the Funds showing credits and debits to the Funds and the purpose for which each debit to the Funds was made. The Funds are pledged as additional security for the sums secured by this Deed of Trust.

If the amount of the Funds held by Lender, together with the future monthly installments of Funds payable prior to the due dates of taxes, assessments, insurance premiums and ground rents, shall exceed the amount required to pay said taxes, assessments, insurance premiums and ground rents as they fall due, such excess shall be, at Borrower's option, either promptly repaid to Borrower or credited to Borrower on monthly installments of Funds. If the amount of the Funds held by Lender shall not be sufficient to pay taxes, assessments, insurance premiums and ground rents as they fall due, Borrower shall pay to Lender any amount necessary to make up the deficiency within 30 days from the date notice is mailed by Lender to Borrower requesting payment thereof.

Upon payment in full of all sums secured by this Deed of Trust, Lender shall promptly refund to Borrower any Funds held by Lender. If under paragraph 18 hereof the Property is sold or the Property is otherwise acquired by Lender, Lender shall apply, no later than immediately prior to the sale of the Property or its acquisition by Lender, any Funds held by Lender at the time of application as a credit against the sums secured by this Deed of Trust.

3. Application of Payments. Unless applicable law provides otherwise, all payments received by Lender under the Note and paragraphs 1 and 2 hereof shall be applied by Lender first in payment of amounts payable to Lender by Borrower under paragraph 2 hereof, then to interest payable on the Note, then to the principal of the Note, and then to interest and principal on any Future Advances.

4. Charges; Liens. Borrower shall pay all taxes, assessments and other charges, fines and impositions attributable to the Property which may attain a priority over this Deed of Trust, and leasehold payments or ground rents, if any, in the manner provided under paragraph 2 hereof or, if not paid in such manner, by Borrower making payment, when due, directly to the payee thereof. Borrower shall promptly furnish to Lender all notices of amounts due under this paragraph, and in the event Borrower shall make payment directly, Borrower shall promptly furnish to Lender receipts evidencing such payments. Borrower shall promptly discharge any lien which has priority over this Deed of Trust; provided, that Borrower shall not be required to discharge any such lien so long as Borrower shall agree in writing to the payment of the obligation secured by such lien in a manner acceptable to Lender, or shall in good faith contest such lien by, or defend enforcement of such lien in, legal proceedings which operate to prevent the enforcement of the lien or forfeiture of the Property or any part thereof.

5. Hazard Insurance. Borrower shall keep the improvements now existing or hereafter erected on the Property insured against loss by fire, hazards included within the term "extended coverage", and such other hazards as Lender may require and in such amounts and for such periods as Lender may require; provided, that Lender shall not require that the amount of such coverage exceed that amount of coverage required to pay the sums secured by this Deed of Trust.

The insurance carrier providing the insurance shall be chosen by Borrower subject to approval by Lender; provided, that such approval shall not be unreasonably withheld. All premiums on insurance policies shall be paid in the manner provided under paragraph 2 hereof or, if not paid in such manner, by Borrower making payment, when due, directly to the insurance carrier.

All insurance policies and renewals thereof shall be in form acceptable to Lender and shall include a standard mortgage clause in favor of and in form acceptable to Lender. Lender shall have the right to hold the policies and renewals thereof, and Borrower shall promptly furnish to Lender all renewal notices and all receipts of paid premiums. In the event of loss, Borrower shall give prompt notice to the insurance carrier and Lender. Lender may make proof of loss if not made promptly by Borrower.

Unless Lender and Borrower otherwise agree in writing, insurance proceeds shall be applied to restoration or repair of the Property damaged, provided such restoration or repair is economically feasible and the security of this Deed of Trust is not thereby impaired. If such restoration or repair is not economically feasible or if the security of this Deed of Trust would be impaired, the insurance proceeds shall be applied to the sums secured by this Deed of Trust, with the excess, if any, paid to Borrower. If the Property is abandoned by Borrower, or if Borrower fails to respond to Lender within 30 days from the date notice is mailed by Lender to Borrower that the insurance carrier offers to settle a claim for insurance benefits, Lender is authorized to collect and apply the insurance proceeds at Lender's option either to restoration or repair of the Property or to the sums secured by this Deed of Trust.

Unless Lender and Borrower otherwise agree in writing, any such application of proceeds to principal shall not extend or postpone the due date of the monthly installments referred to in paragraphs 1 and 2 hereof or change the amount of such installments. If under paragraph 18 hereof the Property is acquired by Lender, all right, title and interest of Borrower in and to any insurance policies and in and to the proceeds thereof resulting from damage to the Property prior to the sale or acquisition shall pass to Lender to the extent of the sums secured by this Deed of Trust immediately prior to such sale or acquisition.

6. Preservation and Maintenance of Property; Leaseholds; Condominiums; Planned Unit Developments. Borrower shall keep the Property in good repair and shall not commit waste or permit impairment or deterioration of the Property and shall comply with the provisions of any lease if this Deed of Trust is on a leasehold. If this Deed of Trust is on a unit in a condominium or a planned unit development, Borrower shall perform all of Borrower's obligations under the declaration or covenants creating or governing the condominium or planned unit development, the by-laws and regulations of the condominium or planned unit development, and constituent documents. If a condominium or planned unit development rider is executed by Borrower and recorded together with this Deed of Trust, the covenants and agreements of such rider shall be incorporated into and shall amend and supplement the covenants and agreements of this Deed of Trust as if the rider were a part hereof.

7. Protection of Lender's Security. If Borrower fails to perform the covenants and agreements contained in this Deed of Trust, or if any action or proceeding is commenced which materially affects Lender's interest in the Property, including, but not limited to, eminent domain, insolvency, code enforcement, or arrangements or proceedings involving a bankrupt or decedent, then Lender at Lender's option, upon notice to Borrower, may make such appearances, disburse such sums and take such action as is necessary to protect Lender's interest, including, but not limited to, disbursement of reasonable attorney's fees and entry upon the Property to make repairs. If Lender required mortgage insurance as a condition of making the loan secured by this Deed of Trust, Borrower shall pay the premiums required to maintain such insurance in effect until such time as the requirement for such insurance terminates in accordance with Borrower's and

Deed of Trust (continued)

Lender's written agreement or applicable law. Borrower shall pay the amount of all mortgage insurance premiums in the manner provided under paragraph 2 hereof.

Any amounts disbursed by Lender pursuant to this paragraph 7, with interest thereon, shall become additional indebtedness of Borrower secured by this Deed of Trust. Unless Borrower and Lender agree to other terms of payment, such amounts shall be payable upon notice from Lender to Borrower requesting payment thereof, and shall bear interest from the date of disbursement at the rate payable from time to time on outstanding principal under the Note unless payment of interest at such rate would be contrary to applicable law, in which event such amounts shall bear interest at the highest rate permissible under applicable law. Nothing contained in this paragraph 7 shall require Lender to incur any expense or take any action hereunder.

8. Inspection. Lender may make or cause to be made reasonable entries upon and inspections of the Property, provided that Lender shall give Borrower notice prior to any such inspection specifying reasonable cause therefor related to Lender's interest in the Property.

9. Condemnation. The proceeds of any award or claim for damages, direct or consequential, in connection with any condemnation or other taking of the Property, or part thereof, or for conveyance in lieu of condemnation, are hereby assigned and shall be paid to Lender.

In the event of a total taking of the Property, the proceeds shall be applied to the sums secured by this Deed of Trust, with the excess, if any, paid to Borrower. In the event of a partial taking of the Property, unless Borrower and Lender otherwise agree in writing, there shall be applied to the sums secured by this Deed of Trust such proportion of the proceeds as is equal to that proportion which the amount of the sums secured by this Deed of Trust immediately prior to the date of taking bears to the fair market value of the Property immediately prior to the date of taking, with the balance of the proceeds paid to Borrower.

If the Property is abandoned by Borrower, or if, after notice by Lender to Borrower that the condemnor offers to make an award or settle a claim for damages, Borrower fails to respond to Lender within 30 days after the date such notice is mailed, Lender is authorized to collect and apply the proceeds, at Lender's option, either to restoration or repair of the Property or to the sums secured by this Deed of Trust.

Unless Lender and Borrower otherwise agree in writing, any such application of proceeds to principal shall not extend or postpone the due date of the monthly installments referred to in paragraphs 1 and 2 hereof or change the amount of such installments.

10. Borrower Not Released. Extension of the time for payment or modification of amortization of the sums secured by this Deed of Trust granted by Lender to any successor in interest of Borrower shall not operate to release, in any manner, the liability of the original Borrower and Borrower's successors in interest. Lender shall not be required to commence proceedings against such successor or refuse to extend time for payment or otherwise modify amortization of the sums secured by this Deed of Trust by reason of any demand made by the original Borrower and Borrower's successors in interest.

11. Forbearance by Lender Not a Waiver. Any forbearance by Lender in exercising any right or remedy hereunder, or otherwise afforded by applicable law, shall not be a waiver of or preclude the exercise of any such right or remedy. The procurement of insurance or the payment of taxes or other liens or charges by Lender shall not be a waiver of Lender's right to accelerate the maturity of the indebtedness secured by this Deed of Trust.

12. Remedies Cumulative. All remedies provided in this Deed of Trust are distinct and cumulative to any other right or remedy under this Deed of Trust or afforded by law or equity, and may be exercised concurrently, independently or successively.

13. Successors and Assigns Bound; Joint and Several Liability; Captions. The covenants and agreements herein contained shall bind, and the rights hereunder shall inure to, the respective successors and assigns of Lender and Borrower, subject to the provisions of paragraph 17 hereof. All covenants and agreements of Borrower shall be joint and several. The captions and headings of the paragraphs of this Deed of Trust are for convenience only and are not to be used to interpret or define the provisions hereof.

14. Notice. Except for any notice required under applicable law to be given in another manner, (a) any notice to Borrower provided for in this Deed of Trust shall be given by mailing such notice by certified mail addressed to Borrower at the Property Address or at such other address as Borrower may designate by notice to Lender as provided herein, and (b) any notice to Lender shall be given by certified mail, return receipt requested, to Lender's address stated herein or to such other address as Lender may designate by notice to Borrower as provided herein. Any notice provided for in this Deed of Trust shall be deemed to have been given to Borrower or Lender when given in the manner designated herein.

15. Uniform Deed of Trust; Governing Law; Severability. This form of deed of trust combines uniform covenants for national use and non-uniform covenants with limited variations by jurisdiction to constitute a uniform security instrument covering real property. This Deed of Trust shall be governed by the law of the jurisdiction in which the Property is located. In the event that any provision or clause of this Deed of Trust or the Note conflicts with applicable law, such conflict shall not affect other provisions of this Deed of Trust or the Note which can be given effect without the conflicting provision, and to this end the provisions of the Deed of Trust and the Note are declared to be severable.

16. Borrower's Copy. Borrower shall be furnished a conformed copy of the Note and of this Deed of Trust at the time of execution or after recordation hereof.

17. Transfer of the Property; Assumption. If all or any part of the Property or an interest therein is sold or transferred by Borrower without Lender's prior written consent, excluding (a) the creation of a lien or encumbrance subordinate to this Deed of Trust, (b) the creation of a purchase money security interest for household appliances, (c) a transfer by devise, descent or by operation of law upon the death of a joint tenant or (d) the grant of any leasehold interest of three years or less not containing an option to purchase, Lender may, at Lender's option, declare all the sums secured by this Deed of Trust to be immediately due and payable. Lender shall have waived such option to accelerate if, prior to the sale or transfer, Lender and the person to whom the Property is to be sold or transferred reach agreement in writing that the credit of such person is satisfactory to Lender and that the interest payable on the sums secured by this Deed of Trust shall be at such rate as Lender shall request. If Lender has waived the option to accelerate provided in this paragraph 17, and if Borrower's successor in interest has executed a written assumption agreement accepted in writing by Lender, Lender shall release Borrower from all obligations under this Deed of Trust and the Note.

If Lender exercises such option to accelerate, Lender shall mail Borrower notice of acceleration in accordance with paragraph 14 hereof. Such notice shall provide a period of not less than 30 days from the date the notice is mailed within which Borrower may pay the sums declared due. If Borrower fails to pay such sums prior to the expiration of such period, Lender may, without further notice or demand on Borrower, invoke any remedies permitted by paragraph 18 hereof.

NON-UNIFORM COVENANTS. Borrower and Lender further covenant and agree as follows:

18. Acceleration; Remedies. Except as provided in paragraph 17 hereof, upon Borrower's breach of any covenant or agreement of Borrower in this Deed of Trust, including the covenants to pay when due any sums secured by this Deed of Trust, Lender prior to acceleration shall mail notice to Borrower as provided in paragraph 14 hereof specifying: (1) the breach; (2) the action required to cure such breach; (3) a date, not less than 30 days from the date the notice is mailed to Borrower, by which such breach must be cured; and (4) that failure to cure such breach on or before the date specified in the notice may result in acceleration of the sums secured by this Deed of Trust and sale of the Property. The notice shall further inform Borrower of the right to reinstate after acceleration and the right to assert in the foreclosure proceeding the non-existence of a default or any other defense of Borrower to acceleration and sale. If the breach is not cured on or before the date specified in the notice, Lender at Lender's option may declare all of the sums secured by this Deed of Trust to be immediately due and payable without further demand and may invoke the power of sale and any other remedies permitted by applicable law. Lender shall be entitled to collect all reasonable costs and expenses incurred in pursuing the remedies provided in this paragraph 18, including, but not limited to, reasonable attorney's fees.

Deed of Trust (continued)

If Lender invokes the power of sale, Lender shall give written notice to Trustee of the occurrence of an event of default and of Lender's election to cause the Property to be sold. Lender shall mail a copy of such notice to Borrower as provided in paragraph 14 hereof. Trustee shall record a copy of such notice in the county in which the Property is located. Trustee shall publish a notice of sale for the time and in the manner provided by applicable law and shall mail copies of such notice of sale in the manner prescribed by applicable law to Borrower and to the other persons prescribed by applicable law. After the lapse of such time as may be required by applicable law, Trustee, without demand on Borrower, shall sell the Property at public auction to the highest bidder for cash at the time and place and under the terms designated in the notice of sale in one or more parcels and in such order as Trustee may determine. Trustee may postpone sale of all or any parcel of the Property by public announcement at the time and place of any previously scheduled sale. Lender or Lender's designee may purchase the Property at any sale.

Trustee shall deliver to the purchaser Trustee's certificate describing the Property and the time when the purchaser will be entitled to Trustee's deed thereto. The recitals in Trustee's deed shall be prima facie evidence of the truth of the statements made therein. Trustee shall apply the proceeds of the sale in the following order: (a) to all reasonable costs and expenses of the sale, including, but not limited to, reasonable Trustee's and attorney's fees and costs of title evidence; (b) to all sums secured by this Deed of Trust; and (c) the excess, if any, to the person or persons legally entitled thereto.

19. Borrower's Right to Reinstate. Notwithstanding Lender's acceleration of the sums secured by this Deed of Trust, Borrower shall have the right to have any proceedings begun by Lender to enforce this Deed of Trust discontinued at any time prior to the earlier to occur of (i) the fifth day before sale of the Property pursuant to the power of sale contained in this Deed of Trust or (ii) entry of a judgment enforcing this Deed of Trust if: (a) Borrower pays Lender all sums which would be then due under this Deed of Trust, the Note and notes securing Future Advances, if any, had no acceleration occurred; (b) Borrower cures all breaches of any other covenants or agreements of Borrower contained in this Deed of Trust; (c) Borrower pays all reasonable expenses incurred by Lender and Trustee in enforcing the covenants and agreements of Borrower contained in this Deed of Trust and in enforcing Lender's and Trustee's remedies as provided in paragraph 18 hereof, including, but not limited to, reasonable attorney's fees and Trustee's expenses and withdrawal fee; and (d) Borrower takes such action as Lender may reasonably require to assure that the lien of this Deed of Trust, Lender's interest in the Property and Borrower's obligation to pay the sums secured by this Deed of Trust shall continue unimpaired. Upon such payment and cure by Borrower, this Deed of Trust and the obligations secured hereby shall remain in full force and effect as if no acceleration had occurred.

20. Assignment of Rents; Appointment of Receiver; Lender in Possession. As additional security hereunder, Borrower hereby assigns to Lender the rents of the Property, provided that Borrower shall, prior to acceleration under paragraph 18 hereof or abandonment of the Property, have the right to collect and retain such rents as they become due and payable.

Upon acceleration under paragraph 18 hereof or abandonment of the Property, Lender, in person, by agent or by judicially appointed receiver, shall be entitled to enter upon, take possession of and manage the Property and to collect the rents of the Property including those past due. All rents collected by Lender or the receiver shall be applied first to payment of the costs of management of the Property and collection of rents, including, but not limited to, receiver's fees, premiums on receiver's bonds and reasonable attorney's fees, and then to the sums secured by this Deed of Trust. Lender and the receiver shall be liable to account only for those rents actually received.

21. Future Advances. Upon request of Borrower, Lender, at Lender's option prior to release of this Deed of Trust, may make Future Advances to Borrower. Such Future Advances, with interest thereon, shall be secured by this Deed of Trust when evidenced by promissory notes stating that said notes are secured hereby.

22. Release. Upon payment of all sums secured by this Deed of Trust, Lender shall request Trustee to release this Deed of Trust and shall produce for Trustee duly cancelled all notes evidencing indebtedness secured by this Deed of Trust. Trustee shall release this Deed of Trust without further inquiry or liability. Borrower shall pay all costs of recordation, if any, and shall pay the statutory Trustee's fees.

23. Waiver of Homestead. Borrower hereby waives all right of homestead exemption in the Property.

IN WITNESS WHEREOF, Borrower has executed this Deed of Trust.

.... /s/ Marvin J. Miller ....
—Borrower

.... /s/ Cynthia Miller ....
—Borrower

(Acknowledgment)

Deed of Trust (concluded)

APPENDIX B

Tables

The basic equations for Tables 1, 2, 3, and 4 are as follows:

Table 1: The basic equation for finding the future value interest factor (FVIF) of $1 is:

$$FVIF = (1 + i)^n$$

where i is the interest rate and n is the number of periods in years. More frequent than annual compounding would require adjustment of the FVIF equation for m, the number of times compounding will take place within one year, as follows:

$$= (1 + i/m)^{n \times m}$$

Table 2: The basic equation for finding the present value interest factor (PVIF) of $1 is:

$$PVIF = \frac{1}{(1 + i)^n}$$

where i is the interest or discount rate and n is the number of periods in years. More frequent than annual discounting would require adjustment of the PVIF equation for m, the number of times discounting will take place within one year, as follows:

$$= \frac{1}{(1 + i/m)^{n \times m}}$$

Table 3: The basic equation for finding the future value interest factor of an ordinary annuity (FVIFA) is:

$$FVIFA = \sum_{t=1}^{n} (1 + i)^{t-1} = \frac{(1 + i)^n - 1}{i}$$

where i is the interest rate and n is the number of periods in years. More frequent than annual compounding would require adjustment of the FVIFA equation for m, the number of times compounding will take place within one year, as follows:

$$= \frac{(1 + i/m)^{n \times m} - 1}{i/m}$$

Table 4: The basic equation for finding the present value interest factor of an annuity (PVIFA) is:

$$\text{PVIFA} = \sum_{t=1}^{n} \frac{1}{(1 + i)^t} = \frac{1 - \dfrac{1}{(1 + i)^n}}{i}$$

where i is the interest or discount rate and n is the number of periods in years. More frequent than annual discounting would require adjustment of the PVIFA equation for m, the number of times discounting will take place within one year, as follows:

$$= \frac{1 - \dfrac{1}{(1 + i/m)^{n \times m}}}{i/m}$$

TABLE 1. Future Value of $1

Year	1%	2%	3%	4%	5%	6%	7%	8%	9%	10%	12%	14%	15%	16%	18%	20%	25%	30%
1	1.010	1.020	1.030	1.040	1.050	1.060	1.070	1.080	1.090	1.100	1.120	1.140	1.150	1.160	1.180	1.200	1.250	1.300
2	1.020	1.040	1.061	1.082	1.102	1.124	1.145	1.166	1.188	1.210	1.254	1.300	1.322	1.346	1.392	1.440	1.563	1.690
3	1.030	1.061	1.093	1.125	1.158	1.191	1.225	1.260	1.295	1.331	1.405	1.482	1.521	1.561	1.643	1.728	1.953	2.197
4	1.041	1.082	1.126	1.170	1.216	1.262	1.311	1.360	1.412	1.464	1.574	1.689	1.749	1.811	1.939	2.074	2.441	2.856
5	1.051	1.104	1.159	1.217	1.276	1.338	1.403	1.469	1.539	1.611	1.762	1.925	2.011	2.100	2.288	2.488	3.052	3.713
6	1.062	1.126	1.194	1.265	1.340	1.419	1.501	1.587	1.677	1.772	1.974	2.195	2.313	2.436	2.700	2.986	3.815	4.827
7	1.072	1.149	1.230	1.316	1.407	1.504	1.606	1.714	1.828	1.949	2.211	2.502	2.660	2.826	3.185	3.583	4.768	6.276
8	1.083	1.172	1.267	1.369	1.477	1.594	1.718	1.851	1.993	2.144	2.476	2.853	3.059	3.278	3.759	4.300	5.960	8.157
9	1.094	1.195	1.305	1.423	1.551	1.689	1.838	1.999	2.172	2.358	2.773	3.252	3.518	3.803	4.435	5.160	7.451	10.604
10	1.105	1.219	1.344	1.480	1.629	1.791	1.967	2.159	2.367	2.594	3.106	3.707	4.046	4.411	5.234	6.192	9.313	13.786
11	1.116	1.243	1.384	1.539	1.710	1.898	2.105	2.332	2.580	2.853	3.479	4.226	4.652	5.117	6.176	7.430	11.642	17.922
12	1.127	1.268	1.426	1.601	1.796	2.012	2.252	2.518	2.813	3.138	3.896	4.818	5.350	5.936	7.288	8.916	14.552	23.298
13	1.138	1.294	1.469	1.665	1.886	2.133	2.410	2.720	3.066	3.452	4.363	5.492	6.153	6.886	8.599	10.699	18.190	30.288
14	1.149	1.319	1.513	1.732	1.980	2.261	2.579	2.937	3.342	3.797	4.887	6.261	7.076	7.988	10.147	12.839	22.737	39.374
15	1.161	1.346	1.558	1.801	2.079	2.397	2.759	3.172	3.642	4.177	5.474	7.138	8.137	9.266	11.974	15.407	28.422	51.186
16	1.173	1.373	1.605	1.873	2.183	2.540	2.952	3.426	3.970	4.595	6.130	8.137	9.358	10.748	14.129	18.488	35.527	66.542
17	1.184	1.400	1.653	1.948	2.292	2.693	3.159	3.700	4.328	5.054	6.866	9.276	10.761	12.468	16.672	22.186	44.409	86.504
18	1.196	1.428	1.702	2.026	2.407	2.854	3.380	3.996	4.717	5.560	7.690	10.575	12.375	14.463	19.673	26.623	55.511	112.46
19	1.208	1.457	1.754	2.107	2.527	3.026	3.617	4.316	5.142	6.116	8.613	12.056	14.232	16.777	23.214	31.948	69.389	146.19
20	1.220	1.486	1.806	2.191	2.653	3.207	3.870	4.661	5.604	6.728	9.646	13.743	16.367	19.461	27.393	38.338	86.736	190.05
25	1.282	1.641	2.094	2.666	3.386	4.292	5.427	6.848	8.623	10.835	17.000	26.462	32.919	40.874	62.669	95.396	264.70	705.64
30	1.348	1.811	2.427	3.243	4.322	5.743	7.612	10.063	13.268	17.449	29.960	50.950	66.212	85.850	143.371	237.376	807.79	2620.00

TABLE 2. Present Value of $1

Year	1%	2%	3%	4%	5%	6%	7%	8%	9%	10%	12%	14%	15%	16%	18%	20%	25%	30%
1	.990	.980	.971	.962	.952	.943	.935	.926	.917	.909	.893	.877	.870	.862	.847	.833	.800	.769
2	.980	.961	.943	.925	.907	.890	.873	.857	.842	.826	.797	.769	.756	.743	.718	.694	.640	.592
3	.971	.942	.915	.889	.864	.840	.816	.794	.772	.751	.712	.675	.658	.641	.609	.579	.512	.455
4	.961	.924	.888	.855	.823	.792	.763	.735	.708	.683	.636	.592	.572	.552	.516	.482	.410	.350
5	.951	.906	.863	.822	.784	.747	.713	.681	.650	.621	.567	.519	.497	.476	.437	.402	.328	.269
6	.942	.888	.837	.790	.746	.705	.666	.630	.596	.564	.507	.456	.432	.410	.370	.335	.262	.207
7	.933	.871	.813	.760	.711	.665	.623	.583	.547	.513	.452	.400	.376	.354	.314	.279	.210	.159
8	.923	.853	.789	.731	.677	.627	.582	.540	.502	.467	.404	.351	.327	.305	.266	.233	.168	.123
9	.914	.837	.766	.703	.645	.592	.544	.500	.460	.424	.361	.308	.284	.263	.225	.194	.134	.094
10	.905	.820	.744	.676	.614	.558	.508	.463	.422	.386	.322	.270	.247	.227	.191	.162	.107	.073
11	.896	.804	.722	.650	.585	.527	.475	.429	.388	.350	.287	.237	.215	.195	.162	.135	.086	.056
12	.887	.788	.701	.625	.557	.497	.444	.397	.356	.319	.257	.208	.187	.168	.137	.112	.069	.043
13	.879	.773	.681	.601	.530	.469	.415	.368	.326	.290	.229	.182	.163	.145	.116	.093	.055	.033
14	.870	.758	.661	.577	.505	.442	.388	.340	.299	.263	.205	.160	.141	.125	.099	.078	.044	.025
15	.861	.743	.642	.555	.481	.417	.362	.315	.275	.239	.183	.140	.123	.108	.084	.065	.035	.020
16	.853	.728	.623	.534	.458	.394	.339	.292	.252	.218	.163	.123	.107	.093	.071	.054	.028	.015
17	.844	.714	.605	.513	.436	.371	.317	.270	.231	.198	.146	.108	.093	.080	.060	.045	.023	.012
18	.836	.700	.587	.494	.416	.350	.296	.250	.212	.180	.130	.095	.081	.069	.051	.038	.018	.009
19	.828	.686	.570	.475	.396	.331	.276	.232	.194	.164	.116	.083	.070	.060	.043	.031	.014	.007
20	.820	.673	.554	.456	.377	.312	.258	.215	.178	.149	.104	.073	.061	.051	.037	.026	.012	.005
25	.780	.610	.478	.375	.295	.233	.184	.146	.116	.092	.059	.038	.030	.024	.016	.010	.004	.001
30	.742	.552	.412	.308	.231	.174	.131	.099	.075	.057	.033	.020	.015	.012	.007	.004	.001	.000

TABLE 3. Future Value of a $1 Ordinary Annuity

Year	1%	2%	3%	4%	5%	6%	7%	8%	9%	10%	12%	14%
1	1.000	1.000	1.000	1.000	1.000	1.000	1.000	1.000	1.000	1.000	1.000	1.000
2	2.010	2.020	2.030	2.040	2.050	2.060	2.070	2.080	2.090	2.100	2.120	2.140
3	3.030	3.060	3.091	3.122	3.152	3.184	3.215	3.246	3.278	3.310	3.374	3.440
4	4.060	4.122	4.184	4.246	4.310	4.375	4.440	4.506	4.573	4.641	4.779	4.921
5	5.101	5.204	5.309	5.416	5.526	5.637	5.751	5.867	5.985	6.105	6.353	6.610
6	6.152	6.308	6.468	6.633	6.802	6.975	7.153	7.336	7.523	7.716	8.115	8.536
7	7.214	7.434	7.662	7.898	8.142	8.394	8.654	8.923	9.200	9.487	10.089	10.730
8	8.286	8.583	8.892	9.214	9.549	9.897	10.260	10.637	11.028	11.436	12.300	13.233
9	9.369	9.755	10.159	10.583	11.027	11.491	11.978	12.488	13.021	13.579	14.776	16.085
10	10.462	10.950	11.464	12.006	12.578	13.181	13.816	14.487	15.193	15.937	17.549	19.337
11	11.567	12.169	12.808	13.486	14.207	14.972	15.784	16.645	17.560	18.531	20.655	23.044
12	12.683	13.412	14.192	15.026	15.917	16.870	17.888	18.977	20.141	21.384	24.133	27.271
13	13.809	14.680	15.618	16.627	17.713	18.882	20.141	21.495	22.953	24.523	28.029	32.089
14	14.947	15.974	17.086	18.292	19.599	21.015	22.550	24.215	26.019	27.975	32.393	37.581
15	16.097	17.293	18.599	20.024	21.579	23.276	25.129	27.152	29.361	31.772	37.280	43.842
16	17.258	18.639	20.157	21.825	23.657	25.673	27.888	30.324	33.003	35.950	42.753	50.980
17	18.430	20.012	21.762	23.698	25.840	28.213	30.840	33.750	36.974	40.545	48.884	59.118
18	19.615	21.412	23.414	25.645	28.132	30.906	33.999	37.450	41.301	45.599	55.750	68.394
19	20.811	22.841	25.117	27.671	30.539	33.760	37.379	41.466	46.018	51.159	63.440	78.969
20	22.019	24.297	26.870	29.778	33.066	36.786	40.995	45.762	51.160	57.275	72.052	91.025
25	28.243	32.030	36.459	41.646	47.727	54.865	63.249	73.106	84.701	98.347	133.334	181.871
30	34.785	40.568	47.575	56.805	66.439	79.058	94.461	113.283	136.308	164.494	241.333	356.787

TABLE 3. Future Value of a $1 Ordinary Annuity (concluded)

Year	16%	18%	20%	25%	30%
1	1.000	1.000	1.000	1.000	1.000
2	2.160	2.180	2.200	2.250	2.300
3	3.506	3.572	3.640	3.813	3.990
4	5.066	5.215	5.368	5.766	6.187
5	6.877	7.154	7.442	8.207	9.043
6	8.977	9.442	9.930	11.259	12.756
7	11.414	12.142	12.916	15.073	17.583
8	14.240	15.327	16.499	19.842	23.858
9	17.518	19.086	20.799	25.802	32.015
10	21.321	23.521	25.959	33.253	42.619
11	25.733	28.755	32.150	42.566	56.405
12	30.850	34.931	39.580	54.208	74.327
13	36.786	42.219	48.497	68.760	97.625
14	43.672	50.818	59.196	86.949	127.91
15	51.660	60.965	72.035	109.69	167.29
16	60.925	72.939	87.442	138.11	218.47
17	71.673	87.068	105.931	173.64	285.01
18	84.141	103.740	128.117	218.05	371.52
19	98.603	123.414	154.740	273.56	483.97
20	115.380	146.628	186.688	342.95	630.17
25	249.214	342.603	471.981	1054.80	2348.80
30	530.312	790.948	1181.882	3227.20	8730.00

TABLE 4. Present Value of a $1 Annuity

Year	1%	2%	3%	4%	5%	6%	7%	8%	9%	10%	12%	14%
1	0.990	0.980	0.971	0.962	0.952	0.943	0.935	0.926	0.917	0.909	0.893	0.877
2	1.970	1.942	1.913	1.886	1.859	1.833	1.808	1.783	1.759	1.736	1.690	1.647
3	2.941	2.884	2.829	2.775	2.723	2.673	2.624	2.577	2.531	2.487	2.402	2.322
4	3.902	3.808	3.717	3.630	3.546	3.465	3.387	3.312	3.240	3.170	3.037	2.914
5	4.853	4.713	4.580	4.452	4.329	4.212	4.100	3.993	3.890	3.791	3.605	3.433
6	5.795	5.601	5.417	5.242	5.076	4.917	4.767	4.623	4.486	4.355	4.111	3.889
7	6.728	6.472	6.230	6.002	5.786	5.582	5.389	5.206	5.033	4.868	4.564	4.288
8	7.652	7.325	7.020	6.733	6.463	6.210	5.971	5.747	5.535	5.335	4.968	4.639
9	8.566	8.162	7.786	7.435	7.108	6.802	6.515	6.247	5.995	5.759	5.328	4.946
10	9.471	8.983	8.530	8.111	7.722	7.360	7.024	6.710	6.418	6.145	5.650	5.216
11	10.368	9.787	9.253	8.760	8.306	7.887	7.499	7.139	6.805	6.495	5.938	5.453
12	11.255	10.575	9.954	9.385	8.863	8.384	7.943	7.536	7.161	6.814	6.194	5.660
13	12.134	11.348	10.635	9.986	9.394	8.853	8.358	7.904	7.487	7.103	6.424	5.842
14	13.004	12.106	11.296	10.563	9.899	9.295	8.745	8.244	7.786	7.367	6.628	6.002
15	13.865	12.849	11.938	11.118	10.380	9.712	9.108	8.559	8.061	7.606	6.811	6.142
16	14.718	13.578	12.561	11.652	10.838	10.106	9.447	8.851	8.313	7.824	6.974	6.265
17	15.562	14.292	13.166	12.166	11.274	10.477	9.763	9.122	8.544	8.022	7.120	5.373
18	16.398	14.992	13.754	12.659	11.690	10.828	10.059	9.372	8.756	8.201	7.250	6.467
19	17.226	15.678	14.324	13.134	12.085	11.158	10.336	9.604	8.950	8.365	7.366	6.550
20	18.046	16.351	14.877	13.590	12.462	11.470	10.594	9.818	9.129	8.514	7.469	6.623
25	22.023	19.523	17.413	15.622	14.094	12.783	11.654	10.675	9.823	9.077	7.843	6.873
30	25.808	22.397	19.600	17.292	15.372	13.765	12.409	11.258	10.274	9.427	8.055	7.003

TABLE 4.   Present Value of a $1 Annuity (concluded)

Year	16%	18%	20%	25%	30%
1	0.862	0.847	0.833	.800	.769
2	1.605	1.566	1.528	1.440	1.361
3	2.246	2.174	2.106	1.952	1.816
4	2.798	2.690	2.589	2.362	2.166
5	3.274	3.127	2.991	2.689	2.436
6	3.685	3.498	3.326	2.951	2.643
7	4.039	3.812	3.605	3.161	2.802
8	4.344	4.078	3.837	3.329	2.925
9	4.607	4.303	4.031	3.463	3.019
10	4.833	4.494	4.193	3.571	3.092
11	5.029	4.656	4.327	3.656	3.147
12	5.197	4.793	4.439	3.725	3.190
13	5.342	4.910	4.533	3.780	3.223
14	5.468	5.008	4.611	3.824	3.249
15	5.575	5.092	4.675	3.859	3.268
16	5.668	5.162	4.730	3.887	3.283
17	5.749	4.222	4.775	3.910	3.295
18	5.818	5.273	4.812	3.928	3.304
19	5.877	5.316	4.843	3.942	3.311
20	5.929	5.353	4.870	3.954	3.316
25	6.097	5.467	4.948	3.985	3.329
30	6.177	5.517	4.979	3.995	3.332

TABLE 5. Monthly Present Values

		12% Annual Interest Rate					13% Annual Interest Rate		
Years	Months	Present Value of $1	Present Value Annuity of $1 Per Period	Loan Constant	Years	Months	Present Value of $1	Present Value Annuity of $1 Per Period	Loan Constant
1	12	.887449	11.255077	.088849	1	12	.878710	11.196042	.089317
2	24	.787566	21.243387	.047073	2	24	.772130	21.034112	.047542
3	36	.698925	30.107505	.033214	3	36	.678478	29.678917	.033694
4	48	.620260	37.973959	.026334	4	48	.596185	37.275190	.026827
5	60	.550450	44.955038	.022244	5	60	.523874	43.950107	.022753
6	72	.488496	51.150391	.019550	6	72	.460333	49.815421	.020074
7	84	.433515	56.648453	.017653	7	84	.404499	54.969328	.018192
8	96	.384723	61.527703	.016253	8	96	.355437	59.498115	.016807
9	108	.341422	65.857790	.015184	9	108	.312326	63.477604	.015754
10	120	.302995	69.700522	.014347	10	120	.274444	66.974419	.014931
11	132	.268892	73.110752	.013678	11	132	.241156	70.047103	.014276
12	144	.238628	76.137157	.013134	12	144	.211906	72.747100	.013746
13	156	.211771	78.822939	.012687	13	156	.186204	75.119613	.013312
14	168	.187936	81.206434	.012314	14	168	.163619	77.204363	.012953
15	180	.166783	83.321664	.012002	15	180	.143774	79.036253	.012652
16	192	.148012	85.198824	.011737	16	192	.126336	80.645952	.012400
17	204	.131353	86.864707	.011512	17	204	.111012	82.060410	.012186
18	216	.116569	88.343095	.011320	18	216	.097548	83.303307	.012004
19	228	.103449	89.655089	.011154	19	228	.085716	84.395453	.011849
20	240	.091806	90.819416	.011011	20	240	.075319	85.355132	.011716
25	300	.050534	94.946551	.010532	25	300	.039458	88.665428	.011278
30	360	.027817	97.218331	.010286	30	360	.020671	90.399605	.011062
35	420	.015312	98.468831	.010155	35	420	.010829	91.308095	.010952
40	480	.008428	99.157169	.010085	40	480	.005673	91.784030	.010895

TABLE 5. Monthly Present Values (concluded)

		14% Annual Interest Rate					15% Annual Interest Rate		
Years	Months	Present Value of $1	Present Value Annuity of $1 Per Period	Loan Constant	Years	Months	Present Value of $1	Present Value Annuity of $1 Per Period	Loan Constant
1	12	.870063	11.137455	.089787	1	12	.861509	11.079312	.090258
2	24	.757010	20.827743	.048013	2	24	.742197	20.624235	.048487
3	36	.658646	29.258904	.034178	3	36	.639409	28.847267	.034665
4	48	.573064	36.594546	.027326	4	48	.550856	35.931481	.027831
5	60	.498601	42.977016	.023268	5	60	.474568	42.034592	.023790
6	72	.433815	48.530168	.020606	6	72	.408844	47.292474	.021145
7	84	.377446	53.361760	.018740	7	84	.352223	51.822185	.019297
8	96	.328402	57.565549	.017372	8	96	.303443	55.724570	.017945
9	108	.285730	61.223111	.016334	9	108	.261419	59.086509	.016924
10	120	.248603	64.405420	.015527	10	120	.225214	61.982847	.016133
11	132	.216301	67.174230	.014887	11	132	.194024	64.478068	.015509
12	144	.188195	69.583269	.014371	12	144	.167153	66.627722	.015009
13	156	.163742	71.679284	.013951	13	156	.144004	68.479668	.014603
14	168	.142466	73.502950	.013605	14	168	.124061	70.075134	.014270
15	180	.123954	75.089654	.013317	15	180	.106879	71.449643	.013996
16	192	.107848	76.470187	.013077	16	192	.092078	72.633794	.013768
17	204	.093834	77.671337	.012875	17	204	.079326	73.653950	.013577
18	216	.081642	78.716413	.012704	18	216	.068340	74.532823	.013417
19	228	.071034	79.625696	.012559	19	228	.058875	75.289980	.013282
20	240	.061804	80.416829	.012435	20	240	.050722	75.942278	.013168
25	300	.030815	83.072966	.012038	25	300	.024071	78.074336	.012808
30	360	.015365	84.397320	.011849	30	360	.011423	79.086142	.012644
35	420	.007661	85.057645	.011757	35	420	.005421	79.566313	.012568
40	480	.003820	85.386883	.011711	40	480	.002573	79.794186	.012532

TABLE 6. Monthly Payments Needed to Amortize a $1,000 Loan

Year	6.0%	6.5%	7.0%	7.5%	8.0%	8.5%	9.0%	9.5%	10.0%	10.5%
1	86.08	86.31	86.54	86.77	86.99	87.22	87.45	87.69	87.92	88.15
2	44.33	44.55	44.78	45.00	45.23	45.46	45.69	45.92	46.15	46.38
3	30.43	30.65	30.88	31.11	31.34	31.57	31.80	32.03	32.27	32.50
4	23.49	23.72	23.95	24.18	24.41	24.65	24.89	25.12	25.36	25.60
5	19.34	19.57	19.80	20.04	20.28	20.52	20.76	21.00	21.25	21.49
6	16.58	16.81	17.05	17.29	17.53	17.78	18.03	18.28	18.53	18.78
7	14.61	14.85	15.09	15.34	15.59	15.84	16.09	16.34	16.60	16.86
8	13.14	13.39	13.63	13.88	14.14	14.39	14.65	14.91	15.17	15.44
9	12.01	12.26	12.51	12.76	13.02	13.28	13.54	13.81	14.08	14.35
10	11.10	11.36	11.61	11.87	12.13	12.40	12.67	12.94	13.22	13.49
11	10.37	10.62	10.88	11.15	11.42	11.69	11.96	12.24	12.52	12.80
12	9.76	10.02	10.28	10.55	10.82	11.10	11.38	11.66	11.95	12.24
13	9.25	9.51	9.78	10.05	10.33	10.61	10.90	11.19	11.48	11.78
14	8.81	9.08	9.35	9.63	9.91	10.20	10.49	10.78	11.08	11.38
15	8.44	8.71	8.99	9.27	9.56	9.85	10.14	10.44	10.75	11.05
16	8.12	8.39	8.67	8.96	9.25	9.55	9.85	10.15	10.46	10.77
17	7.83	8.11	8.40	8.69	8.98	9.28	9.59	9.90	10.21	10.53
18	7.58	7.87	8.16	8.45	8.75	9.05	9.36	9.68	10.00	10.32
19	7.36	7.65	7.94	8.24	8.55	8.85	9.17	9.49	9.81	10.14
20	7.16	7.46	7.75	8.06	8.36	8.68	9.00	9.32	9.65	9.98
25	6.44	6.75	7.07	7.39	7.72	8.05	8.39	8.74	9.09	9.44
30	6.00	6.32	6.65	6.99	7.34	7.69	8.05	8.41	8.78	9.15
35	5.70	6.04	6.39	6.74	7.10	7.47	7.84	8.22	8.60	8.98
40	5.50	5.85	6.21	6.58	6.95	7.33	7.71	8.10	8.49	8.89

TABLE 6. Monthly Payments Needed to Amortize a $1,000 Loan (concluded)

Year	11.0%	11.5%	12.0%	13%	14%	15%	16%	17%	18%
1	88.39	88.62	88.85	89.32	89.79	90.26	90.73	91.21	91.68
2	46.61	46.84	47.08	47.54	48.01	48.49	48.96	49.44	49.93
3	32.74	32.98	33.22	33.70	34.18	34.67	35.16	35.65	36.15
4	25.85	26.09	26.34	26.83	27.33	27.83	28.34	28.86	29.38
5	21.74	21.99	22.25	22.75	23.27	23.79	24.32	24.85	25.39
6	19.04	19.29	19.55	20.07	20.61	21.15	21.69	22.25	22.81
7	17.12	17.39	17.65	18.19	18.74	19.30	19.86	20.44	21.02
8	15.71	15.98	16.25	16.81	17.37	17.95	18.53	19.12	19.72
9	14.63	14.90	15.18	15.75	16.33	16.92	17.53	18.14	18.76
10	13.78	14.06	14.35	14.93	15.53	16.13	16.75	17.38	18.02
11	13.09	13.38	13.68	14.28	14.89	15.51	16.14	16.79	17.44
12	12.54	12.83	13.13	13.75	14.37	15.01	15.66	16.32	16.99
13	12.08	12.38	12.69	13.31	13.95	14.60	15.27	15.94	16.63
14	11.69	12.00	12.31	12.95	13.61	14.27	14.95	15.64	16.34
15	11.37	11.68	12.00	12.65	13.32	14.00	14.69	15.39	16.10
16	11.09	11.41	11.74	12.40	13.08	13.77	14.47	15.19	15.91
17	10.85	11.18	11.51	12.19	12.87	13.58	14.29	15.02	15.76
18	10.65	10.98	11.32	12.00	12.70	13.42	14.14	14.88	15.63
19	10.47	10.81	11.15	11.85	12.56	13.28	14.02	14.76	15.52
20	10.32	10.66	11.01	11.72	12.44	13.17	13.91	14.67	15.43
25	9.80	10.16	10.53	11.28	12.04	12.81	13.59	14.38	15.17
30	9.52	9.90	10.29	11.06	11.85	12.64	13.45	14.26	15.07
35	9.37	9.76	10.16	10.95	11.76	12.57	13.38	14.21	15.03
40	9.28	9.68	10.09	10.90	11.71	12.53	13.36	14.18	15.01

Note: This table indicates the required monthly payment necessary to amortize each $1,000 in loans. Thus, to find the monthly payment on, say, a $20,000, 25-year, 9 percent loan, we take the monthly payment on a $1,000, 25-year, 9 percent loan which is $8.39 and then multiply it by a factor of 20. This, in turn, results in a monthly payment of $167.80 for the $20,000 loan.

TABLE 7. Annual Constant Percentages

Year	6%	7%	8%	9%	10%	11%	12%	13%	14%	15%	16%	17%	18%
1	103.30	103.84	104.39	104.95	105.50	106.07	106.63	107.19	107.75	108.31	108.88	109.45	110.02
2	53.19	53.73	54.28	54.82	55.37	55.93	56.49	57.05	57.62	58.18	58.76	59.33	59.91
3	36.51	37.06	37.61	38.16	38.72	39.29	39.86	40.43	41.01	41.60	42.19	42.79	43.38
4	28.19	28.74	29.30	29.86	30.44	31.02	31.60	32.19	32.79	33.40	34.01	34.63	35.25
5	23.20	23.76	24.33	24.91	25.50	26.09	26.69	27.30	27.92	28.55	29.18	29.82	30.47
6	19.89	20.46	21.04	21.63	22.23	22.84	23.46	24.09	24.73	25.37	26.03	26.70	27.37
7	17.53	18.11	18.70	19.31	19.92	20.55	21.18	21.83	22.49	23.16	23.83	24.52	25.22
8	15.77	16.36	16.96	17.58	18.21	18.85	19.50	20.17	20.85	21.53	22.23	22.95	23.67
9	14.41	15.01	15.62	16.25	16.89	17.55	18.22	18.90	19.60	20.31	21.03	21.76	22.51
10	13.32	13.93	14.56	15.20	15.86	16.53	17.22	17.92	18.63	19.36	20.10	20.86	21.62
11	12.44	13.06	13.70	14.35	15.02	15.71	16.41	17.13	17.86	18.61	19.37	20.15	20.93
12	11.71	12.34	12.99	13.66	14.34	15.04	15.76	16.50	17.25	18.01	18.79	19.58	20.39
13	11.10	11.74	12.40	13.08	13.77	14.49	15.22	15.97	16.74	17.52	18.32	19.13	19.96
14	10.58	11.23	11.90	12.59	13.30	14.03	14.78	15.54	16.33	17.12	17.94	18.77	19.61
15	10.13	10.79	11.47	12.17	12.90	13.64	14.40	15.18	15.98	16.80	17.62	18.47	19.33
16	9.74	10.41	11.10	11.81	12.55	13.31	14.09	14.88	15.69	16.52	17.37	18.22	19.10
17	9.40	10.08	10.78	11.51	12.25	13.03	13.81	14.62	15.45	16.29	17.15	18.02	18.91
18	9.10	9.79	10.50	11.24	12.00	12.78	13.58	14.41	15.24	16.10	16.97	17.86	18.75
19	8.83	9.53	10.25	11.00	11.78	12.57	13.38	14.22	15.07	15.94	16.82	17.72	18.63
20	8.60	9.30	10.04	10.80	11.58	12.39	13.21	14.06	14.92	15.80	16.70	17.60	18.52
25	7.73	8.48	9.26	10.07	10.90	11.76	12.64	13.53	14.45	15.37	16.31	17.25	18.21
30	7.20	7.98	8.81	9.66	10.53	11.43	12.34	13.27	14.22	15.17	16.14	17.11	18.09
35	6.84	7.67	8.52	9.41	10.32	11.24	12.19	13.14	14.11	15.08	16.06	17.05	18.03
40	6.60	7.46	8.34	9.26	10.19	11.14	12.10	13.07	14.05	15.04	16.03	17.02	18.01

Note: An annual constant percentage value is calculated by first taking the sum of 12 monthly payments and then expressing this sum as a percentage of the principal loan amount. In formula fashion this becomes: Annual Constant = (12 × Monthly Payment × 100)/Principal Loan Amount.

The 100 factor is used to express the annual constant in percentage form. For example, the monthly payment on a $20,000, 25-year, 9 percent loan is $167.80 (calculated from Table 6 in the Appendix). The monthly payment times 1200 is $201,360. This figure divided by the $20,000 loan gives an annual constant value of 10.07 (see year 25 at 9 percent in the above table).

TABLE 8. Remaining Loan Balances (Percentage of Original Loan Amount)

Age of Loan in Years	6% Rate					7%				
	Original Loan Length in Years					Original Loan Length in Years				
	10	15	20	25	30	10	15	20	25	30
1	92.5%	95.8%	97.3%	98.2%	98.8%	92.8%	96.1%	97.6%	98.5%	99.0%
2	84.5	91.3	94.5	96.3	97.5	85.2	91.9	95.1	96.8	97.9
3	76.0	86.5	91.5	94.3	96.1	76.9	87.4	92.3	95.1	96.7
4	67.0	81.4	88.3	92.2	94.6	68.1	82.6	89.4	93.2	95.5
5	57.4	76.0	84.9	89.9	93.1	58.6	77.4	86.3	91.2	94.1
10	0.0	43.6	64.5	76.3	83.7	·0.0	45.4	66.8	78.6	85.8
15		0.0	37.0	58.0	71.0		0.0	39.1	60.9	74.0
20			0.0	33.3	54.0			0.0	35.7	57.3
25				0.0	31.0				0.0	33.6
30					0.0					0.0

Years	8% Rate					9% Rate				
	10	15	20	25	30	10	15	20	25	30
1	93.2%	96.4%	97.9%	98.7%	99.2%	93.5%	96.7%	98.1%	98.9%	99.3%
2	85.8	92.5	95.6	97.3	98.3	86.5	93.1	96.1	97.7	98.6
3	77.8	88.3	93.1	95.7	97.3	78.7	89.1	93.8	96.3	97.8
4	69.2	83.7	90.4	94.1	96.2	70.3	84.8	91.4	94.9	96.9
5	59.8	78.8	87.5	92.3	95.1	61.0	80.1	88.7	93.3	95.9
10	0.0	47.1	68.9	80.8	87.7	0.0	48.9	71.0	82.7	89.4
15		0.0	41.2	63.6	76.8		0.0	43.3	66.2	79.3
20			0.0	38.1	60.5			0.0	40.4	63.5
25				0.0	36.2				0.0	38.8
30					0.0					0.0

Years	10% Rate					11% Rate				
	10	15	20	25	30	10	15	20	25	30
1	93.9%	97.0%	98.3%	99.1%	99.4%	94.2%	97.2%	98.5%	99.2%	99.5%
2	87.1	93.6	96.5	98.0	98.8	87.7	94.1	96.9	98.3	99.0
3	79.6	89.9	94.5	96.9	98.2	80.4	90.7	95.1	97.3	98.5
4	71.3	85.8	92.3	95.3	97.4	72.4	86.8	93.1	96.2	97.9
5	62.2	81.3	89.8	94.2	96.6	63.3	82.5	90.8	95.0	97.2
10	0.0	50.6	73.0	84.6	90.9	0.0	52.3	74.9	86.2	92.3
15		0.0	45.4	68.8	81.7		0.0	47.5	71.1	83.8
20			0.0	42.8	66.4			0.0	45.1	69.1
25				0.0	41.3				0.0	43.8
30					0.0					0.0

TABLE 8. Remaining Loan Balances (Percentage of Original Loan Amount) (concluded)

Age of Loan in Years	12% Rate Original Loan Length in Years					13% Rate Original Loan Length in Years				
	10	15	20	25	30	10	15	20	25	30
1	94.5%	97.5%	98.7%	99.3%	99.6%	94.8%	97.7%	98.9%	99.4%	99.7%
2	88.3	94.6	97.3	98.6	99.2	88.8	95.0	97.6	98.8	99.4
3	81.3	91.4	95.6	97.7	98.8	82.1	92.0	96.1	98.1	99.0
4	73.4	87.7	93.8	96.7	98.2	74.4	88.6	94.5	97.2	98.6
5	64.5	83.6	91.7	95.7	97.7	65.6	84.7	92.6	96.3	98.1
10	0.0	53.9	76.7	87.8	93.4	0.0	55.6	78.5	89.1	94.4
15		0.0	49.5	73.4	85.7		0.0	51.5	75.5	87.4
20			0.0	47.3	71.7			0.0	49.6	74.1
25				0.0	46.2				0.0	48.6
30					0.0					0.0

Years	14% Rate					15% Rate				
	10	15	20	25	30	10	15	20	25	30
1	95.1%	97.9%	99.0%	99.5%	99.8%	95.3%	98.1%	99.1%	99.6%	99.8%
2	89.4	95.5	97.9	99.0	99.5	89.9	95.8	98.1	99.1	99.6
3	82.9	92.7	96.6	98.4	99.2	83.6	93.3	97.0	98.6	99.3
4	75.3	89.5	95.1	97.6	98.8	76.3	90.2	95.6	98.0	99.1
5	66.7	85.8	93.4	96.8	98.4	67.8	86.7	94.1	97.3	98.7
10	0.0	57.2	80.1	90.4	95.3	0.0	58.8	81.6	91.5	96.0
15		0.0	53.4	77.5	89.0		0.0	55.3	79.4	90.3
20			0.0	51.7	76.3			0.0	53.8	78.4
25				0.0	50.9				0.0	53.1
30					0.0					0.0

Years	16% Rate				
	10	15	20	25	30
1	95.6%	98.3%	99.3%	99.7%	99.9%
2	90.4	96.2	98.4	99.3	99.7
3	84.3	93.8	97.3	98.8	99.5
4	77.2	91.0	96.1	98.3	99.2
5	68.9	87.7	94.7	97.7	99.0
10	0.0	60.4	83.1	92.5	96.7
15		0.0	57.2	81.1	91.6
20			0.0	55.9	80.3
25				0.0	55.3
30					0.0

Note: This table indicates the loan balance remaining on a previously made mortgage loan. For example, the remaining loan balance on a $20,000, 25-year, 9 percent loan that has been outstanding for 5 years can be found by first turning to the 9% rate. Then, begin by reading across at the 5-year "age of the loan" row until the 25-year original loan column is found. This indicates that 93.3 percent (or $18,660) of the $20,000 loan will still be outstanding.

APPENDIX C
Major Legislation Affecting Real Estate Finance

Date	Legislation
Date	**Legislation**

1932   Federal Home Loan Bank Act
Established the Federal Home Loan Bank System in form similar to the Federal Reserve System. There is a Federal Home Loan Bank Board and 12 regional banks. This Act provided a central credit structure to assist institutions engaged in making home mortgage loans.

1933   Home Owners' Loan Act
Provided for the creation of a system of federal savings and loan associations. These federal associations were to be chartered and supervised by the Federal Home Loan Bank Board.

1934   National Housing Act
Created the Federal Housing Administration. Also provided for the establishment of privately-owned mortgage institutions to operate a national secondary mortgage market. Not only was the Federal Housing Administration established to insure home mortgages, but this Act also provided for the creation of the Federal Savings and Loan Insurance Corporation. The FSLIC provides insurance for savings accounts held at member associations.

1938   Federal National Mortgage Association (creation of)
The Reconstruction Finance Corporation provided capital for the establishment of the Federal National Mortgage Association which was to operate as a government-sponsored secondary mortgage market.

1944   Servicemen's Readjustment Act
Frequently referred to as the G.I. Bill of Rights. This Act established a program for the guarantee of mortgage loans made to veterans of the armed services. The Veterans Administration guarantees these home mortgage loans.

1949   Housing Act
Provided for national housing goals. Also aided municipalities to clear slum areas and provide public housing through federal grants. Rural areas also received financial assistance.

1950   Federal National Mortgage Association (transference of)
            Provision was made to move the FNMA from under the Recon-
            struction Finance Corporation to the Housing and Home Finance
            Agency which was created in 1942 to coordinate federal home fi-
            nancing activities.

1950   Regulation X (real estate credit—not currently operational)
            The Board of Governors of the Federal Reserve System, with con-
            currence of the Housing and Home Finance Administration, was
            authorized to regulate real estate credit. Maximum loan amounts,
            minimum down payments, and maximum repayment periods were
            set to restrain construction expansion and the related inflationary
            pressures during the Korean War. These restrictions were removed
            in 1952.

1954   Federal National Mortgage Association Charter Act
            The FNMA was rechartered as a federal agency with some corpo-
            rate structural characteristics. It continued as an agency of the
            Housing and Home Finance Agency but was to become privately-
            owned.

1961   Housing Act
            Provided for further federal government involvement in housing.
            New programs included subsidized rental housing for low- to
            moderate-income families and FHA-insured loans for home repair
            and modernization for homes located in certain urban areas.

1968   Housing and Urban Development Act
            Authorized further federal government participation in housing.
            Two new programs were created for home ownership (Section 235)
            and rental housing (Section 236) assistance in the form of subsidies
            whereby the federal government paid a portion of loan interest
            costs.
            The FNMA was reorganized as a separate privately-owned corpo-
            ration. At the same time, the Government National Mortgage As-
            sociation was created as a wholly-owned government corporation
            under the direction of the Department of Housing and Urban De-
            velopment.

1968   Truth in Lending Act (Regulation Z)
            Established under the Consumer Credit Protection Act of 1968.
            The Board of Governors of the Federal Reserve System was given
            authority to regulate (Regulation Z) consumer credit costs in a way
            so as to make the cost statements more meaningful. Both the
            amount of finance charges and the effective annual percentage in-
            terest rate must be stated.

1970   Emergency Home Finance Act
Created the Federal Home Loan Mortgage Corporation for purposes of providing a secondary mortgage market for savings and loan association members of the Federal Home Loan Bank System. The secondary market was to be for FHA, VA, and conventional mortgages. The Act also provided for the Federal National Mortgage Association to purchase and sell conventional mortgages.

1974   Equal Credit Opportunity Act
Prohibits discrimination in the decision to grant credit on the basis of sex or marital status.

1974   Real Estate Settlement Procedures Act
Provided a comprehensive set of guidelines to be used for handling loan closing costs and settlement practices and procedures.

1976   Equal Credit Opportunity Act Amendments
Broadened the scope of the Equal Credit Opportunity Act. Prohibits discrimination in the granting of credit on the basis of sex, marital status, race, color, religion, national origin, age, source of income, and the exercise of rights in good faith under the Consumer Protection Act of 1968.

1976   Real Estate Settlement Procedures Act Amendments
Made some of the requirements under the Real Estate Settlement Procedures Act less stringent. Lenders can provide good-faith estimates of closing costs (instead of actual costs) and can tie disclosure timing to when loan applications are received (instead of at the closing date).

1978   Financial Institutions Regulatory and Interest Rate Control Act
Authorized the FHLMC to purchase packages of home improvement loans.

1980   Housing and Community Development Act
Created a secondary market for FNMA mobile home loans and property improvement loans.

1980   Depository Institutions Deregulation and Monetary Control Act
One portion of the Act was directed toward the improvement of monetary control procedures by the Federal Reserve. A second portion was directed at deregulation by allowing increased competition in the financial markets amongst depository institutions and by expanding the powers of thrift institutions. The Act is discussed in detail in Chapter 5.

1981   Economic Recovery Tax Act
Provision was made for cutting individual and corporate income tax rates to encourage increased saving. In addition, the Act provided for a major overhauling of acceptable methods for depreciating personal and real property by instituting the accelerated cost recovery system. Implications pertaining to real estate are discussed in Chapter 4.

1982   Garn-St. Germain Depository Institutions Act
Principal focus was on aid to the savings and loan industry. Savings and Loans were permitted to make commercial loans and nonresidential real estate loans, as well as to issue variable-rate mortgages. Depository institutions could issue new money market deposit accounts with no interest rate ceilings. State due-on-sale clauses were preempted or severely restricted.

1984   Secondary Mortgage Market Enhancement Act
Secondary mortgage market issuers were exempted from state securities registration laws and the secondary mortgage market powers of Freddie Mac (FHLMC) and Fannie Mae (FNMA) were broadened.

1986   Tax Reform Act
Provision was made for a lowering of both corporate and individual income tax rates. However, because this Act was to be revenue neutral, many previously allowed deductions were eliminated or sharply reduced. The taxpayer's ability to depreciate real property was severely altered. Residential rental property must be depreciated using the straight-line method over a 27.5-year period, while nonresidential real estate must be depreciated over 31.5 years.

APPENDIX D

The Real Estate Settlement Procedures Act

The Real Estate Settlement Procedures Act (RESPA) was first passed by Congress in 1974 and amended in 1975. The result was chaos—within six months its provisions were suspended.

In June 1976 the Act was amended in its current form. The Act must be complied with by all federally regulated lenders. It covers all federally regulated mortgages secured by single-family dwellings, condominiums, and cooperatives occupied by one to four families.

Exempt from the Act are properties in excess of 25 acres, construction loans, and loans on vacant lots.

The lender is required to furnish the borrower a copy of a HUD approved information booklet at the time application is made for the loan or within three days. This booklet entitled, *Settlement Procedures Special Information Booklet,* specifies the main procedures cited by the Act and lists unfair practices prohibited under the Act.

Furthermore, the lender must furnish a "good faith" estimate of settlement costs to the loan applicant within three days of the written loan application. The standard "good faith" estimate is shown in Figure 17–5 in Chapter 17.

The third requirement under the Act is to furnish the borrower a standard form to be used in all regulated settlements (or closings). If the borrower requests it, the settlement costs, to the extent known, must be made available to the borrower 24 hours before settlement. This settlement form is shown in Figure 17–6 in Chapter 17.

The following excerpts from the HUD information booklet discuss each specific settlement service as shown on Section L of the Uniform Settlement Statement form.

700. Sales/Broker's Commission. This is the total dollar amount of sales commission, usually paid by the seller. Fees are usually a percentage of the selling price of the house, and are intended to compensate brokers or salesmen for their services. Custom and/or the negotiated agreement between the seller and the broker determine the amount of the commission.

701–702. Division of Commission. If several brokers or salesmen work together to sell the house, the comn.ission may be split among them. If they are paid from funds collected for settlement, this is shown on lines 701–702.

703. Commission Paid at Settlement. Sometimes the broker will retain the earnest money deposit to apply towards his commission. In this case, line 703 will show only the remainder of the commission which will be paid at settlement.

800. Items Payable in Connection with Loan. These are the fees which lenders charge to process, approve and make the mortgage loan.

801. Loan Origination. This fee covers the lender's administrative costs in processing the loan. Often expressed as a percentage of the loan, the fee will vary among lenders and from locality to locality. Generally the buyer pays the fee unless another arrangement has been made with the seller and written into the sales contract.

802. Loan Discount. Often called "points," a loan discount is a one-time charge used to adjust the yield on the loan to what market conditions demand. It is used to offset constraints placed on the yield by state or federal regulations. Each "point" is equal to one percent of the mortgage amount. For example, if a lender charges four points on a $30,000 loan this amounts to a charge of $1,200.

803. Appraisal Fee. This charge, which may vary significantly from transaction to transaction, pays for a statement of property value for the lender, made by an independent appraiser or by a member of the lender's staff. The lender needs to know if the value of the property is sufficient to secure the loan if you fail to repay the loan according to the provision of your mortgage contract, and the lender must foreclose and take title to the house. The appraiser inspects the house and the neighborhood, and considers sales prices of comparable houses and other factors in determining the value. The appraisal report may contain photos and other information of value to you. It will provide the factual data upon which the appraiser based the appraised value. Ask the lender for a copy of the appraisal report or review the original.

The appraisal fee may be paid by either the buyer or the seller, as agreed in the sales contract. In some cases this fee is included in the Mortgage Insurance Application Fee. See line 806.

804. Credit Report Fee. This fee covers the cost of the credit report, which shows how you have handled other credit transactions. The lender uses this report in conjunction with information you submitted with the application regarding your income, outstanding bills, and employment, to determine whether you are an acceptable credit risk and to help determine how much money to lend you.

805. Lender's Inspection Fee. This charge covers inspections, often of newly constructed housing, made by personnel of the lending institution or an outside inspector. (Pest or other inspections made by companies other than the lender are discussed in connection with line 1302.)

806. Mortgage Insurance Application Fee. This fee covers processing the application for private mortgage insurance which may be required on certain loans. It may cover both the appraisal and application fee.

807. Assumption Fee. This fee is charged for processing papers for cases in which the buyer takes over payments on the prior loan of the seller.

900. Items Required by Lender to be Paid in Advance. You may be required to prepay certain items, such as interest, mortgage insurance premium and hazard insurance premium, at the time of settlement.

901. Interest. Lenders usually require that borrowers pay at settlement the interest that accrues on the mortgage from the date of settlement to the beginning of the period covered by the first monthly payment. For example, suppose your settlement takes place on April 16, and your first regular monthly payment will be due June 1, to cover interest charges for the month of May. On the settlement date, the lender will collect interest for the period from April 16 to May 1. If you borrowed $30,000 at 9% interest, the interest item would be $112.50. This amount will be entered on line 901.

902. Mortgage Insurance Premium. Mortgage insurance protects the lender from loss due to payment default by the home owner. The lender may require you to pay your first premium in advance, on the day of settlement. The premium may cover a specific number of months or a year in advance.

903. Hazard Insurance Premium. This premium prepayment is for insurance protection for you and the lender against loss due to fire, windstorm, and natural hazards. This coverage may be included in a Homeowners Policy which insures against additional risks which may include personal liability and theft. Lenders often require payment of the first year's premium at settlement.

1000. Reserves Deposited with Lenders. Reserves (sometimes called "escrow" or "impound" accounts) are funds held in an account by the lender to assure future payment for such recurring items as real estate taxes and hazard insurance.

You will probably have to pay an initial amount for each of these items to start the reserve account at the time of settlement. A portion of your regular monthly payment will be added to the reserve account. RESPA places limitations on the amount of reserve funds which may be required by the lender.

1001. Hazard Insurance. The lender determines the amount of money that must be placed in the reserve in order to pay the next insurance premium when due.

1002. Mortgage Insurance. The lender may require that part of the total annual premium be placed in the reserve account at settlement. The portion to be received in reserve may be negotiable.

1003–1004. City/County Property Taxes. The lender may require a regular monthly payment to the reserve account for property taxes.

1005. Annual Assessments. The reserve item covers assessments that may be imposed by subdivisions or municipalities for special improvements (such as sidewalks, sewers or paving) or fees (such as homeowners association fees).

1100. Title Charges. Title charges may cover a variety of services performed by the lender or others for handling and supervising the settlement transaction and services related thereto. The specific charges discussed in connection with lines 1101 through 1109 are those most frequently incurred at settlement. Due to the great diversity in practice from area to area, your particular settlement may not include all these items or may include others not listed.

1101. Settlement or Closing Fee. This fee is paid to the settlement agent. Responsibility for payment of this fee should be negotiated between the seller and buyer, at the time the sales contract is signed.

1102–1104. Abstract or Title Search, Title Examination, Title Insurance Binder. These charges cover the costs of the search and examination of records of previous ownership, transfers, etc., to determine whether the seller can convey clear title to the property, and to disclose any matters on record that could adversely affect the buyer or the lender. Examples of title problems are unpaid mortgages, judgment or tax liens, conveyances of mineral rights, leases, and power line easements or road right-of-ways that could limit use and enjoyment of the real estate. In some areas, a title insurance binder is called a commitment to insure.

1105. Document Preparation. There may be a separate document fee that covers preparation of final legal papers, such as a mortgage, deed of trust, note, or deed. You should check to see that these services, if charged for, are not also covered under some other service fees; ask the settlement agent.

1106. Notary Fee. This fee is charged for the cost of having a licensed person affix his or her name and seal to various documents authenticating the execution of these documents by the parties.

1107. Attorney's Fees. You may be required to pay for legal services provided to the lender in connection with the settlement, such as examination of the title binder or sales contract. Occasionally this fee can be shared with the seller, if so stipulated in the sales contract. If a lawyer's involvement is required by the lender, the fee will appear on this part of the form. The buyer and seller may each retain an attorney to check the various documents and to represent them at all stages of the transaction including settlement. Where this service is not required and is paid for outside of closing, the person conducting settlement is not obligated to record the fee on the settlement form.

1108. Title Insurance. The total cost of owner's and lender's title insurance is shown here. The borrower may pay all, a part or none of this cost depending on the terms of the sales contract or local custom.

1109. Lender's Title Insurance. A one-time premium may be charged at settlement for a lender's title policy which protects the lender against loss due to problems or defects in connection with the title. The insurance is usually written for the amount of the mortgage loan and covers losses due to defects or problems not identified by title search and examination. In most cases this is customarily paid by the borrower unless the seller agrees in the sales contract to pay part or all of it.

1110. Owner's Title Insurance. This charge is for owner's title insurance protection and protects you against losses due to title defects. In some areas it is customary for the seller to provide the buyer with an owner's policy and for the seller to pay for this policy. In other areas, if the buyer desires an owner's policy he must pay for it.

1200. Government Recording and Transfer Charges.

These fees may be paid either by borrower or seller, depending upon your contract when you buy the house or accept the loan commitment. The borrower usually pays the fees for legally recording the new deed and mortgage (item 1201). These fees, collected when property changes hands or when a mortgage loan is made, may be quite large and are set by state and/or local governments. City, county and/or state tax stamps may have to be purchased as well (items 1201 and 1203).

1300. Additional Settlement Charges

1301. Survey. The lender or the title insurance company may require that a surveyor conduct a property survey to determine the exact location of the house and the lot line, as well as easements and rights of way. This is a protection to the buyer as well. Usually the buyer pays the surveyor's fees, but sometimes this may be handled by the seller.

1302. Pest and Other Inspections. This fee is to cover inspections for termite or other pest infestation of the house. This may be important if the sales contract included a promise by the seller to transfer the property free from pests or pest-caused damage. Be sure that the inspection shows that the property complies with the sales contract before you complete the settlement. If it does not you may wish to require a bond or other financial assurance that the work will be completed. This fee can be paid either by the borrower or seller depending upon the terms of the sales contract. Lenders vary in their requirements as to such an inspection.

Fees for other inspections, such as the structural soundness, are entered on line 1303.

1400. Total Settlement Charges.

All the fees in the borrower's column entitled "Paid from Borrower's Funds at Settlement" are totaled here and transferred to line 103 of Section J, "Settlement charges to borrower" in the *Summary of Borrower's Transaction* on page 1 of the Uniform Settlement Statement. All the settlement fees paid by the seller are transferred to line 502 of Section K, *Summary of Seller's Transaction* on page 1 of the Uniform Settlement Statement.

APPENDIX E

Guidelines for Preparation of FHLMC Form 70 and FNMA Form 1004

I. Lender's (Seller's) Section

All of the information requested in the section at the top of page 1 is to be furnished by the seller prior to giving the form to the appraiser for a particular assignment. The property rights appraised are to be indicated by checking the appropriate box and the sale price of the subject property, loan charges to be paid by the seller of the property, and other sales concessions, are to be entered in the spaces provided.

Instructions to the appraiser will generally consist of directions to the property and the means of gaining access thereto.

II. Neighborhood Description and Analysis

Nothing in the form or the attachments thereto is intended to preclude the appraiser from considering the social and economic characteristics of the neighborhood to the extent that they presently, or are likely to, affect the value of the subject property. However, the appraiser is to report detrimental neighborhood conditions in factual, specific terms by giving the addresses of the affected properties and an exact description of the nature of the conditions involved in each case. For example: "There are junked and abandoned cars (or refrigerators, etc.) in the front (or rear) yards of the properties at (addresses);" or, "the houses at (addresses) are vacant (or boarded up, or vandalized as evidenced by broken windows, etc.);" or, "a lack of maintenance is evident in the neighborhood by uncut grass (or peeling paint, or fallen gutters and downspouts, etc.) at (addresses)." Furthermore, if the value trend in the neighborhood is declining as a result of detrimental conditions, statements to that effect must be supported by reporting actual property sales which demonstrate the trend. Such information may be provided in the comment section or in an addendum to the report.

Major considerations in this section of the form which may require further explanation and instruction are:

1. *Present Land Use*—enter the estimated percentage of each type of property in the neighborhood. If the use is other than one of those indicated on the form, enter the percentage and state the type in the spaces provided. Use "0" where none of the listed uses are in evidence. The total of uses must equal 100%.

2. *Change in Present Land Use*—indicate by checking the appropriate box what your professional judgment indicates to be the

RESIDENTIAL APPRAISAL REPORT

File No _____

To be completed by Lender

Borrower	Census Tract _____ Map Reference _____
Property Address	
City	County _____ State _____ Zip Code _____
Legal Description	

Sale Price $ _____ Date of Sale _____ Loan Term _____ yrs. Property Rights Appraised ☐ Fee ☐ Leasehold ☐ DeMinimis PUD

Actual Real Estate Taxes $ _____ (yr) Loan charges to be paid by seller $ _____ Other sales concessions _____

Lender/Client _____ Address _____

Occupant _____ Appraiser _____ Instructions to Appraiser _____

NEIGHBORHOOD

Location	☐ Urban	☐ Suburban	☐ Rural
Built Up	☐ Over 75%	☐ 25% to 75%	☐ Under 25%
Growth Rate ☐ Fully Dev.	☐ Rapid	☐ Steady	☐ Slow
Property Values	☐ Increasing	☐ Stable	☐ Declining
Demand/Supply	☐ Shortage	☐ In Balance	☐ Over Supply
Marketing Time	☐ Under 3 Mos.	☐ 4-6 Mos.	☐ Over 6 Mos.

Present Land Use ____ % 1 Family ____ % 2-4 Family ____ % Apts. ____ % Condo ____ % Commercial ____ % Industrial ____ % Vacant ____ %

Change in Present Land Use ☐ Not Likely ☐ Likely (-) ☐ Taking Place (-)
(-) From _____ To _____

Predominant Occupancy ☐ Owner ☐ Tenant ____ % Vacant

Single Family Price Range $ _____ to $ _____ Predominant Value $ _____

Single Family Age _____ yrs. to _____ yrs. Predominant Age _____ yrs.

Rating	Good	Avg	Fair	Poor
Employment Stability	☐	☐	☐	☐
Convenience to Employment	☐	☐	☐	☐
Convenience to Shopping	☐	☐	☐	☐
Convenience to Schools	☐	☐	☐	☐
Adequacy of Public Transportation	☐	☐	☐	☐
Recreational Facilities	☐	☐	☐	☐
Adequacy of Utilities	☐	☐	☐	☐
Property Compatibility	☐	☐	☐	☐
Protection from Detrimental Conditions	☐	☐	☐	☐
Police and Fire Protection	☐	☐	☐	☐
General Appearances of Properties	☐	☐	☐	☐
Appeal to Market	☐	☐	☐	☐

Note: FHLMC/FNMA do not consider race or the racial composition of the neighborhood to be reliable appraisal factors.

Comments including those factors, favorable or unfavorable, affecting marketability (e.g. public parks, schools, view, noise) _____

SITE

Dimensions _____ = _____ Sq. Ft. or Acres ☐ Corner Lot

Zoning classification _____ Present improvements ☐ do ☐ do not conform to zoning regulations

Highest and best use ☐ Present use ☐ Other (specify) _____

	Public	Other (Describe)	OFF SITE IMPROVEMENTS	
Elec.	☐	_____	Street Access: ☐ Public ☐ Private	Topo _____
Gas	☐	_____	Surface _____	Size _____
Water	☐	_____	Maintenance: ☐ Public ☐ Private	Shape _____
San. Sewer	☐	_____	☐ Storm Sewer ☐ Curb/Gutter	View _____
	☐ Underground Elect. & Tel.	☐ Sidewalk ☐ Street Lights	Drainage _____

Is the property located in a HUD Identified Special Flood Hazard Area? ☐ No ☐ Yes

Comments (favorable or unfavorable including any apparent adverse easements, encroachments or other adverse conditions) _____

IMPROVEMENTS

☐ Existing ☐ Proposed ☐ Under Constr. No. Units _____ Type (det, duplex, semi/det, etc.) _____ Design (rambler, split level, etc.) _____ Exterior Walls _____

Yrs. Age: Actual _____ Effective _____ to _____ No. Stories _____

Roof Material _____ Gutters & Downspouts ☐ None

Window (Type): _____ ☐ Storm Sash ☐ Screens ☐ Combination Insulation ☐ None ☐ Floor ☐ Ceiling ☐ Roof ☐ Walls

☐ Manufactured Housing

Foundation Walls _____

BSMT. ____ % Basement ☐ Outside Entrance ☐ Concrete Floor ____ % Finished ☐ Floor Drain ☐ Sump Pump Finished Ceiling _____ Finished Walls _____ Finished Floor _____

☐ Slab on Grade ☐ Crawl Space Evidence of: ☐ Dampness ☐ Termites ☐ Settlement

Comments _____

ROOM LIST

Room List	Foyer	Living	Dining	Kitchen	Den	Family Rm.	Rec. Rm.	Bedrooms	No. Baths	Laundry	Other
Basement											
1st Level											
2nd Level											

Finished area above grade contains a total of _____ rooms _____ bedrooms _____ baths. Gross Living Area _____ sq. ft. Bsmt Area _____ sq ft

INTERIOR FINISH & EQUIPMENT

Kitchen Equipment: ☐ Refrigerator ☐ Range/Oven ☐ Disposal ☐ Dishwasher ☐ Fan/Hood ☐ Compactor ☐ Washer ☐ Dryer ☐ _____

HEAT: Type _____ Fuel _____ Cond. _____ AIR COND: ☐ Central ☐ Other _____ ☐ Adequate ☐ Inadequate

Floors	☐ Hardwood	☐ Carpet Over _____ ☐ _____
Walls	☐ Drywall	☐ Plaster ☐ _____
Trim/Finish	☐ Good	☐ Average ☐ Fair ☐ Poor
Bath Floor	☐ Ceramic	☐ _____
Bath Wainscot	☐ Ceramic	☐ _____

Special Features (including energy efficient items) _____

ATTIC: ☐ Yes ☐ No ☐ Stairway ☐ Drop-stair ☐ Scuttle ☐ Floored
Finished (Describe) _____ ☐ Heated

CAR STORAGE: ☐ Garage ☐ Built-in ☐ Attached ☐ Detached ☐ Car Port
No. Cars _____ ☐ Adequate ☐ Inadequate Condition _____

PROPERTY RATING

	Good	Avg	Fair	Poor
Quality of Construction (Materials & Finish)	☐	☐	☐	☐
Condition of Improvements	☐	☐	☐	☐
Room Sizes and Layout	☐	☐	☐	☐
Closets and Storage	☐	☐	☐	☐
Insulation—adequacy	☐	☐	☐	☐
Plumbing—adequacy and condition	☐	☐	☐	☐
Electrical—adequacy and condition	☐	☐	☐	☐
Kitchen Cabinets—adequacy and condition	☐	☐	☐	☐
Compatibility to Neighborhood	☐	☐	☐	☐
Overall Livability	☐	☐	☐	☐
Appeal and Marketability	☐	☐	☐	☐

Yrs Est Remaining Economic Life _____ to _____ . Explain if less than Loan Term

FIREPLACES, PATIOS, POOL, FENCES, etc. (describe) _____

COMMENTS (including functional or physical inadequacies, repairs needed, modernization, etc.) _____

FHLMC Form 70 Rev. 7/79 12 Ch. ATTACH DESCRIPTIVE PHOTOGRAPHS OF SUBJECT PROPERTY AND STREET SCENE FFFP FNMA Form 1004 Rev 7/79

Residential Appraisal Report

VALUATION SECTION

Purpose of Appraisal is to estimate Market Value as defined in Certification & Statement of Limiting Conditions (FHLMC Form 439/FNMA Form 1004B). If submitted for FNMA, the appraiser must attach (1) sketch or map showing location of subject, street names, distance from nearest intersection, and any detrimental conditions and (2) exterior building sketch of improvements showing dimensions.

COST APPROACH

Measurements	No. Stories	Sq. Ft.
___ x ___	x ___	= ___
___ x ___	x ___	= ___
___ x ___	x ___	= ___
___ x ___	x ___	= ___
___ x ___	x ___	= ___
___ x ___	x ___	= ___

Total Gross Living Area (List in Market Data Analysis below) _____

Comment on functional and economic obsolescence: _____

ESTIMATED REPRODUCTION COST — NEW — OF IMPROVEMENTS:

Dwelling _____ Sq. Ft. @ $ _____ = $ _____
_____ Sq. Ft. @ $ _____ = _____
Extras _____ = _____
_____ = _____
Special Energy Efficient Items _____ = _____
Porches, Patios, etc. _____ = _____
Garage/Car Port _____ Sq. Ft. @ $ _____ = _____
Site Improvements (driveway, landscaping, etc. _____ = _____
Total Estimated Cost New . . . . = $ _____

	Physical	Functional	Economic
Less
Depreciation $ _____ | $ _____ | $ _____ | = $ (_____)
Depreciated value of improvements . . . . = $ _____
ESTIMATED LAND VALUE . . . . = $ _____
(If leasehold, show only leasehold value)

INDICATED VALUE BY COST APPROACH . . . . . $ _____

MARKET DATA ANALYSIS

The undersigned has recited three recent sales of properties most similar and proximate to subject and has considered these in the market analysis. The description includes a dollar adjustment, reflecting market reaction to those items of significant variation between the subject and comparable properties. If a significant item in the comparable property is superior to, or more favorable than, the subject property, a minus (-) adjustment is made, thus reducing the indicated value of subject, if a significant item in the comparable is inferior to, or less favorable than, the subject property, a plus (+) adjustment is made, thus increasing the indicated value of the subject.

ITEM	Subject Property	COMPARABLE NO.1	COMPARABLE NO. 2	COMPARABLE NO 3
Address				
Proximity to Subj.				
Sales Price	$	$	$	$
Price/Living area	$	$	$	$
Data Source				

Date of Sale and	DESCRIPTION	DESCRIPTION	+(-)$ Adjustment	DESCRIPTION	+(-)$ Adjustment	DESCRIPTION	+(-)$ Adjustment
Time Adjustment							
Location							
Site/View							
Design and Appeal							
Quality of Const.							
Age							
Condition							
Living Area Room Count and Total	Total	B-rms	Baths	Total	B-rms	Baths	Total	B-rms	Baths	Total	B-rms	Baths
Gross Living Area	Sq. Ft.	Sq. Ft.		Sq. Ft.		Sq. Ft.	
Basement & Bsmt. Finished Rooms							
Functional Utility							
Air Conditioning							
Garage/Car Port							
Porches, Patio Pools, etc.							
Special Energy Efficient Items							
Other (e.g. fire-places, kitchen equip., remodeling)							
Sales or Financing Concessions							
Net adj. (Total)		Plus	Minus $	Plus	Minus $	Plus	Minus $
Indicate Value of Subject		$	$	$

Comments on Market Data _____

INDICATED VALUE BY MARKET DATA APPROACH . . . . $ _____

INDICATED VALUE BY INCOME APPROACH (If applicable Economic Market Rent $ _____ /Mo. x Gross Rent Multiplier _____ = $ _____

This appraisal is made ☐ "as is" ☐ subject to the repairs, alterations, or conditions listed below ☐ completion per plans and specifications.

Comments and Conditions of Appraisal: _____

Final Reconciliation: _____

Construction Warranty ☐ Yes ☐ No Name of Warranty Program _____ Warranty Coverage Expires _____

This appraisal is based upon the above requirements, the certification, contingent and limiting conditions, and Market Value definition that are stated in

☐ FHLMC Form 439 (Rev. 10/78)/FNMA Form 1004B (Rev. 10/78) filed with client _____ 19___ ☐ attached

I ESTIMATE THE MARKET VALUE, AS DEFINED, OF SUBJECT PROPERTY AS OF _____ 19___ to be $ _____

Appraiser(s) _____

Review Appraiser (if applicable) _____ ☐ Did ☐ Did Not Physically Inspect Property

FHLMC Form 70 Rev. 7/79   Forms and Worms, Inc 315 Whitney Ave . New Haven CT 06511 1 (800) 243 4545   REVERSE   FFFP   FNMA Form 1004 Rev. 7/79

Residential Appraisal Report (concluded)

trend of change in land uses in the neighborhood. Major factors to be considered in this category include present uses, market supply and demand, and zoning. If change is likely or is already taking place, state from what use and give the use to which the neighborhood is in transition. Elaborate further on such changes in the comment section or in a separate addendum.

3. *Predominant Occupancy*—indicate the predominant type of occupancy by checking the appropriate box or giving the estimated percentage of vacancy. It should be emphasized that this question refers to occupancy rather than to building types. For example, if the neighborhood consists of two-family properties of which 90% are owner-occupied, then the owner box should be checked. If there is only a relatively small preponderance of owners over tenants (e.g. 60% owners vs. 40% tenants), then this situation should be reported in the comment section since the long term stability of the neighborhood could be adversely affected for single family residential purposes.

4. *Single-Family Price Range*—enter the lowest and highest typical prevailing prices of single-family residential properties in the neighborhood. However, isolated extremes at either end of the range should not be reported. Also, state the predominant price most frequently found.

5. *Single-Family Age*—give the typical age range of single-family properties in the neighborhood together with the predominant age. Do not report occasional extremes at either end of the range.

Neighborhood Rating Grid—as part of the neighborhood analysis, the appraiser is also to rate the various characteristics of the neighborhood in terms of good, average, fair, or poor. These ratings are to be based on comparison by the appraiser of the subject neighborhood with comparison neighborhoods as to the present and probable future characteristic factors while recognizing the effect of these factors upon continued market appeal for residential purposes.

The quality ratings which the appraiser is being asked to provide are defined as follows:

Good—this rating is to be applied when the characteristics being considered are outstanding and superior to those found in competing neighborhoods.

Average—this indicates that the factors being rated are equal to the norm found to be acceptable in competing neighborhoods.

Fair—this rating is to be used where the factors concerned are below what is typical for comparable neighborhoods.

Poor—a rating of this nature is appropriate if the characteristics under consideration are either nonexistent or in such small supply that single-family residential values are, or may be, adversely affected.

In connection with these ratings, it should be noted that the appraiser must explain in the comment section the reasons for any ratings of "fair" or "poor." A separate addendum to the report should be used for this purpose if necessary.

Neighborhood Rating Factors—the following represent some of the considerations which should enter into rating the various aspects of the neighborhood. In this connection, the appraiser should remember that these ratings are based upon competitive locations and, therefore, should never rate a neighborhood in one price range against a noncompetitive area. It should also be noted that different income and user groups may place more weight on some factors than others.

Employment Stability—consideration should be given to the number of employment opportunities and the variety and type of industries in the community. One-industry or cyclical industry areas would normally not be rated as favorably as those having a broader variety of employment with greater stability.

Convenience to Employment—the distance, both in terms of time and mileage, is to be considered here. This factor is particularly important in view of the increasing cost of gasoline. The availability, cost, and convenience of public transportation is also to be considered as an alternative to customary means of private transportation.

Convenience to Shopping—rate the neighborhood in terms of distance, time, and required means of transportation, to shopping for daily necessities.

Convenience to Schools—consider the time and distance to schools. If bus transportation is required, travel time is a factor.

Quality of Schools—the reputation of neighborhood schools and/or the school system as a whole for quality education to the extent that it affects real estate value is to be considered here.

Recreational Facilities—consider the number, type, and quality of such facilities available in the neighborhood as compared to competing neighborhoods. The extent to which such facilities are expected by the market for properties in the subject's price range is also a consideration.

Adequacy of Utilities—rate the extent to which the utility systems (water, sewer, electricity, and gas, if the latter is available) serving the neighborhood are adequate to serve the residents' needs as compared to similar neighborhoods. Consideration of utilities include public, private (community or subdivision) and individual.

Property Compatibility—factors to be considered in this category include the types of land uses prevalent in the neighborhood, lot sizes, price ranges, and building ages and styles.

Protection from Detrimental Conditions—the appraiser is to consider here the extent to which present, or probable future, land uses or environmental conditions presently, or are likely to, adversely affect single-family residential property values in the neighborhood.

Police and Fire Protection—this rating covers the extent to which these services are adequate and equivalent to those provided for competing neighborhoods.

General Appearance of Properties—consider the extent to which properties in the subject neighborhoods are receiving proper maintenance (both buildings and yards) to preserve property values.

Appeal to Market—this is essentially an overall summary rating of the extent to which all aspects of the property and the neighborhood will appeal to the market—i.e. an indication of the marketability of the subject property and the neighborhood. ·

Comments—in addition to the factors already mentioned, about which further explanation is to be given, this section should be used to elaborate upon any favorable or unfavorable aspects of the neighborhood which have not been adequately covered in the preceding analysis and which are likely to affect the long-term stability of property values in the neighborhood. In summary, the basis for any deductions for economic obsolescence in the Cost Approach should be made evident in this section.

III. Site Description and Analysis

Detailed instructions are being given herein only for those items which may not be self-explanatory.

Zoning Classification—state the zoning category as designated by the local zoning code and the major permitted uses.

Highest and Best Use—this factor is critical and deserving of thorough analysis. Do not automatically check the box indicating the present use. If some other use would be more appropriate on the basis of zoning, market demand, and predominant land uses in the neighborhood, state the use specifically. Further explanation should then be provided in the comment section.

Electricity, Water, Sewer, etc.—"public" means governmentally supplied and regulated. It does not, therefore, include community systems sponsored, owned, or operated by the developer or a private company not subject to government regulation or financial assistance. If such systems are found, further explanation thereof must be given in the comment section or an addendum to the report.

Off-Site Improvements—if access to the subject property is by private street or other such right-of-way, describe the nature thereof and provision for maintenance in the comment section or attach an addendum giving details.

Topo, Size, Shape, etc.—provide a brief description of these features of the subject site and how they compare to other sites in the neighborhood. Elaborate under comments if additional information is needed to clarify an item.

Comments—this space is for further explanation of favorable and unfavorable factors which affect the value of the site. The appraiser should also describe any easements, encroachments, or other detrimental conditions.

IV.   Description of Improvements

Detailed instructions are set forth herein only to the extent that the information desired in the form may need clarification.

Number of Units—this should be one unit in all cases since a different appraisal form is required for a greater number of units.

Number of Stories—this is the number of above-grade floors of finished living area and should be the same number used to calculate the gross living area in the Cost Approach.

Exterior Walls—specify the material used for the exterior wall covering, such as wood siding (e.g.—clapboard, board and batten, etc.), shingles, or brick. If the latter, specify whether veneer or solid masonry (either brick or brick on some form of masonry).

Roof Material—state the material used for roof covering—e.g. wood shingles or shakes, asphalt or asbestos shingles, tile, etc.

Gutters and Downspouts—specify the material used for both. If none are present, the appraiser should state the width of the roof overhang and note the site grading around the foundation walls together with any evidence of dampness in the basement.

Windows—list the type of windows—e.g. casement (wood or metal), sliding, double hung (wood or metal), etc.

Insulation—the appraiser should make every effort to determine and report the extent and adequacy of insulation since this is likely to have an increasing effect upon the value of the property due to the high cost of energy.

Foundation Walls—specify the material used—e.g. poured concrete, cinder or concrete block, etc.

Basement—calculate and enter the percentage of basement area in relation to first floor area and indicate the various features requested on the form to the extent present. Also, indicate the existence of any adverse conditions by checking the boxes provided. If the basement is partially finished, estimate and state the percentage of finished area to total area. Also, state the materials used for ceiling, wall, and floor finish.

Comments—the appraiser should here describe any physical deterioration or functional inadequacy found in the basic structure. Such conditions should then be reflected in the estimate of depreciation in the Cost Approach.

Room List—enter the number of each type of room on every level. For this purpose, baths are calculated as follows: three plumbing fixtures (wash bowl, toilet, tub or shower) constitute one bathroom, two fixtures are a half bathroom, one fixture (toilet only) is a quarter bathroom, and one fixture (wash bowl only) is a wash room and is listed under "other." The total count of rooms, bedrooms, and baths is to be reported for the finished area above grade only. These totals will then be used for the subject in the Market Data Analysis.

Interior Finish and Equipment:

1. *Floors*—this is intended to describe the floor finish in the major portion of the house. If hardwood, so indicate by checking the box provided for this purpose. If wall-to-wall carpeting, state the material over which the carpet is installed. If some other type of floor covering prevails, check the third box on the line and state the material. Floor covering in the kitchen or other areas such as the foyer may be described under special features.

2. *Trim/Finish*—this question refers to the sufficiency of this item as well as the quality of materials and workmanship. The definitions of good, average, fair, and poor to be applied in rating this item are the same as set forth in the section on Neighborhood Description.

3. *Bath Floor and Wainscot*—if other than ceramic, check the appropriate box and state the material.

4. *Special Features*—describe any features not mentioned previously in the report such as other floor finish, fireplaces (including location thereof), and built-ins (e.g. cabinets, bookcases, etc.).

Property Rating Grid—the property ratings indicate how the subject property compares to competing properties as to quality and soundness of construction, convenience of living, and appeal to the market. All of these factors have a major effect upon the marketability of any single-family property. The rating factors of good, average, fair and poor are the same as previously defined in the instructions or the Neighborhood Description.

Quality of Construction—consideration is to be given to the quality of workmanship throughout and the quality and durability of materials used in all components of the building.

Condition of Improvements—the appraiser is to rate the condition of the building and is to take note of all aspects of physical depreciation and report these in the comment section.

Room Sizes and Layout—this item includes consideration of the adequacy of room sizes as well as proportions of the rooms and sufficient wall area to permit appropriate furniture groupings. The layout is to be rated as to the extent to which it facilitates the proper flow of traffic, privacy of sleeping areas, and easy access to all rooms without interfering with the intended use of other rooms. Stairways, halls, and doors must also have inadequate width. A rating below average should be reflected by an estimate for functional obsolescence in the Cost Approach. Conversely, if a deduction is made for functional obsolescence, it should be supported by appropriate ratings in this item and "Overall liveability."

Closets and Storage—rate the adequacy and convenience of closets and general storage as compared to competing properties. This is an important item which can have a substantial effect on liveability and marketability and should, therefore, not be ignored by the appraiser.

Plumbing—Adequacy and Condition—considerations affecting this item include the number, style, and condition of plumbing fixtures; the materials used for piping and the condition thereof; and the proper operation of any on-site water or septic systems. In the event that the evaluation of adequacy and condition does not permit a single rating, the appraiser should give two ratings and explain or indicate which rating applies to each factor.

Electrical—Adequacy and Condition—this rating includes the adequacy of electrical service available within the building, the number and location of outlets and switches, the quality and condition of the wiring, and the adequacy and style of lighting fixtures. Split ratings are to be handled in the manner described above.

Kitchen Cabinets—rate the adequacy of the amount of kitchen storage space provided in relation to the likely number of occupants of the house. The style, quality, and condition of the cabinets are also factors in the rating to be given.

Compatibility to Neighborhood—this rating is to indicate the extent to which the size, age, price, architectural design, and construction of the subject property conform to the neighborhood.

Overall Liveability—this rating basically represents a composite of all of the above factors to the extent that they contribute to the sense of comfort and satisfaction likely to be experienced by an owner/occupant of the property.

Appeal and Marketability—consideration is to be given here to the overall appeal of the subject property to the market based on the above factors together with the architectural attractiveness of the property and, therefore, the demand which will probably be generated by the particular combination of these factors.

Effective Age—the appraiser is to report the estimated effective age of the subject property, as distinct from its chronological age, based on its utility and condition.

Remaining Economic Life—state here the estimated remaining number of years over which the improvements can still be expected to make a contribution to the value of the property.

Porches, Patios, Pools, Fences, etc.—describe all improvements which have not previously been mentioned and which will be included in the cost and market approaches.

Comments—the appraiser is to make specific, factual comments here on the reasons for any ratings of fair or poor. Furthermore, it is in this space that the appraiser must specifically describe all items of physical depreciation, whether curable or incurable, and provide an itemized listing of repairs needed to cure deferred maintenance together with the cost thereof.

If more space is required, a separate addendum sheet should be attached to the report. The appraiser should bear in mind at all times that the comments in this section will form the basis and support for the estimate of physical depreciation in the Cost Approach. If new construction, the appraiser is also to comment on whether the property is covered by the Home Owner's Warranty program.

V.   Required Attachments to Form

Photos—attach to the report on a separate sheet, quality (sharp and clear) photos of the front and rear of the subject property as well as at least one street scene which includes the subject property. It is not necessary or even desirable to attach the photos in the margin at the bottom of page one of the form as indicated on the form.

Location map—submit, as an attachment to the report, a sketch or copy of a map showing the location of the subject property, its relation to major traffic arteries, distance to the nearest intersection, and the location of any favorable factors or detrimental conditions as previously reported in the neighborhood description.

Exterior Building Sketch—submit, as an attachment to the report, a perimeter plan of the building (not necessarily to scale) showing the exterior building lines with dimensions which must correspond to those used in the gross building, area calculations set forth in the Cost Approach. In both cases, inches should be converted to *tenths of a foot.* Dimensions must be shown for every exterior wall. An exterior layout would be helpful to the reviewer and may be provided in conjunction with the sketch but is optional.

VI.   Cost Approach

Building Area Calculations—measurements must be exact and be the same as those shown in the exterior building sketch. The total gross building area thus calculated is to be entered on the line calling for "Total Gross Living Area." This is to include finished and habitable above-grade living area only. Finished basement or attic areas are to be calculated and shown separately for use in the cost estimate but are not to be included in the total gross living area.

Comment on Functional & Economic Obsolescence—use this space to fully describe the causes of these forms of obsolescence and support the estimate of the loss in value. No comment as to physical depreciation is needed here since it will already have been explained and estimated in the comment section of the building description.

Estimate of Reproduction Cost New—note that what is required here is reproduction cost—i.e. the cost of reproducing the subject structure using the same materials and workmanship as well as the same layout. It is, however, recognized that in some cases typically involving older buildings containing obsolete materials or unusual functional features, it will be difficult, if not impossible, to estimate reproduction cost new with any reasonable degree of accuracy. In such cases, therefore, replacement cost may be used but then this should be specifically stated along with a description of the materials and quality upon which the estimate of replacement cost is based as well as the functional deficiencies thereby eliminated.

Extras—these are to include such items as finished basement or attic areas and baths. Show square foot areas and cost factors.

Depreciation—this estimate is to reflect, and be supported by, the comments and calculations made previously on the form. In all instances, the depreciation estimate must be allocated to one of the three types shown on the form. A lump-sum total estimate combining several forms of depreciation will not be acceptable.

Land Value—this will normally be estimated on the basis of comparison to sales of similar lots or, in the case of built-up neighborhoods, by extraction from sales of improved properties.

If the final value estimated by the appraiser is the value indicated by the Cost Approach, then the appraiser should also state on an attachment the source of data as to the cost factors and recite comparable land sales.

VII.   Market Data Analysis and Approach to Value

It is expected that the appraiser will use comparables which have sold as recently as possible (usually no earlier than six months prior to the date of the appraisal), are located in the same neighborhood as the property being appraised and therefore subject to the same locational influences, and as similar as possible in size and physical features. If this is not possible, the appraiser shall attach an explanation as to the reasons for selecting comparables which do not meet the above criteria. Listings are not considered as indicative as actual sales but, in the absence of a sufficient number of truly comparable sales, no more than one listing may be used if accompanied by an explanation of the reason for the use of such listing and a complete analysis of the listing which shall include a supported estimate of the probable selling price.

Sales of properties of FHA or VA financing will not be acceptable unless an appropriate downward adjustment has been made to reflect the loan discount paid by the seller.

If the total adjustments for all factors exceed 25% of the sale price of the comparable, then the appraiser should reconsider whether the comparable is, in fact, truly comparable and should, therefore, be replaced by another, more indicative sale.

The appropriate descriptive information (or a rating as to good, fair, etc. as defined in the neighborhood description) is to be entered in the subject property column for each property characteristic set forth in the "Item" column. This is to assist the appraiser and the reviewer in relating the comparables to the subject property. In view of the brevity of the form, it is mandatory that the appraiser complete the analysis of all items.

It is felt that further explanation would be beneficial as to the following specific items in the market data analysis:

Address—identify location of subject property and all comparables with exact street number and name as well as the name of the town or city in which the property is located.

Proximity to Subject—give the distance of the comparable from the subject property in terms of blocks, fractions of a mile or miles as the case may be as well as the direction.

Sale Price—state the price for which the subject property and the comparables sold.

Price/Living Area—calculate the total sales price per square foot of gross above-grade building (living) area in order to provide this indicator of value.

Data Source—give the source from which the data pertaining to each comparable were obtained—e.g. deed records, recordation tax stamps, brokers, multiple listings, data bank, buyer or seller, etc.

Date of Sale and Time Adjustment—provide the month, day, and year of sale for the subject property and each comparable. Then proceed to make the appropriate adjustment indicated by the market for the time difference between the date of sale and the date of appraisal. Of course, the comparables should be as current as possible in order to reduce the risk of error in making the adjustment.

Location—give an overall quality rating (e.g. good, average, etc.) for the subject and a comparison rating (e.g. superior, equal, inferior) for the comparables and make the adjustment indicated by the market for differences between the comparables and the subject property.

Site/View—an overall quality rating of good, average, fair or poor is to be given for the subject property and a comparison rating, as indicated under "location" above, should be provided for both site and view for each comparable. However, if an adjustment is being made for site features but not for view or vice-versa, enter the item in the box in lieu of the comparison rating so that the reviewer will know for what specific factor the adjustment was made. Factors to be considered by the appraiser under site include size, shape, topography, drainage, encroachments, easements or any detrimental site conditions.

Design and Appeal—this adjustment category considers such aspects of the property as appeal of exterior design, inferior attractiveness and special features, and any other characteristics which would make the property attractive or unattractive to purchasers in general and otherwise enhance, or detract from, its marketability. The appraiser is to rate the subject property in accordance with the ratings given in the building description on page 1 of the form and is to give comparison ratings, as indicated for the preceding items above, for each of the comparables. The appropriate adjustments may then be made.

Quality of Construction—this item covers quality of materials and workmanship in all respects, including exterior walls, roof covering, framing (walls, floor, and roof), finish flooring, interior walls, trim, doors, hardware, plumbing and electrical systems, baths, kitchen, and mechanical equipment. The appraiser is to indicate an overall quality rating for the subject property commensurate with the rating shown on page 1 of the form and is to give comparison ratings, as indicated previously, for each of the comparables. The adjustments are to reflect the market's monetary reaction based on these comparisons.

Age—the appraiser is to report the effective age of the subject property as well as that of the comparables and make the necessary adjustments indicated by the market.

Condition—the appraiser's opinion of the condition of the subject property (whether good, average, fair or poor) is to be stated whereas for the comparables, comparison ratings of superior, equal, or inferior are to be reported and adjustments are to be made as indicated by the market.

Living Area, Room Count, and Total Living Area—the appraiser is to report the total room count (number of finished, above-grade rooms as indicated on page 1 of the form), the number of bedrooms and baths, and the total square foot living area (above grade—as obtained from the calculations in the Cost Approach) for the subject property and for each comparable. Adjustments which are reflective of the market are to be made for each item as indicated.

Basement and Basement Finished Rooms—the appraiser is to report basement improvements such as finished rooms, recreation room, etc. found in the subject property and the comparables. If there is no basement (slab or crawl space) or a partial basement, this should also be indicated. Appropriate adjustments are to be made to reflect differences between the comparables and the subject property.

Functional Utility—this item refers to room sizes and layout and, therefore, overall liveability. A rating should be given for the subject property which will summarize the ratings for these factors found on page 1 of the form. Comparison ratings such as those indicated previously are to be given for the comparables and appropriate adjustments made to represent the market's reaction to any differences.

Air Conditioning—the presence or absence of this feature and the type thereof (central, sleeve or window units) are to be noted for the subject property as well as the comparables and adjustments made accordingly.

Garage/Car Port—the appraiser is to report and make adjustments on the basis of whether the subject property and the comparables have garages or carports and, if so, the capacity in terms of the number of cars. This increase or decrease in value should not necessarily represent the cost of construction but should rather be based on the market's response.

Porches, Patio, Pools, etc.—the appraiser should indicate the presence or absence of these or similar exterior building or site improvements and make the necessary adjustments indicated by the market. Cost data may, at times, serve as a guide but are not necessarily indicative since improvements such as pools may not return their entire cost upon resale as added value.

Other—the items under this heading are to be reported for the subject property and the comparables whether or not adjustments are being made. The items shown are simply intended to illustrate some of the more common features which may be found and for which adjustments may be appropriate. Therefore, the appraiser should not feel constrained to consider only the physical features shown.

Sales or Financing Concessions—the monetary value of concessions such as builder or seller price discounts, financing charges or benefits (e.g. loan points which are included in the sale price, "buy-downs" of the mortgage interest rate by the builder), gifts of merchandise (e.g. "a free new car in the garage with every purchase") must be reported for the subject property and the comparables and the value adjusted accordingly. It is not acceptable for the appraiser to simply ignore these items and say that they have no effect upon value.

The two blank lines following the above item are for such other adjustments as the appraiser feels are appropriate under the circumstances of the particular appraisal assignment and are intended to provide the appraiser with sufficient flexibility to do a professional job.

Net Adjustments (Total)—report the net total of the adjustments made for all the above items and indicate whether, on balance, the total is plus or minus. If the total adjustments appear excessive in relation to the sale price, the appraiser would be well advised to re-examine the comparable for comparability.

Indicated Value of Subject—add or subtract the net total adjustments from the sale price at the top of each column to arrive at the value of the subject property indicated by each of the comparables. It is expected that the indicated values will not be identical for all comparables.

Comments on Market Data—reconcile the values indicated by the comparables as adjusted in the market data analysis above and explain the reasons for giving more weight to one comparable over the others.

Indicated Value by Market Data Approach—the estimated value resulting from reconciliation.

VIII.   Indicated Value by the Income Approach

If the subject property is located in a neighborhood where rentals predominate and rental data are readily available together with sales, then this approach to value should be used prior to final reconciliation. If the final estimate of value is based upon the Income Approach, the supporting rental and sales data along with calculations of the indicated rent multipliers must be attached as an addendum to the report.

IX.   Requirements of the Appraisal, Comments, and Final Reconciliation

Indicate by checking the appropriate box whether the subject property was appraised in "as is" condition or whether the appraisal is based on certain repairs, alterations, or other conditions in order to achieve the estimated value. Also, if the property being appraised is proposed or under construction, indicate that the valuation is subject to satisfactory completion in accordance with plans and specifications.

Comments and Conditions of Appraisal—this space is to be used to itemize in detail the required repairs or other conditions as indicated above together with the estimated cost thereof. Comments on any portion of the report are also appropriate in this section if further explanation is needed to support the property analysis or the value estimate. If the space provided is not sufficient, attach an addendum to the report.

Final Reconciliation—the appraiser is to explain in this space the relevance and validity of each approach to value and present justification for the value selected as the final value estimate. It should be emphasized that final reconciliation is not an averaging process.

X.   Other Requirements for Completion of Form

The appraiser is to indicate, by checking the appropriate box, whether FNMA Form 1004B (Certification, Contingent and Limiting Conditions, and Market Value Definition) has previously been filed with the client (seller) and, if so, on what date. This procedure may be followed only if these items are applicable to the appraisal at hand and do not vary from the previous appraisal for which Form 1004B was submitted. The date of such filing must then be given in every instance. Otherwise, since it is recognized that a particular appraisal assignment may require different or additional limiting conditions, the appraiser may add these to Form 1004B and file it with the report. However, if there are no such changes, the appraiser may prefer, as a matter of practice, to file Form 1004B with the client in connection with each report. This, of course, will also be acceptable.

The appraiser is expected to be familiar with these instructions for proper completion of the appraisal report and, by signing the report, certifies that it is in compliance with the instructions.

The estimated market value is to be reported as of a specific date and in numbers which have been rounded off to the nearest one hundred dollars.

The space for the signature of a review appraiser has been provided only in recognition of the fact that some appraisals will be performed by multi-appraiser firms which require that the principal of the firm co-sign each report. Only in such instances will a review appraiser's signature be applicable. In this event, it should be indicated whether the review appraiser co-signing the report has personally inspected the property.

SUGGESTED READINGS
BY SELECTED TOPICS

Adjustable-Rate Mortgages

Bible, Douglas S. "Adjustable Mortgage Loans as Shaped by FHLMC." *Real Estate Review* (Spring 1982): 70–74.

Goodman, John, and Charles Luckett. "Adjustable-Rate Financing in Mortgage and Consumer Credit Markets." *Federal Reserve Bulletin* (November 1985): 823–835.

Naiman, Judith. "ARMs Poised for Big Gains." *Freddie Mac Reports* (August 1987): 1–2.

Stamper, Michael K. "Building ARM Strength." *Freddie Mac Reports* (February 1988): 1–2.

Apartment Building Financing

Smith, Charles C., and Harold A. Lubell. "New Look at Apartment House Financing." *Real Estate Review* (Spring 1977): 13–16.

Bankruptcy and Default

Pace, Kelly, Clifford Cox, and Henry Wichman. "The Adverse Tax Consequences of a Real Estate Loan Default." *Real Estate Review* (Fall 1987): 92–95.

Rasmussen, Vaughn B., II. "Dealing with the Buyer of Property in Trouble." *Real Estate Review* (Winter 1976): 39–44.

Smith, Charles C., and Harold A. Lubell. "Lender Looks at Bankruptcy." *Real Estate Review* (Fall 1976): 7–11.

Collateralized Mortgage Obligations

Bergman, Dru. "CMO Conduits Provide New Routes to the Capital Markets." *Freddie Mac Reports* (October 1985): 1–2.

Bergman, Dru. "Highs and Lows for CMOs." *Freddie Mac Reports* (November 1986): 1–2.

Condominiums and Cooperatives

Cirz, Raymond T. "Valuation and Condominium Conversion." *The Appraisal Journal* (January 1982): 43–56.

Levin, Michael R. "Financing the Commercial Condominium." *Real Estate Review* (Winter 1975): 71–77.

Pollack, Bruce. "Valuation of Cooperative Apartment Buildings." *The Appraisal Journal* (April 1982): 243–252.

Rosenstein, James. "New Tax Advantages of Condo and Co-op Conversions." *Real Estate Review* (Fall 1987): 42–45.

Weiss, Stephen J. "The Legal Corner: When Co-op. Shares and Condominiums Constitute Securities." *Real Estate Review* (Winter 1976): 15–17.

Construction Loans

Goldberg, Alfred M. "How HUD Handles Its Problem Construction Loans." *Real Estate Review* (Winter 1976): 45–48.

Hall, Cary H. "Successful Construction Loan Demands Expert Supervision, Careful Planning." *The Mortgage Banker* (October 1976): 92–98.

Roberts, Paul E. "Working Out the Construction Mortgage Loan." *Real Estate Review* (Summer 1975): 50–57.

Tockarshewsky, J. B. "Reducing the Risks in Construction Lending." *Real Estate Review* (Spring 1977): 59–63.

Wilner, Alfred. "Five Trouble Spots in Construction." *Real Estate Review* (Winter 1977): 54–57.

Convertible Adjustable-Rate Mortgages

McElhone, Josie. "Convertibles Cruise to New Popularity." *Freddie Mac Reports* (November 1987): 1–2.

Convertible Mortgages

Vitt, Lois A., and Joel H. Berstein. "Convertible Mortgages: New Financing Tool?" *Real Estate Review* (Spring 1976): 33–37.

Zachary, Peter L. "The Appraisal Implications of a Convertible Mortgage." *The Appraisal Journal* (April 1982): 182–186.

Depository Institutions Deregulation and Monetary Control Act of 1980

Gilbert, R. Alton. "Will the Removal of Regulation Q Raise Mortgage Interest Rates?" *Review,* Federal Reserve Bank of St. Louis (December 1981): 3–12.

McNeill, Charles R., and Denise M. Rechter. "The Depository Institutions Deregulation and Monetary Control Act of 1980." *Federal Reserve Bulletin* (June 1980): 444–453.

Moulton, Janice M. "Implementing the Monetary Control Act in a Troubled Environment for Thrifts." *Business Review,* Federal Reserve Bank of Philadelphia (July–August 1982): 13–21.

West, Robert Craig. "The Depository Institutions Reregulation Act of 1980: A Historical Perspective." *Economic Review,* Federal Reserve Bank of Kansas City (February 1982): 3–13.

Discount Points

Bouillon, Marvin, David Newbery, and Kanalis Ockree. "Should Points be Paid for a Lower Home Mortgage Interest Rate?" *Real Estate Issues* (Fall–Winter 1987): 25–28.

Zerbst, Robert, and William B. Brueggeman. "FHA and VA Mortgage Discount Points and Housing Prices." *Journal of Finance* (December 1977): 1766–1773.

Disintermediation

Smith, David. "Regional Impact of Disintermediation." *Journal of the Federal Home Loan Bank Board* (June 1977): 20–24.

Economic Recovery Tax Act of 1981

Brueggeman, William B., Jeffrey D. Fisher, and Jerrold J. Stern. "Choosing the Optional Depreciation Method Under 1981 Tax Legislation." *Real Estate Review* (Winter 1982): 32–37.

Brumbaugh, Mark, and Saul Fenichel. "Special Features and Opportunities in the New Tax Act." *Real Estate Review* (Winter 1982): 40–42.

Kendall, Donald R., Jr. "Give Me Shelter: The Economic Recovery Tax Act of 1981." *Real Estate Review* (Winter 1982): 24–30.

Farm Real Estate Financing

Duncan, Marvin. "Farm Real Estate: Who Buys and How?" *Monthly Review,* Federal Reserve Bank of Kansas City (June 1977): 3–9.

Federal Housing Administration

Cunningham, Robert P. "Requiem for FHA Is Premature." *The Appraisal Journal* (January 1977): 95–102.

Federal National Mortgage Association

Eisman, Eugene R. "Getting it Together: FNMA Conventional Mortgage-Backed Securities." *Seller/Servicer* (October 1981): 1–3.

Kaufman, Herbert M. "FNMA Auction Results as a Forecaster of Residential Mortgage Yields." *Journal of Money, Credit, and Banking* (August 1981): 352–364.

"Participations: A New Way to Do Business with FNMA." *Seller/Servicer* (October 1981): 10.

Financial Futures

Chicago Board of Trade. *An Introduction to Financial Futures* (Chicago 1982).

Chicago Board of Trade. *Financial Instruments Markets: Cash-Futures Relationships* (Chicago 1980).

Chicago Mercantile Exchange. *Treasury Bill Futures* (Chicago 1979).

Ederington, Louis H. "The Hedging Performance of the New Futures Markets." *Journal of Finance* (March 1979): 157–170.

McCarthy, Michael P., and William C. Handorf. "Successful Developers Are Trading in Interest Rate Futures." *Real Estate Review* (Winter 1980): 29–34.

Financing (General)

Smith, Charles C., and Harold A. Lubell. "Real Estate Financing: Handling Condemnation Awards and Insurance Proceeds." *Real Estate Review* (Winter 1976): 8–10.

Smith, Charles C., and Harold A. Lubell. "Real Estate Financing: Protecting the Lender." *Real Estate Review* (Summer 1977): 14–16.

Government National Mortgage Association

Connally, James J. "Historical Analysis of GNMA's Activity Can Clarify Current Yields." *The Mortgage Banker* (May 1977): 83–93.

Mitchell, Douglas W. "GNMA Pass-Through Certificates." *Journal of Banking and Finance* (Spring 1981): 547–556.

Senft, Dexter E. "The 'True Yield' of a Pass-Through Security." *The Mortgage Banker* (September 1979): 15–19.

Stuckey, Richard. "GNMA Options Markets." *Seller/Service* (October 1981): 20–23.

The Ginnie Mae Manual. GNMA Mortgage-Backed Securities Dealers Association. Homewood, Ill.: Dow Jones-Irwin, 1978.

Historic Properties

Oldham, Sally G. "Historic Properties: Variable Valuations." *The Appraisal Journal* (July 1982): 364–377.

Home Equity Loans

Bergman, Dru. "Raising HEL: The Equity Lending Boom." *Freddie Mac Reports* (September 1987): 1–2.

Housing and Mortgage Market Developments

Gabriel, Stuart A. "Housing and Mortgage Markets: The Post-1982 Expansion". *Federal Reserve Bulletin* (December 1987): 893–903.

Housing Costs

Crone, Theodore. "Housing Costs After Tax Reform." *Business Review,* Federal Reserve Bank of Philadelphia (March–April 1987): 3–12.

Housing Patterns and Developments

Cloos, George W., and William R. Sayre. "Bull Market in Homes." *Economic Perspectives,* Federal Reserve Bank of Chicago (July–August 1977): 7–16.

Seiders, David F. "Changing Patterns of Housing Finance." *Federal Reserve Bulletin* (June 1980): 461–472.

Seiders, David F. "Changing Patterns of Housing Finance." *Federal Reserve Bulletin* (June 1981): 461–472.

Stevens, Neil A. "Housing: A Cyclical Industry on the Upswing." *Review,* Federal Reserve Bank of St. Louis (August 1976): 15–20.

Housing Subsidies

Brueggeman, William B. "Federal Housing Subsidies: Conceptual Issues and Benefit Patterns." *Journal of Economics and Business* (Winter 1975): 141–149.

Halperin, Jerome Y., and Michael J. Brenner. "Opportunities Under the New Section 8 Housing Program." *Real Estate Review* (Spring 1976): 67–75.

Shilton, Leon. "Judging Investment Quality of Section 8 Housing." *Real Estate Review* (Spring 1982): 53–60.

Installment Sales

Zerbst, Robert H. "Installment Sales Are Not Always Better." *Real Estate Review* (Spring 1982): 28–32.

Interest Rate Swaps

Szabo, Andrew. "Interest Rate Swaps: A Powerful Tool in Real Estate Finance." *Real Estate Review* (Winter 1988): 37–43.

International Mortgage Markets

Bergman, Dru. "U.S. Mortgage Securities Gaining Foothold in Overseas Markets." *Freddie Mac Reports* (June 1986): 1–2.

Cheng, Anna. "International Debt Financing for Real Estate." *Real Estate Review* (Summer 1982): 40–44.

Interval Ownership

Kirby, Thomas R. "Appraisal of Timeshare Resort Conversions." *The Appraisal Journal* (July 1982): 417–427.

Smith, Jeremy D. "Urban Time-Sharing: A Major Growth Area." *Real Estate Review* (Summer 1982): 69–74.

Investment Analysis

Dickerson, Frederick G. "A Technique for the Analysis of Owner-Financed Sales." *The Appraisal Journal* (January 1976): 55–62.

Webb, James R. "Yields for Selected Types of Real Property vs. the Money and Capital Markets." *The Appraisal Journal* (April 1982): 228–242.

Whisler, William D. "Analyzing the Effects of Deviations from Forecasts in Real Estate Investment Analysis." *The Appraisal Journal* (January 1977): 35–48.

Wiley, Robert J. "Real Estate Investment Analysis: An Empirical Study." *The Appraisal Journal* (October 1976): 586–592.

Investment in Housing

Mills, Edwin S. "Dividing up the Investment Pie: Have we Overinvested in Housing?" *Business Review,* Federal Reserve Bank of Philadelphia (March–April 1987): 13–23.

Joint Ventures

Corgel, John, and Ronald C. Rogers. "Corporate Real Estate Joint Ventures and Security Price Performance." *Real Estate Issues* (Fall–Winter 1987): 1–4.

Leasing

Kalil, Greg. "Lease Valuation and Comparison with ELR." *Real Estate Review* (Summer 1987): 32–38.

Legislation (General)

Duffy, Robert E., Jr. "The Real Estate Settlement Procedures Act of 1974." *Real Estate Review* (Winter 1976): 86–93.

Haney, Richard L., Jr. "ECOA and the Real Estate Broker." *Real Estate Review* (Spring 1982): 108–110.

Lynch, James D. "New Uniform Laws Are Proposed That Will Affect Real Estate Transactions." *Mortgage Banker* (August 1979): 18–22.

Limited Partnerships

Ross, Stan. "Real Estate Master Limited Partnerships: Why Investors Like Them." *Real Estate Review* (Spring 1987): 28–37.

Thompson, Mark. "Valuing Interests in Real Estate Limited Partnerships." *Real Estate Review* (Fall 1987): 36–41.

Loan Assumptions

Roberts, Ralph M. "The Value of an Assumption." *The Appraisal Journal* (July 1982): 428–433.

Mortgage Banking

"Mortgage Banking in the 1980's." Special issue of *Mortgage Banker* (April 1980): 29–51.

Mortgage Futures Market

Stevens, Neil A. "A Mortgage Futures Market: Its Development, Uses, Benefits and Costs." *Review,* Federal Reserve Bank of St. Louis (April 1976): 12–19.

Mortgage Interest Rate Ceilings

Peters, Helen F. "The Mortgage Market: A Place for Ceilings." *Business Review,* Federal Reserve Bank of Philadelphia (July–August 1977): 13–21.

Mortgage Liens

Boyd, Brook. "When the Mortgage Lien Doesn't Protect the Lender." *Real Estate Review* (Summer 1987): 94–97.

Mortgage Prepayments

Kinkade, Maurice E. "Mortgage Prepayments and Their Effects on S & L's." *FHLBB Journal* (January 1976): 12–18.

Mortgage Types

Federal Home Loan Bank of San Francisco. *Solving the Mortgage Menu Problem.* Proceedings of the Tenth Annual Conference, 11–12 December 1984.

Office Buildings and Shopping Centers

Cymrot, Allen, Abraham Gelber, and Lynda L. Cole. "How to Invest in Office Buildings and Shopping Centers." *Real Estate Review* (Summer 1982): 75–82.

Participating Mortgages

Kelly, Peter. "Advantages of Participating Mortgages." *Real Estate Review* (Spring 1987): 54–57.

Pension Funds and Trusts

Cheng, Anna. "Marketing Real Estate to Pension Funds." *Real Estate Review* (Spring 1982): 61–64.

Davidson, Harold A. "The Pension Funds' Increasing Real Estate Commitment." *Real Estate Review* (Spring 1981): 115–119.

Project Analysis

Lewis, Barbara. "Real Estate Project Analysis Using an Annualized Rate of Return." *Real Estate Review* (Winter 1988): 68–72.

Purchase Money Mortgages

Bell, Robert. "Negotiating the Purchase-Money Mortgage." *Real Estate Review* (Spring 1977): 51–58.

Rates of Return

Messner, Stephen D., and M. Chapman Findlay, III. "Real Estate Investment Analysis: IRR versus FMRR." *The Real Estate Appraiser* (July–August 1975).

Raper, Charles F. "Internal Rate of Return—Handle with Care." *The Appraisal Journal* (July 1976): 405–411.

Strung, Joseph. "The Internal Rate of Return and the Reinvestment Presumptions." *The Appraisal Journal* (January 1976): 23–33.

Viscione, Jerry A., and Ronald Porter. "IRR Analysis May Not Yield the Best Results." *Real Estate Review* (Summer 1980): 97–101.

Real Estate Franchises

Dowling, Raymond B., and Mary Alice Hines. "Here Come the Real Estate Franchises." *Real Estate Review* (Summer 1977): 48–52.

Real Estate Investment Trusts

Carrigan, Richard T., and Don M. Enders. "Don't Weep for the REITs: The New Valuation Rules Won't Hurt." *Real Estate Review* (Summer 1977): 65–71.

Hines, Mary Alice. "The REIT Shakeout in 1974." *Real Estate Review* (Winter 1975): 56–59.

Stevenson, Howard H. "What Went Wrong with the REITs?" *The Appraisal Journal* (April 1977): 249–260.

Wurtzebach, Charles H. "An Institutional Explanation of Poor REIT Performance." *The Appraisal Journal* (January 1977): 103–109.

Real Estate Law

Anderson, Ronald A. *Business Law.* Revised Edition. Cincinnati: South-Western Publishing Co., 1987, Part 9.

French, William B., and Harold F. Lusk. *Law of the Real Estate Business.* 5th ed. Homewood, Ill.: Richard D. Irwin, Inc., 1984.

Fusilier, H. L. *Real Estate Law.* Boulder, Col.: Business Research Division, University of Colorado, 1977.

Kratovil, Robert, and Raymond J. Werner. *Real Estate Law.* 7th ed. Englewood Cliffs, N.J.: Prentice-Hall, Inc. 1979.

Real Estate Principles

Unger, Maurice A., and George R. Karvel. *Real Estate: Principles and Practices.* 8th ed. Cincinnati: South-Western Publishing Co., 1987.

Sales and Leasebacks

Handorf, William, and Gordon May. "Making Fixed Assets Work: Sell Your Building and Lease it Back? It's a Possible Source of Investable Funds." *Journal of the Federal Home Loan Bank Board* (October 1976).

Haymes, Allan. "Real Estate Dealing: Survival of a Business with a Sale-Leaseback." *Real Estate Review* (Winter 1976): 12–14.

Sillcocks, H. Jackson. "Financial Sense in Real Estate Sales and Leasebacks." *Real Estate Review* (Spring 1975): 89–95.

Secondary Mortgage Market

"Legislative Changes Broaden Powers of Secondary Market." *Freddie Mac Reports* (November 1984): 1–2.

Wiggin, Charles E. "Doing Business in the Secondary Market." *Real Estate Review* (Summer 1975): 84–95.

Second Mortgages

Bergman, Dru. "Second Mortgages Build Image as First-Class Investments." *Freddie Mac Reports* (November 1985): 1–2.

Securities Innovations

"Securities Innovations Designed to Attract New Investors." *Freddie Mac Reports* (July 1984): 1, 5.

"Mortgage Securities Spur New Financing Techniques." *Freddie Mac Reports* (May 1985): 1–2.

Securitization

Benveniste, Lily and Frank Nothaft. "Mortgage Market Success Spurs Securitization of Other Assets." *Freddie Mac Reports* (May 1987): 1–2.

Wolf, Rosalie. "Securitization of Commercial Real Estate: An opportunity for Pension Funds." *Real Estate Review* (Winter 1988): 52–55.

Subdivisions

Maes, Marvin A. "Subdivision Analysis: A Case Study." *The Appraisal Journal* (January 1982): 100–112.

Tax Exempt Mortgages

Marvel, Josiah, and Peter A. Louis. "The Tax Exempt Mortgage: Solutions to High Interest Rates." *Real Estate Review* (Summer 1977): 44–47.

Williams, Marvin. "Financing Shopping Centers with Tax-Free Funds." *Real Estate Review* (Winter 1976): 67–71.

Tax Reform Act of 1986

Brueggeman, William, and Thomas Thibodeau. "Real Estate Returns and Market Responses to 1986 Tax Reform." *Real Estate Review* (Spring 1987): 69–76.

Rollain, James, Patric Hendershott, and David Ling. "The Impact of the 1986 Tax Reform Act on Real Estate." *Real Estate Review* (Spring 1987): 76–83.

Variable-Rate Mortgages

Brueggeman, William B., and Jerome B. Baesel. "The Mechanics of Variable Rate Mortgages and Implications for Home Ownership as an Inflation Hedge." *The Appraisal Journal* (April 1976): 236–246.

Epley, Donald R. "Variable Mortgage Plans and Their Unsolved Issues." *The Appraisal Journal* (April 1977): 242–248.

Gevedon, Everett B. "Equivalent Constants for Variable Rate Mortgages." *The Appraisal Journal* (July 1982): 403–409.

Lusht, Kenneth M. "A New Twist to the Variable Payment Mortgages." *Real Estate Review* (Summer 1977): 72–76.

Millar, James A., and Stanley R. Stansell. "A Comparison of the Characteristics of Fixed and Variable Rate Mortgages." *The Appraisal Journal* (January 1976): 63–68.

Tucker, Donald P. "The Variable-Rate Graduated-Payment Mortgage." *Real Estate Review* (Spring 1975): 71–80.

Wraparound Mortgages

Leider, Arnold. "How to Wrap Around a Mortgage." *Real Estate Review* (Winter 1975): 29–34.

Valachi, Donald. "Calculating True Yields on Wrap-Arounds." *Real Estate Review* (Winter 1977): 92–99.

GLOSSARY OF SELECTED TERMS

Abstract of Title. A condensed history of recorded documents affecting title to a specific parcel of real estate.

Accelerated Cost Recovery System (ACRS). A system developed under the Economic Recovery Tax Act of 1981 to depreciate recovery property (i.e., property held to produce income or used in a business that is tangible and depreciable).

Accelerated Depreciation. A method for writing-off the value of an asset over time such that larger deductions occur during the early years of the asset's economic life and lower deductions occur during later years.

Acceleration Clause. In the event of default by the borrower in terms of interest and/or principal, this clause in a mortgage instrument provides for the entire debt to be immediately due.

Adjustable-Rate Mortgage (ARM). A mortgage where the interest rate varies with changes in some predetermined index reflecting the cost of funds. Also referred to as a variable-rate mortgage.

Advance Commitment. A forward commitment from a permanent investor (often an insurance company or mutual savings bank) to purchase mortgage loans which will be placed on a property. This is done in advance of construction.

After-Tax Cash Flow. After-tax profit plus depreciation charges (which are noncash write-offs).

Amortization. The systematic repayment of a loan in which the principal amount is repaid in installments over the life of the loan.

Annual Percentage Rate. The effective annualized interest cost that must be reported under Truth in Lending requirements.

Annuity. A term used to describe a series of payments or receipts of a fixed amount that will continue over several time periods.

Annuity Due. An annuity involving fixed periodic payments or receipts that occur at the beginning of each period.

Assets. Anything of economic value such as real and personal property.

Assignment. The transfer of contract rights associated with a mortgage or other instrument such as a bond or lease by an assignor to an assignee.

Assumption. A contractual arrangement whereby a purchaser of property takes over or assumes the obligations of an existing mortgage.

Balloon Payment. A final large payment that results at maturity when the periodic installment payments are not adequate to retire the principal amount of debt.

Banking System. A financial system comprised of the four basic depository institutions (commercial banks, savings and loan associations, mutual savings banks, and credit unions).

Bankruptcy. A legal procedure, carried out under the jurisdiction of courts of law, whereby a debtor's property is taken over for the benefit of the creditors.

Basis. The difference between the cash price and the futures price for a commodity.

Basket Loan. A loan made as a result of a provision in the regulatory acts governing investments by insurance companies allowing for a percentage of total assets to be placed in otherwise unauthorized or illegal investments.

Beneficiary. The lender in a deed of trust.

Blanket Mortgage. A mortgage that is secured by the pledge of more than one parcel of property.

Bondable Lease. This lease must be noncancellable by the tenant for any default on the part of the landlord. Security to the lender is provided by both the real estate and the high credit rating of the tenant.

Book Value. The value of an asset remaining after accumulated depreciation has been deducted from the asset's original cost.

Buy-Down Mortgage. A process of putting money "up front" to reduce monthly mortgage payments.

Call Second Mortgage. A second mortgage giving the lender the right to "call" it at a time prior to its termination date.

Capitalization Rate. A discount or interest rate used to find the present value of a series of future cash flows. This also is commonly referred to as the *discount rate*.

Chattel Mortgage. A mortgage on personal property such as equipment.

Collateral. Assets used as security for a loan.

Collateralized Mortgage Obligation (CMO). A variation of the mortgage-backed security which was designed to offer cash flows to investors more like those received by holders of government and corporate bonds. An investor in a CMO owns one of several classes of "bonds" that are backed by a pool of mortgages, or even mortgage-backed securities. Interest is paid on all existing bonds, while principal repayments are made class by class.

Compound Interest. Interest is earned on the original principal and on accrued interest (i.e., interest on interest). Through the process of compounding, a current investment will increase in value over time.

Condominium. An ownership in fee simple by an individual of a single unit in a multi-unit structure, coupled with ownership of an undivided interest in the land and other elements of the structure held in common with other unit owners of the building.

Construction Loan. Usually a short-term mortgage loan designed to finance construction of buildings on a property whereby periodic advances are made by the lender to the builder as the work progresses.

Conventional Mortgage. A mortgage loan without governmental backing in the form of Federal Housing Administration insurance or Veterans Administration guarantees.

Conventionally-Insured Mortgage. A conventional mortgage which is insured by a private mortgage company.

Convertible Adjustable-Rate Mortgage. A variation of the standard adjustable-rate mortgage (ARM) where the buyer is given the option to convert an ARM to a fixed-rate mortgage.

Cooperative Dwelling. A building in which a tenant purchases stock in the corporation that owns the building rather than renting an individual unit in the building.

Cost-to-Replace Approach (to appraisal). Generally, the replacement cost of the building minus depreciation plus the value of the land equals the estimated value of the property.

Covenants. Detailed clauses in loan agreements that are designed to protect lenders.

Debt Service. The periodic payment of principal and interest required in the loan agreement.

Deed. A written instrument by which title to real property is transferred from one person to another person.

Deed of Trust. A deed absolute to secure the payment of a debt.

Default. The failure to fulfill a contractual obligation when it comes due such as the failure to make interest and/or principal payments.

Depository Institutions Deregulation Act. An act whose purpose was to phase out and finally eliminate interest rate ceilings on interest and dividends that could be paid by depository institutions.

Depository Institutions Deregulation and Monetary Control Act of 1980 (DIDMCA). Significant banking legislation providing for the deregulation of depository institution activities and operations, and for improved monetary policy control by the Federal Reserve System.

Depreciation. The decline in the value over time of an asset as it is used or depreciates. This also refers to the writing-off of the value of the asset over time.

Discount Points. Mortgages that are issued below market interest rates are discounted in terms of points, where 1 point equals 1 percent, in order to increase the effective yield. Points are subtracted from the face value of the loan.

Discount Rate. The interest rate used to find the present worth or value of a series of future cash flows. It is often called the *capitalization rate*.

Disintermediation. The process whereby savings are withdrawn from thrift institutions and commercial banks and are channeled into alternative investments.

Due-on-Sale Clause. A clause which is inserted by lenders in conventional mortgages stating that the mortgagor cannot have a buyer assume the mortgage without the consent of the lender. Also called a non-assumption clause.

Earnest Money. Money deposited by the purchaser to show evidence of good faith and intent to complete an agreement.

Economic Life. The useful life of a property.

Economic Recovery Tax Act of 1981. Legislation providing for a reduction in individual and corporate income taxes as well as a major over-hauling of acceptable methods for depreciating personal and real property in the form of the accelerated cost recovery system.

Eminent Domain. The right of the government or a governmental agency to take private property for public use, provided just compensation is paid to the owner.

Equal Credit Opportunity Act. Regulation B of the Federal Reserve Board prohibiting discrimination in lending on the basis of sex or marital status.

Equity. The owner's interest or share of value in a property. This is determined as the difference between the current market value of the property and any outstanding loans or mortgage debt.

Escalator Clause. A clause in a loan instrument that permits the lender to raise or lower the rate of interest in a loan agreement on the basis of some schedule or index.

Escrow. Something of value such as real or personal property held by a third party until the performance of certain conditions or the happening of some act.

Estoppel Certificate. An instrument executed by a mortgagor showing the amount of the unpaid balance due on a mortgage and stating that the mortgagor will furnish a written statement, duly acknowledged, of the amount due on the mortgage and whether any offsets or defenses exist against the mortgage debt.

Extension Agreement. As an alternative to foreclosure, this device is used to extend the due date of the mortgage, and in some cases to modify the original note and mortgage.

Facilitating Function. An intermediary function in the overall or broad mortgage market performed by mortgage banking firms.

Federal Deposit Insurance Corporation (FDIC). This agency insures deposits and supervises member commercial banks.

Federal Funds. Short-term loans, usually on a daily basis, from one bank to another bank.

Federal Home Loan Bank System. This system, which is headed by the Federal Home Loan Bank Board (FHLBB), supervises and regulates member savings and loan associations.

Federal Home Loan Mortgage Corporation (FHLMC). This agency provides a secondary market for the mortgages written by savings and loan associations that are members of the Federal Home Loan Bank System.

Federal Housing Administration (FHA). This agency provides mortgage loan insurance on homes that meet FHA requirements and standards.

Federal Land Bank. An agency under which mortgages are given to buy land for agricultural use and to provide buildings.

Federal National Mortgage Association (FNMA). This corporation purchases and sells mortgages in the secondary mortgage market. Although privately owned, the corporation is government regulated.

Federal Reserve System. This system, which is headed by the Federal Reserve Board, sets monetary policy and supervises and regulates member commercial banks.

Federal Savings and Loan Insurance Corporation (FSLIC). This agency insures deposits and supervises member savings and loan associations.

Fee Simple. A title to property without restrictions. This legal term indicates absolute ownership.

FHA-Insured Mortgage. A mortgage loan that is insured by the Federal Housing Administration.

First Mortgage. The first mortgage in point of time recorded by the holder thereof, which mortgage has priority over any subsequently recorded mortgage.

Fiscal Policy. Efforts to "manage" the economy through government spending, taxation of individuals and institutions, and public debt management. Fiscal policy is established by the executive and legislative branches of government.

Flexible Payment Mortgage. A mortgage designed for young homeowners where payments will increase as earning power increases.

Foreclosure. Legal action to collect a debt against property secured by a mortgage.

Fractional Reserve System. A portion of deposits at commercial banks and other depository institutions that must be held as required reserves so that 100 percent of deposits are not available for lending or investing.

Fully Modified Passthrough Securities. Monthly fixed payments of principal and interest are paid to certificate holders whether or not the payments have been collected from the mortgagors on these GNMA securities.

Future Value. The worth at a specific point in the future of an amount received or paid today.

Futures Contract. A standardized agreement to make or take delivery of a specified amount and quality of the commodity, at a specified future time and price, and at a place designated by the originating commodity exchange.

Gap Financing. A form of financing sometimes called "bridge" or "swing" financing and in effect a second or junior lien which is paid off when a permanent lender pays the full amount of the money due under a first mortgage.

Garn-St. Germain Act. A banking act which focused primarily on assisting savings and loan associations by permitting them to issue adjustable-rate mortgages, commercial loans, and nonresidential real estate loans.

General Monetary Controls. Controls used by the Federal Reserve to regulate and control the level and changes in the supply of money and the availability of credit. The general controls involve reserve requirements, the discount rate, open-market operations, and moral suasion.

Government National Mortgage Association (GNMA). A government-owned corporation that participates in the secondary mortgage market.

Graduated Payment Mortgage. A mortgage that calls for small payments in the beginning and larger payments at the end.

Gross Lease. A type of lease, also called a flat lease, in which the premises are rented at a fixed rate.

Ground Lease. A device permitting the ground and the improvements to be owned by different persons.

Growing Equity Mortgage (GEM). A mortgage that provides for accelerated principal repayments because there is a "step-up" in monthly mortgage payments each year, with all of the increase being used to pay off the principal.

Guaranteed Mortgage Certificate (GMC). An instrument which gives ownership interest in a pool of mortgages under which interest payments are received semiannually (as is the case with most bonds) and principal payments are passed through annually to investors by the FHLMC.

Hedging. The process of buying or selling a futures contract to "lock-in" a current commodity price, or a financial instrument price, even though interest rates may change.

Home Equity Mortgage. A revolving line of credit based on the equity in a home. These loans are sometimes referred to as home equity loans or HELs.

Housing and Urban Development, Department of (HUD). Created in 1965, HUD has a wide range of responsibilities including the regulation of the Federal Housing Administration and the Government National Mortgage Association.

Income Approach (to appraisal). This approach assumes that the property value is equal to the present worth of future income.

Indexed Lease. A lease with a clause providing for periodic rental increases based on a well-defined index.

Initial Margin. The portion of the commodity contract price that is deposited with a commodities broker at the time the contract is entered into.

Installment Land Contract. A contract used in the sale of property whereby the title is not conveyed until the installment payments are completed.

Interest-Only Loans. These loans, as their name implies, require payment over a number of years of interest only.

Intermediation. The process of accumulating savings in financial institutions and then lending or investing (supplying) funds.

Internal Rate of Return (IRR). This is the actual compound rate of return on an investment and is found by determining the discount rate which equates the present value of future cash flows with the investment's cost.

Interstate Land Sales Full Disclosure Act. Legislation passed in 1969 requiring subdividers of certain real property to make full disclosure of relevant information to buyers prior to a sale.

Junior Lien. A lien that is subordinate to another lien or mortgage. Examples of a junior lien include a second purchase money mortgage, a second contract for deed, and a wraparound mortgage.

Junior Mortgage. A mortgage that is subordinate to another mortgage. A similar relationship would hold in terms of a *junior lien*.

Lease. A contract creating a landlord and tenant relationship.

Lessee. This is the tenant in a lease contract which creates a landlord and tenant relationship.

Lessor. This is the landlord in a lease contract which creates a landlord and tenant relationship.

Leverage. The use of borrowed funds that have a fixed cost to purchase property.

Lien. A legal claim that is placed against property as security for payment of a debt.

Limited Partnership. A partnership consisting of a general partner with unlimited liability and limited partners who are equity investors. Limited partner liability is generally limited to the amount of the equity investment.

Loan-To-Value Ratio. The percentage relationship between the amount of a mortgage loan and value of the property.

Market Data Approach (to appraisal). This is sometimes called the "sales-comparison approach" and it involves a comparison of sales prices that have been obtained for like properties.

Master Limited Partnership (MLP). A large partnership with interests (shares) that are sold in organized securities markets. The MLP has many corporate characteristics but also provides limited partnership attributes such as the pass through of certain deductions and avoidance of double taxation.

Mechanic's Lien. This device gives the right of lien to those persons (e.g., contractors, laborers, engineers, etc.) who have furnished work or materials for the improvement of real property.

Monetary Control Act. Through this Act efforts were made to improve the Fed's ability to control the nation's money supply and to implement monetary policy. Provision was made for imposing universal reserve requirements on all depository institutions.

Monetary Policy. Policy established by the Federal Reserve which involves efforts to "manage" the economy by controlling the supply and cost of money and the availability of credit.

Money Market Certificates. Certificates issued by depository institutions. Rates are determined based on Treasury bill auction results and once issued the certificates carry a fixed interest rate until maturity.

Mortgage. A pledge of property as security for the payment of a debt.

Mortgage-Backed Security. A security or investment instrument representing shares in an underlying pool of FHA, VA, or conventional mortgage loans. The security issued against the pool of mortgages is "collateralized" by the underlying mortgage loans which, in turn, are said to be "securitized."

Mortgage Banker. A financial intermediary that originates mortgage loans and services mortgage loans.

Mortgage Broker. An agent that brings together buyers and sellers for real estate loans but does not service the mortgages.

Mortgage Loan Participations. Joint participation in a mortgage loan by several lenders, which often occurs when a single lender cannot meet the total amount requested.

Mortgage Market. Broadly defined, this market involves three types of transactions—the primary mortgage market, the facilitating function, and the secondary mortgage market.

Mortgage Participation Certificate (PC). An instrument which gives an ownership interest in a pool of mortgages and provides for the passing through of monthly interest and principal payments to the security holder with the payments being guaranteed by the FHLMC.

Mortgage Pass-Through Securities. Securities that provide for the "passing-through" to security holders of interest and principal amortization payments made on the underlying mortgages.

Mortgagee. The lender of money secured by the mortgage.

Mortgagor. The borrower of the money secured by the mortgage.

Movable Mortgage. A commercial-type mortgage which permits the borrower to transfer the balance of his or her income property loan to another property without paying points, or if the loan is increased, the points are paid only on the incremental amount.

Net Lease. A type of lease in which the tenant pays taxes, assessments, and all operating expenses in connection with the use of the premises and the landlord receives a net figure.

Net Operating Income. Gross income less operating expenses before depreciation and capital recovery.

Net Present Value (NPV) Method. This is a method for evaluating alternative investment proposals. The NPV is equal to the present value of future cash flows, discounted at a specified interest rate, minus the present value of the investment's cost.

Nominal Interest Rate. The stated interest rate in a contract.

Open-End Mortgage. A mortgage that can be increased by subsequent advances of principal after part of the original loan has been repaid.

Open Market Operations. This is the Federal Reserve System's most important general credit tool whereby the Federal Reserve influences bank credit through the process of buying and selling U.S. government securities.

Option. The right to purchase or lease property at a specific price for a designated time period.

Origination Fee. An amount charged by a financial institution for handling mortgage loan applications and the processing of the loan.

Package Mortgage. A mortgage secured by both real and personal property.

Partial Release. The instrument that is employed to release part of the mortgaged premises from the terms of the mortgage. It recites the mortgage, the amount paid for the release, and a description of the part of the mortgaged premises that has been released.

Partially Amortized Mortgage. A mortgage which will not be fully amortized at maturity and thus will require a *balloon payment* of the remaining principal at maturity.

Participation Mortgage. Several lenders have a share in a single mortgage.

Pass-Through Security. a mortgage-backed security whereby the payments received by the trustee are passed through to the security holders in proportion to their ownership in the mortgage pool.

Percentage Lease. A lease where the rental amount is stated as a percentage of business transacted on the leased property. This is usually a percentage of gross sales.

Personal Property. An item of value that is not real property or real estate.

Personal Savings Rate. Personal savings divided by disposable personal income.

Prepayment Clause. A mortgage clause that permits the payment of the mortgage principal, in part or in full, prior to the maturity date. This clause frequently provides for a penalty payment if the clause is exercised.

Present Value. The worth today of an amount to be received (or paid) in the future, and thus the opposite of future value.

Price Risk. Risk caused by fluctuations in interest rates due to the fact that prices of fixed-income securities move inversely with changes in market interest rates.

Primary Mortgage Market. A market involving the creation or origination of new mortgages.

Prime Contractor. A person hired directly by an owner or builder-developer.

Prime Rate. The rate of interest charged by large banks to their most creditworthy customers.

Principal. The amount of a loan or debt.

Principle of Matching Maturities. The practice of matching a firm's average maturity of its assets with the average maturity of its liabilities.

Promissory Note. A written or signed instrument that acknowledges a debt and promises repayment.

Property Report. A report of information on subdivision lots subject to the Interstate Land Sales Full Disclosure Act.

Property Tax. A tax levied against the owner of real and/or personal property based on the value of the owned property.

Purchase Money Mortgage. A mortgage given by the borrower to the seller as part of the purchase price of the real property.

Quit Claim Deed. A deed conveying the grantor's interest in real property without warranty in that the grantor is not responsible for failure to convey a clear title.

Real Estate. Land and its attachments. It also is referred to as *realty* or *real property*.

Real Estate Investment Trust (REIT). A trust authorized to invest in real estate that is managed and controlled by trustees and is exempt from federal corporate income taxes.

Real Property. Land and its attachments. It is used synonymously with *realty* and *real estate*.

Recapture. Excess depreciation which is recouped upon the sale of property.

Redemption. The right of the original owner of property to reclaim the property in the event of default by paying the loan principal and all related costs.

Regular or Ordinary Annuity. An annuity involving fixed periodic payments or receipts that occur at the end of each period.

Release Clause. A provision that, upon payment of a specific amount of money, a stipulated lien will be removed from the property.

Renegotiable Rate Mortgage. A mortgage wherein lenders are permitted to renegotiate interest rates periodically.

Replacement Cost. The current cost of replacing an existing property with a new property that has equivalent utility value.

Return on Assets or Investment (ROA or ROI). This is the income or yield on an investment expressed as a percentage of the total investment in assets.

Return on Equity (ROE). This is the income or yield on an investment expressed as a percentage of the owner's investment in assets. Since a portion of the investment in assets is frequently financed with debt, this use of *leverage* often causes ROE to differ from ROA.

Reversion Value. The value of property at some future date when the property reverts back to the owner in the case of a lease or to the grantor of the property.

Rolling Option. An option designed to permit a developer to free capital and minimize risk.

Sale-Buyback. A financing arrangement whereby property is sold by a developer to an investor who in turn sells it back to the developer under a long-term sales arrangement. Title is retained by the investor.

Sale-Leaseback. A financing arrangement whereby a business sells real estate it owns and uses to an investor who in turn leases back the real estate to the business firm. This method of financing is usually on a long-term basis.

Satisfaction of Mortgage. A receipt signed by a mortgagee stating that the amount due under a mortgage has been paid and may be discharged of record.

Savings. The accumulation of cash and other financial assets such as savings accounts, insurance policies, and pension plan reserves.

Second Mortgage. A mortgage that is subordinate to another mortgage (i.e., a first mortgage). This would be an example of a *junior mortgage*.

Secondary Mortgage Market. The market where the buying and selling of existing mortgage loans and mortgage-backed securities takes place.

Security. Property used as collateral for a loan.

Selective Credit Controls. Controls designed to operate directly on the availability of credit in contrast with the general monetary controls which operate on bank reserves. An example would be the use of margin requirements (i.e., the minimum down payment required to purchase securities).

Servicing Fee. A fee charged by a financial intermediary to cover collection of mortgage payments, property inspection, payment of property taxes, and possible foreclosure expenses.

Shared Appreciation Mortgage. A mortgage wherein the lender shares in any capital appreciation upon the sale of a residence.

Shared Equity Financing. An agreement under which two or more persons acquire qualified ownership interests in a dwelling unit as a principal residence, and occupant-owners are required to pay rent to the nonoccupant co-owners.

Simple Interest. Interest computed on the loan's remaining principal balance.

Spreading Agreement. An instrument used by a mortgagee to incorporate other lands owned by the mortgagor under the terms of an existing mortgage.

Statute of Frauds. A law involving contracts which must be in writing to be enforceable. One section specifically states that contracts relating to real property must be in writing in order to be enforceable.

Straight Hedge. A hedge that involves the same commodity in both the cash and futures markets. This contrasts with a "cross hedge" which uses two different debt instruments.

Straight-Line Depreciation. The writing-off of the value of an asset in equal amounts over the life of the asset. This assumes a level decline in the value of the asset over time.

Subordination Clause. A clause in a mortgage or lease that places the holder in a secondary or subordinate position to the claims of another mortgagor.

Take-Out Commitment. A loan commitment on the part of a lender to provide back-up support for construction financing until permanent financing is arranged.

Take-Out Letter. An agreement for an advance commitment which covers the delivery date, amount of loans, and fees connected with the long-term mortgages.

Tandem Plan. A secondary mortgage market plan that combines GNMA guarantees with FNMA activities.

Tax Shelter. A taxable loss that may be used to reduce taxable income earned from other sources.

Term Mortgage. A mortgage that does not provide for amortization of principal over the life of the mortgage but rather requires payment of the total principal at maturity.

Time-Sharing. A method of providing multiple use and/or use of vacation and recreational properties. An individual may purchase the ownership or the right to use a property for a fraction of time during the year and for a fraction of the cost of purchasing the entire unit.

Time Value of Money. A concept involving both the "cost" of money and "when" money flows in, or is paid out.

Title. The means whereby the owner of lands has the just possession of the property.

Title Theory of Mortgages. A concept wherein, upon making the mortgage, the mortgagor passes title to the property, the subject of the mortgage, to the mortgagee subject to a condition subsequent.

Tract Development Loan. A loan which is given to a developer or subdivider to put in streets and utilities after the acquisition of raw land. Also called a land development loan.

Treasury Bills. Short-term U.S. government securities with maturities ranging up to one year. Treasury notes and bonds have longer maturities.

Trust Deed. A deed that conveys title to real estate to a third party trustee to be held for the benefit of a lender or beneficiary. This also is often referred to as a deed of trust.

Trustee. One of the three parties in a deed of trust. In the event of default, the trustee forecloses for the benefit of the beneficiary.

Trustor. The borrower in a deed of trust.

Usury. Interest rates deemed to be excessive by state laws.

VA-Guaranteed Mortgage. A mortgage where a portion of an eligible veteran's loan is guaranteed in terms of repayment to the lender by the Veterans Administration.

Variable Payment Mortgage. A mortgage that requires a constant payment of principal over the life of the mortgage (i.e., the mortgage is amortized in equal payments of principal).

Variable-Rate Mortgage. A mortgage where the interest rate can be changed over time in relation to changes in a specified index. Also called an adjustable-rate mortgage.

Warranty Deed. A deed under which the grantor guarantees title to the real property that is being sold. In the event of a bad title, the grantee has the right to sue the grantor for breach of warranty.

Wraparound Mortgage. A second or junior mortgage designed to encompass an existing mortgage. Payment on the existing mortgage is continued while a new, larger (in dollar amount and often in terms of the interest rate) mortgage is given to the borrower. Thus, the new mortgage "wraps around" the original mortgage.

Yield Curve. A graphic depiction of the relationship between interest rate levels and time to maturity for comparable quality securities.

INDEX